THE COLLECTED PLAYS OF
EMLYN WILLIAMS

VOLUME I

Plays by Emlyn Williams

Accolade
Beth
The Druid's Rest
He Was Born Gay
The Light of Heart
The Morning Star
A Murder Has Been Arranged
Night Must Fall
Pepper and Sand (*One Act*)
Someone Waiting
Spring, 1600
Thinking Aloud (*One Act*)
Trespass
Vigil (*One Act*)
The Wind of Heaven

Adaptations

The Late Christopher Bean (Fauchois)
A Month in the Country (Turgenev)
Readings From Dickens

EMLYN WILLIAMS

THE
COLLECTED
PLAYS

VOLUME ONE

NIGHT MUST FALL
HE WAS BORN GAY
THE CORN IS GREEN
THE LIGHT OF HEART

With an Introduction by
THE AUTHOR

RANDOM HOUSE · NEW YORK

Selection © Emlyn Williams 1961

First published 1961

The plays were first published
individually in Great Britain as follows:

Night Must Fall, 1935   *He Was Born Gay*, 1937
The Corn is Green, 1938   *The Light of Heart*, 1940

PRINTED IN GREAT BRITAIN
BY THE WINDMILL PRESS LTD
KINGSWOOD, SURREY

CONTENTS

CONTENTS

AUTHOR'S INTRODUCTION

A host presents a fellow-guest to you by name, and adds 'I *know* you'll enjoy being talked to by Thompson, he's as witty as he is well-informed, a spell-binder!' Thompson motions you to a conversation-piece away from the herd, and your heart sinks. Whether he knows it or not, he has a hard job ahead; his poker-faced audience is irremediably prejudiced.

Plays, like Thompson, should need introducing only by name; whether on view in the theatre or under scrutiny on the page, they ought to speak for themselves. Scenes are either moving, or they are not; they are either funny, or they are not. 'You see, the *reason* why in my play the scene in Act Three is so peculiarly poignant, is that you can meet my Wilfred and my Hilda next to each other in any tube train in London, their problem has universality.' You go to the play, your heart steeled against both Wilfred and Hilda before the house-lights are lowered. Don't explain, don't excuse, don't coax: write the play, get it on, leave it *alone*. And when I was asked to write an 'introduction' to this book, my instinct was 'No, the plays must speak for themselves, haven't I always tried to help them to do just that on paper – what about "The Curtain Never Goes Up, Compensate the Reader"? No introduction!'

Then I realised that the phrase 'The Curtain Never Goes Up, Compensate the Reader', which I repeat mechanically to myself as I start putting every act on to paper, could do with being explained. . . . And perhaps a couple of details about how the plays came to be

vii

written, how they fared – would that perhaps be of interest? So here I am, introducing. But when it comes to the actual plays, I shall leave you to examine them for yourself, and thank you for wanting to.

When, at the age of eighteen, I was pecking at a second-hand typewriter with undergraduate finger bursting with second-hand dramatic emotions – I gave my mind to the words my characters spoke, and to nothing else; down to brass tacks, the play's the thing. 'Enter HENRY, JOAN. *Joan*: Look at that moon. *Henry*: Yes. (Exeunt.)' What was good enough for Shakespeare, was good enough for G. E. Williams (Ch.Ch.) A couple of years later, I saw Zena Dare, at the New Theatre Oxford, in a new comedy the polish of which dazzled me enough to speed me to Blackwell's to buy it in book form: *The Last of Mrs Cheyney*. With the wonderful ease and dexterity of the play fresh in my blotting-paper mind, I put aside my typewriter, curled up in my window-seat overlooking the Meadows, tossed the twenties hair out of my eye (hair was worn forward then, diagonally down and eyebrow-length on one brow) and settled down to pleasure.

'Act One. Room at Mrs Cheyney's house at Goring. Charles discovered at window up C. Enter George.' Not a word to define the room, not a clue as to Charles (the Ronald Squire part) which seemed a vital omission. I read on, and disillusionment crept over me. Even though the play was still pictorially vivid in my mind, I simply could not believe that these were the scenes which had enchanted me; they read like a crude farce in the hands of amateurs. Gradually I realised why. Lonsdale, man of the theatre as he was, had prepared his play for the stage *only*; the printed version had obviously been taken from the hurriedly punctuated prompt-copy, with no thought whatever of the prospective reader. One peculiarly harmful effect of this, I discovered, was the indiscriminate pepper-pot use of the exclamation-mark, which in dialogue should surely express only positive surprise, or vehemence, the last word to apply to this author's humour. Line after line, which I had seen and heard – on the stage – deliciously shrugged off in the Lonsdale manner, gaining laugh after laugh, I found – on paper – killed dead by this slight but lethal weapon. 'Rumour has it she has remained faithful to her husband!' 'She is either a very good woman, or very nervous!' 'If I may say so, you appear to have rather a low opinion of me!'

And so it went on. I thought, if *The Last of Mrs Cheyney* was a good play in the theatre, the least it deserved was transcription, to the printed page, careful enough for the reader to get the same picture of it – as nearly as stage directions and our inadequate system of punctuation permit – as the audience had been granted. The reader *must* be helped out by the author, who must imagine him as somebody sitting in a theatre, able to hear the words *but to see nothing.* (I am so conscious of a reading audience, it may be noted, that in each play the words 'left' and 'right' refer to the audience's left and right, not to the actors'.) If there is an amusing piece of byplay, it should be described, in plain, grammatical, even elegant English. I invent. 'He takes her glass of whisky, tastes it, rises, walks unsteadily to the sideboard, and pours it into the fruit-salad. She runs across, slaps his face, and runs out.' Not necessarily an unforgettable moment in the theatre, but if it is in the stage action it *must* be thus adequately described in print, and not as 'Roger Xes to sideboard, comedy bus, with whisky & fruit-salad, Iris Xes. Face slap, exit.' You must agree that that sort of

A*   ix

reading is not worth taking out of the library, never mind half-a-guinea a copy.

Not that I advocate the irrelevant extremes to which J. M. Barrie, in his anxiety to make you feel at home, travelled on tiptoe; he was a brilliant playwright who was inclined, in his stage directions, to put his reader to bed under a suffocating eiderdown of sentimental meander, and then tenderly, ruthlessly, to rub syrup into his hair. 'Miss Patty, her dear little head on one thoughtful side, is thinking of her wee dog fifteen miles-and-a-morsel awa'. And wee dog, we may whisper, is thinking of his young mistress, though too far to cock up his ears at what *we* can hear: the slow fall of the curtain.' No, rather than that, 'Policeman Xes to desk, bus. with revolver, sharp exit upstage.'

But there is a lot of territory in between, where I have tried to stake a claim; and as you are presumably planning to sample one or two of the plays in this book, I think I should assure you that the stage-directions are throughout written with as much care as the dialogue. Even as I work on the first draft – when I know from experience that before and during production there will be many changes, large and small – I carefully type out essential stage-directions. And after production, the preparation of the final script for the printer has always been for me a major responsibility which I try scrupulously to carry out; I make it a rule that every alteration of dialogue made over the months of gestation, every cut, every inserted piece of business which has in the course of performance become an integral part of the play, must be incorporated, not only for the potential reader but for the potential producer; dialogue is carefully examined for lines which are perfectly clear to an audience, but can cause endless perplexity to a reader, needing only a simple emendation. Let me make up a quick example:

JANE (*at the telephone*): I'll meet you Friday. This is an appointment I *won't* keep. I'll be there.

Cryptic? This can so easily read:

JANE (*at the telephone*): I'll meet you Friday. (*To the others, covering the receiver.*) This is an appointment I *won't* keep. . . . (*Back into the telephone.*) I'll be there.

This 'keeping the script up to date' is a back-breaking job, but one which only the author can do. And one of the pleasures of a playwright – almost a physical one – after sending to the printer an exhausted typescript, dog-eared, travel-stained, hideously scarred across and across with the wounds of parturition – one of the pleasures, weeks later, is to turn page after page of virgin print, running as smooth as water. For the reader, 'the Curtain Never Rises, Compensate'.

What else? Like all playwrights, I am constantly asked how I ever 'do it'. I suppose it's an occupational hazard, for I never heard of an architect being cornered at a cocktail party as to how in the world he had managed to erect a block of flats without a couple of storeys collapsing like a pack of cards, and would he care to see some sketches my Wendy made for a cathedral when she had flu on her last hols, and could he recommend where she should send them, are agents any good? '*How* do you start writing a play?'

Well . . . A theme occurs to me, half-subconsciously sometimes; my mind is set ticking by a book I have read, or even a chance remark, a news item, a face in the street. I examine the theme, think hard to find out if it's been used before, four times out of five decide that it has, settle on the fifth, sketch in the characters roughly, christen them temporarily on a sort of shadow theatre-programme, then write a synopsis. This is never more than five hundred words, and is purely for my own guidance – a bare statement of the situation, the problem it poses, and the development and solution of that problem. From then on, in a little notebook, I make constant illegible notes of scraps of dialogue, sketchy turns of action, details of clothes, furniture, 'props', turns of phrase, mannerisms – anything that may become grist to the mill which is going to grind laboriously during the ensuing weeks. Many of these notes, when consulted later, have disconcertingly turned into one of those garbled telegrams. 'Plant black stockings party apples help comedy water routine.'

I make it a rule not to tell anybody anything about a play until it is finished; even to my wife, I will only say 'Oh it's a thriller about spiritualism, set in a castle', or 'It's a comedy set in a village inn'. It's a prejudice, I know, but I find it hard to believe that anybody who will read out his new play bit by bit to an admiring circle (whether the circle sits speechless with admiration or buzzing with nebulous and contradictory suggestions for the next and unwritten scene) is anything but an amateur. This is superstition as well as prejudice, for like every playwright, I have a dread of getting bogged half-way through a play; and the only time I have ever done this, was when I had described scenes not yet tackled. They never were.

Having finished my synopsis and started the notebook, I type the title, which I have nearly always settled already;

I find that this gives to the unborn play a shadowy existence, and moreover feel much encouraged if I have hit on a good one. I would find it vexing to leave this to the last, and quite intolerable then, as sometimes happens, to give a 'working title', which is a provisional name till somebody comes along with something better. I attach enormous, perhaps too special, importance to this matter, believing the title should be euphonious, easy to say and remember, not to be confused with other titles, short if possible (I always count the letters, and hope they won't add up to more than fourteen), impossible to misinterpret, striking without being eccentric, and the right title for the play *after* it has been seen; not an easy problem. In milling over a title, I say aloud, over an imaginary ticket-counter, something like 'Have you by any chance two seats left for *The Boy Fred*?' '*The Boy Fred*,' says a testy voice, '*The Boy Fred*? What a funny name, don't you mean *The Boy Friend*, that came off years ago. . . .' From which you somehow feel you haven't got the ideal thing, yet. I do not myself like using quotations as titles, feeling, I suppose, that one shouldn't borrow. *Night Must Fall* and *The Corn is Green* sound like quotations, but are not; the latter is a phrase used in the play itself. I doubt if I would have called a play *The Wind of Heaven* if I had remembered (from *Hamlet*) 'the winds of heaven'. I will never listen to, never mind ask for, titles suggested by friends. I deserve no marks for this, it is foolish pride. (I also avoid any contingency at rehearsal in which anybody might suggest a better line than the one in question. 'No no' I say, as lips are tentatively opening, 'I'll think it over at home and we'll have something tomorrow.' From the reading to the first night in London, I will act upon any sensible suggestion as to cuts or rewriting, but I will *not* allow one line into the script which has been thought of by somebody else. Foolish pride.)

Having typed out the title, I then write the whole play (first draft) straight on to the typewriter, double-spacing, using the blank spaces for amendments as I go along, but (so as not to be held up) not crossing out till I have finished the day's work. When I do come to cross out – going through with a pencil – until I have sorted out what is meant to go and what is meant to stay, each page reads like gibberish. I do not like to think what any other eye would make of it. For instance (note that the second line is the 'blank' one, there to be filled in with emendations, as I go along):

THE MAN: You say that I reminded me that I have made a fool of that twice since Christmas you arrived I have made a fool of you. That is not exactly quite quite untrue, though an exaggeration.

You see what I mean? Corrected, this will read:

THE MAN: You ~~say that I~~ reminded me ~~that I have made a fool of~~ that twice since ~~Christmas~~ you arrived I have made a fool of you. That is ~~not exactly quite quite untrue, though~~ an exaggeration.

or more clearly

THE MAN: You reminded me that twice since you arrived I have made a fool of you. That is an exaggeration.

Except for this mechanical correcting, I make it a rule (another superstition?) not to look back at anything until the first draft is completed: not even in order to check names and dates, or to bring an early scene up to date when later I have changed the whole basis of a character or even cut one out. This comes partly from the inner urge to get to the end as soon as decently possible, and partly from the wish to review the first draft freshly, as a finished whole, before relaxing and starting to revise. This re-reading can turn out a perplexing affair. A character will suddenly pipe up who has apparently soared into the room, unnoticed, through a trap-door, with in the margin a furtive 'Get him on'. Other pencillings: 'Put all this earlier, see asterisk p. 4.' . . . 'Work in a reference to murder' . . . 'Plant somewhere here that O. writes ptry.' Things can look even more puzzling. Having 'finished' *Night Must Fall* (the first draft) and turning back with some trepidation to the half-forgotten first act, I was taken aback to find that Hubert had a talkative wife, who mysteriously stopped talking in the middle of page 7, apparently remained standing in the middle of the stage for the rest of the act, and was never mentioned again.

From this it will be gathered that the hard work comes after the first draft; in any of the amended second drafts, it is rare for a page not to be pasted over or even re-typed, often twice. This continues right until the script goes to the printer. Weigh every word, cross out, cut, transpose, clarify – clarify, transpose, cut, cross out, weigh every word – each beautifully tidy page in this book, as it meets your eye, will be invisibly scored with preliminary travail. I hope invisibly.

Why so much work? Well, you see, in order for you to smile at Hilda's line 4 on page 84, there has to have been a line by Wilfred on page 81 to . . . I leave it to you.

───────────

NIGHT MUST FALL I started in November 1934, on

the eve of my twenty-ninth birthday, and finished in January. For a month, night and day, I revised, and the play went to the typist.

For eighteen months, I had been under contract, as actor and writer, to a major British film company, and the daily possibility of being telephoned for extra jokes for Yvonne Arnaud, George Robey, and Cicely Court-neidge, was beginning to lose its glow. (Would you like a sample? Right. Louise has been supplanted by a rival. Fade in, Louise at grand piano. She stops playing, angrily: 'Franz, I weel amuse you wiz piano, but I weel *not* play second feedle!' Well, you asked for it.) Looking back from 1934, into my mistily dim past (covering four years, in those days) I'd had five plays produced in London, with varying degrees of success; I now badly wanted to write a new one. Just as badly, I wanted to play the leading part in it, for I was beginning to feel sure, sitting in the studios being made up as one bank-clerk and petty blackmailer after another, that there was only one living playwright sufficiently interested in my acting to write a part which only I could play. Me.

For years I had been fascinated by real-life murders, and accounts of murder trials: I found myself wanting to write a play in which the audience knew as the curtain rose, that the murderer had not only 'done it', but was to be hanged for his crime – I longed to go on from there. I had thought of dramatising De Quincey's *Murder as a Fine Art*, then let the idea go – I wanted to write a play of my very own, starring my very own self. Then, just as I opened my typewriter, the telephone would ring. 'This is Princess Charming, could you slip along and inject some verbal warmth into Miss Evelyn Laye's love scenes?' The summer of 1934 was, for me, one of megalomania burrowing underground: though they knew it not, Gaumont-British had, under contract, a Welsh mole.

Several years before, above ground, megalomania of a more sinister sort had been rearing its head. In Margate, on the night of 23 October 1929, Sidney Fox, aged twenty-eight, had murdered his invalid mother by setting fire to her for the insurance. Some time in the summer of 1934, an evening paper brought this up in a crime series; 'Monster!' screamed the headline in the tube. 'Good gracious,' said the woman opposite me, 'look at his photo, you wouldn't think butter would . . .' Then she stared again. 'Good gr . . . but it's the Sidney somebody brought to tea at my auntie's in Surbiton the week before it happened, and he had a glass of milk instead of tea – but he was so nice and *ordinary*. . . .' 'Monster!' screamed the front page. The train stopped, she got out. I did not know it, but I had the play.

I started off with Dan and his victim as mother and son, but (as often happens) absolute truth in the theatre can be too shocking. I started notes. Notes about Fox, Patrick Mahon (the Crumbles murderer, who dismembered his victim), Mancini (of Brighton, who lost his nerve to the point of keeping the dead body in his room for weeks) and for physical characteristics and idiom, a contemporary I knew who was not a criminal but might have been. For the facial picture of Dan, I did not have to look far: I put a fag-end between my lips and looked in the mirror.

The only important change I made after the first draft of this play, was to settle for a musical effect at the opening and between scenes only, and to discard (as too fanciful, too 'filmish') an idea I had developed of using weirdly dramatic background music, whenever the murderer was moved to remember or talk of the murder. I was reminded of this years later, when I saw the wonderful use made of the device in *A Streetcar Named Desire*. But I still feel it would have been wrong for *Night Must Fall*.

The script went to the typist in February 1935, the curtain rose on 29 April: a tour of three major cities in which we did so badly that till the last minute, it was a toss-up whether the play should be granted a London verdict. (Several years later, it returned to one of these cities, and played to twenty pounds more on the Saturday night than it had on the whole of the week of the first visit. So when theatregoers in that city remind me that 'What London'll think tomorrow, we in the provinces think today!' I tend to look rather abstracted.) The gamble was undertaken, and the play opened in London, at the Duchess Theatre, where it ran for over a year, then transferring (over a week-end) to the Cambridge Theatre for a further six months. As most of the original cast were contracted for New York, this transfer was effected with an entirely new cast, headed by Esmond Knight, and a new director, Glen Byam Shaw: his first assignment. This, I understand, was the first time this had ever been done in London.

Ironically (the theatre is an amalgam of sugar and spice and all that's iron) we ran eight weeks on Broadway; I had arrived to find the play billed as 'The Spine-Chilling British Melodrama!' which I knew was a bad sign. However, I have since met so many Americans who genuinely believe we were a success that I almost believe it myself. The play was well received in Paris, as *L'Homme qui se Donnait la Comédie*, and Pierre Brasseur made one of his first successes as Dan. A film was made in Hollywood in

1937, with Robert Montgomery, who gave a fine performance; I was oddly gratified, moreover, to see my part undertaken by a star with glamour and looks. Since then, I am assured, there has not been, anywhere on the face of the globe, any aspiring young character actor, professional or amateur, who has not played the part. I believe it, when I recall the Dans who have since called to see me in every dressing-room from Wolverhampton to Woollangong.

When reviews and letters referred to Dan as 'a study in schizophrenia', I had to look the word up. And when, the other day, I read in an article that 'looking back, one realises that *Night Must Fall* started a fashion; Dan was one of the first, if not the first, of a long line of psychopathic killers of stage and screen', I was gratified enough to want to slip the quotation unobtrusively into this introduction. I trust that I have done just that. In fairness I must add that the German film 'M' ante-dated my play by several years.

Not long ago I received a letter from an American composer. When I had first tapped out 'The action takes place in the sitting-room of a bungalow in Essex', I had little thought that I would one day be approached with the idea of having *Night Must Fall* turned into an opera. I am flattered, but I just do not know what to say. A *musical* hat-box?

HE WAS BORN GAY was written during the run of *Night Must Fall*. John Gielgud, making up as Noah for his matinée, looked at me in the mirror. 'Why don't you write a play for me?' A week later, I happened to be reading a book called *The Son of Marie Antoinette*. This was it, I thought; I've paid fifteen shillings for an idea, not bad. I would write a play round the Lost Dauphin. The part would fit J.G. like a glove.

It did, so tightly that neither he nor I was able to pull it off. When, on the first night in Glasgow in April 1937, he made his first unobtrusive entrance, as an anonymous music-master in a snobbish household, his innate nobility was such that he wore, blazing invisibly on his brow, the diadem of France; the play was over before it had started, a great actor was miscast in a part written for him.

This was not immediately too evident, for on its preliminary tour the production played to record business, in the same towns where *Night Must Fall* had made such a lamentable start. A couple of weeks before *He Was Born Gay* was due to open in Shaftesbury Avenue, my cautious country-born Welsh mother was preparing tea. 'How is it going,' she said, 'in Manchester?' 'Sold out,' I said, laconically, 'standing-room.' 'Ah,' said my mother, making an absent dab at the butter, 'London's the mischief.' It was. *He Was Born Gay* ran two weeks, and as I had invested money in it, *The Son of Marie Antoinette* had cost me not fifteen shillings, but nine hundred pounds. 'London's the mischief.' Dorothy Parker could not have uttered a more devastating theatrical mot.

There is a great deal wrong with *He Was Born Gay*, but its critical reception was particularly severe because Gielgud and I stood labelled as successes. If we had been unknown, the play would have been quite differently received, and possibly over-praised; I was yet another playwright learning the lesson of the theatre. The graph is a familiar one: the author's first play (with all its faults) is lauded for its merits; the second turns out 'right', and wins deserved success; the third, which is 'not right', finds itself, in spite of quite a few merits, unreservedly damned for its faults. It is the penalty of success, and cannot be helped. Success, in the meantime, is very pleasant.

Should I define more specifically what is wrong with *He Was Born Gay*? Well, it is, I suppose a none-too-easy mixture of realistic comedy, romance, poetry, near-farce, besides being – but judge for yourself. It taught me that as a playwright I had to be absolutely sure beforehand of what I was setting out to achieve, and it meant working again with John Gielgud. So I have not regretted it.

THE CORN IS GREEN. The summer of 1937 I spent waiting to go to the Old Vic, to play in *Ghosts* and *Richard the Third*. And waiting meant, quite a lot of the time, mooning. Said my wife one day, sitting on the lawn, 'Why don't you write a play about Miss Cooke?' Miss Cooke is the English schoolmistress who taught me, in Wales, and prepared me for a scholarship to Oxford. I was not immediately fired to open the typewriter; it seemed uncomfortably near real life – I did not get the idea of putting the period well back into the last century till I started writing it – and I let the idea lie fallow till after the Old Vic and a subsequent film. With Sybil Thorndike shadowily in mind (but *not* 'writing a play for her') I finished the first act in Kitzbühel, in February 1938, the second in Monte Carlo (of all places) and the third off (and even on) a film set; the play was revised and back from the typist in April.

I wrote to Miss Cooke, 'I've written a play, it's no good pretending she isn't meant to be you, though all the rest is pretty well dramatic licence. Anything you don't like, I'll change.' She wrote back, 'Well! I can't imagine the

public being faintly interested in a play about education.'
I sent her the script. She wired back, 'No objection, but
don't think Sybil Thorndike's mouth is right.' This
obscure quibble was overruled, and plans went ahead.

The casting of the boy was a problem; while writing
the play, I had steadily avoided the idea of playing it
myself because I wanted to direct the production un-
fettered by a second – no, a third – heavy responsibility,
and also I felt I was too old (thirty-three); Marius Goring
was unavailable, and I finally agreed. (It was by no means
the last time, by the way, that I was to play a part which
I had written with another actor in view.) The play was
produced in London in September 1938, ran a year till the
outbreak of war, when – like everything else – it closed.
It went on tour till Christmas, reopened in London and
ran till the fall of France in June. The American company
opened in the States in November 1940, with Ethel
Barrymore as Miss Moffat, and ran, in New York and on
the road, for two years, being subsequently filmed with
Bette Davis. For a couple of years there has been talk of
making a musical play of it. Should I try and do the book
and lyrics myself? I don't know . . . I was taken aback at
first by the idea of a 'musical', but now that I am faced
with *Night Must Fall* as an opera, I am ready for anything.

As one question about *The Corn is Green* crops up with
fair frequency from certain earnest producers, I may as
well answer it once and for all. 'In spite of everything,
you do mean Miss Moffat to be a *bit* in love with the boy,
don't you – sort of repressed?' The answer is NO. Also
I have never been down a coal-mine in my life: I was
never a miner. I am so often reminded that I was, that
by now I almost believe it. Also I am frequently told
that it is a play with a message. I never meant it to

be, and even labelled it, at first, a 'comedy'. So you never know.

THE LIGHT OF HEART was written during the run of *The Corn is Green*, during the summer of 1939. I wanted to write a play about the theatre as I know it, from the inside, and yet in a way understandable to the audience, a way to which I hoped they would warm; the character of Maddoc was based partly on Henry Ainley, partly on two other actors I knew well. The play had an exciting but bumpy two years: produced in London in February 1940, it closed temporarily in June, went on tour, closed again at Streatham Hill Theatre in early September, on the night the London blitz broke out. It had been scheduled to reopen at the Savoy Theatre, and all through that historic winter, the Savoy façade flaunted the dilapidated sign 'The Light of Heart'. The play toured for a year, and when Godfrey Tearle left the cast, I was prevailed upon to take over his part. Before doing this, I performed on the play a delicate but impudent piece of surgery the like of which I shall never do again: being too young to play Maddoc as written, I made him Cattrin's brother instead of her father. It made sense to those who did not know the play already, but suited neither me – I was miscast – nor the play, which (though it ran in London a further six months, at the Globe) lost considerably in effect. Let us call it a minor case of war damage. The play was produced in New York in 1942 – with Paul Muni, Jessica Tandy and Alfred Drake – and was a failure; it was subsequently filmed, with Monty Woolley and Ida Lupino, under the title of *Every Night at* 8.30. I only discovered recently, from a biography, that Scott Fitzgerald worked on the script.

The wheel had come round in some sort of circle. 'Mr Fitzgerald in? . . . Scottie, the light of heart speakin', could you slip along and inject some verbal warmth into Miss Lupino's love scenes?'

All these plays were written some years ago. I quote from a London weekly, the recent review of a new play. 'It represents yet another step forward from the West End theatre of the thirties – away from that stockbroker's Sussex drawing-room opening through the inevitable french windows on to the fox-gloved backcloth, away from Lady What-not hovering over the Spode with tea-spoon and epigram, away from that inevitable juvenile in tennis flannels – oh, those thirties!' Reading this as I finish preparing this introduction, I seem to hear an usher call my name, and feel impelled to sidle, for a moment, into a sort of witness-box (dock?).

'No, your worship, I don't recall any french windows in any plays of mine with a modern setting, unless you count the glass doors into the sun-room in *Night Must Fall* but, your worship, they're there because the old lady is in a wheel-chair, and so couldn't get from . . . Tea, your worship? No, no tea. . . . Am I sure? Oh – there's tea brought on at the end of the first scene of *The Corn is Green*, but that's because the schoolmistress is addicted to it, but only in separate cups. . . . No, no stockbrokers, though Hubert *may* be one, it doesn't say, and no fox-gloves, just a geranium on the window sill. . . . No, not a single titled character, your worship, not even the Squire – oh, Barty's grandmother in *The Light of Heart*, she *may* have been, but then she never comes on. The Lost Dauphin, of course, was titled, in a way. . . . Sorry. . . . Oh, but scattered among the plays there's – let me see – a bell-boy in a roadhouse who was once a seaman and a blackmailer and a ponce before he took to murder, your worship, does *he* help? Plus several grubby and under-privileged miners, a village slut who's having a baby, a kleptomaniac ex-Salvation Army lass, a Coventry-Street tart, a night-school policeman, a London landlady with a retarded daughter of thirty-seven, and a re-mittance-man with no trousers on who's left his bowler hat in the sink and doesn't play tennis.... Dustbins, your worship? Oh yes, there's one just outside the kitchen in *Night Must Fall*, AND *The Corn is Green*. . . . No, not on stage, I'm afraid, and not inhabited, sorry. . . . Oh, in *Night Must Fall* there's a rubbish heap, with a broken lipstick in it and a woman's dismembered and decom-posing body.... No, that's not on stage either, sorry....'

E.W.

London, 1961

NIGHT MUST FALL

To
My Wife

CHARACTERS

The Lord Chief Justice
Mrs Bramson
Olivia Grayne
Hubert Laurie
Nurse Libby
Mrs Terence
Dora Parkoe
Inspector Belsize
Dan

PROLOGUE
The Court of Criminal Appeal

The action of the play takes place in the sitting-room of 'Forest Corner', Mrs Bramson's bungalow in Essex

ACT ONE
A fine morning in October

ACT TWO
Scene 1: An afternoon, twelve days later
Scene 2: Late afternoon, two days later

ACT THREE
Scene 1: Half an hour later
Scene 2: Half an hour later

NIGHT MUST FALL *was first produced in London by J. P Mitchelhill at the Duchess Theatre, on 31 May 1935 with the following cast:*

THE LORD CHIEF JUSTICE	Eric Stanley
MRS BRAMSON	May Whitty
OLIVIA GRAYNE	Angela Baddeley
HUBERT LAURIE	Basil Radford
NURSE LIBBY	Dorothy Langley
MRS TERENCE	Kathleen Harrison
DORA PARKOE	Betty Jardine
INSPECTOR BELSIZE	Matthew Boulton
DAN	Emlyn Williams

The play directed by
MILES MALLESON

BEFORE THE PLAY

The orchestra plays light tunes until the house lights are turned down; the curtain rises in darkness, accompanied by solemn music: the opening chords of Holst's 'The Perfect Fool'. A small light grows in the middle of the stage and shows the LORD CHIEF JUSTICE *sitting in judgment wearing wig and red robes of office, in the Court of Criminal Appeal. His voice, cold and disapproving, gradually swells up with the light as he reaches his peroration.*

LORD CHIEF JUSTICE: . . . and there is no need to re-capitulate here the arguments for and against this point of law, which we heard in the long and extremely fair summing up at the trial of the appellant at the Central Criminal Court. The case was clearly put to the jury; and it is against sentence of death for these two murders that the prisoner now appeals. Which means that the last stage of this important and extremely horrible case has now been reached. On a later page in the summing up, the learned judge, said this . . . (*Turning over papers*) . . . 'This case has, through the demeanour of the prisoner in the witness-box, obtained the most widespread and scandalous publicity, which I would beg you most earnestly, members of the jury, to forget.' I cannot help but think that the deplorable atmosphere of sentimental melodrama which has pervaded this trial has made the *theatre* a more fitting background for it than a court of law; but we are in a court of law, nevertheless, and the facts have been placed before the court. A remarkable and in my opinion praiseworthy feature of the case has been that the *sanity* of the prisoner has never been called into question; and, like the learned judge, the Court must dismiss as mischievous pretence the attitude of this young man who stands convicted of two brutal murders in cold blood. This case has, from beginning to end, exhibited no feature calling for sympathy; the evidence has on every point been conclusive, and on this evidence the jury have convicted the appellant. In the opinion of the Court there is no reason to interfere with that conviction, and this appeal must be dismissed.

The chords of solemn music are heard again, and the stage gradually darkens. A few seconds later the music merges into the sound of church bells playing far away, and the lights come up on

ACT I

*The sitting-room of Forest Corner, Mrs Bramson's bungalow in
a forest in Essex. A fine morning in October.*

*Centre back, a small hall; in its left side the front door
of the house (throughout the play, 'left' and 'right' refer to
the audience's left and right). Thick plush curtains can be
drawn across the entrance to the hall; they are open at the
moment. Windows, one on each side of the hall, with
window-seats and net curtains beyond which can be glimpsed
the pine-trees of the forest. In the left wall, upstage, a door
leading to the kitchen. In the left wall, downstage, the fireplace; above it, a cretonne-covered sofa, next to a very solid
cupboard built into the wall; below it a cane arm-chair. In
the right wall, upstage, a door leading to* MRS BRAMSON'S
*bedroom. In the right wall downstage, wide-open paned
doors leading to the sun-room. Right downstage, next the
sun-room, a large dining-table with four straight chairs
round it. Between the bedroom and the sun-room, a desk
with books on it, a cupboard below it, and a hanging mirror
on the wall above. Above the bedroom, a corner medicine
cupboard. Between the hall and the right window, an
occasional table.*

*The bungalow is tawdry but cheerful; it is built entirely
of wood, with an oil lamp fixed in the wall over the
occasional table. The room is comfortably furnished, though
in fussy and eccentric Victorian taste: stuffed birds, High-
land cattle in oils, antimacassars, and wax fruit are unobtrusively in evidence. On the mantelpiece, an ornate chiming
clock. The remains of breakfast on a tray on the table.*

MRS BRAMSON *is sitting in a wheeled chair in the centre*

*of the room. She is a fussy, discontented, common woman of
fifty-five, old-fashioned both in clothes and coiffure;* NURSE
LIBBY, *a kindly, matter-of-fact young north-country
woman in district nurse's uniform, is sitting on the sofa,
massaging one of her hands.* OLIVIA GRAYNE *sits on*
MRS BRAMSON'S *right, holding a book; she is a subdued
young woman of twenty-eight, her hair tied severely in a
knot, wearing horn-rimmed spectacles; there is nothing in
any way remarkable about her at the moment.* HUBERT
LAURIE *is sitting in the arm-chair, scanning the 'Daily
Telegraph'. He is thirty-five, moustached, hearty and
pompous, wearing plus fours and smoking a pipe.*

A pause. The church bells die away.

MRS BRAMSON (*sharply*): Go on.

OLIVIA (*reading*): '. . . Lady Isabel humbly crossed her
attenuated hands upon her chest. "I am on my way to
God," she whispered, "to answer for all my sins and
sorrows." "Child," said Miss Carlyle, "had I anything to
do with sending you from . . . (*turning over*) . . . East
Lynne?" Lady Isabel shook her head and cast down her
gaze.'

MRS BRAMSON (*aggressively*): Now that's what I call a
beautiful character.

NURSE: Very pretty. But the poor thing'd have felt
that much better tucked up in 'ospital instead of lying
about her own home, gassing her 'ead off——

MRS BRAMSON: Sh!

NURSE: Sorry.

OLIVIA (*reading*): ' "Thank God," inwardly breathed
Miss Corny. . . . "Forgive me," she said loudly and in
agitation. "I want to see Archibald," whispered Lady
Isabel.'

8

MRS BRAMSON: You don't see many books like *East Lynne* about nowadays.

HUBERT: No, you don't.

OLIVIA (*reading*): ' "I want to see Archibald," whispered Lady Isabel. "I have prayed Joyce to bring him to me, and she will not——" '

MRS BRAMSON (*sharply*): Olivia!

OLIVIA: Yes, auntie?

MRS BRAMSON (*craftily*): You're not skipping, are you?

OLIVIA: Am I?

MRS BRAMSON: You've missed out about Lady Isabel taking up her cross and the weight of it killing her. I may be a fool, but I do know *East Lynne*.

OLIVIA: Perhaps there were two pages stuck together.

MRS BRAMSON: Very convenient when you want your walk, eh? Yes, I *am* a fool, I suppose, as well as an invalid.

OLIVIA: But I thought you were so much better——

NURSE: You'd two helpings of bacon at breakfast, remember——

MRS BRAMSON: Doctor's orders. You know every mouthful's agony to me.

HUBERT (*deep in his paper*): There's a man here in Weston-super-Mare who stood on his head for twenty minutes for a bet and he hasn't come to yet.

MRS BRAMSON (*sharply*): I thought this morning I'd never be able to face the day.

HUBERT: But last night when you opened the port——

MRS BRAMSON: I've had a relapse since then. My heart's going like anything. Give me a chocolate.

   OLIVIA *rises and fetches her a chocolate from a large box on the table.*

NURSE: How does it feel?

MRS BRAMSON: Nasty. (*Munching her chocolate.*) I *know* it's neuritis.

NURSE: You know, Mrs Bramson, what you want isn't massage at all, only exercise. Your body——

MRS BRAMSON: Don't you dictate to me about my body. Nobody here understands my body or anything else about me. As for sympathy, I've forgotten the meaning of the word. (*To* OLIVIA.) What's the matter with your face?

OLIVIA (*startled*): I – I really don't know.

MRS BRAMSON: It's as long as my arm.

OLIVIA (*dryly*): I'm afraid it's made like that. (*She crosses the room, and comes back again.*)

MRS BRAMSON: What are you walking up and down for? What's the matter with you? Aren't you happy here?

OLIVIA: It's a bit lonely, but I'll get used to it.

MRS BRAMSON: Lonely? All these lovely woods? What *are* you talking about? Don't you like nature?

NURSE: Will that be all for today?

MRS BRAMSON: I suppose it'll have to be.

NURSE (*rising and taking her bag from the sofa*): Well, I've that confined lady still waiting in Shepperley. (*Going into the hall.*) Toodle-oo!

MRS BRAMSON: Mind you call Wednesday. In case my neuritis sets in again.

NURSE (*turning in the hall*): I will that. And if paralysis pops up, let me know. Toodle-oo!

> *She marches cheerily out of the front door.* MRS BRAM-SON *cannot make up her mind if the last remark is sarcastic or not. She concentrates on* OLIVIA.

MRS BRAMSON: You know, you mustn't think just because this house is lonely you're going to get a rise in salary. Oh no . . . I expect you've an idea I'm worth a good bit of money, haven't you? . . . It isn't my money you're after, is it?

OLIVIA (*setting chairs to rights round the table*): I'm sorry, but my sense of humour can't stand the strain. I'll have to go.

MRS BRAMSON: Can you afford to go?

OLIVIA (*after a pause, controlling herself*): You know I can't.

MRS BRAMSON: Then don't talk such nonsense. Clear the breakfast things.

OLIVIA *hesitates, then crosses to the kitchen door.*

(*Muttering.*) Sense of humour indeed, never heard of such a thing.

OLIVIA (*at the door*): Mrs Terence, will you clear away? (*She goes to the left window, and looks out.*)

MRS BRAMSON: You wait, my girl. Pride comes before a fall. Won't catch a husband with your nose in the air, you know.

OLIVIA: I don't want a husband.

MRS BRAMSON: Don't like men, I suppose? Never heard of them, I suppose? Don't believe you. See?

OLIVIA (*resigned*): I see. It's going to be a fine day.

MRS BRAMSON (*taking up 'East Lynne' from the table*): It'll cloud over, I expect.

OLIVIA: I don't think so. The trees look beautiful with the sun on them. Everything looks so clean. (*Lifting up three books from the window-seat.*) Shall I pack the other half of Mrs Henry Wood?

MRS BRAMSON: Mrs Henry Wood? Who's Mrs Henry Wood? Pack the other half of Mrs Henry Wood? What *are* you talking about?

OLIVIA: She wrote your favourite book – *East Lynne*.

MRS BRAMSON (*looking at her book*): Oh . . . (*Picking a paper out of it.*) What's this? (*Reading ponderously.*) A sonnet. 'The flame of passion is not red but white, not quick but slow——'

OLIVIA (*going to her and snatching it from her with a cry*): Don't!

MRS BRAMSON: Writing *poetry*! That's a hobby and a half, I must say! 'Flame of passion . . .' *Well!*

OLIVIA (*crossing to the fireplace*): It's only a silly poem I amused myself with at college. It's not meant for anybody but me.

MRS BRAMSON: You're a dark horse, you are.

> MRS TERENCE *enters from the kitchen. She is the cook, middle-aged, Cockney and fearless. She carries a bunch of roses.*

MRS TERENCE (*grimly*): Would you be wanting anything?

MRS BRAMSON: Yes. Clear away.

MRS TERENCE: That's Dora's job. Where's Dora?

OLIVIA: She's gone into the clearing for some firewood.

MRS BRAMSON: You can't expect the girl to gather firewood with one hand and clear breakfast with the other. Clear away.

MRS TERENCE (*crossing to the table, under her breath*): All right, you sour-faced old hag.

> HUBERT *drops his pipe.* MRS BRAMSON *winces and looks away.* MRS TERENCE *clears the table.*

HUBERT (*to* OLIVIA): What – what was that she said?

MRS TERENCE: She 'eard. And then she 'as to save 'er face and pretend she 'asn't. She knows nobody but me'd stay with 'er a day if I went.

MRS BRAMSON: She oughtn't to talk to me like that. I know she steals my sugar.

MRS TERENCE: That's a living lie. (*Going round to her.*) Here are your roses.

MRS BRAMSON: You've cut them too young. I knew you would.

MRS TERENCE (*taking up her tray and starting for the kitchen*): Then you come out and pick the ones you want, and you'll only 'ave yourself to blame.

MRS BRAMSON: That's a nice way to talk to an invalid.

MRS TERENCE: If you're an invalid, I'm the Prince of Wales. (*She goes back into the kitchen.*)

OLIVIA: Would you like me to read some more?

MRS BRAMSON: No. I'm upset for the day now. I'd better see she does pick the right roses. (*Wheeling herself, muttering.*) That woman's a menace. Good mind to bring an action against her. She ought to be put away. . . . (*Shouting.*) Wait for me, wait for me!

    Her voice dies away in the kitchen. The kitchen door closes. HUBERT *and* OLIVIA *are alone.*

OLIVIA: That's the fifth action she threatened to bring this week. (*She crosses to the right window.*)

HUBERT: She's a good one to talk about putting away. Crikey! She'll be found murdered one of these days. . . . (*Suddenly reading from his paper.*) 'In India a population of three and a half hundred million is loyal to Britain; now——'

OLIVIA: Oh, Hubert! (*Good-humouredly.*) I thought I'd cured you of that.

HUBERT: Sorry.

OLIVIA: You've only had two weeks of her. I've had six. (*A pause. She sighs restlessly.*)

HUBERT: Fed up?

OLIVIA: It's such a very inadequate expression, don't you think; . . . (*After a pause.*) How bright the sun is today. . . . (*She is pensive, far-away, smiling.*)

HUBERT: A penny for 'em.

OLIVIA: I was just thinking . . . I often wonder on a very fine morning what it'll be like . . . for night to come. And I never can. And yet it's got to. . . . (*Looking at his perplexed face.*) It *is* silly, isn't it?

> DORA *comes in from the kitchen with a duster and crosses towards the bedroom. She is a pretty, stupid, and rather sluttish country girl of twenty, wearing a maid's uniform. She looks depressed.*

Who are those men, Dora?

DORA: What men, miss?

OLIVIA: Over there, behind the clearing.

DORA: Oh. . . . (*Peering past her.*) Oh. 'Adn't seen them. What are they doing poking about in that bush?

OLIVIA (*absently*): I don't know. I saw them yesterday, too, further down the woods.

DORA (*lamely*): I expect they're looking for something. (*She goes into the kitchen.*)

HUBERT: She looks a bit off-colour, doesn't she?

OLIVIA: The atmosphere must be getting her down, too.

HUBERT: I'm wondering if I'm going to be able to stand it myself. Coming over here every day for another week.

OLIVIA (*smiling*): There's nothing to prevent you staying at *home* every day for another week . . . is there?

HUBERT (*still apparently reading the paper*): Oh yes, there is. What d'you think I invite myself to lunch every day for? You don't think it's the old geyser, do you?

OLIVIA (*smiling*): No. (*She comes down to the table.*)

HUBERT: Don't want to sound rude, et cetera, but women don't get men proposing to them every day, you know. . . . (*Turning over a page.*) Gosh, what a wizard machine——

OLIVIA (*sitting at the left of the table*): I can't think *why* you want to marry me, as a matter of fact. It isn't the same as if I were very pretty, or something.

HUBERT: You do say some jolly rum things, Olivia, upon my soul.

OLIVIA: I'll tell *you* why, then, if it makes you feel any better. You're cautious; and you want to marry me because I'm quiet. I'd make you a steady wife, and run a home for you

HUBERT: There's nothing to be ashamed of in being steady. I'm steady myself.

OLIVIA: I know you are.

HUBERT: Then why aren't you keen?

OLIVIA (*after a pause, tolerant but weary*): Because you're an unmitigated bore.

HUBERT: A bore? (*Horrified.*) *Me*, a bore? Upon my word, Olivia, I think you're a bit eccentric, I do really. Sorry to be rude, and all that, but that's put the kybosh on it! People could call me a thing or two, but I've never been called a bore!

OLIVIA: Bores never are. People are too bored with them to call them anything.

HUBERT: I suppose you'd be more likely to say 'Yes' if I were an unmitigated bounder?

OLIVIA (*with a laugh*): Oh, don't be silly. . . .

HUBERT (*going to her*): You're a rum girl, Olivia, upon my soul you are. P'raps that's why I think you're so jolly attractive. Like a mouse one minute, and then this straight-from-the-shoulder business. . . . What *is* a sonnet?

OLIVIA: It's a poem of fourteen lines.

HUBERT: Oh yes, Shakespeare. . . . Never knew you did a spot of rhyming, Olivia! Now that's what I mean about you. . . . We'll have to start calling you Elizabeth Brontë! (*She turns away. He studies her.*) You *are* bored, aren't you?

> *He walks to the sun-room. She rouses herself and turns to him impetuously.*

OLIVIA: I'm being silly, I know – of course I *ought* to get married, and *of course* this is a wonderful chance, and——

HUBERT (*moving to her*): Good egg! Then you will?

OLIVIA (*stalling*): Give me a – another week or two – will you?

HUBERT: Oh. My holiday's up on the twenty-seventh.

OLIVIA: I know I'm being tiresome, but——

MRS BRAMSON (*in the kitchen*): The most disgraceful thing I've ever heard——

HUBERT: She's coming back. . . .

> OLIVIA *rises and goes to the right window.* HUBERT *hurries into the sun-room.* MRS BRAMSON *is wheeled back from the kitchen by* MRS TERENCE, *to the centre of the room. She* (MRS BRAMSON) *has found the pretext for the scene she has been longing to make since she got up this morning.*

MRS BRAMSON: Fetch that girl here. This minute.

MRS TERENCE: Oh, leave the child alone.

MRS BRAMSON: Leave her alone, the little sneak-thief? Fetch her here.

MRS TERENCE (*at the top of her voice*): Dora! (*Opening the front door and calling into the trees.*) Dora!

OLIVIA: What's Dora done now?

MRS BRAMSON: Broken three of my Crown Derby,

that's all. Thought if she planted them in the rose-bed I wouldn't be well enough to see them, I suppose. Well, I *have* seen.

MRS TERENCE (*crossing and calling to the bedroom*): You're wanted.

DORA'S VOICE: What for?

MRS TERENCE: She wants to kiss you good morning, what d'you think. . . .

> *She collects the table cloth, fetches a vase from the mantelpiece, and goes into the kitchen.* DORA *enters gingerly from the bedroom carrying a cup and saucer on a tray.*

DORA: Did you want me, mum?

MRS BRAMSON: Crown Derby to you, my girl.

DORA (*uncertain*): Beg pardon, mum?

MRS BRAMSON: I suppose you think that china came from Marks and Spencer?

DORA: Oh . . . (*Snivelling.*) Oh . . . oh . . .

OLIVIA (*coming between* DORA *and* MRS BRAMSON): Come along, Dora, it's not as bad as all that.

DORA: Oh yes, it is. . . . Oh . . .

MRS BRAMSON: You can leave, that's all. You can leave.

> *Appalled,* DORA *drops the tray and breaks the saucer.*

That settles it. Now you'll *have* to leave.

DORA (*with a cry*): Oh, please I . . . (*Kneeling and collecting broken china.*) Oh, ma'am – I'm not meself, you see. . . . (*Snivelling.*) I'm in – terrible trouble. . . .

MRS BRAMSON: Have you been stealing?

DORA (*shocked*): Oh no!

OLIVIA (*after a pause*): Are you going to have a baby?

> *After a pause,* DORA *nods.*

DORA (*putting the china in her apron*): The idea of me stealing . . . I do go to Sunday School anyways. . . .

MRS BRAMSON: So that's the game. Wouldn't think

butter would melt in her mouth. . . . You'll have to go, of course; I can't have that sort of thing in this house – and stop squeaking! You'll bring my heart on again. It's all this modern life. I've always said so. All these films and rubbish.

OLIVIA: My dear auntie, you can't have a baby by just sitting in the pictures.

MRS BRAMSON: Go away, and don't interefere.

OLIVIA *goes to the left window.* DORA *rises.* (*Triumphantly.*) So you're going to have a child. When?

DORA (*sniffling*): Last August Bank Holiday. . . .

MRS BRAMSON: What? . . . Oh!

DORA: I 'aven't got a penny only what I earn – and if I lose my job 'ere——

MRS BRAMSON: He'll have to marry you.

DORA: Oh, I don't think he's keen. . . .

MRS BRAMSON: I'll *make* him keen. Who is the gentleman?

DORA: A boy I know; Dan his name is – leas' 'e's not a gentleman. He's a page-boy at the Tallboys.

MRS BRAMSON: The Tallboys? D'you mean that newfangled place all awnings and loud-speakers and things?

DORA: That's right. On the by-pass.

MRS BRAMSON: Just the nice ripe sort of place for mischief, it always looked to me. All those lanterns. . . . What's his character, the good-for-nothing scoundrel?

DORA: Oh, he's nice, really. He done the wrong thing by me, but he's all right, if you know what I mean. . . .

MRS BRAMSON: No, I don't. Where does he come from?

DORA: He's sort of Welsh, I think. 'E's been to sea, too. He's funny of course. Ever so open. Baby-face, they call him. Though I never seem to get 'old of what 'e's thinking somehow——

MRS BRAMSON: I'll get hold of what he's thinking, all right. I've had my knife into that sort ever since I was a girl.

DORA: Oh, mum, if I got him to let you speak to him – d'you think, I could stay on?

MRS BRAMSON (*after a pause*): If he marries you at once.

DORA: Shall I—— (*Eagerly.*) As a matter of fact, ma'am, he's gone on a message on his bicycle to Payley Hill this morning, and he said he might pop in to see me on the way back——

MRS BRAMSON: That's right; nothing like visitors to brighten your mornings, eh? I'll deal with him.

DORA: Yes. . . . (*Going, and turning at the kitchen door, in impulsive relief.*) Oh, ma'am——

MRS BRAMSON: And I'll stop the Crown Derby out of your wages.

DORA (*crestfallen*): Oh!

MRS BRAMSON: What were you going to say?

DORA: Well, ma'am, I *was* going to say I don't know how to thank you for your generosity. . . .

She goes into the kitchen. The clock chimes.

MRS BRAMSON: Olivia!

OLIVIA: Yes, auntie?

MRS BRAMSON: You've forgotten again. Medicine's overdue. Most important.

OLIVIA *crosses to the medicine cupboard and fetches the medicine.* MRS TERENCE *comes in from the kitchen with a vase of flowers and barges between the sofa and the wheel-chair.*

MRS TERENCE (*muttering*): All this furniture. . . .

MRS BRAMSON (*to her*): Did *you* know she's having a baby?

MRS TERENCE (*coldly*): She did mention it in conversation.

MRS BRAMSON: Playing with fire, that's the game nowadays.

MRS TERENCE (*arranging flowers as* OLIVIA *gives* MRS BRAMSON *her medicine*): Playing with fiddlesticks. We're only young once; that 'ot summer too. She's been a fool, but she's no criminal. And, talking of criminals, there's a p'liceman at the kitchen door.

MRS BRAMSON: A what?

MRS TERENCE: A p'liceman. A bobby.

MRS BRAMSON: What does he want?

MRS TERENCE: Better ask 'im. I know *my* conscience is clear; I don't know about other people's.

MRS BRAMSON: But I've never had a policeman coming to see me before!

DORA *runs in from the kitchen.*

DORA (*terrified*): There's a man there! From the p'lice! 'E said something about the Tallboys! 'E—'e 'asn't come about me, 'as 'e?

MRS TERENCE: Of course, he 'asn't——

MRS BRAMSON: He may have.

MRS TERENCE: Don't frighten the girl; she's simple enough now.

MRS BRAMSON (*sharply*): It's against the law, what she's done, isn't it? (*To* DORA.) Go back in there till he sends for you.

DORA *creeps back into the kitchen.*

OLIVIA (*at the left window*): He isn't a policeman, as a matter of fact. He must be a plain-clothes man.

MRS TERENCE (*sardonically*): Scotland Yard, I should think.

BELSIZE *is seen outside, crossing the left window to the front door.*

Mrs Bramson: That place in those detective books? Don't be so silly.

Mrs Terence: He says he wants to see you very particular——

A sharp rat-tat at the front door.

(*Going to the hall.*) On a very particular matter. . . . (*Turning on* Mrs Bramson.) And don't you start callin' me silly! (*Going to the front door, and opening it.*) This way, sir. . . .

Belsize *enters, followed by* Mrs Terence. *He is an entirely inconspicuous man of fifty, dressed in tweeds; his suavity hides an amount of strength.*

Belsize: Mrs Bramson? I'm sorry to break in on you like this. My card . . .

Mrs Bramson (*taking it, sarcastically*): I suppose you're going to tell me you're from Scotland Ya—— (*She sees the name on the card.*)

Belsize: I see you've all your wits about you!

Mrs Bramson: Oh. (*Reading incredulously.*) Criminal Investigation Department!

Belsize (*smiling*): A purely informal visit, I assure you.

Mrs Bramson: I don't like having people in my house that I don't know.

Belsize (*the velvet glove*): I'm afraid the law sometimes makes it necessary.

Mrs Terence *gives him a chair next the table. He sits.* Mrs Terence *stands behind the table.*

Mrs Bramson (*to her*): You can go.

Mrs Terence: I don't want to go. I might 'ave to be arrested for stealing sugar.

Belsize: Sugar? . . . As a matter of fact you might be useful. Any of you may be useful. Mind my pipe?

MRS BRAMSON *blows in disgust and waves her hand before her face.*

MRS BRAMSON: Is it about my maid having an illegitimate child?

BELSIZE: I beg your pardon? ... Oh no! That sort of thing's hardly in my line, thank God. ... Lonely spot. ... (*To* MRS TERENCE.) Long way for you to walk every day, isn't it?

MRS TERENCE: I don't walk. I cycle.

BELSIZE: Oh.

MRS BRAMSON: What's the matter?

BELSIZE: I just thought if she walked she might use some of the paths, and have seen – something.

MRS BRAMSON: Something of what?

MRS TERENCE: Something?

BELSIZE: I'll tell you. I——

A piano is heard in the sun-room, playing the 'Merry Widow' waltz.

(*Casually.*) Other people in the house?

MRS BRAMSON (*calling sharply*): Mr Laurie!

The piano stops.

HUBERT'S VOICE (*as the piano stops in the sun-room*): Yes?

MRS BRAMSON (*to* OLIVIA *sourly*): Did *you* ask him to play the piano?

HUBERT *comes back from the sun-room.*

HUBERT (*breezily*): Hello, house on fire or something?

MRS BRAMSON: Very nearly. This is Mr-er-Bel——

BELSIZE: Belsize.

MRS BRAMSON (*dryly*): Of Scotland Yard.

HUBERT: Oh ... (*Apprehensive.*) It isn't about my car, is it?

BELSIZE: No.

HUBERT: Oh. (*Shaking hands affably.*) How do you do?

22

BELSIZE: How do you do, sir . . .

MRS BRAMSON: He's a friend of Miss Grayne's here. Keeps calling.

BELSIZE: Been calling long?

MRS BRAMSON: Every day for two weeks. Just before lunch.

HUBERT: Well——

OLIVIA (*sitting on the sofa*): Perhaps I'd better introduce myself. I'm Olivia Grayne, Mrs Bramson's niece. I work for her.

BELSIZE: Oh, I see. Thanks. Well now . . .

HUBERT (*sitting at the table, effusively*): I know a chap on the Stock Exchange who was taken last year and shown over the Black Museum at Scotland Yard.

BELSIZE (*politely*): Really——

MRS BRAMSON: And what d'you expect the policeman to do about it?

HUBERT: Well, it was very interesting, he said. Bit ghoulish, of course——

BELSIZE: I expect so. . . . (*Getting down to business.*) Now I wonder if any of you've seen anything in the least out of the ordinary round here lately? Anybody called – anybody strange wandering about in the woods – overheard anything?

They look at one another.

MRS BRAMSON: The only visitor's been the doctor – and the district nurse.

MRS TERENCE: Been ever so gay.

HUBERT: As a matter of fact, funny thing did happen to me. Tuesday afternoon it was, I remember now.

BELSIZE: Oh?

HUBERT(*graphically*): I was walking back to my cottage

23

from golf, and I heard something moving stealthily behind a tree, or a bush, or something.

BELSIZE (*interested*): Oh, yes?

HUBERT: Turned out to be a squirrel.

MRS BRAMSON (*in disgust*): Oh! ...

HUBERT: No bigger than my hand! Funny thing to happen, I thought.

BELSIZE: Very funny. Anything else?

HUBERT: Not a thing. By Jove, fancy walking in the woods and stumbling over a dead body! Most embarrassing!

MRS TERENCE: I've stumbled over bodies in them woods afore now. But they wasn't dead. Oh no.

MRS BRAMSON: Say what you know, and don't talk so much.

MRS TERENCE: Well, I've told 'im all I've seen. A bit o' love now and again. Though 'ow they make do with all them pine-needles beats me.

BELSIZE: Anything else?

MRS BRAMSON: Miss Grayne's always moping round the woods. Perhaps *she* can tell you something.

OLIVIA: I haven't seen anything, I'm afraid. .... Oh – I saw some men beating the undergrowth——

BELSIZE: Yes, I'm coming to that. But no tramps, for instance.

OLIVIA: N-No. I don't think so.

HUBERT: Always carry a stick's my motto, I'd like to see a tramp try anything on with me. A-ha! Swish!

MRS BRAMSON: What's all the fuss about? Has there been a robbery, or something?

BELSIZE: There's a lady missing.

MRS TERENCE: Where from?

BELSIZE: The Tallboys.

MRS BRAMSON: That Tallboys again——
BELSIZE: A Mrs Chalfont.
MRS TERENCE: Chalfont? Oh yes! Dyed platinum blonde – widow of a colonel, so she says, livin' alone, so she says, always wearing them faldalaldy open-work stockings. Fond of a drop too. That's 'er.
HUBERT: Why, d'you know her?
MRS TERENCE: Never set eyes on 'er. But you know how people talk. Partial to that there, too, I'm told.
MRS BRAMSON: What's that there?
MRS TERENCE: Ask no questions, I'll tell no lies.
BELSIZE (*quickly*): Well, anyway . . . Mrs Chalfont left the Tallboys last Friday afternoon without a hat, went for a walk through the woods in this direction, and has never been seen since. (*He makes his effect.*)
MRS BRAMSON: I expect she was so drunk she fell flat and never came to.
BELSIZE: We've had the woods pretty well thrashed. (*To* OLIVIA.) Those would be the men you saw. Now she was . . .
HUBERT (*taking the floor*): She may have had a brainstorm, you know, and taken a train somewhere. That's not uncommon you know, among people of her sort. (*Airing knowledge.*) And if what we gather from our friend here's true – and she's both a dipsomaniac *and* a nymphomaniac——
MRS BRAMSON: Hark at the walking dictionary!
BELSIZE: We found her bag in her room; and maniacs can't get far without cash . . . however dipso or nympho they may be. . . .
HUBERT: Oh.
BELSIZE: She was a very flashy type of wo—she *is* a flashy type, I should say. At least I hope I should say. . . .

Mrs Bramson: What d'you mean? Why d'you hope?

Belsize: Well . . .

Olivia: You don't mean she may be . . . she mayn't be alive?

Belsize: It's possible.

Mrs Bramson: You'll be saying she's been murdered next!

Belsize: That's been known.

Mrs Bramson: Lot of stuff and nonsense. From a policeman, too. Anybody'd think you'd been brought up on penny dreadfuls.

Olivia *turns and goes to the window.*

Belsize (*to* Mrs Bramson): Did you see about the fellow being hanged for the Ipswich murder? In last night's papers?

Mrs Bramson: I've lived long enough not to believe the papers.

Belsize: They occasionally print facts. And murder's occasionally a fact.

Hubert: Everybody likes a good murder, as the saying goes! Remember those trials in the *Evening Standard* last year! Jolly interesting. I followed——

Belsize (*rising*): I'd be very grateful if you'd all keep your eyes and ears open, just in case. . . . (*Shaking hands.*) Good morning . . . good morning . . . good morning, Mrs Bramson. I must apologise again for intruding——

He *turns to* Olivia *who is still looking out of the window.*

Good morning, Miss . . . er . . .

A pause.

Olivia (*starting*): I'm so sorry.

Belsize: Had you remembered something?

Olivia: Oh no . . .

MRS BRAMSON: What were you thinking, then?

OLIVIA: Only how . . . strange it is.

BELSIZE: What?

OLIVIA: Well, here we all are, perfectly ordinary English people. We woke up . . . no, it's silly.

MRS BRAMSON: Of course it's silly.

BELSIZE (*giving* MRS BRAMSON *an impatient look*): No, go on.

OLIVIA: Well, we woke up this morning, thinking, 'Here's another day.' We got up, looked at the weather, and talked; and here we all are, still talking. . . . And all that time——

MRS BRAMSON: My dear girl, who are you to expect a policeman——

BELSIZE (*quelling her sternly*): If you please! I want to hear what she's got to say. (*To* OLIVIA.) Well?

OLIVIA: All that time . . . there may be something . . . lying in the woods. Hidden under a bush, with two feet just showing. Perhaps one high heel catching the sunlight, with a bird perched on the end of it; and the other – a stockinged foot, with blood . . . that's dried into the openwork stocking. And there's a man walking about somewhere, and talking, like us; and he woke up this morning, and looked at the weather. . . . And he killed her. . . . (*Smiling, looking out of the window.*) The cat doesn't believe a word of it anyway. It's just walking away.

MRS BRAMSON: Well!

MRS TERENCE: Ooh, Miss Grayne, you give me the creeps! I'm glad it *is* morning, that's all I can say. . . .

BELSIZE: I don't think the lady can quite describe *herself* as ordinary, after that little flight of fancy!

MRS BRAMSON: Oh, that's nothing; she writes poetry. Jingle jingle——

27

BELSIZE: I can only hope she's wrong, or it'll mean a nice job of work for us! . . . Well, if anything funny happens, nip along to Shepperley police station. Pity you're not on the phone. Good morning. . . . Good morning.

MRS TERENCE: This way. . . . (*She follows* BELSIZE *into the hall.*)

BELSIZE: No, don't bother. . . . Good morning. . . .

He goes out. MRS TERENCE *shuts the door after him.*

MRS BRAMSON (*to* HUBERT): What are *you* staring at?

HUBERT (*crossing to the fireplace*): Funny, I can't get out of my mind what Olivia said about the man being somewhere who's done it.

MRS TERENCE (*coming into the room*): Why, Mr Laurie, it might be you! After all, there's nothing in your face that *proves* it isn't!

HUBERT: Oh, come, come! You're being a bit hard on the old countenance, aren't you?

MRS TERENCE: Well, 'e's not going to walk about with bloodshot eyes and a snarl all over his face, is he? (*She goes into the kitchen.*)

HUBERT: That's true enough.

MRS BRAMSON: Missing woman indeed! She's more likely than not at this very moment sitting in some saloon bar. On the films, I shouldn't wonder. (*To* OLIVIA.) Pass me my wool, will you . . .

OLIVIA *crosses to the desk. A knock at the kitchen door.* DORA *appears, cautiously.*

DORA: *Was* it about me?

OLIVIA: Of course it wasn't.

DORA (*relieved*): Oh . . . please, mum, 'e's 'ere.

MRS BRAMSON: Who?

DORA: My boy fr—my gentleman friend, ma'am, from the Tallboys.

MRS BRAMSON: I'm ready for him. (*Waving aside the wool which* OLIVIA *brings to her.*) The sooner he's made to realise what his duty is, the better. I'll give him baby-face!

DORA: Thank you, ma'am. (*She goes out through the front door.*)

HUBERT: What gentleman? What duty?

OLIVIA: The maid's going to have a baby. (*She crosses and puts the wool in the cupboard of the desk.*)

HUBERT: Is she, by Jove! . . . Don't look at me like that, Mrs Bramson! I've only been in the country two weeks. . . . But is *he* from the Tallboys?

MRS BRAMSON: A page-boy or something of the sort.

DORA *comes back to the front door, looks back and beckons. She is followed by* DAN, *who saunters past her into the room. He is a young fellow wearing a blue pill-box hat, uniform trousers, a jacket too small for him, and bicycle-clips: the stub of a cigarette dangles between his lips. He speaks with a rough accent, indeterminate, but more Welsh than anything else.*

His personality varies very considerably as the play proceeds: the impression he gives at the moment is one of totally disarming good humour and childlike unself-consciousness. It would need a very close observer to suspect that there is something wrong somewhere – that this per-sonality is completely assumed. DORA *shuts the front door and comes to the back of the sofa.*

MRS BRAMSON (*sternly*): Well?

DAN (*saluting*): Mornin', all!

MRS BRAMSON: So you're Baby-face?

DAN: That's me. (*Grinning*). Silly name, isn't it? (*After*

29

a pause.) I must apologise to all and sundry for this fancy dress, but it's my working togs. I been on duty this mornin', and my hands isn't very clean. You see, I didn't know as it was going to be a party.

MRS BRAMSON: Party?

DAN (*looking at* OLIVIA): Well, it's ladies, isn't it?

HUBERT: Are you shy with ladies?

DAN (*smiling at* OLIVIA): Oh yes.

    OLIVIA *moves away coldly.* DAN *turns to* MRS BRAMSON.

MRS BRAMSON (*cutting*): You smoke, I see.

DAN: Yes. (*Taking the stub out of his mouth with alacrity and taking off his hat.*) Oh, I'm sorry. I always forget my manners with a cigarette when I'm in company. . . . (*Pushing the stub behind his ear, as* OLIVIA *crosses to the armchair.*) I always been clumsy in people's houses. I am sorry.

MRS BRAMSON: You know my maid, Dora Parkoe, I believe?

DAN: Well, we have met, yes. . . . (*With a grin at* DORA.)

MRS BRAMSON (*to* DORA): Go away!

    DORA *creeps back into the kitchen.*

You walked out with her last August Bank Holiday?

DAN: Yes. . . . Excuse me smiling, but it sounds funny when you put it like that, doesn't it?

MRS BRAMSON: You ought to be ashamed of yourself.

DAN (*soberly*): Oh, I am.

MRS BRAMSON: How did it happen?

DAN (*embarrassed*): Well . . . we went . . . did *you* have a nice Bank Holiday?

MRS BRAMSON: Answer my question!

HUBERT: Were you in love with the wench?

DAN: Oh yes!

Mrs Bramson (*triumphantly*): *When* did you first meet her?

Dan: Er-Bank Holiday morning.

Mrs Bramson: Picked her up, I suppose?

Dan: Oh no, I didn't pick her up! I asked her for a match, and then I took her for a bit of a walk, to take her mind off her work——

Hubert: You seem to have succeeded.

Dan (*smiling at him, then catching* Mrs Bramson's *eye*): I've thought about it a good bit since, I can tell you. Though it's a bit awkward talking about it in front of strangers; though you all look very nice people; but it is a *bit* awkward——

Hubert: I should jolly well think it is awkward for a chap! Though of course, never having been in the same jam myself——

Mrs Bramson: I haven't finished with him yet.

Hubert: In that case I'm going for my stroll. . . . (*He makes for the door to the hall.*)

Olivia: You work at the Tallboys, don't you?

Dan: Yes, miss. (*Grinning.*) Twenty-four hours a day, miss.

Hubert (*coming to* Dan's *left*): Then perhaps you can tell us something about the female who's been murdered.

> *An unaccountable pause.* Dan *looks slowly from* Olivia *to* Hubert *and back again.*

Well, *can* you tell us? You know there was a Mrs Chalfont staying at the Tallboys who went off one day?

Dan: Yes.

Hubert: And nobody's seen her since?

Dan: I know.

Mrs Bramson: What's she like?

31

DAN (*to* MRS BRAMSON): But I thought you said – or somebody said – something about – a murder?

HUBERT: Oh, we don't *know*, of course, but there *might* have been, mightn't there?

DAN (*suddenly effusive*): Yes, there might have been, yes!

HUBERT: Ever seen her?

DAN: Oh, yes. I used to take cigarettes an' drinks for her.

MRS BRAMSON (*impatiently*): What's she *like*?

DAN: What's she like? . . . (*To* MRS BRAMSON.) She's . . . on the tall side. Thin ankles, with one o' them bracelets on one of 'em. (*Looking at* OLIVIA.) Fair hair—— (*A sudden thought seems to arrest him. He goes on looking at* OLIVIA.)

MRS BRAMSON: Well? Go on!

DAN (*after a pause, in a level voice*): Thin eyebrows, with white marks, where they was pulled out . . . to be in the fashion, you know. . . . Her mouth . . . a bit thin as well, with red stuff painted round it, to make it look more; you can rub it off . . . I suppose. Her neck . . . rather thick. Laughs a bit loud; and then it stops. (*After a pause.*) She's . . . very lively. (*With a quick smile that dispels the atmosphere he has unaccountably created.*) You can't say I don't keep my eyes skinned, can you?

HUBERT: I should say you do! A living portrait, if ever there was one, what? Now——

MRS BRAMSON (*pointedly*): Weren't you going for a walk?

HUBERT: So I was, by Jove! Well, I'll charge off. Bye-bye. (*He goes out of the front door.*)

OLIVIA (*her manner faintly hostile*): You're very observant.

DAN: Well, the ladies, you know . . .

MRS BRAMSON: If he weren't so observant, that Dora mightn't be in the flummox she is now.

DAN (*cheerfully*): That's true, ma'am.

OLIVIA (*rising*): You don't sound very repentant.

DAN (*as she crosses, stiffly*): Well, what's done's done's my motto, isn't it?

> *She goes into the sun-room. He makes a grimace after her and holds his left hand out, the thumb pointing downward.*

MRS BRAMSON: And what does that mean?

DAN: She's a nice bit of ice for next summer, isn't she?

MRS BRAMSON: You're a proper one to talk about next summer when Dora there'll be up hill and down dale with a perambulator. Now look here, young man, immorality——

> MRS TERENCE *comes in from the kitchen.*

MRS TERENCE: The butcher wants paying. And 'e says there's men ferreting at the bottom of the garden looking for that Mrs Chalfont and do you know about it.

MRS BRAMSON (*furious*): Well, they won't ferret long, not among my pampas grass!...(*Calling.*) Olivia!...Oh, that girl's never there. (*Wheeling herself furiously towards the kitchen as* MRS TERENCE *makes a move to help her.*) Leave me alone. I don't want to be pushed into the nettles today thank you. . . . (*Shouting loudly as she disappears into the kitchen.*) Come out of my garden, you! Come out!

MRS TERENCE (*looking towards the kitchen as* DAN *takes the stub from behind his ear and lights it*): Won't let me pay the butcher, so I won't know where she keeps 'er purse; but I do know, so put that in your pipe and smoke it!

DAN (*going to her and jabbing her playfully in the arm*): They say down at the Tallboys she got enough inside of 'er purse, too.

Mrs Terence: Well, nobody's seen it open. If *you* 'ave a peep inside, young fellow, you'll go down in 'istory, that's what you'll do. (Dan *salutes her. She sniffs.*) Something's boiling over.

> *She rushes back into the kitchen as* Olivia *comes back from the sun-room.*

Olivia: Did Mrs Bramson call me, do you know?

> *A pause. He surveys her from under drooping lids, rolling his cigarette on his lower lip.*

Dan: I'm sorry. I don't know your name.

Olivia: Oh. (*She senses his insolence, goes self-consciously to the desk and takes out the wool.*)

Dan: Not much doin' round here for a girl, is there?

> *No answer.*

It is not a very entertaining quarter of the world for a young lady, is it?

> *He gives it up as a bad job.* Dora *comes in from the kitchen.*

Dora (*eagerly*): What did she . . . (*Confused, seeing* Olivia.) Oh, beg pardon, miss. . . .

> *She hurries back into the kitchen.* Dan *jerks his head after her with a laugh and looks at* Olivia.

Olivia (*arranging wool at the table*): I'm not a snob, but in case you ever call here again, I'd like to point out that though I'm employed by my aunt, I'm not quite in Dora's position.

Dan: Oh, I hope not. . . . (*She turns away, confused. He moves to her.*) Though I'll be putting it all right for Dora. I'm going to marry her. And I——

Olivia (*coldly*): I don't believe you.

Dan (*after a pause*): You don't like me, do you?

Olivia: No.

Dan (*with a smile*): Well, everybody else does!

OLIVIA (*absorbed in her wool-sorting*): Your eyes are set quite wide apart, your hands are quite good . . . I don't really know what's wrong with you.

DAN *looks at his outspread hands. A pause. He breaks it and goes nearer to her.*

DAN (*persuasively*): You know, I've been looking at you, too. You're lonely, aren't you? I could see——

OLIVIA: I'm sorry, it's a waste of time doing your stuff with me. I'm not the type. (*Crossing to the desk and turning suddenly to him.*) Are you playing up to Mrs Bramson?

DAN: Playin' up?

OLIVIA: It crossed my mind for a minute. You stand a pretty poor chance there, you know.

DAN (*after a pause, smiling*): What d'you bet me?

OLIVIA *turns from him, annoyed, and puts the wool away.* MRS BRAMSON *careers in from the kitchen in her chair.*

MRS BRAMSON: They say they've got permits to look for that silly woman – who are *they*, I'd like to know? If there's anything I hate, it's these men who think they've got authority.

OLIVIA: I don't think they're quite as bad as men who think they've got charm. (*She goes back into the sun-room.* DAN *whistles.*)

MRS BRAMSON: What did she mean by that?

DAN: Well, it's no good her thinkin' *she's* got any, is it?

MRS BRAMSON (*sternly*): Now, young man, what about Dora? I——

DAN: Wait a minute. . . . (*Putting his hat on the table and going to her.*) Are you sure you're comfortable like that? Don't you think, Mrs Bramson, you ought to be facin' . . . a wee bit more this side, towards the sun more, eh? (*He moves her chair round till she is in the centre of the room,*

35

facing the sun-room.) You're looking pale you know. (*As she stares at him, putting the stub in an ash-tray on the table.*) I am sorry. Excuse rudeness. . . . Another thing, Mrs Bramson – you don't mind me sayin' it, do you? – but you ought to have a rug, you know. This October weather's very treacherous.

MRS BRAMSON (*blinking*): Pale? Did you say pale?

DAN: Washed out. (*His wiles fully turned on, but not over-done in the slightest.*) The minute I saw you just now, I said to myself – now there's a lady that's got a lot to contend with.

MRS BRAMSON: Oh . . . Well, I have. Nobody knows it better than me.

DAN: No, I'm sure. . . . Oh, it must be terrible to watch everybody else striding up and down enjoying every-thing, and to see everybody tasting the fruit——

> *As she looks at him, appreciation of what he is saying grows visibly in her face.*

I'm sorry. . . . (*Diffidently.*) I didn't ha' ought to say that.

MRS BRAMSON: But it's true! As true as you are my witness, and nobody else—— (*Pulling herself together.*) Now look here, about that girl——

DAN: Excuse me a minute. . . . (*Examining her throat, like a doctor.*) Would you mind sayin' something?

MRS BRAMSON (*taken aback*): What d'you want me to say?

DAN: Yes . . .

MRS BRAMSON: Yes. What?

DAN: There's a funny twitching in your neck when you talk – very slight, of course – nerves, I expect—— But I hope your doctor knows all about it. . . . D'you mind if I ask what your ailments are?

MRS BRAMSON: . . . Hadn't you better sit down?

DAN (*sitting*): Thank you.

MRS BRAMSON: Well, I have the most terrible palpitations. I——

DAN: Palpitation? (*Whistling.*) But the way you get about!

MRS BRAMSON: Oh?

DAN: It's a pretty bad thing to have, you know. D'you know that nine women out of ten in your position'd be just sittin' down giving way?

MRS BRAMSON: Would they?

DAN: Yes, they would ! I do know, as a matter of fact. I've known people with palpitations. Somebody very close to me. . . . (*After a pause, soberly.*) They're dead now. . . .

MRS BRAMSON (*startled*): Oh!

DAN: My mother, as a matter of fact. . . . (*With finely controlled emotion, practically indistinguishable from the real thing.*) I can just remember her.

MRS BRAMSON: Oh?

DAN: She died when I was six. I know that, because my dad died two years before that.

MRS BRAMSON (*vaguely*): Oh.

DAN (*studying her*): As a matter o' fact——

MRS BRAMSON: Yes?

DAN: Oh, no, it's a daft thing——

MRS BRAMSON (*the old tart note creeping back*): Come along now! Out with it!

DAN: It's only fancy, I suppose . . . but . . . you remind me a bit of her.

MRS BRAMSON: Of your mother? (*As he nods simply, her sentimentality stirring.*) Oh . . .

DAN: Have *you* got a son?

MRS BRAMSON (*self-pityingly*): I haven't anybody at all.

37

DAN: Oh . . . But I don't like to talk too much about my mother. (*Putting a finger unobtrusively to his eye.*) Makes me feel . . . sort of sad. . . . (*With a sudden thought.*) She had the same eyes very wide apart as you, and – and the same very good hands.

MRS BRAMSON (*looking interestedly at her fingers*): Oh? . . . And the same palpitations?

DAN: And the same palpitations. You don't mind me talking about your health, do you?

MRS BRAMSON: No.

DAN: Well, d'you know you ought to get used to letting *other* people do things for you.

MRS BRAMSON (*a great truth dawning on her*): Yes!

DAN: You ought to be *very* careful.

MRS BRAMSON: Yes! (*After a pause, eyeing him as he smiles at her.*) You're a funny boy to be a page-boy.

DAN (*shyly*): D'you think so?

MRS BRAMSON: Well, now I come to talk to you, you seem so much better class – I mean, you know so much of the world.

DAN: I've knocked about a good bit, you know. Never had any advantages, but I always tried to do the right thing.

MRS BRAMSON (*patronisingly*): I think you deserve better—— (*Sharply again.*) Talking of the right thing, what about Dora?

DAN (*disarming*): Oh, I know I'm to blame; I'm not much of a chap, but I'd put things straight like a shot if I had any money. . . . But, you see, I work at the Tall-boys, get thirty bob a week, with tips – but listen to me botherin' you with my worries and rubbish the state you're in . . . well!

MRS BRAMSON: No! I can stand it.

OLIVIA *comes back from the sun-room.*
(*Pursing her lips, reflectively.*) I've taken a liking to you.

DAN: Well. . . . (*Looking round at* OLIVIA.) That's very kind of you, Mrs Bramson.

MRS BRAMSON: It's the way you talked about your mother. That's what it was.

DAN: Was it?

OLIVIA (*at the left window*): Shall I pack these books?

DAN (*going to her with alacrity, taking the parcel from her*): I'll post them for you.

OLIVIA: Oh . . .

DAN: I'm passing Shepperley post office on the bike before post time tomorrow morning. With pleasure!

MRS BRAMSON: Have you got to go back?

DAN: Now? Well no, not really . . . I've finished my duty now I done that errand, and this is my half-day.

MRS BRAMSON (*imperiously*): Stay to lunch.

DAN (*apparently taken aback, after a look at* OLIVIA): Well – I don't like to impose myself——

MRS BRAMSON: In the kitchen, of course.

DAN: Oh, I know——

MRS BRAMSON: There's plenty of food! Stay to lunch!

DAN: Well – I don't know . . . all right, so long as you let me help a bit this morning. . . . Don't you want some string for this? Where's it kep'?

MRS BRAMSON: That woman knows. In the kitchen somewhere.

DAN: Through here?

    He tosses the books on the sofa and hurries into the kitchen. MRS BRAMSON *holds out her hands and studies them with a new interest.*

MRS BRAMSON: That boy's got understanding.

OLIVIA: Enough to marry Dora?

MRS BRAMSON: You ought to learn to be a little less bitter, my dear. Never hook a man if you don't. With him and that Dora, I'm not so sure it wasn't six of one and half a dozen of the other. I know human nature, and mark my words, that boy's going to do big things.

A scurry in the garden. MRS TERENCE *rushes in from the front door, madly excited.*

MRS TERENCE: The paper-boy's at the back gate, and says there's a placard in Shepperley, and it's got 'News of the World – Shepperley Mystery' on it!

MRS BRAMSON: What!

OLIVIA: They've got it in the papers!

MRS TERENCE: They've got it in the papers! D'ye want any? (*Beside herself.*)

MRS BRAMSON: Catch him quick!

MRS TERENCE: First time I ever 'eard of Shepperley being in print before – hi! (*She races out of the front door.*)

MRS BRAMSON: Running around the house shouting like a lunatic! Sensation mad! Silly woman!

DORA *runs in from kitchen.*

DORA: They've got it in the papers!

MRS BRAMSON: Go away!

MRS TERENCE (*off*): I've bought three!

MRS BRAMSON (*shouting*): Be QUIET!

MRS TERENCE *runs back with three Sunday news-papers and gives one to* OLIVIA *and one to* MRS BRAMSON.

OLIVIA (*sitting left of the table*): I expect it is a bit of an event.

MRS TERENCE (*leaning over the table, searching in her paper*): 'E says they're selling like ninepins——

MRS BRAMSON (*turning pages over, impatiently*): Where *is* it? . . .

MRS TERENCE: Oh, I expect it's nothink after all. . . .

OLIVIA: Here it is. . . . (*Reading*.) 'Disappeared mysteriously . . . woods round the village being searched' . . . then her description . . . tall . . . blonde. . . .

MRS TERENCE: Blonde? I should think she is . . . I can't find it!

OLIVIA: Here's something . . . 'A keeper in the Shepperley woods was closely questioned late last night, but he has heard nothing, beyond a woman's voice in the woods on the afternoon in question, and a man's voice, probably with her, singing "Mighty Lak a Rose". Inquiries are being pursued. . . .'

MRS BRAMSON: 'Mighty Lak a Rose'. What rubbish! . . .

MRS TERENCE: Oh yes. . . . It's the 'eadline in this one. (*Humming the tune absently as she reads*.) 'Don't know what to call you, but you're mighty lak a rose.' . . . Those men have done rummaging in the garden, anyway.

MRS BRAMSON: I must go this minute and have a look at my pampas grass. And if they've damaged it I'll bring an action.

MRS TERENCE: Fancy Shepperley bein' in print——

MRS BRAMSON: Wheel me out, and don't talk so much.

MRS TERENCE (*manœuvring her through the front door*): I could talk me 'ead off and not talk as much as some people I could mention.

> OLIVIA *is alone. A pause. She spreads her paper on the table and finds* DAN's *hat under it. She picks it up and looks at it;* DAN *comes in from the kitchen with a ball of tangled string, a cigarette between his lips. He is about to take the books into the kitchen, when he sees her. He crosses to her.*

DAN: Excuse me. . . . (*Taking the hat from her, cheerfully*.) I think I'll hang it in the hall, same as if I was a visitor. . . . (*He does so, then takes up the books, sits on the sofa, and begins to unravel the string. A pause.*) You don't mind me stayin' and havin' a bit o' lunch . . . in the kitchen, do you?

OLIVIA: It's not for me to say. As I told you before I'm really a servant here.

DAN (*after a pause*): You're not a very ordinary servant, though, are you?

OLIVIA (*turning over a page*): N-no. . . .

DAN: Neither am I.

> *He unpicks a knot, and begins to hum absent-mindedly. The humming gradually resolves itself into faint singing.*

(*Singing.*) 'I'm a pretty little feller . . . everybody knows. . . .'

> OLIVIA *looks up; a thought crosses her mind. She turns her head and looks at him. The curtain begins to fall slowly.*

(*Singing, as he intently unravels the string.*) 'Don't know what to call me – but I'm mighty lak a rose. . . .'

THE CURTAIN IS DOWN

ACT II

SCENE 1

An afternoon twelve days later. The weather is a little duller.
MRS BRAMSON *is sitting on the right of the table in
her invalid chair, puzzling out a game of patience. She has
smartened up her appearance in the interval and is wearing
purple, and ear-rings.* OLIVIA *is sitting opposite her,
smoking a cigarette, a pencil and pad on the table in front of
her; and is pondering and writing. A portable gramophone
on a small table next the desk is playing the H.M.V. dance
record of 'Dames', or any jaunty tune with suitable words.*
A pause. MRS BRAMSON *coughs. She coughs again, and
looks at* OLIVIA, *waving her hand before her, clearing away
billows of imaginary smoke.*

OLIVIA: I'm sorry. Is my cigarette worrying you?
MRS BRAMSON (*temper*): Not at all. I like it!
   OLIVIA *stubs out her cigarette with a resigned look and
goes on making notes.* DAN *enters from the kitchen, keeping
time to the music, carrying a bunch of roses, wearing overalls
over flannel trousers and a brown golf jacket, and smoking.
He goes to the fireplace and clumps the roses into a vase on
the mantelpiece, humming the tune. He crosses to the gramophone, still in rhythm,* MRS BRAMSON *keeping time skit-
tishly with her hands. He turns the gramophone and looks
over* OLIVIA'S *shoulder at what she is writing.*
DAN (*singing*): 'Their home addresses . . . and their

43

caresses . . . linger in my memory of . . . those beautiful
dames' . . . (*His hand to his forehead.*) That's me!

> OLIVIA *looks at him coldly and continues her notes.*

MRS BRAMSON: It won't come out. . . .

> DAN *shrugs his shoulders, stands behind* MRS BRAM-
> SON's *chair, and studies her play.* OLIVIA *follows his
> example from her side.*

OLIVIA (*pointing to two cards*): Look.

MRS BRAMSON (*infuriated*): I saw that! Leave me alone,
and don't interfere.

> *A pause,* DAN *makes a quick movement and puts one
> card on another.*

(*Pleased and interested, quite unconscious of the difference in
her attitude.*) Oh yes, dear, of course.

OLIVIA (*as* MRS BRAMSON *makes a move*): No, that's a
spade.

MRS BRAMSON (*sharply*): No such thing; it's a club. It's
got a wiggle on it.

DAN: They both got wiggles on 'em. (*Pointing to
another card.*) This is a club.

MRS BRAMSON: Oh, yes, dear, so it is!

OLIVIA (*writing*): The ironmonger says there *were* two
extra gallons of paraffin not paid for.

MRS BRAMSON: And they *won't* be paid for either – not
if I have to go to law about it. (*A pause. She coughs absently.*)

DAN: I'm sorry. Is my cigarette worrying you!

MRS BRAMSON: Oh no, dear.

> *This has its effect on* OLIVIA. DAN *sits on the left of
> the table, where 'East Lynne' is open on the table.*

MRS BRAMSON: I'm sick of patience.

DAN (*reading laboriously*): 'You old-fashioned child——'

MRS BRAMSON: What?

DAN: *East Lynne.*

44

MRS BRAMSON: Oh . . .

DAN (*reading*): ' "You old-fashioned child!" retorted Mrs Vane, "Why did you not put on your diamonds?" "I – did – put on my diamonds," stay-mered Lady Isabel. "But I – took them off again." "What on earth for?" ' That's the other lady speaking there——

MRS BRAMSON: Yes dear. . . .

DAN: ' "What on earth for?" . . . "I did not like to be too fine," answered Lady Isabel, with a laugh' – (*turning over*) – 'and a blush. "They glittered so! I feared it might be thought I had put them on to look fine." '

MRS BRAMSON (*absently*): Good, isn't it?

DAN (*flicking ash*): Oh, yes, realistic. . . . (*Reading.*) " 'I see you mean to set up among that class of people who pree-tend to dee-spise ornyment," scornfully ree-marked Mrs Vane. "It is the ree-finement of aff-affectation, Lady Isabel——" '

> *An excited knock at the kitchen door.* DORA *enters.* DAN *turns back the page and surveys what he has been reading, scratching his head.*

MRS BRAMSON (*the old edge to her voice*): What is it?

DORA: Them men's in the wood again.

MRS BRAMSON: What men?

DORA: The men lookin' for that Mrs Chalfont.

> *A pause.* DAN *hums under his breath.*

MRS BRAMSON: You don't mean to tell me they're still at it? But they've been pottering about since . . . when was that day Mr Dan left the Tallboys?

DORA (*stressing a little bitterly*): *Mister* Dan?

DAN (*smiling*): Ahem! . . .

DORA: *Mister* Dan first came to work for you, mum, a week last Monday. . . .

MRS BRAMSON: Well, I think it's a disgrace——

DORA: *I've* found something!

> DAN'S *humming stops abruptly; he swivels round and looks at* DORA, *his face unseen by the audience.* OLIVIA *and* MRS BRAMSON *stare at* DORA; *a pause.*

MRS BRAMSON: *You've* found something?

OLIVIA: What?

DORA (*excitedly*): This!

> *She holds out her left arm and lets fall from her fist the length of a soiled belt. A pause.* OLIVIA *puts down her pencil and pad, goes to her, and looks at the belt.*

OLIVIA: Yes, of course, it's mine! I missed it last week. . . .

MRS BRAMSON (*baulked of excitement*): Oh yes, I thought I recognised it. . . . What nonsense! . . .

> DAN *looks at her chuckling.*

DORA (*going, dolefully*): I'm ever so disappointed. . . .

> *She goes into the kitchen.* OLIVIA *goes to the arm-chair by the fireplace.*

MRS BRAMSON: She'll be joining Scotland Yard next . . . Go on, dear.

DAN (*reading*): ' "It is the ree-finement of affectation, Lady Isabel——" ' (*The clock chimes. Clapping his hands, to* MRS BRAMSON.) Ah!

MRS BRAMSON (*pleased*): Oh, Danny. . . .

> *He hurries to the medicine cupboard and pours medicine into a spoon.* HUBERT *comes in from the front door.*

HUBERT (*eagerly*): Have you heard?

MRS BRAMSON (*eagerly*): What?

HUBERT: Dora's found a belt!

MRS BRAMSON (*disappointed again*): Oh. . . . It was Olivia's.

HUBERT: I say, what a shame! . . .

MRS BRAMSON: Tch, tch! . . . All this sensation-mong—— (DAN *drowns her speech by deftly pouring the spoonful of medicine down her throat. He pushes her chocolate-box towards her, and strides briskly into the hall.*) Horrid. . . .

DAN (*taking a soft hat from the rack and putting it on*): Good for you, though, the way you are. . . .

MRS BRAMSON: Yes, dear.

DAN (*coming into the room, and beginning to take off his overalls.*) And now it's time for your walk. . . . (*Smiling at* OLIVIA.) It's all right, I got trousers on. . . . (*Peeling the overalls over his feet and tossing them on to the left window-seat.*) Listen to me talking about your walk, when you'll be in a chair all the time. . . . (*Chuckling, to* HUBERT.) That's funny, isn't it! . . . (*Going to* MRS BRAMSON.) Come on, I got your shawl and your rug in the hall. . . .

MRS BRAMSON (*as he wheels her into the hall*): Have you got my pills?

DAN: I got them in my pocket.

MRS BRAMSON: And my chocolates?

DAN: I got them in my pocket, too. Here's your hat – better put it on yourself.

MRS BRAMSON: Yes, dear.

DAN: And here's your shawl.

MRS BRAMSON: It isn't a shawl, it's a cape.

DAN: Well, I don't know, do I? And I carry your rug on my shoulder. . . . (*To the others.*) See you later! Be good!

> *Shutting the front door, his voice dying, as the chair passes the left window.*

Down this way today. . . .

> *A pause.* HUBERT *and* OLIVIA *look at each other.*

OLIVIA (*suddenly*): What do *you* think of him?

HUBERT (*a little taken aback*): Him? Grannie's white-headed boy, you mean? Oh, he's all right. (*Heavily.*) A bit slow in the uptake, of course. I wish he'd occasionally take that fag-end out of his mouth.

OLIVIA: He does. For *her.*

HUBERT: That's true. That's why he's made such a hit with her. Funny I haven't been able to manage it. In two weeks too ... it's uncanny.

OLIVIA: Uncanny? ... I think it's clever.

HUBERT: You don't think he's a wrong 'un, do you?

OLIVIA: What do we know about him?

HUBERT: Why ... his Christian name——

OLIVIA: And that's all.

HUBERT: He looks pretty honest.

OLIVIA: Looks? (*After a pause.*) It's rather frightening to think what a face can hide ... I sometimes catch sight of one looking at me. Careful lips, and blank eyes. ... And then I find I'm staring at myself in the glass ... and I realise how successfully I'm hiding the thoughts I know so well ... and then I know we're all ... strangers. What's behind *his* eyes? (*After a pause, with a smile.*) You're quite right, it *is* morbid.

HUBERT: D'you think he's a thief or something? By Jove, I left my links on the wash-stand before lunch——

OLIVIA: He's acting ... every minute of the time. I know he is! But he's acting pretty well, because I don't know *how* I know. ... He's walking about here all day, and talking a little, and smiling, and smoking cigarettes. ... Impenetrable ... that's what it is! What's going on – in his mind? What's he thinking of? (*Vehemently.*) He *is* thinking of something! All the time. What is it?

> DAN *enters from the front door and smiles broadly at them.*

DAN: Anybody seen my lady's pills? It's a matter of life and death ... I thought I had 'em.

HUBERT *chuckles.*

OLIVIA (*after a pause, in a level voice*): Oh yes. They're in the top drawer of the desk. I'm so sorry.

DAN: Thank you. (*He salutes her, goes to the desk, and takes out the pills. They watch him.*)

MRS BRAMSON (*off*): Danny!

HUBERT (*to say something*): Is she feeling off colour again?

DAN (*on his way to the front door*): Off colour? She'd never been on it, man! To hear her go on you'd think the only thing left is artificial respiration. *And* chocolates. . . . (*Laughing and calling.*) Coming! (*He goes, shutting the front door behind him.*)

HUBERT: No, really, you have to laugh!

OLIVIA: But what you've just seen . . . that's exactly what I mean! It's acting! He's not being himself for a minute – it's all put on for our benefit . . . don't you see?

HUBERT (*banteringly*): D'you know, I think you're in love with him.

OLIVIA (*with rather more impatience than is necessary*): Don't be ridiculous.

HUBERT: I was only joking.

OLIVIA: He's common and insolent, and I dislike him intensely.

MRS TERENCE *comes in from the kitchen.*

MRS TERENCE: What'll you 'ave for tea, scones or crumpets? Can't make both.

OLIVIA: What *d'you* think of Dan?

MRS TERENCE: Dan? Oh, 'e's all right. Bit of a mystery.

HUBERT: Oh.

MRS TERENCE (*shutting the kitchen door and coming into the middle of the room*): Terrible liar, o' course. But then a lot of us are. Told me he used to 'unt to 'ounds and 'ave

49

'is own pack. Before 'e went up in the world and went as a page-boy I suppose.

OLIVIA (*to* HUBERT): You see? He wouldn't try that on with us, but couldn't resist it with her.

HUBERT: I wonder how soon the old girl'll get his number? . . . Oh, but fair play, we're talking about the chap as if he were the most terrible——

MRS TERENCE: Why, what's 'e done?

HUBERT: Exactly.

OLIVIA: I don't know, but I feel so strongly. . . . Is Dora there? . . . (*Calling cautiously.*) Dora!

MRS TERENCE: Oh, she won't know anything. She's as 'alf-witted as she's lazy, and that's sayin' a lot. She'd cut 'er nose off to stop the dust-bin smelling sooner than empty it, she would.

>DORA *comes in from the kitchen, wiping her hands on her apron.*

DORA: Did somebody say Dora?

OLIVIA: Has Dan said any more about marrying you?

DORA: No. *She* 'asn't brought it up again, either.

OLIVIA: Does he talk to you at all?

DORA (*perplexed*): Oh . . . only how-do-you-do and beg-your-pardon. I've never really spent any time in 'is company, you see. Except, o' course——

HUBERT: Quite. What's your idea of him?

DORA: Oh . . . (*Moving to the centre of the room.*) 'E's all right. Takes 'is fun where 'e finds it. And leaves it. . . . Cracks 'imself up, you know. Pretends 'e doesn't care a twopenny, but always got 'is eye on what you're thinking of 'im . . . if you know what I mean.

OLIVIA: Yes, I do. That incredible vanity . . . they always have it. Always.

HUBERT: Who? (*A pause.*)

OLIVIA: Murderers.

A pause. They stare at her.

HUBERT: Good God! . . .

MRS TERENCE: D'you mean . . . this woman they're looking for?

OLIVIA: I'm sure of it.

MRS TERENCE: But 'e's such a – such a ordinary boy——

OLIVIA: That's just it – and then he's suddenly so . . . extraordinary. I've felt it ever since I heard him sing that song – I told you——

HUBERT: That 'mighty-lak-a-rose' thing, you mean? Oh, but it's a pretty well-known one——

OLIVIA: It's more than that. I've kept on saying to myself: No, murder's a thing we read about in the papers; it isn't real life; it can't touch us . . . but it can. And it's here. All round us. In the forest . . . in this house. We're . . . living with it. (*After a pause, rising decisively.*) Bring his luggage in here, will you, Mrs Terence?

MRS TERENCE (*staggered*): 'Is luggage? (*Recovering, to* DORA.) Give me a 'and. (*Wide-eyed, she goes into the kitchen, followed by* DORA.)

HUBERT: I say, this is a bit thick, you know – spying——

OLIVIA (*urgently*): We may never have the house to ourselves again.

She runs to each window and looks across the forest. MRS TERENCE *returns carrying luggage; one large and one small suitcase.* DORA *follows, lugging an old-fashioned thick leather hat-box.* MRS TERENCE *places the suitcase on the table;* DORA *plants the hat-box in the middle of the floor.*

MRS TERENCE (*in a conspiratorial tone*): This is all.

HUBERT: But look here, we can't do this——

   OLIVIA *snaps open the lid of the larger suitcase with a jerk. A pause. They look, almost afraid.* DORA *moves to the back of the table.*

MRS TERENCE (*as* OLIVIA *lifts it gingerly*): A dirty shirt. . . .

HUBERT: That's all right.

OLIVIA: A clean pair of socks . . . packet of razor-blades. . . .

HUBERT: We shouldn't be doing this – I feel as if I were at school again.

MRS TERENCE: Singlet. . . .

OLIVIA: Half ticket to Shepperley Palais de Danse. . . .

MRS TERENCE: Oh, it's a proper 'aunt!

DORA: Oh, 'ere's a pocket-book. With a letter. (*She gives the letter to* MRS TERENCE *and the pocket-book to* OLIVIA.)

HUBERT: Look here, this is going a bit too far – you can't do this to a chap——

MRS TERENCE (*taking the letter from the envelope*): Don't be silly, dear, your wife'll do it to you 'undreds of times. . . . (*Sniffing the notepaper.*) Pooh . . . (*Reading, as they crane over her shoulder.*) 'Dear Baby-Face my own . . .' Signed Lil. . . .

OLIVIA: What awful writing. . . .

MRS TERENCE (*reading, heavily*): '. . . Next time you strike Newcastle, O.K. by me, baby. . . .' Ooh!

HUBERT: Just another servant-girl. . . . Sorry, Dora. . . .

DORA (*lugubriously*): O.K.

OLIVIA (*rummaging in the pocket-book*): Bus ticket to Thorburton, some snaps. . . .

MRS TERENCE: Look at 'er *bust!*

OLIVIA: Here's a group. . . . Look, Hubert. . . .

HUBERT *joins her in front of the table.*

HUBERT: This wench is rather fetching.

MRS TERENCE (*coming between them*): Look at 'er! . . .
The impudence, 'er being taken in a bathing suit! . . .

DORA: He's not in this one, is 'e?

HUBERT (*impressed*): Oh, I say . . . there *she* is!

MRS TERENCE: } Who?
DORA:

HUBERT: The missing female! In front of the tall man.
. . . You remember the photograph of her in the
Mirror?

DORA: It's awful to think she may be dead. Awful. . . .

MRS TERENCE: Looks ever so sexy, doesn't she?

DORA: 'Ere's one of a little boy——

OLIVIA: How extraordinary. . . .

HUBERT: What?

OLIVIA: It's himself.

DORA: The little Eton collar. . . . Oh dear . . . ever so
sweet, isn't it?

MRS TERENCE: Now that's what I call a real innocent
face. . . .

HUBERT (*going to the centre of the room*): Well, that's
that. . . .

OLIVIA: Wait a minute, wasn't there another one?
(*Seeing the hat-box.*) Oh yes. . . .

HUBERT (*lifting it on to the chair*): Oh, this; yes. . . .

DORA: Old-fashioned, isn't it?

MRS TERENCE: I should think he got it from a box-
room at the Tallboys——

OLIVIA (*puzzled*): But it looks extraordinary—— (*She
gives a sudden gasp. They look at her. She is staring at the box.
A pause.*)

HUBERT: What is it?

53

OLIVIA: I don't know. . . . Suppose there is something . . . inside it?

> *A pause. They stare at her, fascinated by her thought. The front door bangs. They are electrified into action; but it is too late. It is* DAN. *He goes briskly to the table.*

DAN: She wants to sit in the sun now and have a bit of *East Lynne*. Talk about changin' her mind——

> *He sees the suitcase on the table before him, and is motionless and silent. A pause. The others dare not move. He finally breaks the situation, takes up 'East Lynne' from the table, and walks slowly back to the front door. He stops, looks at* HUBERT, *smiles and comes down to him. His manner is normal – too normal.*

Could I have it back, please? It's the only one I got. . . .

HUBERT: Oh . . . yes, of course. . . . (*Handing him the pocket-book.*)

DAN (*taking it*): Thank you very much.

HUBERT: Not at all . . . I . . . (*To* OLIVIA.) Here, you deal with this. It's beyond me.

DAN (*to him*): Did you see the picture of me when I was a little fellow?

HUBERT: Yes . . . Very jolly.

DAN (*turning to* MRS TERENCE): Did *you*? It was in the inside of my wallet.

MRS TERENCE: Oh . . . was it?

DAN: Yes. Where I should be keeping my money, only any bit of money I have I always keep *on* me. (*Turning to* HUBERT.) Safer, don't you think?

HUBERT (*smiling weakly*): Ye'es. . . .

DAN: I only keep one ten-bob note in this wallet, for emergencies. . . . (*Looking.*) That's funny, it's gone. (*He looks at* HUBERT. *The others look blankly at one another.*) . . .

I expect I dropped it somewhere . . . what did you think
of the letter?

HUBERT: Letter?

DAN: You got it in your hand.

HUBERT: Well, I didn't – er——

DAN: Means well, does Lil; but we had a row. (*Taking
back the letter.*) She would spy on me. And if there's anything I hate, it's spyin'. Don't you agree?

HUBERT: Ye'es.

DAN: I'd sooner have anything than a spy. (*To* MRS
TERENCE.) Bar a murderer, o' course.

A pause. He is arranging his property in his wallet.

HUBERT (*incredulous*): What – what did you say?

DAN (*turning to him, casually*): Bar a murderer, o' course.

OLIVIA *steps forward.* MRS TERENCE *steps back from
the chair on which the hat-box has been placed.*

OLIVIA (*incisively*): Talking of murder, do you know
anything about Mrs Chalfont's whereabouts at the
moment?

DAN *turns to her, and for the first time sees the hat-box.
He stands motionless. A pause.*

DAN: Mrs Who?

OLIVIA: You can't pretend you've never heard of her.

DAN (*turning to* HUBERT, *recovering himself*): Oh, Mrs
Chalfont's whereabouts! I thought she said her name was
Mrs Chalfontswear. (*Profusely.*) Silly. . . . Swear – about –
couldn't think——

OLIVIA: Well?

DAN (*still looking at* HUBERT, *brightly after a pause*): I've
nothin' to go on, but I think she's been . . . murdered.

HUBERT: Oh, you do?

DAN: Yes, I do.

MRS TERENCE: Who by?

DAN: They say she had several chaps on a string, and—— (*Suddenly.*) There was one fellow, a London chap, a bachelor, very citified – with a fair moust—— (*He stares at* HUBERT.)

HUBERT (*touching his moustache, unconsciously*): What are you looking at me for?

DAN: Well . . . you wasn't round these parts the day she bunked, was you?

HUBERT: Yes, I was, as a matter of fact.

DAN (*significantly*): Oh. . . .

MRS BRAMSON'S VOICE (*calling in the garden*): Danny!

HUBERT(*flustered*): What in God's name are you getting at?

> DAN *smiles, shrugs his shoulders regretfully at him, and goes out through the front door.* OLIVIA *sits at the table.*

MRS TERENCE (*to* HUBERT, *perplexed*): Are you *sure* you didn't do it, sir?

HUBERT: I'm going out for a breath of air. (*He takes his hat and stick as he goes through the hall, and goes out through the front door.*)

MRS TERENCE (*to* OLIVIA): You don't still think——

OLIVIA: I won't say any more. I know how silly it sounds.

> DORA *runs into the kitchen, snivelling.*

MRS TERENCE (*to* OLIVIA): The way you worked us all up. Doesn't it all go to show——

> *She hears* DAN *return, and looks round apprehensively. He goes to the table slowly and looks at the two suitcases.*

DAN (*smiling to* MRS TERENCE): Would you mind please givin' me a hand with the tidyin' up. . . . (*Taking up the suitcases.*) And carryin' the other one? . . . (*Going into the*

kitchen, followed by MRS TERENCE *carrying the hat-box.*)
Looks as if we're goin' on our holidays, doesn't
it? . . .

> OLIVIA *is alone for a moment. She stares before her,
> perplexed.* DAN *returns. She looks away. He looks at her,
> his eyes narrowed. A pause. Studying her, he takes from
> the pocket of his jacket a formidable-looking clasp-knife,
> unclasps it, and tests the blade casually with his fingers. He
> glances at the mantelpiece, crosses to it, takes down a stick
> and begins to sharpen the end of it.* OLIVIA *watches him.
> A pause.*

OLIVIA: Did you do it?

> *He whittles at the stick.*

DAN: You wouldn't be bad-lookin' without them
glasses.

OLIVIA: It doesn't interest me very much what I look
like.

DAN: Don't you believe it. . . . (*Surveying the shavings in
the hearth.*) Tch! . . . Clumsy. . . . *Looking round and seeing
a newspaper lying on the table.*) Ah. . . . (*Crossing to the table,
then smiling, with the suspicion of a mock-bow.*) Excuse
me. . . . (*He unfolds the newspaper on the table and begins to
whittle the stick over it.*)

OLIVIA: You're very conceited, aren't you?

DAN (*reassuringly*): Yes. . . .

OLIVIA: And you *are* acting all the time, aren't you?

DAN (*staring at her, as if astonished*): Actin'? Actin' what?
(*Leaning over the table, on both arms.*) Look at the way I can
look you in the eyes. I'll stare you out. . . .

OLIVIA (*staring into his eyes*): I have a theory it's the
criminals who *can* look you in the eyes, and the honest
people who blush and look away.

DAN (*smiling*): Oh. . . .

OLIVIA (*after a pause, challenging*): It's a very blank look, though, isn't it?

DAN (*smiling*): Is it?

OLIVIA: You *are* acting, aren't you?

DAN (*after a pause, in a whisper, almost joyfully*): Yes!

OLIVIA (*fascinated*): And what are you like when you stop acting?

DAN: I dunno, it's so long since I stopped.

OLIVIA: But when you're alone?

DAN: Then I act more than ever I do.

OLIVIA: Why?

DAN: I dunno; 'cause I like it. . . . (*Breaking the scene, pulling a chair round to the table.*) Now what d'ye say if I ask a question or two for a change? (*Sitting in the chair, facing her.*) Just for a change . . . Why can't you take a bit of an interest in some other body but me?

OLIVIA (*taken aback*): I'm not interested in you. Only you don't talk. That's bound to make people wonder.

DAN: I can talk a lot sometimes. A drop o' drink makes a power o' difference to me. (*Chuckling.*) You'd be surprised. . . . Ah. . . . (*He returns to his work.*)

OLIVIA: I wonder if I would . . . .

DAN: I know you would. . . .

OLIVIA: I think I can diagnose you all right.

DAN: Carry on.

OLIVIA: You haven't any feelings . . . at all. . . .

He looks slowly up at her. She has struck home.

But you live in a world of your own. . . . A world of your own imagination.

DAN: I don't understand so very well, not bein' so very liter-er-airy.

OLIVIA: You follow me perfectly well.

He shrugs his shoulders, laughs, and goes on whittling.

58

DAN: D'you still think there's been a bit o' dirty work?

OLIVIA: I don't know what to think now. I suppose not.

DAN (*intent on his work, his back to the audience*): Disappointed?

OLIVIA: What on earth do you mean?

DAN: Disappointed?

OLIVIA (*laughing, in spite of herself*): Yes, I suppose I am.

DAN: Why?

OLIVIA (*the tension at last relaxed*): Oh, I don't know.... Because nothing much has ever happened to me, and it's a dull day, and it's the depths of the country. ... I don't know. ...

> *A piercing scream from the bottom of the garden. A pause.*

MRS BRAMSON (*shrieking, from the other side of the house*): Danny! ... Danny!

> *The clatter of footsteps in the garden.* DORA *runs in from the hall, breathless and terrified.*

DORA: They're diggin' ... in the rubbish-pit....

OLIVIA: Well?

DORA: There's something sticking out. ...

OLIVIA: What?

DORA: A hand.... Somebody's hand! ... Oh, Miss Grayne ... somebody's hand. ... (*She runs whimpering into the kitchen, and* OLIVIA *rises and runs to the left window and looks out.*)

MRS BRAMSON'S VOICE (*calling off*): Danny!

> DAN *rises slowly, his back to the audience.* OLIVIA *turns and suddenly sees him. Horror grows in her face.*
> *The blare of music.*
> *The lights dim out.*

SCENE II

*The music plays in darkness for a few bars, then the curtain rises
    again. The music fades away.*

> *Late afternoon, two days later.* OLIVIA *is seated above
> the table snipping long cuttings from newspapers and past-
> ing them into a ledger. A knock at the front door. She starts
> nervously. Another knock.* MRS TERENCE *comes in from
> the kitchen carrying a smoothing-iron.*

MRS TERENCE: If it's the police again, I'll bash their
helmets in with this. If it lands me three months, I
will.

OLIVIA: They're from Scotland Yard, and they don't
wear helmets.

MRS TERENCE: Then they're going to get 'urt. . . .
(*Going into the hall.*) I can tell by their looks what they
think. And they better not think it, neither.

OLIVIA: And what do they think?

MRS TERENCE (*over her shoulder*): They think it's me. I
know they think it's me. (*She goes into the hall and opens the
front door.*)

HUBERT (*outside*): Good afternoon, Mrs Terence.

MRS TERENCE: Oh . . . come in, sir. (*Coming back into
the room.*) It's a civilian for a change. (*She is followed by
HUBERT.*)

HUBERT (*to* OLIVIA): I say, this is all getting pretty
terrible, isn't it?

OLIVIA: Yes, terrible.

MRS TERENCE: Oh, terrible, terrible. There's one word
for it; it's terrible. Forty-eight hours since they found
'er. They'll never get 'im now.

HUBERT: Terrible.

MRS TERENCE: There was another charabanc load just after two o'clock. All standing round the rubbish 'eap eating sandwiches. Sensation, that's what it is.

OLIVIA: Would you like some food, Hubert?

HUBERT: Well, I——

MRS TERENCE: They're still looking for the 'ead.

HUBERT (*to* OLIVIA, *with a slight grimace*): No, thanks. I had lunch.

MRS TERENCE: Mangled, she was, mangled. . . . Did you see your name in the paper, sir?

HUBERT: I – er – did catch a glimpse of it, yes.

MRS TERENCE: Little did you think, sir, when you was digging that pit for my rubbish, eh? 'E may 'ave been watching you digging it . . . ooh! I have to sit in my kitchen and think about it.

HUBERT: Then why don't you leave?

MRS TERENCE (*indignantly*): How can I leave with the whole village waitin' on me to tell 'em the latest? (*Going towards the kitchen.*) I 'eard 'er 'ead must have been off at one stroke. One stroke. . . .

HUBERT: Really . . .

MRS TERENCE (*turning at the door*): She wasn't interfered with, though. (*She goes into the kitchen.*)

HUBERT: How they all love it. . . . How's the old lady bearing up in the invalid chair, eh?

OLIVIA: She's bursting out of it with health. And loving it more than anybody. This is my latest job – a press-cutting book. There was a picture of her in the *Chronicle* yesterday; she bought twenty-six copies.

HUBERT (*taking his pipe out*): She'll get to believe she did it herself in the end. . . . Is she in?

OLIVIA: She's gone over to Breakerly to interview a local paper.

HUBERT: The lad pushing the go-cart? . . . He's the devoted son all right, isn't he?

OLIVIA (*after a pause*): I don't talk to him much.

HUBERT: Nice fellow. I've thought a lot about that prying into his things – pretty bad show, you know. (*Going to the left window.*) I wonder if they'll ever nab him?

OLIVIA (*with a start*): What do you mean?

HUBERT: The fellow who did it. . . . Wonder what he's doing now.

OLIVIA: I wonder.

HUBERT: Damn clever job you know, quietly. . . . That was a rum touch, finding that broken lipstick in the rubbish-heap. . . . You know, the fact they still have no idea where this woman's head is——

OLIVIA (*convulsively*): Don't. . . .

HUBERT: Sorry.

OLIVIA (*after a pause*): It's a bit of a strain.

HUBERT (*earnestly*): Then why don't you leave?

OLIVIA: I – I couldn't afford it.

HUBERT: But you *could* if you married me! Now, look here—— (*Going to her.*) You said you'd tell me today. So here I am – er – popping the question again. There's nothing much to add, except to go over the old ground again, and say that I'm not what you'd call a terrible brainy chap, but I am straight.

OLIVIA: Yes, I know.

HUBERT: Though, again, I'm not the sort that gets into corners with a pipe, and never opens his mouth from one blessed year's end to the other. I can talk.

OLIVIA: Yes, you can.

HUBERT: An all-round chap, really – that's me.

OLIVIA: Yes.

HUBERT: Well?

OLIVIA: I'm sorry, Hubert, but I can't.

HUBERT: You can't? But you told me that day we might make a go of it, or words to that effect——

OLIVIA: I've thought it over since then, and I'm afraid I can't.

A pause.

HUBERT: What's changed you?

OLIVIA: Nothing's changed me, Hubert. I've just thought the matter over, that's all.

A pause. He crosses towards the fireplace.

HUBERT: Is it another man?

OLIVIA (*startled*): Don't be silly. (*Collecting herself.*) What man could I possibly meet cooped up here?

HUBERT: Sorry. Can't be helped. Sorry.

DAN (*in the garden*): There we are. Nice outing, eh——

OLIVIA: So am I.

The front door opens and DAN *wheels in* MRS BRAM-SON. *He is as serene as ever, but more animated than before. He is dressed the same as in the previous scene, and is smoking his usual cigarette.* HUBERT *sits at the table.*

DAN (*hanging up her rug in the hall*): Back home again – I put your gloves away——

MRS BRAMSON (*as he wheels her in*): I feel dead. (*To* HUBERT.) Oh, it's you . . . I feel dead.

DAN (*sitting beside her on the sofa, full of high spirits*): Don't you be a silly old 'oman, you look as pretty as a picture – strawberries and cream in your face, and not a day over forty; and when I've made you a nice cup of tea you'll be twenty-five in the sun and eighteen with your back to the light, so you think yourself lucky!

MRS BRAMSON (*as he digs her in the side*): Oh, Danny, you are a terror! (*To the others.*) He's been at me like this all the way. I must say it keeps me alive.

DAN (*as she hands him her hat and cape*): But you feel dead. I get you.

MRS BRAMSON (*kittenish*): Oh, you caution! You'll be the death of me.

DAN (*wagging his finger at her*): Ah-ha! (*Hanging up her things in the hall.*) Now what'd you like a drop of in your tea – gin, whisky, liqueur brandy, or a nice dollop of sailor's rum, eh?

MRS BRAMSON: Just listen to him! Now don't make me laugh, dear, because there's always my heart.

DAN (*sitting beside her again*): You've lost your heart, you know you have to the little feller that pushes your pram – you know you have!

MRS BRAMSON (*laughing shrilly*): Pram! Well! (*Her laugh cut short.*) It's wicked to laugh, with this – this thing all round us.

DAN (*sobering portentously*): I forgot. (*As she shivers.*) Not in a draught, are you? (*Shutting the front door and coming down to* HUBERT.) D'you remember, Mr Laurie, me, pulling your leg about you havin' done it? Funniest thing out! . . . Talk about laugh!

MRS BRAMSON (*fondly*): Tttt! . . .

DAN (*a glint of mischief in his eyes*): I think I better get the tea before I get into hot water. (*He goes towards the kitchen.*)

OLIVIA: Mrs Terence is getting the tea.

DAN (*at the door*): She don't make tea like me. I'm an old sailor, Miss Grayne. Don't you forget that. (*He goes into the kitchen.*)

OLIVIA: I'm not interested, I'm afraid.

MRS BRAMSON (*wheeling herself to the front of the table*): Look here, Olivia, you're down right rude to that boy, and if there's one thing that never gets a woman anywhere, it's rudeness. What have you got against him?

HUBERT: Surely he's got more to say for himself today then when I met him before.

MRS BRAMSON: Oh, he's been in rare spirits all day.

HUBERT: Johnny Walker, judging by the whiff of breath I got just now.

MRS BRAMSON: Meaning whisky?

HUBERT: Yes.

OLIVIA: I've never heard you make a joke before, Hubert.

HUBERT: Didn't realise it was one till I'd said it. Sorry.

MRS BRAMSON: It's not a joke; it's a libel. (*A knock at the front door.*) Come in. The boy's a teetotaller.

> NURSE LIBBY *enters from the front door.*

HUBERT: Sorry, my mistake.

NURSE: Good afternoon. Shall I wait for you in your bedroom?

MRS BRAMSON: Yes. I feel absolutely dead.

NURSE (*turning at the bedroom, eagerly*): Anything new *re* the murder?

HUBERT: I believe her head was cut off at one stroke.

NURSE (*brightly*): Oh, poor thing. . . .

> She goes into the bedroom. DAN *returns from the kitchen, carrying a tray of tea and cakes.*

DAN: There you are, fresh as a daisy. Three lumps, as per usual, and some of the cakes you like——

MRS BRAMSON (*as he pours out her tea*): Thank you, dear. . . . Let me smell your breath. (*After smelling it.*) Clean as a whistle. Smells of peppermints.

OLIVIA: Yes. There were some in the kitchen.

HUBERT: Oh.

MRS BRAMSON (*to* HUBERT, *as* DAN *pours out two more cups*): So you won't stay to tea, Mr – er——

HUBERT: Er – (*rising*) – no thank you. . . . (DAN *sits in* HUBERT's *chair*.) I think I'll get off before it's dark. Good-bye, Mrs Bramson. Good-bye, Mr – er——

DAN (*grinning and saluting*): Dan. Just Dan. (*He opens the press-cutting ledger*.)

HUBERT (*to* OLIVIA): Good-bye.

OLIVIA (*rises*): Good-bye, Hubert. I'm sorry.

      DAN *raises his cup as if drinking a toast to* MRS BRAMSON. *She follows suit.*

HUBERT: Can't be helped. . . . It'll get dark early today, I think. Funny how the evenings draw in this time of year. Good night.

DAN: Good night.

HUBERT (*to* OLIVIA): Good-bye.

OLIVIA: Good-bye. (*She goes to the right window-seat*.)

MRS BRAMSON: Johnny Walker, indeed! Impertinence!

DAN (*drinking tea and scanning press-cuttings*): Johnny Walker?

MRS BRAMSON: Never you mind, dear. . . . Any more of those terrible people called? Reporters? Police?

DAN (*gaily*): There's a definite fallin' off in attendance today. Sunday, I expect.

MRS BRAMSON: Hush, don't talk like that, dear.

DAN: Sorry, mum.

MRS BRAMSON: And don't call me 'mum'!

DAN: Well, if I can't call you Mrs. Bramson, what can I call you.

MRS BRAMSON: If you were very good, I might let you call me . . . mother!

DAN (*mischievously, his hand to his forehead*): O.K., mother.

MRS BRAMSON (*joining in his laughter*): Oh, you are in a mood today! (*Suddenly, imperiously*.) I want to be read to, now.

DAN (*crossing to the desk in mock resignation*): Your servant, mother o' mine. . . . What'll you have? *The Channings? The Red Court Farm?*

MRS BRAMSON. I'm tired of them.

DAN: Well . . . oh! (*Taking a large Bible from the top of the desk.*) What about the Bible?

MRS BRAMSON: The Bible?

DAN: It's Sunday, you know. I was brought up to it!

MRS BRAMSON: So was I . . . *East Lynne's* nice, though.

DAN: Not so nice as the Bible.

MRS BRAMSON (*doubtfully*): All right, dear; makes a nice change. . . . Not that I don't often dip into it.

DAN: I'm sure you do. (*Blowing the dust off the book.*) Now where'll I read?

MRS BRAMSON (*unenthusiastic*): At random's nice, don't you think, dear?

DAN: At random. . . . Yes. . . .

MRS BRAMSON: The Old Testament.

DAN (*turning over leaves thoughtfully*): At random in the Old Testament's a bit risky, don't you think so?

    MRS TERENCE *comes in from the kitchen.*

MRS TERENCE (*to* MRS BRAMSON): The paper-boy's at the door again and says you're in the *News of the World* again.

MRS BRAMSON (*interested*): Oh! . . . (*Simulating indifference.*) That horrible boy again, when the one thing I want is to blot the whole thing out of my mind.

MRS TERENCE: 'Ow many copies d'you want?

MRS BRAMSON: Get three.

MRS TERENCE: *And* 'e says there's a placard in Shepperley with your name on it.

MRS BRAMSON: What does it say?

MRS TERENCE: 'Mrs Bramson Talks'. (*She goes back towards the kitchen.*)

MRS BRAMSON: Oh. (*As* MRS TERENCE *reaches the kitchen door.*) Go at once into Shepperley and order some. At once!

MRS TERENCE: Can't be done.

MRS BRAMSON: Can't be done? What d'you mean, can't be done? It's a scandal. What are you paid for?

MRS TERENCE (*coming back, furious*): I'm not paid! And 'aven't been for two weeks! And I'm not coming to-morrow unless I am. Put that in your copybook and blot it. (*She goes into the kitchen, banging the door.*)

MRS BRAMSON: Isn't paid? Is she mad? (*To* OLIVIA.) Are you mad? Why don't you pay her?

OLIVIA (*coming down*): Because you don't give me the money to do it with.

MRS BRAMSON: I – (*fumbling at her bodice*) – wheel me over to that cupboard.

> OLIVIA *is about to do so, when she catches* DAN'S *eye.*

OLIVIA (*to* DAN *pointedly*): Perhaps *you'd* go into the kitchen and get the paper from Mrs Terence?

DAN (*after a second's pause, with a laugh*): Of course I will, madam! Anythin' you say! Anythin' you say!

> *He careers into the kitchen, still carrying the Bible.* MRS BRAMSON *has fished up two keys on the end of a long black tape.* OLIVIA *wheels her over to the cupboard above the fireplace.*

OLIVIA: If you give me the keys, I'll get it for you.

MRS BRAMSON: No fear! (*She unlocks the cupboard; it turns out to be a small but very substantial safe. Unlocking the safe, muttering to herself.*) Won't go into Shepperley, indeed . . . never heard of such impertinence. . . . (*She takes out a cash-box from among some deeds, unlocks it with the smaller key, and takes out a mass of five-pound and pound notes.*) The way these servants – what are you staring at?

OLIVIA: Isn't it rather a lot of money to have in the house?

MRS BRAMSON: 'Put not your trust in banks' is my motto, and always will be.

OLIVIA: But that's hundreds of pounds! It——

MRS BRAMSON (*handing her two notes*): D'you wonder I wouldn't let you have the key?

OLIVIA: Has . . . anybody else asked you for it?

MRS BRAMSON (*locking the cash-box and putting it back in the safe*): I wouldn't let a soul touch it. Not a soul. Not even Danny. (*She snaps the safe, locks it, and slips the keys back into her bosom.*)

OLIVIA: Has *he* asked you for it?

MRS BRAMSON: It's enough to have these policemen prying, you forward girl, without——

OLIVIA (*urgently*): Please! Has he?

MRS BRAMSON: Well, he did offer to fetch some money yesterday for the dairy. But I wouldn't give him the key. Oh no!

OLIVIA: Why?

MRS BRAMSON: Do I want to see him waylaid and attacked, and my key stolen? Oh no, I told him, that key stays on me——

OLIVIA: Did he – know how much money there is in there?

MRS BRAMSON: I told him. Do you wonder I stick to the key, I said – what *is* the matter with you, all these questions?

OLIVIA: Oh, it's no use——

    She goes to the arm-chair below the fireplace and sits in it. DAN *returns from the kitchen, with a copy of the 'News*

*of the World'; the Bible tucked under his arm, a cigarette
stub between his lips.*

DAN: He says they're sellin' like hot cakes! (*Handing
the paper to* MRS BRAMSON.) There you are, I've found the
place for you – whole page, headlines an' all. . . .

MRS BRAMSON: Oh yes. . . .

 DAN *stands with one knee on the sofa, and turns over
the pages of his Bible.*

(*Reading breathlessly, her back to the fireplace.*) '. . . The
Victim's Past' . . . with another picture of me underneath!
(*Looking closer, dashed.*) Oh, taken at Tonbridge the year
before the war; really it isn't right. . . . (*To* OLIVIA,
savouring it.) 'The Bungalow of Death! . . . Gruesome
finds. . . . Fiendish murderer still at large. . . . The enigma
of the missing head . . . where is it buried ? . . .' Oh yes!
(*She goes on reading silently to herself.*)

DAN (*suddenly in a clear voice*): '. . . Blessed is the man
. . . that walketh not in the counsel of the ungodly . . .
nor standeth in the way of sinners . . . nor sitteth in the
seat of the scornful. . . .'

MRS BRAMSON (*impatiently*): Oh, the print's too
small. . . .

DAN (*firmly*): Shall I read it to you ?

MRS BRAMSON: Yes dear, do. . . .

 *He shuts the Bible with a bang, throws it on the sofa,
and takes the paper from her.* OLIVIA *watches him intently;
he smiles at her slowly and brazenly as he shakes out the
paper.*

DAN (*reading laboriously*): '. . . The murderer com-
mitted the crime in the forest most – in the forest, most
likely strippin' beforehand——

 DORA *comes in from the kitchen, and stands at the door,
arrested by his reading. She is dressed in Sunday best.*

(*Reading.*) '. . . and cleansin' himself afterwards in the forest lake——

MRS BRAMSON: Tch! tch!

DAN (*reading*): '. . . He buried the body shallow in the open pit, cunnin'ly chancin' it bein' filled, which it was next day, the eleventh——' (*Nodding to* OLIVIA.) That was the day 'fore I come here. . . .

MRS BRAMSON: So it was. . . .

DAN (*reading*): 'The body was nude. Attempts had been made to . . . turn to foot of next column. . . .' (*Doing so.*) 'Attempts had been made to . . . era-eradicate finger-prints with a knife. . . .'

Far away, the tolling of village bells.

(*Reading.*) '. . . The head was severed by a skilled person, possibly a butcher. The murderer——' (*He stops suddenly, raises his head, smiles, takes the cigarette stub, puts it behind his ear, and listens.*)

OLIVIA: What's the matter?

MRS BRAMSON: Can you hear something? Oh, I'm scared.

DAN: I forgot it was Sunday. . . . They're goin' to church in the villages. All got up in their Sunday best, with prayer-books, and the organ playin', and the windows shinin'. Shinin' on holy things, because holy things isn't afraid of the daylight.

MRS BRAMSON: But Danny, what on earth are you——

DAN (*quelling her*): But all the time, the daylight's movin' over the floor, and by the end of the sermon the air in the church is turning grey. . . . And people isn't able to think of holy things so much no more, only of the terrible things that's goin' on outside, that everybody's readin' about in the papers! (*Looking at* OLIVIA.) Because they know that though it's still daylight, and everythin's or'nary and quiet . . . today will be the same as all the other days, and come to an end, and it'll be night. . . . (*After a pause, coming to earth again with a laugh at the others, throwing the newspaper on the sofa.*) I forgot it was Sunday!

MRS BRAMSON (*overawed*): Good gracious . . . what's come over you, Danny?

DAN (*with exaggerated animation*): Oh, I speechify like anything when I'm roused! I used to go to Sunday School, see, and the thoughts sort of come into my head. Like as if I was reading' off a book! (*Slapping the Bible.*)

MRS BRAMSON: Dear, dear. . . . You should have been a preacher. You should!

DAN *laughs loudly and opens the Bible.*

DORA (*going to the table and collecting the tea-tray*): I never knew 'e 'ad so many words in 'is 'ead. . . .

MRS BRAMSON (*suddenly*): I want to lie down now, and be examined.

DAN (*rising*): Anything you say, mother o' mine. . . . Will you have your medicine in your room as well, eh?

MRS BRAMSON: Yes, dear. . . . Olivia, you *never* got a new bottle yesterday!

DAN (*as he wheels her into her bedroom*): I got it today while you were with the chap. . . . Popped in at the chemist's.

MRS BRAMSON: Oh, thank you, dear. The one by the mortuary? . . . Oh, my back. . . . Nurse!

> *Her voice is lost in the bedroom. The daylight begins to fade. The church bells die away.*

DORA: My sister says all this is wearin' me to a shadow.

OLIVIA: It is trying, isn't it?

DORA: You look that worried, too, Miss Grayne.

OLIVIA: Do I?

DORA: As if you was waiting for something to 'appen.

OLIVIA: Oh?

DORA: Like an explosion. A bomb, or something.

OLIVIA (*smiling*): I don't think that's very likely. . . .
(*Lowering her voice.*) Have you talked to Dan at all this
week?

DORA: Never get the chance. 'E's too busy dancin'
attendance on Madam Crocodile. . . .

> DAN *comes back from the bedroom, his cigarette-stub*
> *between his lips.*

(*Going towards the kitchen.*) I'm off. You don't catch me
'ere after dark.

DAN: Why, will ye be late for courting?

DORA: If I was, they'd wait for me. Good afternoon,
Miss Grayne. Good afternoon . . . *sir.*

DAN (*winking at* OLIVIA): Are you sure they'd wait?

DORA: You ought to know.

> *She goes into the kitchen.* DAN *and* OLIVIA *are alone.*
> DAN *crosses to the sofa with a laugh, humming gaily.*

DAN: 'Their home addresses . . . and their caresses. . . .'
(*He sits on the end of the sofa.*)

OLIVIA: You've been drinking, haven't you?

DAN (*after a pause, quizzically*): You don't miss much,
do you?

OLIVIA (*significantly*): No.

DAN (*rubbing his hands*): I've been drinking, and I feel
fine! . . . (*Brandishing the Bible.*) You wouldn't like another
dose of reading?

OLIVIA: I prefer talking.

DAN (*putting down the Bible*): Carry on.

OLIVIA: Asking questions.

DAN (*catching her eye*): Carry on! (*He studies his outspread
hands.*)

OLIVIA (*crisply*): Are you sure you were ever a sailor! Are you sure you weren't a butcher?

> *A pause. He looks at her, slowly, then breaks the look abruptly.*

DAN (*rising with a smile and standing against the mantelpiece*): Aw, talkin's daft! *Doin's* the thing!

OLIVIA: You can talk too.

DAN: Aw, yes! D'you hear me just now? She's right, you know, I should ha' been a preacher. I remember, when I was a kid, sittin' in Sunday school – catching my mother's eye where she was sitting by the pulpit, with the sea behind her; and she pointed to the pulpit, and then to me, as if to say, that's the place for you. . . . (*Far away, pensive.*) I never forgot that.

> *A pause.*

OLIVIA: I don't believe a word of it.

DAN: Neither do I, but it sounds wonderful. (*Leaning over confidentially.*) I never saw my mam, and I never had a dad, and the first thing I remember is . . . Cardiff Docks. And you're the first 'oman I ever told that, so you can compliment yourself. Or the drink. (*Laughing.*) I think it's the drink.

OLIVIA: You *do* live in your imagination, don't you?

DAN (*reassuringly*): Yes. . . . It's the only way to bear with the awful things you have to do.

OLIVIA: What awful things?

DAN: Well. . . . (*Grinning like a child and going back to the sofa.*) Ah-ha! . . . I haven't had as much to drink as all that! (*Sitting on the sofa.*) Ah-ha! . . .

OLIVIA: You haven't a very high opinion of women, have you?

DAN *makes a gesture with his hands, pointing the thumbs downwards with a decisive movement.*

DAN: Women don't have to be drunk to talk. . . . You don't talk that much though, fair play. (*Looking her up and down, insolently.*) You're a dark horse, you are.

A pause. She rises abruptly and stands at the fireplace, her back to him. She takes off her spectacles.

Ye know, this isn't the life for you. What is there to it? Tell me that.

OLIVIA (*sombrely*): What is there to it . . . ?

DAN: Yes. . . .

OLIVIA: Getting up at seven, mending my stockings or washing them, having breakfast with a vixenish old woman and spending the rest of the day with her, in a dreary house in the middle of a wood and going to bed at eleven. . . . I'm plain, I haven't got any money, I'm shy, and I haven't got any friends.

DAN (*teasing*): Don't you *like* the old lady?

OLIVIA: I could kill her. (*A pause. She realises what she has said.*)

DAN (*with a laugh*): Oh no, you couldn't! . . . Not many people have it in them to kill people. . . . Oh no!

She looks at him. A pause. He studies the palms of his hands, chuckling to himself.

OLIVIA: And what was there to *your* life at the Tall-boys?

DAN: My life? Well. . . . The day don't start so good, with a lot of stuck-up boots to clean, and a lot of silly high heels all along the passage waitin' for a polish, and a lot of spoons to clean that's been in the mouths of gapin' fools that looks through me as if I was a dirty window hadn't been cleaned for years. . . . (*Throwing his stub into the fire in a sudden crescendo of fury.*) Orders, orders, orders;

75

go here, do this, don't do that you idiot, open the door for me, get a move on – I was never meant to take orders, never! . . . Down in the tea-place there's an old white beard wigglin'. 'Waiter, my tea's stone cold.' (*Furiously.*) I'm not a waiter, I'm a millionaire, and everybody's under me! . . . And just when I think I got a bit o' peace . . . (*his head in his hands*) . . . there's somebody . . . lockin' the the bedroom door . . . (*raising his head*) . . . won't let me get out; talk, talk, talk, won't fork out with no more money, at me, at me, at me, won't put no clothes on, calls me everythin', lie on the floor and screams and screams, so nothin' keeps that mouth shut only . . . (*A pause.*) It's raining out of the window, and the leaves is off the trees . . . oh, Lord . . . I wish I could hear a bit o' music . . . (*smiling, slowly*) . . . And I do, inside o' myself! And I have a drop of drink . . . and everything's fine! (*Excited.*) And when it's the night . . .

OLIVIA (*with a cry*): Go on!

    A pause. He realises she is there, and turns slowly and looks at her.

DAN (*wagging his finger with a sly smile*): Aha! I'm too fly for you! You'd like to know, wouldn't you? Aha! *Why* would you like to know? (*Insistently, mischievously.*) Why d'you lie awake . . . all night?

OLIVIA: Don't! . . . I'm frightened of you! . . .

DAN (*triumphantly, rising and facing her, his back half to the audience*): Why?

OLIVIA (*desperate*): How do you know I lie awake at night? Shall I tell you why? Because you're awake yourself. You *can't sleep*! There's one thing that keeps you awake . . . isn't there? One thing you've pushed into the back of your mind and you can't do any more about it,

and you never will. . . . And do you know what it is? . . .
It's a little thing. A box. Only a box. But it's . . . rather
heavy. . . .

> DAN *looks at her. A long pause. He jerks away with a*
> *laugh and sits at the sofa again.*

DAN (*quietly, prosaically*): The way you was going
through my letters the other day – that had to make me
smile. . . .

> *His voice dies away. Without warning, as if seeing*
> *something in his mind which makes him lose control, he*
> *shrieks loudly, clapping his hands over his eyes: then is*
> *silent. He recovers slowly and stares at her. After a*
> *pause, in a measured voice.*

It's the only thing that keeps me awake, mind you! The
only thing! (*Earnestly.*) But I don't know what to do. . . .
You see, nothing worries me, nothing in the world, only
. . . I don't like a pair of eyes staring at me . . . (*his voice*
trailing away) . . . with no look in them. I don't know what
to do . . . I don't know. . . .

> *Without warning he bursts into tears. She sits beside*
> *him and seems almost about to put her arms about him.*
> *He feels she is there, looks into her eyes, grasps her arm,*
> *then pulls himself together, abruptly.*

(*Rising.*) But it's the only thing! I live by myself . . .
(*slapping his chest*) . . . inside here – and all the rest of you
can go to hang. *After* I've made a use of you, though!
Nothing's going to stop me! I feel fine! I——

> BELSIZE *crosses outside. A sharp knock at the front*
> *door. She half rises. He motions her to sit again.*

(*With his old swagger.*) All right! Anybody's there, I'll
deal with 'em——— I'll manage myself all right! You watch
me! (*He goes to the front door and opens it.*)

BELSIZE (*at the door, jovially*): Hello Dan! How's things?

DAN (*letting him in and shutting the door*): Not so bad. . . .
(*He brings* BELSIZE *into the room.*)

BELSIZE (*as* OLIVIA *goes*): Afternoon, Miss Grayne!

OLIVIA (*putting on her spectacles*): How do you do . . . .
(*She makes an effort to compose herself and hurries across to the sun-room.*)

BELSIZE'S *attitude is one of slightly exaggerated breeziness:* DAN'S *is one of cheerful naïveté almost as limpid as on his first appearance.*

BELSIZE: Bearing up, eh?

DAN: Yes, sir, bearin' up, you know. . . .

BELSIZE: We haven't scared you all out of the house, yet, I see!

DAN: No chance!

BELSIZE: All these blood-curdlers, eh?

DAN: I should say so!

BELSIZE: No more news for me, I suppose?

DAN: No chance!

BELSIZE: Ah . . . too bad. Mind if I sit down?

DAN (*pointing to the sofa*): Well, this is the nearest you get to comfort in this house, sir.

BELSIZE: No, thanks, this'll do. . . . (*Sitting on a chair at the table, and indicating the cuttings.*) I see you keep apace of the news.

DAN: I should say so! They can't hardly wait for the latest on the case in this house, sir.

BELSIZE: Ah, well, it's only natural . . . I got a bit of a funny feeling bottom of my spine myself crossing by the rubbish heap.

DAN: Well, will you have a cigarette, sir? . . . (*His hand to his jacket pocket.*) Only a Woodbine——

BELSIZE: No, thanks.

DAN (*after a pause*): Would you like to see Mrs Bramson, sir?

BELSIZE: Oh, plenty of time. How's she bearing up?

DAN: Well, it's been a bit of a shock for her, them finding the remains of the lady at the bottom of her garden, you know.

BELSIZE: The remains of the lady! I wish you wouldn't talk like that. I've seen 'em.

DAN (*looking over his shoulder at the cuttings*): Well, you see, I haven't.

BELSIZE: You know, I don't mind telling you, they reckon the fellow that did this job was a bloodstained clever chap.

DAN (*smiling*): You don't say?

BELSIZE (*casually*): He was blackmailing her, you know.

DAN: Tch! tch! Was he?

BELSIZE: Whoever he was.

DAN: She had a lot of fellows on a string, though, didn't she?

BELSIZE (*guardedly*): That's true.

DAN: Though this one seems to have made a bit more stir than any of the others, don't he?

BELSIZE: Yes. (*Indicating the cuttings.*) Regular film star. Made his name.

DAN (*abstractedly*): If you *can* make your name without nobody knowin' what it is, o' course.

BELSIZE (*slightly piqued*): Yes, of course. . . . But I don't reckon he's been as bright as all that.

DAN (*after a pause*): Oh, you don't?

BELSIZE: No! They'll nab him in no time.

DAN: Oh . . . Mrs Bramson'll be that relieved. And the whole country besides. . . .

BELSIZE: Look here, Dan, any self-respecting murderer

would have taken care to mutilate the body to such a degree that nobody could recognise it – and here we come and identify it first go!

    DAN *folds his arms and looks thoughtful.*

Call that clever? . . . What d'you think?

    DAN *catches his eye and crosses to the sofa.*

DAN: Well sir, I'm a slow thinker, I am, but though it might be clever to leave the lady unide – unide——

BELSIZE: Unidentified.

DAN (*sitting on the edge of the sofa*): Thank you, sir. . . . (*Laboriously.*) Well, though it be clever to leave the lady unidentified and not be caught . . . hasn't he been more clever to leave her identified . . . and still not be caught?

BELSIZE: Why didn't you sleep in your bed on the night of the tenth?

    A pause. DAN *stiffens almost imperceptibly.*

DAN: What you say?

BELSIZE: Why didn't you sleep in your bed on the night of the murder?

DAN: I did.

BELSIZE (*lighting his pipe*): You didn't.

DAN: Yes, I did. Oh – except for about half an hour – that's right. I couldn't sleep for toffee and I went up the fire-escape – I remember thinkin' about it next day when the woman was missing, and trying to remember if I could think of anything funny——

BELSIZE: What time was that? (*He rises, crosses to the fireplace, and throws his match into it.*)

DAN: Oh, about . . . oh, you know how you wake up in the night and don't know what time it is. . . .

BELSIZE (*staring at him doubtfully*): Mmm. . . .

DAN: I could never sleep when I was at sea, neither, sir.

BELSIZE: Mmm. (*Suddenly.*) Are you feeling hot?

DAN: No.

BELSIZE: Your shirt's wet through.

DAN (*after a pause*): I've been sawin' some wood.

BELSIZE: Why didn't you tell us you were having an affair with the deceased woman?

DAN: Affair? What's that?

BELSIZE: Come along, old chap, I'll use a straighter word if it'll help you. But you're stalling. She was seen by two of the maids talking to you in the shrubbery. Well?

> *A pause.* DAN *bursts into tears, but with a difference. His breakdown a few minutes ago was genuine; this is a good performance, very slightly exaggerated.* BELSIZE *watches him dispassionately, his brows knit.*

DAN: Oh, sir . . . it's been on my conscience . . . ever since. . . .

BELSIZE: So you did have an affair with her?

DAN: Oh no, sir, not that! I avoided her ever after that day she stopped me, sir! . . . You see, sir, a lady stayin' where I was workin', an' for all I knew married, an' all the other fellers she'd been after, and the brazen way she went on to me. . . . You're only human, aren't you, sir, and when they asked me about her, I got frightened to tell about her stopping me. . . . But now you know about it, sir, it's a weight off my mind, you wouldn't believe. . . . (*Rising, after seeming to pull himself together.*) As a matter of fact, it was the disgust-like of nearly gettin' mixed up with her that was keepin' me awake at nights.

BELSIZE: I see. . . . You're a bit of a milk-sop, aren't you?

DAN (*apparently puzzled*): Am I, sir?

BELSIZE: Yes. . . . That'll be all for today. I'll let you off this once.

DAN: I'm that relieved, sir!

BELSIZE (*crossing to the table for his hat*): But don't try and keep things from the police another time.

DAN: No chance!

BELSIZE: They always find out, you know.

DAN: Yes, sir. Would you like a cup o' tea, sir?

BELSIZE: No, thanks. I've got another inquiry in the village. . . . (*Turning back, with an after thought.*) Oh, just one thing – might as well just do it, we're supposed to with all the chaps we're questioning, matter of form – if you don't mind, I'll have a quick look through your luggage. Matter of form. . . .

DAN: Oh yes.

BELSIZE: Where d'you hang out?

DAN (*tonelessly*): Through the kitchen . . . here, sir. . . . First door facin'. . . .

BELSIZE: First door, facing——

DAN: You can't miss it.

BELSIZE: I'll find it.

DAN: It's open, I think.

> BELSIZE *goes into the kitchen. A pause.* DAN *looks slowly round the room.*

(*Turning mechanically to the kitchen door.*) You can't miss it. . . .

> *A pause. The noise of something being moved, beyond the kitchen.* DAN *sits on the sofa with a jerk, looking before him. His fingers beat a rapid tattoo on the sides of the sofa. He looks at them, rises convulsively and walks round the room, grasping chairs and furniture as he goes. He returns to the sofa, sits, and begins the tattoo again. With a sudden wild automatic movement he beats his closed fists*

in rapid succession against the sides of his head. BELSIZE
returns carrying the hat-box.

BELSIZE (*crossing and placing the hat-box on the table*): This
one's locked. Have you got the key?

DAN *rises, and takes a step into the middle of the room.*
He looks at the hat-box at last.

DAN (*in a dead voice*): It isn't mine.

BELSIZE: Not yours?

DAN: No.

BELSIZE: Oh? . . . Whose is it, then?

DAN: I dunno. It isn't mine.

OLIVIA *stands at the sun-room door.*

OLIVIA: I'm sorry, I thought . . . Why, Inspector, what
are you doing with my box?

BELSIZE: Yours?

OLIVIA: It's got all my letters in it!

BELSIZE: But it was in . . .

OLIVIA: Oh, Dan's room used to be the box-
room.

BELSIZE: Oh, I see. . . .

OLIVIA: I'll keep it in my wardrobe; it'll be safer
there. . . .

With sudden feverish resolution, she picks up the box
and carries it into the kitchen. DAN *looks the other way as*
she passes him.

BELSIZE: I'm very sorry, miss. (*Scratching his head.*) I'm
afraid I've offended her. . . .

DAN (*smiling*): She'll be all right, sir. . . .

BELSIZE: Well, young feller, I'll be off. You might tell
the old lady I popped in, and hope she's better.

DAN (*smiling and nodding*): Thank you, sir. . . . Good
day, sir.

BELSIZE: Good day.

He goes out through the front door into the twilight, closing it behind him.

DAN: Good day, sir. . . .

A pause. DAN *crumples to the floor in a dead faint.*

QUICK CURTAIN

ACT III

*Half an hour later. The light has waned; the fire is lit and throws
a red reflection into the room.* DAN *is lying on the sofa, eyes
closed.* NURSE LIBBY *sits at the end of the sofa holding his
pulse.* MRS TERENCE *stands behind the sofa with a toby
jug of water.*

NURSE: There, lovey, you won't be long now. . . .
Ever so much steadier already. . . . What a bit o' luck me
blowin' in today! . . . Tt! tt! Pouring with sweat, the lad
is. Whatever's he been up to?

MRS TERENCE: When I walked in that door and saw
'im lyin' full stretch on that floor everything went topsy-
wopsy. (*Pressing the jug to* DAN's *lips.*) It did! The room
went round and round. . . .

NURSE (*as* DAN *splutters*): Don't choke 'im, there's a
love. . . .

MRS TERENCE: D'you know what I said to meself
when I saw 'im lyin' there?

NURSE: What?

MRS TERENCE: I said, 'That murderer's been at 'im,'
I said, 'and it's the next victim.' I did!

NURSE: So you would! Just like the pictures. . . . 'Old
your 'ead up, love. . . .

MRS TERENCE (*as* NURSE LIBBY *supports* DAN's *head*):
Got a *nice* face, 'asn't he?

NURSE: Oh *yes*! . . . (*As* DAN's *eyes flicker.*) Shh, he's

85

coming to. . . . (DAN *opens his eyes and looks at her.*) Welcome back to the land of the living!

MRS TERENCE: Thought the murderer'd got you!

A pause. DAN *stares, then sits up abruptly.*

DAN: How long I been like that?

NURSE: We picked you up ten minutes ago, and I'd say it was twenty minutes before that, roughly-like, that you passed away.

MRS TERENCE: Passed away, don't frighten the boy! . . . Whatever come over you, dear!

DAN: I dunno. Felt sick, I think. (*Recovering himself.*) Say no more about it, eh? Don't like swinging the lead. . . . (*His head in his hand.*)

MRS TERENCE: Waiting 'and and foot on Madam Crocodile, enough to wear King Kong out. . . .

NURSE: That's better, eh?

DAN: It is really getting dark?

MRS TERENCE: It's a scandal the way the days are drawin' in. . . . 'Ave another sip——

DAN (*as she makes to give him more water, to* NURSE LIBBY): You haven't such a thing as a nip of brandy?

NURSE (*opening her bag*): Yes, lovey, I nearly gave you a drop just now——

DAN *takes a flask from her and gulps; he takes a second mouthful. He gives it back, shakes himself, and looks before him.*

MRS TERENCE: Better?

DAN: Yes. . . . Clears the brain no end. . . . Makes you understand better. . . . (*His voice growing in vehemence.*) Makes you see what a damn silly thing it is to get the wind up about anything. *Do* things! Get a move on! Show 'em what you're made of! Get a move on! . . . Fainting indeed. . . . Proper girl's trick, I'm ashamed o'

meself. . . . (*Looking round, quietly.*) The light's going . . .
the daytime's as if it's never been; it's dead. . . . (*Seeing
the others stare, with a laugh.*) Daft, isn't it?

> DORA *brings in an oil lamp from the kitchen; she is
> wearing her outdoor clothes. She crosses to the table, strikes
> a match with her back to the audience and lights the lamp,
> then the wall light. The twilight is dispelled.*

NURSE (*shutting her bag, rising*): You'll be all right; a bit
light-headed after the fall I expect. (*Going to the hall.*) Well,
got an abscess the other side of Turneyfield, *and* a slow
puncture. So long, lovey.

DAN (*sitting up*): So long!

NURSE: Be good, all!

> *She bustles out of the front door. A pause.* DAN *sits
> looking before him, drumming his fingers on the sofa.*

DORA (*closing the right window-curtains*): What's the
matter with him?

MRS TERENCE: Conked out.

DORA: Conked out? Oh, dear. . . . D'you think 'e see'd
something? I'll tell you what it is!

MRS TERENCE (*closing the left window-curtains*): What?

DORA: The monster's lurking again.

> *Mechanically* DAN *takes a box of matches and a
> cigarette from his pocket.*

MRS TERENCE: I'll give you lurk, my girl, look at the
egg on my toby! Why don't you learn to wash up, instead
of walkin' about talking like three-halfpennyworth of
trash?

DORA: I can't wash up properly in that kitchen; with
that light. Them little oil lamps isn't any good except to
set the place on fire. (*She goes into the kitchen.*)

> DAN *drums his fingers on the sofa.* MRS BRAMSON
> *wheels herself from the bedroom.*

87

MRS BRAMSON: I dropped off. Why didn't somebody wake me? Have I been missing something?

MRS TERENCE: That Inspector Belsize called.

MRS BRAMSON (*testily*): Then why didn't somebody wake me? Dan, what did he want?

DAN: Just a friendly call.

MRS BRAMSON: You seem very far away, dear. What's the matter with you? . . . Dan!

DAN: Bit of an 'eadache, that's all.

MRS BRAMSON: Doesn't make you deaf, though, dear, does it?

MRS TERENCE: Now, now, turnin' against the apple of your eye; can't 'ave that goin' on——

> *A sharp knock at the front door.* DAN *starts up and goes towards the hall.*

MRS BRAMSON (*to* MRS TERENCE): See who it is.

MRS TERENCE (*at the front door, as* DAN *is about to push past her*): Oh . . . it's only the paraffin boy. . . . (*To the boy outside, taking a can from him.*) And you bring stuff on a Saturday night another time.

> DAN *is standing behind* MRS BRAMSON'S *chair.*

MRS BRAMSON: I should think so——

> MRS TERENCE *comes into the room.* DAN *strikes a match for his cigarette.*

MRS TERENCE (*with a cry*): Oh! Can't you see this is paraffin? (*She puts the can on the floor just outside the hall.*)

MRS BRAMSON: You went through my side like a knife——

MRS TERENCE: If people knew what to do with their money, they'd put electric light in their 'omes 'stead of dangerin' people's lives.

> *She goes into the kitchen.* DAN *stares before him, the match flickering.*

MRS BRAMSON (*blowing out the match*): You'll burn your fingers! Set yourself on fire! Absent-minded! . . . I woke up all of a cold shiver. Had a terrible dream.

DAN (*mechanically*): What about?

MRS BRAMSON: Horrors . . . I'm freezing. Get me my shawl off my bed, will you, dear? . . . (*As he does not move.*) My shawl, dear!

> DAN *starts, collects himself, and smiles his most ingratiating smile.*

DAN: I *am* sorry, mum. In the Land of Nod, I was! Let me see, what was it your highness was after? A shawl? No sooner said than done. . . . You watch me! One, two, three! (*He runs into the bedroom.*)

MRS BRAMSON: Silly boy . . . silly boy. . . .

> OLIVIA *comes in quickly from the kitchen. She is dressed to go out and carries a suitcase.*

Where are you off to?

OLIVIA: I've had a telegram. A friend of mine in London's very ill.

MRS BRAMSON: What's the matter with her?

OLIVIA: Pneumonia.

MRS BRAMSON: Where's the telegram?

OLIVIA: I – I threw it away.

MRS BRAMSON: Where d'you throw it?

OLIVIA: I – I threw it away.

MRS BRAMSON: You haven't had any telegram.

OLIVIA (*impatiently*): No, I haven't!

MRS BRAMSON: What's the matter with you?

OLIVIA: I can't stay in this house tonight.

MRS BRAMSON: Why not?

OLIVIA: I'm frightened.

MRS BRAMSON: Oh, don't be——

OLIVIA: Listen to me. I've never known before what

it was to be terrified. But when I saw today beginning to end, and tonight getting nearer and nearer . . . I felt my finger-tips getting cold. And I knew it was fright . . . stark fright. I'm not a fool, and I'm not hysterical . . . but I've been sitting in my room looking at myself in the glass, trying to control myself, telling myself what are real things . . . and what aren't. I don't know any longer. The day's over. The forest's all round us. Anything may happen. . . . You shouldn't stay in this house tonight. That's all.

MRS BRAMSON (*blustering*): It's very silly of you, trying to scare an old woman with a weak heart. What have you to be frightened of?

OLIVIA: There's been a murder, you know.

MRS BRAMSON: Nobody's going to murder *you*! Besides, we've got Danny to look after us. He's as strong as an ox, and no silly nerves about him . . . what *is* it you're afraid of?

OLIVIA: I——

MRS BRAMSON: Shy, aren't you? . . . Where are you staying tonight?

OLIVIA: In Langbury, with Hubert Laurie and his sister.

MRS BRAMSON: Not too frightened to make arrangements with *him*, eh.

OLIVIA: Arrangements?

MRS BRAMSON: Well, some people would call it something else.

OLIVIA (*losing her temper*): Oh, won't you see. . . .

MRS BRAMSON: I'm very annoyed with you. How are you going to get there?

OLIVIA: Walking.

MRS BRAMSON: Through the forest? Not too frightened for that, I see.

OLIVIA: I'd rather spend tonight in the forest than in this house.

MRS BRAMSON: That sounds convincing, I must say. Well, you can go, but when you come back, I'm not so sure I shall answer the door. Think that over in the morning.

OLIVIA: The morning? . . .

DAN'S VOICE (*in the bedroom, singing*): '. . . their home addresses . . . and their caresses . . . linger in my memory of those beautiful dames. . . .'

> OLIVIA *listens, holding her breath; she tries to say something to* MRS BRAMSON, *and fails. She makes an effort, and runs out of the front door. It bangs behind her.* DAN *comes back from the bedroom, carrying the shawl.*

DAN (*over-casual*): What was that at the door?

MRS BRAMSON: My niece. Gone for the night, if you please.

DAN: Gone . . . for the night? (*He stares before him.*)

MRS BRAMSON: Would you believe it? Says she's frightened. . . . (*A pause.*) Come along with the shawl, dear, I'm freezing. . . .

DAN (*with a laugh, putting the shawl round her*): Don't know what's up with me——

> *He goes to the table and looks at a newspaper.* MRS TERENCE *comes in from the kitchen, her coat on.*

MRS TERENCE: Well, I must go on my way rejoicin'.

MRS BRAMSON: Everybody seems to be going. What *is* all this?

MRS TERENCE: What d'you want for lunch tomorrow?

MRS BRAMSON: Lunch tomorrow? . . . Let me see. . . .

DAN: Lunch? Tomorrow? . . . (*After a pause.*) What about a nice little steak?

MRS BRAMSON: A steak, let me see. . . . Yes, with baked potatoes——

DAN: And a nice roly-poly puddin', the kind you like?

MRS BRAMSON: I think so.

MRS TERENCE: Something light. O.K. Good night.

> *She goes back into the kitchen.* DAN *scans the newspaper casually.*

MRS BRAMSON (*inquisitive*): What are you reading, dear?

DAN (*breezily*): Only the murder again. About the clues that wasn't any good.

MRS BRAMSON (*suddenly*): Danny, *d'you* think Olivia's a thief?

DAN: Shouldn't be surprised.

MRS BRAMSON: What!

DAN: Her eyes wasn't very wide apart.

MRS BRAMSON (*working herself up*): Goodness me . . . my jewel-box . . . what a fool I was to let her go – my ear-rings . . . the double-faced——

> *She wheels herself furiously into her bedroom.* DORA, *her hat and coat on, comes in from the kitchen in time to see her go.*

DORA: What's up with her?

DAN (*still at his paper*): Think's she been robbed.

DORA: Oh, is that all. . . . That's the fourth time this month she's thought that. One of these days something *will* 'appen to her and will I be pleased? Oh, baby! . . . Where's Mrs Terence?

DAN: Gone, I think.

DORA (*frightened*): Oh, law, no! (*Calling.*) Mrs Terence!

MRS TERENCE (*calling in the kitchen*): Ye'es!

DORA: You 'aven't gone without me, 'ave you?

MRS TERENCE (*appearing at the kitchen door, spearing a hatpin into her hat.*) Yes, I'm 'alf-way there, what d'you think?

DORA: You did give me a turn! (*Going to the table and taking the box.*) I think I'll 'ave a choc. (*Walking towards the hall.*) I couldn't 'ave walked a step in those trees all by myself. Coming?

DAN (*suddenly*): I'd have come with you with pleasure, only I'm going the other direction. Payley Hill way.

MRS TERENCE (*surprised*): *You* going out?

DORA: Oh?

DAN (*in the hall, putting on hat and mackintosh*): Yes, I still feel a bit funny.

MRS TERENCE: But you can't leave 'er 'ere by herself!

DORA: She'll scream the place down!

DAN (*over-explanatory*): I asked her, this very minute, and she don't seem to mind. You know what she is. Said it'll do me good, and won't hear of my stayin'. It's no good arguin' with her.

> DORA *puts the chocolates down on the occasional table.*
> *She and* MRS TERENCE *follow* DAN *into the hall.*

DORA: No good arguin' with her – don't I know it!

MRS TERENCE: You 'ave a nice walk while you get the chance; you wait on 'er too much. . . . (*Closing the plush curtains so that they are all out of sight.*) Ooh, ain't it dark. . . . Got the torch, Dora?

DORA: O.K., honey.

MRS TERENCE: Laws, I'd be frightened goin' off by meself. . . . Well, we'd best 'urry, Dora. . . . Good night, Dan. Pity you aren't coming our way——

DAN'S VOICE: See you in the morning! Good night!

DORA'S VOICE: O.K.! . . . Toodle-oo!

> *The door bangs. A pause.*

DAN'S VOICE (*outside the left window*): Good night!

MRS TERENCE'S VOICE (*outside the right window*): Good night!

DORA (*same*): Good night!
> *Silence.*

MRS TERENCE (*farther away*): Good night!

DORA (*same*): Good night!
> MRS BRAMSON *comes trundling back from the bed-room in her chair.*

MRS BRANSOM: Good night here, good night there; anybody'd think it was the night before Judgement Day. What's the matter with . . . (*Seeing the room is empty.*) Talking to myself. Wish people wouldn't walk out of rooms and leave me high and dry. Don't like it. (*She wheels herself round to the table. A pause. She looks round impatiently.*) Where's my chocolates? . . .
> *She looks round again, gets up out of her chair for the first time in the play, walks quite normally across the room to the mantelpiece, sees her chocolates are not there, walks up to the occasional table, and takes up the box.*

That girl's been at them again . . .
> *She walks back to her chair, carrying the chocolates, and sits in it again. She begins to munch. She suddenly stops, as if she has heard something.*

What's that? . . .
> *She listens again. A cry is heard far away.*

Oh, God . . . Danny!
> *The cry is repeated.*

Danny!
> *The cry is heard a third time.*

It's an owl . . . Oh, Lord!
> *She falls back in relief, and eats another chocolate.*

*The clock strikes the half-hour. Silence. The silence gets
on her nerves.*

(*After a pause, calling softly.*) Danny! . . . (*As there is no
answer.*) What's the boy doing in that kitchen?

> *She takes up the newspaper, sees a headline, and puts
> it down hastily. She sees the Bible on the table, opens it,
> and turns over pages.*

(*After a pause, suddenly.*) I've got the jitters. I've got the
jitters. I've got the jitters. . . . (*Calling loudly.*) Danny!

> *She waits; there is complete silence. She rises, walks
> over to the kitchen door, and flings it wide open.*

(*Shouting.*) Danny! (*No reply.*) He's gone. . . . They've
all gone. . . . They've left me. . . . (*Losing control, beating
her hands wildly on her Bible.*) Oh, Lord, help a poor
woman. . . . They've left me! (*Tottering to the sun-room.*)
Danny . . . where are you? . . . Danny. . . . I'm going to
be murdered. . . . I'm going to be murdered! . . . Danny. . . .
(*Her voice rising, until she is shrieking hysterically.*) Danny!
Danny! Danny!

> *She stops suddenly. Footsteps on the gravel outside
> the front door.*

(*In a strangled whisper.*) There's something outside . . .
something outside. . . . Oh, heavens. . . . (*Staggering
across to the sofa.*) Danny, where are you? Where are
you? There's something outs—

> *The front door bangs. She collapses on the sofa,
> terrified, her enormous Bible clasped to her breast.*

Oh, Lord, help me . . . help me. . . . Oh, Lord, help . . .
(*Muttering, her eyes closed.*) . . . Forgive us our trespasses . . .

> *The curtains are suddenly parted. It is* DAN, *a cigarette
> between his lips. He stands motionless, his feet planted
> apart, holding the curtains. There is murder in his face.
> She is afraid to look, but is forced to at last.*

Danny . . . Oh . . . Oh . . .

DAN (*smiling, suddenly normal and reassuring*): That's all right. . . . It's only Danny. . . .

MRS BRAMSON: Thank God. . . . (*Going off into laughing hysteria.*) Ah . . . ah . . . ah. . . .

> DAN *throws his cigarette away, lays his hat on the occasional table, throws his mackintosh on the left window-seat, and sits beside her, patting her, looking round to see no one has heard her cries.*

I'll never forgive you, never. Oh, my heart. . . . Oh, oh – oh——

> *He runs across to the medicine cupboard and brings back a brandy bottle and two glasses.*

DAN: Now have a drop of this. . . . (*As she winces at the taste.*) Go on, do you good. . . . (*As she drinks.*) I am sorry, I am really. . . . You see, they wanted me to see them to the main path, past the rubbish-heap, see, in case they were frightened. . . . Now, that's better, isn't it?

> *They are seated side by side on the sofa.*

MRS BRAMSON: I don't know yet. . . . Give me some more. . . . (*He pours one out for her, and one for himself. They drink.*) All alone, I was. . . . (*Her face puckering with self pity.*) Just an old woman calling for help . . . (*her voice breaking*) . . . and no answer.

DAN (*putting the bottle on the floor beside him*): Poor old mum, runnin' about lookin' for Danny——

MRS BRAMSON (*sharply*): I wasn't running about as much as all that. . . . Oh, the relief when I saw your face——

DAN: I bet you wasn't half glad, eh?

MRS BRAMSON: You're the only one that understands me, Danny, that's what you are——

DAN (*patting her*): That's right——

MRS BRAMSON: I don't have to tell you everything I've been through. I don't have to tell you about my husband, how unkind and ungodly he was – I wouldn't have minded so much him being ungodly, but oh, he *was* unkind. . . . (*Sipping.*) And I don't have to tell *you* how unkind he was. You know. You just know . . . whatever else I've not been, I was *always* a great one on psychology.

DAN: You was. (*He takes her glass and fills it again, and his own.*)

MRS BRAMSON: I'm glad those other people have gone. Awful screeching common women. Answer back, answer back, answer back. . . . Isn't it time for my medicine? (*He hands her glass back. They both drink. He sits smiling and nodding at her.*) That day you said to me about me reminding you of your mother. . . . (*As he slowly begins to roll up his sleeves a little way.*) These poets and rubbishy people can think all they like about their verses and sonnets and such – that girl Olivia writes sonnets – would you believe it——

DAN: Fancy.

MRS BRAMSON: They can think all they like, that was a beautiful thought. (*Her arm on his shoulder.*) And when you think you're just an ignorant boy, it's . . . it's startling.

DAN (*with a laugh*): That's right.

MRS BRAMSON: I'll never forget that. Not as long as I live. . . . (*Trying to stem the tears.*) I want a chocolate now.

DAN: Right you are! . . . (*Placing her glass and his own on the floor and walking briskly to the table.*) A nice one with a soft centre, the kind you like. . . . Why, here's one straight away. . . . (*He walks slowly to the back of the sofa.*) *In a level voice.*) Now shut your eyes . . . open you mouth. . . .

MRS BRAMSON (*purring*): Oh, Danny. . . . You're the only one. . . .

> *She shuts her eyes. He stands behind her, and puts the chocolate into her mouth. His fingers close slowly and involuntarily, over her neck; she feels his touch, and draws both his hands down, giggling, so that his face almost touches hers.*

(*Maudlin.*) What strong hands they are. . . . You're a pet, my little chubby-face, my baby-face, my Danny. . . . Am I in a draught? (*A pause.* DAN *draws his hands slowly away, walks to the back, and shuts the plush curtains.*) I've got to take care of myself, haven't I?

DAN (*turning slowly and looking at her*): You have.

> *He picks up the paraffin can briskly and goes towards the kitchen.*

MRS BRAMSON: What are you——

DAN: Only takin' the paraffin tin in the kitchen.

> *He goes into the kitchen.*

MRS BRAMSON (*half to herself*): That girl should have carried it in. Anything to annoy me. Tomorrow—— (*Turning and seeing that he is gone.*) Danny! (*Shrieking suddenly.*) Danny!

> DAN *runs back from the kitchen.*

DAN: What's the matter?

> *He looks hastily towards the hall to see no one has heard.*

MRS BRAMSON: Oh dear, I thought——

DAN (*sitting on the back of the sofa*): I was only putting the paraffin away. Now—— (*He leans over the sofa, and raises his arms slowly.*)

MRS BRAMSON (*putting her hand on his arm*): I think I'll go to bed now.

DAN (*after a pause, dropping his arm*): O.K.

MRS BRAMSON: And I'll have my supper-tray in my

room. (*Petulantly.*) Get me back into my chair, dear, will you?

DAN (*jerkily*): O.K. (*He crosses to the invalid chair.*)

MRS BRAMSON: Has she put the glass by the bed for my teeth?

DAN (*bringing over the chair*): I put it there myself. (*He helps her into the chair and pulls it over towards the bedroom.*)

MRS BRAMSON (*suddenly, in the middle of the room*): I want to be read to now.

DAN (*after a pause of indecision*): O.K. (*Clapping his hands, effusively.*) What'll you have? The old *East Lynne*?

MRS BRAMSON: No. I don't feel like anything senti-mental tonight. . . .

DAN (*looking towards the desk*): What'll you have then?

MRS BRAMSON: I think I'd like the Bible.

A pause. He looks at her.

DAN: O.K.

MRS BRAMSON (*as he goes smartly to the sofa, fetches the Bible, pulls up a chair to the right of her, sits and looks for the place*): That piece you were reading. . . . It's Sunday . . . . Isn't that nice . . . all the aches and pains quiet for once . . . pretty peaceful. . . .

DAN (*reading*): 'Blessed is the man that walketh not in the counsel of the ungodly, nor standeth in the way of sinners, nor sitteth in the seat of the scornful. . . .'

MRS BRAMSON (*drowsily*): You read so nicely, Danny.

DAN: Very kind of you, my lady. (*Reading a little breath-lessly.*) 'But his delight is in the law of the Lord; and in His law doth he meditate day and night——'

MRS BRAMSON: Sh!

DAN: What? Can you hear something?

MRS BRAMSON: Yes! A sort of – thumping noise. . . . (*She looks at him suddenly, leans forward, and puts her right*

99

hand inside his jacket.) Why, Danny, it's you! It's your heart . . . beating! (*He laughs.*) Are you all right dear?

DAN: Fine. I been running along the path, see. . . . (*Garrulously.*) I been out of training, I suppose; when I was at sea I never missed a day running round the decks, o' course. . . .

MRS BRAMSON (*sleepily*): Of course. . . .

DAN (*speaking quickly, as if eager to conjure up a vision*): I remember those mornings – on some sea – very misty – pale it is, with the sun like breathing silver where he's coming' up across the water, but not blowin' on the sea at all . . . and the sea-gulls standing on the deck-rail looking at themselves in the water on the deck, and only me about and nothing else. . . .

MRS BRAMSON (*nodding sleepily*): Yes. . . .

DAN: And the sun. Just me and the sun.

MRS BRAMSON (*nodding*): There's no sun now, dear; it's night!

> *A pause. He drums his fingers on the Bible.*

DAN: Yes . . . it's night now. (*Reading, feverishly.*) 'The ungodly are not so, but are like the chaff which the wind driveth away——'

MRS BRAMSON: I think I'll go to bye-byes. . . . We'll have the rest tomorrow, shall we? (*Testily.*) Help me, dear, help me, you know what I am——

DAN (*drumming his fingers: suddenly, urgently*): Wait a minute. . . . I – I've only got two more verses——

MRS BRAMSON: Hurry it up, dear. I don't want to wake up in the morning with a nasty cold.

DAN (*reading slowly*): '. . . Therefore the ungodly shall not stand in the judgment, nor sinners in the congregation of the righteous. . . . For the Lord knoweth the way of the righteous . . . but the way of the ungodly . . . shall perish. . . .'

> *A pause. He shuts the Bible loudly, and lays it on the table.* MRS BRAMSON *can hardly keep awake.*

That's the end.

MRS BRAMSON: Is it? . . . Ah, well, it's been a long day——

DAN: Are you quite comfortable?

MRS BRAMSON: A bit achy. Glad to go to bed. Hope that woman's put my bottle in all right. Bet she hasn't——

DAN: Sure you're comfortable? Wouldn't you like a cushion back of your head?

MRS BRAMSON: No dear, just wheel me——

DAN (*rising*): I think you'll be more comfortable with a cushion. (*Rising, humming.*) 'I'm a pretty little feller, everybody knows . . . dunno what to call me . . .'

> *He goes deliberately across, humming, and picks up a large black cushion from the sofa. His hands close on the cushion and he stands silent a moment. He moves slowly back to the other side of her; he stands looking at her, his back three-quarters to the audience and his face hidden: he is holding the cushion in both hands.*

> MRS BRAMSON *shakes herself out of sleep and looks at him.*

MRS BRAMSON: What a funny look on your face, dear. Smiling like that. . . . (*Foolishly.*) You look so kind. . . .

> *He begins to raise the cushion slowly.*

So kind. . . . (*Absently.*) What are you going to do with that cushion? . . .

> *The lights dim gradually into complete darkness, and the music grows into a thunderous crescendo.*

SCENE II

The music plays a few bars, then dies down proportionately as the lights come up again.

Half an hour later. The scene is the same, with the same lighting; the room is empty and the wheel-chair has been removed.

DAN *comes in from the sun-room, smoking the stub of a cigarette. He crosses smartly, takes the bottle and glasses from the floor by the sofa and places them on the table, pours himself a quick drink, places the bottle on the floor next the desk, throws away his stub, takes another cigarette from his pocket, puts it in his mouth, takes out a box of matches, and lights a match. The clock chimes. He looks at it, seems to make a decision, blows out the match, throws the matchbox on the table, takes Mrs Bramson's tape and keys from his trouser pocket, crosses quietly to the safe by the fireplace, opens it, takes out the cash-box, sits on the sofa, unlocks the cash-box, stuffs the keys back into his trousers, opens the cash-box, takes out the notes, looks at them, delighted, stuffs them into his pockets, hurries into the sun-room, returns a second later with the empty invalid chair, plants it in the middle of the room, picks up the cushion from the floor above the table, looks at it a moment, arrested, throws it callously on the invalid chair, hurries into the kitchen, returns immediately with the paraffin, sprinkles it freely over the invalid chair, places the can under the table, lifts the paraffin lamp from the table, and is just about to smash it over the invalid chair when there is a sound of a chair falling over in the sun-room. His face inscrutable, he looks towards it. He carries the lamp stealthily to the desk, puts it down, looks round, picks a chair from near the table, and stands at the sun-room door with the chair held high above his head.*

The stagger of footsteps; OLIVIA *stands in the doorway to the sun-room. She has been running through the forest; her clothes are wild, her hair has fallen about her shoulders, and she is no longer wearing spectacles. She looks nearly beautiful. Her manner is quiet, almost dazed.* DAN *lowers the chair slowly and sits on the other side of the table. A pause.*

OLIVIA: I've never seen a dead body before . . . I climbed through the window and nearly fell over it. Like a sack of potatoes or something. I thought it was, at first. . . . And that's murder. (*As he looks up at her.*) But it's so ordinary . . . I came back . . . (*as he lights his cigarette*) . . . expecting . . . ha (*laughing hysterically*) . . . I don't know . . . and here I find you, smoking a cigarette . . . you might have been tidying the room for the night. It's so . . . ordinary. . . . (*After a pause, with a cry.*) Why don't you *say* something!

DAN: I thought you were goin' to stay the night at that feller's.

OLIVIA: I was.

DAN: What d'you come back for?

OLIVIA (*the words pouring out*): To find you out. You've kept me guessing for a fortnight. Guessing hard. I very nearly knew, all the time. But not quite. And now I do know.

DAN: Why was you so keen on finding me out?

OLIVIA (*vehemently, coming to the table*): In the same way any sane, decent-minded human would want – would want to have you arrested for the monster you are!

DAN (*quietly*): What d'you come back for?

OLIVIA: I . . . I've told you. . . .

E   103

*He smiles at her slowly and shakes his head. She sits
at the table and closes her eyes.*

I got as far as the edge of the wood. I could see the lights
in the village . . . I came back.

She buries her head in her arms. DAN *rises, looks at
her a moment regretfully, puts away his cigarette, and
stands with both hands over the invalid chair.*

DAN (*casually*): She didn't keep any money anywhere
else, did she?

OLIVIA: I've read a lot about evil——

*DAN realises his hands are wet with paraffin and wipes
them on his trousers.*

DAN: Clumsy. . . .

OLIVIA: I never expected to come across it in real life.

DAN (*lightly*): You didn't ought to read so much. I
never got through a book yet. . . . But I'll read you all
right. . . . (*Crossing to her, leaning over the table, and smiling at
her intently.*) You haven't had a drop of drink, and yet
you feel as if you had. You never knew there was such a
secret part inside of you. All that book-learnin' and
moral-me-eye here and social-me-eye there – you took
that off on the edge of the wood same as if it was an overcoat . . . and you left it there!

OLIVIA: I hate you. I . . . hate you!

DAN (*urgently*): And same as anybody out for the first
time without their overcoat, you feel as light as air! Same
as I feel, sometimes – only I never had no overcoat——
(*Excited.*) Why – this is my big chance! You're the one
I can tell about meself! Oh, I'm sick o' hearin' how clever
everybody else is – I want to tell 'em how clever *I* am for
a change! . . . Money I'm going to have, and people doin'
what they're told, and *me* tellin' them to do it! There
was a 'oman at the Tallboys, wasn't there? She wouldn't

be told, would she? She thought she was up 'gainst a soft fellow in a uniform, didn't she? She never knew it was *me* she was dealin' with – (*striking his chest in a paroxysm of elation*) – Me! And this old girl treatin' me like a son 'cause I made her think she was a chronic invalid – ha! She's been more use to me tonight (*tapping the notes in his jacket pocket, smartly*) than she has to any other body all her life. Stupid, that's what people are . . . stupid. If those two hadn't been stupid they might be breathin' now; you're not stupid; that's why I'm talkin' to you. (*With exaggerated self-possession.*) You said just now murder's ordinary. . . . Well it isn't ordinary at all, see? And I'm not an ordinary chap. There's one big difference 'tween me and other fellows that try this game. I'll *never be found out*. 'Cause I don't care a——(*snapping his fingers, grandly.*) The world's goin' to hear from me. That's me. (*Chuckling.*) You wait. . . . (*After a pause.*) But you can't wait, can you?

OLIVIA: What do you mean?

DAN: Well, when I say I'll never be found out, what I mean is, no living soul will be able to tell any other living soul about me. (*Beginning to roll up a sleeve, nonchalantly.*) Can you think of anybody . . . who can go tomorrow . . . and tell the police the fire at Forest Corner . . . wasn't an accident at all?

OLIVIA: I – I can.

DAN: Oh no, you can't.

OLIVIA: Why can't I?

DAN: Well, I'm up against a very serious problem, I am. But the answer to it is as simple as pie, to a fellow like me, simple as pie. . . . (*Rolling up the other sleeve a little way.*) She isn't going to be the only one . . . found tomorrow . . . in the fire at Forest Corner. . . . (*After a pause.*) Aren't you frightened? You ought to be! (*Smiling.*) Don't you think I'll do it?

OLIVIA: I know you will. I just can't realise it.

DAN: You know, when I told you all that about meself just now, I'd made up my mind then about you. (*Moving slowly after her, round the table, as she steps back towards the window.*) That's what I am, see? I make up me mind to do a thing, and I do it. . . . You remember that first day when I come in here? I said to meself then, There's a girl that's got her wits about her; she knows a thing or two; different from the others. I was right, wasn't I? You——— (*Stopping abruptly, and looking round the room.*) What's that light in here?

OLIVIA: What light?

DAN: There's somebody in this room's holdin' a flashlight.

OLIVIA: It can't be in this room. . . . It must be a light in the wood.

DAN: It can't be.

> *A flashlight crosses the window-curtain.* OLIVIA *turns and stares at it.*

OLIVIA: Somebody's watching the bungalow. . . .

> *He looks at her, as if he did not understand.*

DAN (*fiercely*): Nobody's watching! . . .

> *He runs to the window. She backs into the corner of the room.*

I'm the one that watches! They've got no call to watch me! I'll go out and tell them that, an' all! (*Opening the curtains in a frenzy.*) I'm the one that watches!

> *The light crosses the window again. He stares, then claps his hands over his eyes. Backing to the sofa.*

Behind them trees. (*Clutching the invalid chair.*) Hundreds back of each tree. . . . Thousands of eyes. The whole damn world's on my track! . . . (*Sitting on the edge of the sofa, and listening.*) What's that? . . . Like a big wall fallin' over into the sea. . . . (*Closing his hands over his ears convulsively.*)

OLIVIA (*coming down to him*): They mustn't come in. . . .

DAN (*turning to her*): Yes, but . . . (*Staring.*) You're lookin' at me as if you never seen *me* before. . . .

OLIVIA: I never have. Nobody has. You've stopped acting at last. You're real. Frightened. Like a child. (*Putting her arm about his shoulders.*) They mustn't come in. . . .

DAN: But everything's slippin' away. From underneath our feet. . . . Can't you feel it? Starting slow . . . and then hundreds of miles an hour. . . . I'm goin' backwards! . . . And there's a wind in my ears, terrible blowin' wind. . . . Everything's going past me like the telegraph-poles. . . . All the things I've never seen . . . faster and faster . . . backwards – back to the day I was born. (*Shrieking.*) I can see it coming . . . the day I was born! . . . (*Turning to her, simply.*) I'm goin' to die. (*A pause. A knock at the front door.*) It's getting cold.

Another knock; louder. She presses his head to her.

OLIVIA: It's all right. You won't die. I'll tell them I *made* you do it. I'll tell lies – I'll tell——

A third and louder knock at the front door. She realises that she must answer, goes into the hall, opens the front door, and comes back, hiding DAN *from view.*

BELSIZE (*in the hall*): Good evening. . . . Sorry to pop back like this. . . .

He comes into the room, followed by DORA *and* MRS TERENCE, *both terrified. Looking round.*

Everything looks all right here.

MRS TERENCE: I tell you we *did* 'ear her! Plain as plain! And we'd gone near a quarter of a mile——

DORA: Plain as plain——

MRS TERENCE: Made my blood run cold. 'Danny!' she screamed, 'Danny, where are you?' she said. She wanted 'im back, she did, to save 'er——

DORA: Because she was bein' murdered. I know it! I'd never a' run like that if I 'adn't 'eard——

BELSIZE: We'll soon find out who's right. . . . Now then—— (*As* OLIVIA *steps aside behind the sofa.*) Hello, Dan!

DAN (*quietly, rising and standing by the fireplace*): Hello.

BELSIZE (*standing behind the invalid chair*): Second time today, eh? . . .

DAN: That's right.

BELSIZE: How's the old lady?

DAN (*after a pause*): Not so bad, thanks, inspector! Gone to bed and says she didn't want to be disturbed——

BELSIZE: Smell of paraffin. . . .

DAN (*with a last desperate attempt at bluster*): You know what she's like, inspector, a bit nervy these days—— (*As* BELSIZE *goes to the bedroom and flashes a light into it.*) I'd no sooner got round the corner she screamed for me – 'Danny, Danny, Danny!' she was screaming – Danny she calls me, a pet name for Dan, that is——

BELSIZE *goes into the sun-room.*

(*Rambling on mechanically.*) I told her so then. I said 'It's dangerous, that's what it is, havin' so much paraffin in the house.' That paraffin – she shouldn't ha' had so much paraffin in the house——

His voice trails away. Silence. BELSIZE *comes back, his face intent, one hand in a coat pocket. A pause.*

BELSIZE (*to* OLIVIA): What are you doing here?

OLIVIA: I'm concerned in——

DAN (*loudly, decisively, silencing her*): It's all right. (*Cross-*

ing to BELSIZE *and swaggering desperately, in front of the women.*) I'm the fellow. Anything I'm concerned in, I run all by myself. If there's going to be any putting me on a public platform to answer any questions, I'm going to do it by myself . . . (*looking at* OLIVIA) . . . or not at all. I'll manage meself all right——

BELSIZE: I get you. Like a bit of limelight, eh?

DAN (*smiling*): Well . . .

BELSIZE (*as if humouring him*): Let's have a look at your hands, old boy, will you?

> *With an amused look at* OLIVIA, DAN *holds out his hands. Without warning,* BELSIZE *claps a pair of handcuffs over his wrists.* DAN *stares at them a moment, then sits on the sofa, and starts to pull at them furiously over his knee. He beats at them wildly, moaning and crying like an animal. He subsides gradually, looks at the others and rises.*

DAN (*muttering, holding his knee*): Hurt meself. . . .

BELSIZE: That's better. . . . Better come along quietly. . . .

> *He goes up towards the hall.* DAN *follows him, and takes his hat from the occasional table. As he puts it on he catches sight of his face in the mirror.*

BELSIZE (*to the others, crisply, during this*): I've a couple of men outside. I'll send 'em in. See that nothing's disturbed. . . . Coming, old chap?

DORA: What's 'e doin'?

MRS TERENCE: He's lookin' at himself in the glass. . . .

> *A pause.*

DAN (*speaking to the mirror*): This is the real thing, old boy. Actin'. . . . That's what she said, wasn't it? She was right, you know . . . I've been playing up to you, haven't I? I showed you a trick or two, didn't I? . . . But this is the real thing. (*Swaying.*) Got a cigarette? . . . (*Seeing* OLIVIA.) You're not goin' to believe what she said? About helpin' me?

BELSIZE (*humouring him*): No. (*Putting a cigarette between* DAN's *lips and lighting it.*) Plenty of women get a bit hysterical about a lad in your position. You'll find 'em queueing up all right when the time comes. Proposals of marriage by the score.

DAN (*pleased*): Will they?

BELSIZE: Come along——

  DAN *turns to follow him.* DORA *is in the way.*

DAN: Oh yes . . . I forgot about you. . . . (*Smiling, with a curious detached sadness.*) Poor little fellow. Poor little chap. . . . (*Looking round.*) You know, I'd like somethin' now I never wanted before. A long walk, all by meself. And just when I can't have it. (*Laughing.*) That's contrary, isn't it?

BELSIZE (*sternly*): Coming?

DAN (*looking at* OLIVIA): Just comin'.

  He goes to OLIVIA, *takes out his cigarette, puts his manacled arms round her, and kisses her suddenly and violently on the mouth. He releases her with an air of bravado, puts back his cigarette, and looks at her.*

DAN: Well, I'm goin' to be hanged in the end. . . . But they'll get their money's worth at the trial. You wait!

  He smiles, and raises his hand to his hat-brim with the old familiar jaunty gesture of farewell. He walks past BELSIZE *and out through the front door.* BELSIZE *follows him. The bang of the front door.* OLIVIA *falls to the sofa. The sound of* DORA's *sobbing.*

CURTAIN

HE WAS BORN GAY

A ROMANCE IN THREE ACTS

'. . . *Il est né gai* . . .'
Marie Antoinette, Queen of France,
in a letter to Madame de Tourzel
24 July 1789

E*

To
My Parents

CHARACTERS

PRISSY DELL
FRANCIS
MRS GEORGINA DELL
MISS MASON
LEWIS DELL
LADY ATKYNS
SOPHY RAFFETY
MR LEROY
MASON
LAMBERT

The action of the play takes place in the drawing-room of Mrs Dell's house on the cliffs near Dover

ACT ONE
A late afternoon in the summer of 1815

ACT TWO
A week later. Night

ACT THREE
Immediately afterwards, with no lapse of time

HE WAS BORN GAY *was first produced at the Queen's Theatre, London, on 26 May 1937. It was presented by John Gielgud and Emlyn Williams, with the following cast:*

PRISSY DELL	Betty Jardine
FRANCIS	Harry Andrews
MRS GEORGINA DELL	Elliot Mason
MISS MASON	Gwen Ffrangcon-Davies
LEWIS DELL	Glen Byam Shaw
LADY ATKYNS	Sydney Fairbrother
SOPHY RAFFETY	Carol Goodner
MR LEROY	Frank Pettingell
MASON	John Gielgud
LAMBERT	Emlyn Williams

The play directed by
JOHN GIELGUD
in conjunction with
THE AUTHOR

ACT I

*The drawing-room of Mrs Dell's house on the cliffs near Dover.
A late afternoon in the summer of 1815.*

Before the curtain rises, PRISSY'S *voice is heard singing,
with pretty but facile nostalgia, accompanied by the pianoforte.*

PRISSY: 'Mon coeur m'a trahie plusieurs fois. . . .
Depuis trois mois. . . . Depuis trois mois. . . .'

THE CURTAIN RISES. *Centre back, two steps lead up to
folding doors opening outward on to the hall, in which can
be glimpsed another door leading to the ballroom. To the
left of the hall doors, in an angle of the wall, a small door
leads to an ante-room (throughout the play, 'left' and 'right'
refer to the actors' left and right). To the right of the hall
doors, two steps lead to french windows, with bright striped
curtains, opening on to a balcony which leads down to the
garden; beyond the balcony, the sky. Downstage right, a
smaller window. Downstage left, the fireplace; below it, in
another angle in the wall, and let into the panelling of the
room, a small door leading by a passage to the kitchen
quarters.*

*Right, upstage, in front of the french windows, a small
pianoforte, with a stool, set so that the player faces the
audience; in front of the pianoforte, a Dante chair. Right,
downstage, a desk littered with important-looking papers,
with a chair set so that the person seated at it can look out
of the small window. Centre, downstage, an Empire chaise-
longue set at almost right angles to the audience, the head*

upstage. Left, upstage, a high sofa facing the footlights, just above and near the fireplace. Left, downstage, just above the kitchen door, an arm-chair. Upstage, between the hall doors and the french windows, a console table, with above it a bell handle. Behind the sofa, another smaller table with wine and glasses.

The house is pleasing; a good Georgian specimen, elegantly but comfortably furnished, mostly in Empire style, with light panelling. Pictures and flowers, and a quantity of feminine knick-knacks. Cheerful afternoon sunshine.

PRISSY DELL, *a fat melancholy girl in spectacles, dressed incongruously in floating materials, sits accompanying herself at the pianoforte.* FRANCIS, *the footman, wearing dark uniform, stands immobile behind her.*

PRISSY (*singing*): 'Mes larmes coulent chaque jour. . . . Pour mon amour. . . .'

    FRANCIS *bends forward stiffly and turns over the page for her.*

(*Singing.*) 'Pour mon amour, pour mon amour. . . . Pour mon amour. . . .'

    Her voice trails away on a false pronunciation and a flat note. She looks glumly at FRANCIS. *He gathers up the music, bows, lays the music on a small table next to the kitchen door, and goes into the kitchen. She rises, romantically weary, drapes her long scarf about her, and strikes an attitude in the middle of the room.*

My heart is like a wanton——

    She breaks off abruptly as MRS DELL, *in cap, gloves, and apron, comes in briskly from the ante-room, carrying a vase of flowers. She is a large sensible gentlewoman of middle age, with a constant and fluttering preoccupation*

116

with the proprieties. She stops and fixes her daughter with a look.

MRS DELL: You're talking to yourself again, I can see it in your eye. Don't do it in front of the servants, there's a dear.

> *She puts the vase on the console table and bustles back into the ante-room.* PRISSY *takes a quick glance at an open book on the pianoforte, and recites loudly in a voice tinged with melancholy.*

PRISSY: '... Ah me,

Few earthly things found favour in his sight,
Save concubines and carnal companie. . . .'

> MRS DELL *returns from the ante-room, and looks at her.*

MRS DELL: What *is* the matter with you?

PRISSY: I am in love with Lord Byron.

MRS DELL: Oh, is that all. . . ? (*Taking the volume and looking at the cover.*) *Childe Harold.* I hear it's a dirty book.

> FRANCIS *returns and hands her a bowl of visiting-cards.* PRISSY *takes her book and crosses sulkily to sit at the pianoforte.*

PRISSY: It is a beautiful and licentious poem by a great man. (*Wrapt.*) The Vicar of Dymhurst told me he has a cloven hoof.

MRS DELL: The Vicar?

> *A low rumble, far away. She starts, and listens.*

What's that?

> *She goes to the french windows and looks out.*

FRANCIS: Cannon, madam; they are firing cannon from the castle.

MRS DELL: So they are. They said they would only do that if there was bad news. . . . (*Peering.*) I've never seen Dover so full! And there's another troop-ship leaving. . . . Francis, show me the wine for dinner——

FRANCIS *bows and goes into the kitchen.*

MRS DELL: And I'll wager that's two of my own maids running down the hill. . . . They'll be arrested as spies, and serve them right. . . . (*With a sigh of despair.*) It's the end of the world, that's all. . . . You've forgotten to sort these visiting-cards, I might have known it. . . . And this, if you please, is the day Providence must pick for me to be expecting my visitor. No sign of a coach yet, thank the Lord. . . . We *must* be calm. . . . (*Holding a card.*) Who is Henry de Vere Longworth, Esquire?

PRISSY: The solicitor's clerk from Morningfield.

MRS DELL: Oh. (*Tearing the card.*) He sounded quite the thing. . . . (*Reading from another.*) 'Sir Henry Gortenbury.' (*Laying it aside, carefully.*) Ah. . . .

PRISSY: Mamma, you do not seriously think the visitor will go through old visiting cards?

MRS DELL: *I* always do. And put away that Lord Byron and get on with some literature. (*Going to* FRANCIS, *as he returns from the kitchen, carrying a bottle of wine.*) Francis, tell Miss Priscilla's new music-master to wait for me in the servant's hall, and put him in the blue room, the roof's leaking again. . . . (*Nodding at the wine.*) Yes, that will do——

FRANCIS: Very well, madam——

He bows and goes back to the kitchen. MRS DELL *goes restlessly to the french window.*

PRISSY (*thumping on the pianoforte, bad-tempered*): I shall never be proficient.

MRS DELL: Men love a little singing and playing, it gives them an idea that women are ingenuous. You'll be proficient if I have to glue your fingers to the keys.

PRISSY: Whoever your visitor is, he'll never marry me.

I told you this Empire silhouette would put ten years on my age.

MRS DELL (*sitting on the chaise-longue, busy with her visiting cards*): Your features are excellent, if one analyses them.

PRISSY: Yes, but no man has ever looked at them long enough to do that.

MRS DELL: Try taking your spectacles off.

PRISSY: That doesn't help. If I wear them, the men will not look at me; if I take them off, I cannot see the men. I'm always full of conversation when I'm alone——

The sound of the cannon.

MRS DELL (*starting up*): Lord, what can it be. . . . (*Going towards the hall.*) Lewis must be back by now, he'll know something——

PRISSY: Mamma, does my new music-master look anything at *all* like Lord Byron?

MRS DELL (*coming down to her, exasperated*): I didn't notice what he looked like, and may I remind you that we are at deadly war with the French, and may at any moment lie butchered in our beds?

PRISSY: We've been at deadly war with the French since I was three.

MRS DELL: You wait till Napoleon Bonaparte gets hold of you, my girl——

She hurries into the ante-room, still carrying her visiting cards; PRISSY shrugs her shoulders, takes up her book again, and subsides with it on the chaise-longue. The rumble of cannon again, sharper this time. She turns, a little awed, and looks out of the window.

MISS MASON enters quickly from the hall; she is soberly dressed, in a cloak, like a governess, with a timidity which cannot hide her distinction. She is in her forties, but looks younger, having moments of great and unobtrusive beauty. She stands anxiously in front of the hall doors.

MISS MASON: Oh, what is it——

PRISSY: It's only the war. . . . Why? Who are you?

MISS MASON: I beg your pardon. (*Coming into the room, timidly.*) I was waiting in the hall. . . .

PRISSY: Oh. You're not a spy, are you?

MISS MASON: I think that the servants have forgotten me. I am Miss Mason.

> *She speaks fluent English, with an almost imperceptible French accent.*

PRISSY: Everybody's upside-down today. Except me. (*Blankly pensive.*) I'm a thousand miles from it all. (*Going on with her book.*) Please take a seat. Have you come up from Dover?

MISS MASON: They are all standing in the streets waiting for news. And the militia are everywhere.

PRISSY: You sound quite frightened.

MISS MASON (*smiling, constrainedly*): I suppose it does frighten me. I have lived so long in the country, very quietly. Very securely. . . . And today there is such uncertainty in the world. Dover seems full of intrigue, and danger . . . and death. . . . (*Walking to the smaller window.*) This house especially, hanging in the air like this between two countries——

> *She stops short.*

PRISSY (*looking up at her*): What is it?

MISS MASON: I had forgotten how long it is since I saw the sea.

PRISSY: Oh. (*Reading.*) Sometimes it is clear enough to pick out the coast of France, from that window.

MISS MASON (*after a pause, in a level voice*): Yes. How very near it is.

PRISSY: At a time like this, my brother says, uncomfortably near; but then he's always saying things like that, he's a Member of Parliament. (*Turning over a page, glumly, as* MISS MASON *crosses restlessly towards the fireplace.*) Do take a seat. Mamma will be here in a moment. She's more upside-down than anybody today, she's expecting a visitor.

MISS MASON (*casual, but eyes intent*): A visitor?

PRISSY: Don't ask me who he is, because I don't know, she won't tell me.

MISS MASON: Oh. (*Sitting in the corner of the sofa.*) It sounds very . . . important.

PRISSY: Not to me.

LEWIS'S VOICE (*in the hall*): Mamma!

    A pause. LEWIS *hurries in from the hall. He is a sedate, self-satisfied young man of thirty, soberly dressed, with hat and stick. He is at the moment portentously serious, and carries a newspaper.*

LEWIS: Where's mamma?

PRISSY: Looking for you. She said you might have news.

LEWIS (*laying down hat and stick at the console table, and crossing to the desk*): Well, I have. And any minute I may be summoned to London.

PRISSY: Why?

LEWIS: That rumour was correct. He *has* left Paris. And his army with him.

PRISSY: Who?

LEWIS (*sitting at the desk, studying his newspaper*): Bonaparte, my love, who d'ye think, the Mayor of Dover?

    MISS MASON *listens intently.*

PRISSY (*eating a sweet*): Where's he bound for?

LEWIS: Heading north, that's all we know for sure. Some say the Rhine, others Brussels, and some even

England. And England means Dover. The town's seething with it. Bonaparte, Bonaparte, everywhere you turn. You may live to stand at that window, my dear, and be the first to see the wicked Corsican on Albion's fair horizon.

PRISSY (*munching*): They say he's dreadfully on the short side.

LEWIS: The common man, my dear, is coming into his own. And as a good Liberal I can't help giving Bony a pat on the back.

PRISSY: Is there going to be a battle?

LEWIS: Bound to be. And there'll be no more of that Elba business. He'll win or lose for good this time. I think he'll win.

PRISSY (*wandering to the french windows*): If he lost . . . what would happen to France?

LEWIS (*reading*): Lord knows. I expect Royalty'd rear its head again. (*Sarcastically.*) God save the King!

> *The cannon again, far away. A pause.* LEWIS *rises to go out, and sees* MISS MASON.

I have not the pleasure of this lady's acquaintance.

PRISSY: Well, I haven't either. She came in from the hall.

> LEWIS *crosses to* MISS MASON, *who rises, humbly;* PRISSY *sits at the pianoforte and concentrates on Lord Byron.*

LEWIS: You realise, madam, that by military order every stranger in Dover at the present moment is . . . suspect?

MISS MASON: I beg your pardon, sir, but I called to see my brother, Mr Mason.

LEWIS: Mason? I don't recall the name.

MISS MASON: He has come to teach music here.

PRISSY (*revived*): Oh yes, of course. What does he look like, Lewis?

LEWIS: I really didn't notice. (*To* MISS MASON.) But I did not realise he was a Frenchman.

MISS MASON (*after a slight pause, lightly*): He is not French! Heaven forbid!

LEWIS: You do not sound English, madam.

MISS MASON: We came from Wales. It sounds much the same, sometimes. My brother speaks fine English.

PRISSY: Lewis, what does he *look* like?

MISS MASON: You have not seen him? When did he arrive?

LEWIS: This morning.

PRISSY: Nobody ever tells me anything.

LEWIS: So you followed him?

MISS MASON: Yes.

LEWIS: From beyond Tonbridge? Forty miles away? Why?

    The cannon again.

I am sorry, madam, but these are extraordinary times. . . .

MISS MASON: I am afraid the explanation is very simple. He is very forgetful, and he left behind his identification papers. You know, sir, how important they are.

    MRS DELL *hurries in from the ante-room.*

MRS DELL: Oh, Lewis, thank heaven you're back——

LEWIS: You've heard the news?

MRS DELL: Yes, the carrier just told the coachman, isn't it dreadful, what *is* going to happen about my dinner-party? (*Going up and turning the bell-handle.*)

LEWIS: There's nothing we can do now, but wait——

MRS DELL (*crossing to the small window, agitated*): And Lewis, Francis says those men are there again!

LEWIS (*following her*): What men? Where?

MRS DELL: Down by the sea-wall. (*Pointing.*) There they are! Look!

LEWIS (*looking over her shoulder*): Oh yes. . . .

MRS DELL: They weren't there when the music-master arrived. I saw them twice this morning, it's most peculiar.

FRANCIS *returns from the hall.*

PRISSY: What do they look like?

LEWIS (*still peering out*): Excessively ordinary. . . .

FRANCIS (*taking up* LEWIS's *hat and stick*): Yes, sir?

LEWIS: Oh, Francis, go and watch those two fellows, in case they try and get into the garden. . . . (*Stopping him as he goes.*) Particularly if a coach drives up.

FRANCIS: Very good, sir.

He bows and goes back into the hall.

MRS DELL: Lewis, you don't think they can be anything to do with—— (*Seeing* MISS MASON *and stopping short.*) Oh. Are you the person who is waiting for the music-master?

MISS MASON (*advancing*): Yes, madam. His sister.

MRS DELL: He has arrived on the most inconvenient day of the year. I'll send him to you when he has executed one or two commissions for me. Have the goodness to wait . . . in here. (*Ushering her to the ante-room.*) My son's little sanctum.

MISS MASON: Thank you, madam.

She curtseys and goes into the ante-room.

MRS DELL (*shutting the door after her*): Don't mention it. . . . (*Peering anxiously out of the french windows.*) You don't think they could be watching for . . . the visitor?

LEWIS: I wonder. . . . (*Returning to his reading at the desk.*) Though I doubt if even a French count would attract quite so much attention as that.

PRISSY (*looking up, suddenly*): A French count?

MRS DELL (*too late*): Lewis. . . . (*To* PRISSY.) Get on with your reading. . . .

PRISSY (*rising, excited, for the first time*): Mamma, the visitor is not . . . a count?

MRS DELL: Lewis, I begged you not to say. You know how silly she is——

PRISSY: Mamma, a – count!

MRS DELL: Well, you may as well know – (*settling on the Dante chair*) – his letter said he was 'a distinguished person travelling under an assumed name for political reasons, and that his identity is an important secret,' so I sent off post-haste to Maidstone to find out who he is. And there are strong rumours there that he is a French Count. And he wrote to ask *me* for my hospitality. It's all very private. . . . I've been bursting for a week!

LEWIS: Stuff and nonsense. . . .

MRS DELL: Don't be silly, Lewis, you're as excited as I am, even though you *are* in the House of Commons.

PRISSY (*collapsing in the Dante chair*): I can't believe it. . . . I can't! Why should a French Count want to come and stay with *us*?

LEWIS (*loftily*): He states in his letter that this house is the most suitable in Dover for a person of his rank.

MRS DELL (*radiant*): I'm having the letter framed for Lady Rochman's benefit. Now you know why I want you to get on with your French songs. Though you must not——

PRISSY (*her eyes shining*): A Count! Why . . .

MRS DELL: Lewis, I told you. . . . Prissy, it is madness to go building castles in the air. . . . (*Sitting on the chaise-longue, with a voice of awe.*) Suppose he *married* you! The whole of Kent will call on me in one afternoon. . . .

PRISSY (*transported*): Oh dear. . . . Oh dear. . . .

MRS DELL: See if there is a coach, my love. . . .

LEWIS: There is plenty of time——

FRANCIS'S VOICE (*in the garden, remonstratively*): No, no, madam – if you please – this is a private house——

LADY ATKYN'S VOICE: Private? Never heard of such a thing—— Let me pass——

FRANCIS'S VOICE: But I assure you – you cannot come in here——

> *The occupants of the room listen, puzzled.*
>
> LADY ATKYNS *enters through the french windows. She is an eccentric little old woman, immensely cheerful and self-possessed. She is dressed for travelling; her taste in clothes is odd. Her sense of patronage is so kindly and self-confident as to be inoffensive. She carries books under her arm which she deposits on the pianoforte. She wanders into the middle of the room. The others stare at her, amazed.* PRISSY *has risen.* FRANCIS *follows her and stands at the french windows, confused and irresolute.*

LADY ATKYNS: Now whichever of you owns this délicieuse little villa, it should never have been built on a hill; I've been jolted away. . . . (*Sitting gingerly.*) Oh, this English travelling, mon Dieu! Quelle horreur! I'm getting too old for it, that's what it is.

> *Her French accent is atrocious but fearless. She smiles pleasantly from one to the other.*

MRS DELL: Lewis . . . who is it?

LEWIS: I don't know.

MRS DELL: Madam is – foreign?

LADY ATKYNS: No, sergeant. English as you are. Like a bit o' French, though.

MRS DELL (*at a loss*): Was there no answer, madam, to the front door of what you term my little villa?

One of my servants should have taken your card——

LADY ATKYNS: Damn front doors, I say. Always have. Burst in, make an impression, that's my way. Nothing elegant about me.

MRS DELL: You astonish me.

LEWIS: Francis, I thought I asked you to watch the garden——

FRANCIS (*awkwardly*): I am sorry, sir, but——

LADY ATKYNS: Afraid I threatened him with a pair of scissors. Where a stiletto won't scare a man, never known scissors fail.

MRS DELL (*to* FRANCIS): Show this person out.

LADY ATKYNS: He didn't show me in, blast his eyes, why should he show me out?

FRANCIS *moves towards the hall, in confusion.*

MRS DELL: Because, at the moment when I am expecting a distinguished visitor, I will not tolerate in my house a – a bawdy gipsy!

LADY ATKYNS (*gracious*): Bawdy, perhaps, but gipsy never.

LEWIS: Then what are you, madam?

LADY ATKYNS: Hard to say, really. Been everything in my time. Except one. Might have tried that if I'd had any hips. . . . Got a title, so it's no use looking at me like that.

MRS DELL *motions to* FRANCIS, *who goes into the hall.*

MRS DELL: Madam, are you mad?

LADY ATKYNS: Yes, but a heart of gold. Wish I could put the gold to some practical use.

LEWIS: But you spoke of a title?

LADY ATKYNS: Lady. Atkyns.

MRS DELL: I don't believe it. . . . In the family?

LADY ATKYNS: One up to you, sergeant; marriage. Widow of Sir Edward Atkyns. And not a penny. (*Rising.*) Ever heard of Charlotte Walpole, Drury Lane Theatre?

MRS DELL: Never.

LADY ATKYNS (*pointing triumphantly to herself*): Moi! When I played the heroine they never looked twice, but dressed up as a man I was wonderful. Ma chère, quelle fantaisie en travestie! And once, when I was a drummer boy in the dragoons, caught the eye of the Prince Regent.

PRISSY: What happened?

LADY ATKYNS: Mrs Fitzherbert intercepted my note. So I married Sir Edward.

LEWIS: For his title?

LADY ATKYNS: Can't resist 'em. Can you?

MRS DELL (*coldly*): My son, madam, is well known in Westminster for his democratic convictions.

LADY ATKYNS: Oh yes, I remember, youngest Member of Parliament. (*To* LEWIS, *walking round the room.*) Congratulate you on delightfully luxurious stronghold you've chosen for your convictions. . . . Great success, are you not, sir?

LEWIS: Are you contemptuous of success, then, madam?

LADY ATKYNS: Find it boring.

LEWIS (*offended*): Napoleon Bonaparte, who has just left Paris to defy the whole of Europe – would you call him boring?

LADY ATKYNS: Devilishly. Only become interesting the day of his last defeat. (*Sitting, suddenly thoughtful.*) Failure. Disaster. Sadder. Grander. Wouldn't be here if I didn't feel like that about it.

MRS DELL: Well, Mrs Atkyns . . . (*explosively*) . . . why *are* you here?

128

LADY ATKYNS: To take your visitor away from you.

> *A pause.* MRS DELL *recovers from the shock. A pianoforte is played softly in the ball-room, and continues intermittently for some moments.*

MRS DELL: Lewis, can I have heard right?

LEWIS: How did you know we were to have a visitor?

LADY ATKYNS: Letter from Brussels. Private channels. . . .

MRS DELL: And what do you know of my visitor?

LADY ATKYNS: Well, what do *you* know?

PRISSY: A French count, Mamma thought. . . .

> LADY ATKYNS *smiles, then looks up, listening suddenly to the music.*

MRS DELL: I find it intolerable to be catechised in my own house. And who is that playing in my music-room? Your coachman, I suppose?

LEWIS: It's only the music-master. . . . (*To* LADY ATKYNS.) And what would *you* hazard as the name of this distinguished personage?

> *A pause.* LADY ATKYNS *smiles, rises, listening, and wanders to the pianoforte. Her oddness gradually gives way to a curious dignity.* LEWIS *sits on the chaise-longue, watching her, at a loss.*

MRS DELL: Did you hear my son ask you a question?

LADY ATKYNS: Yes. This music. (*Picking up one of her books from the pianoforte.*) Made me think . . .

LEWIS: Think of what?

LADY ATKYNS: Oh, all sorts of things that don't go with this quiet room. Dripping of blood. Smell of fire. Clatter of sharp knives. Scream of a thousand people.

MRS DELL: What do you mean?

LADY ATKYNS: The French Revolution.

A pause. The music flows on. She turns to the end of the book.

(*Smiling, flapping over pages.*) I was in it. You don't forget. . . . Here we are. . . . Ah, left my spectacles in the coach. . . . (*Handing the book to* Lewis.) There . . .

Lewis (*reading, perplexed*): '. . . On the twenty-first day of January, 1793, Louis the Sixteenth, King of France . . .

> *He looks at* Lady Atkyns, *puzzled, inquiring. She nods, eagerly. He continues.*

. . . was, by his subjects, executed; and so his son, the Dauphin, became at the age of eight the unhappy Louis the Seventeenth, King of France. (*Rising, reading slowly, and crossing to the fireplace.*) For the next two years he was a prisoner of the Revolution in the Temple Tower, where, after untold sufferings, on the eighth day of June 1795, at the age of ten, he . . . (*turning over the page*) is supposed to have died. . . .

Lady Atkyns: That was twenty years ago. (*Huddling on the chaise-longue, speaking quickly, and, for the first time, emotionally.*) He didn't die. It was another boy they buried. The prisoner'd gone. Gone, nobody knows where. . . . (*Almost in tears, the tears of an old woman.*) Riddled with diseases of body and mind. . . . (*Recovering herself.*) And has been gone to this day, when he comes perhaps . . . to knock at your door.

Mrs Dell: You mean . . .

Lady Atkyns: I mean the visitor you expect claims to be Louis the Seventeenth, King of France.

> *A pause. They are dumbfounded. The pianoforte dies away in the ballroom.*

(*Lighter.*) And arrives in Dover on a pretty exciting day for him. See those two fellows watching the house?

Bet you a shilling they know a thing or two. Heard one of 'em talking French. Don't miss a thing. . . .

She rises and goes to the pianoforte.

MRS DELL (*collapsing on the sofa*): Prissy, pass me my salts. . . .

LEWIS (*to* LADY ATKYNS): Madam, I don't believe you——

LADY ATKYNS (*picking up her books*): Young man, see these volumes?

LEWIS: Well?

LADY ATKYNS (*pointing to herself*): Mentioned in every one of 'em.

PRISSY (*running to her, and reading, awed and excited*): 'Lady Atkyns and Louis the Seventeenth, he is alive?' a brochure in fifteen pages——

LADY ATKYNS: Not much of it, but very good. All about me at Versailles, meeting his dear mother, and plotting to get 'em all out of France. Spent a fortune. Still looking for him. Royalist mad, they call me. My little boy is thirty now. (*With a sigh.*) In the last six years, interviewed fourteen young men who all swore they were Louis the Seventeenth.

MRS DELL: Are you accusing my visitor, Mrs Atkyns, of being an impostor?

LEWIS: What sort of young men?

LADY ATKYNS: Tall ones, short ones; some pretty, some horrid; but all pretenders. (*To* PRISSY, *amiably.*) If your mother calls me Mrs Atkyns again, I shall strike her. . . . Had to get here before my visitor.

MRS DELL (*rising, cold and menacing*): *Your* visitor? Lewis, throw this woman out of my house.

LADY ATKYNS: Young man, would it interest you to know that I haven't cut my nails for weeks? (*As* LEWIS *recoils.*) Besides, as a confirmed Republican, it's the visitor you ought to throw out of the house, not me.

PRISSY: But this may be . . . the real one?

LADY ATKYNS: It is more than possible. I'm very curious.

> *A loud rat-tat-tat at the front door. The* DELLS *are transfixed. A pause.*

PRISSY: I think I'm going to faint.

> *A pause.*
>
> *The hall door opens.* FRANCIS *enters, goes to* LEWIS *and holds out a salver on which lies a visiting-card. He raises his hand; it is trembling slightly;* FRANCIS *notices this;* LEWIS *sees him look, steadies himself, takes the card, turns it over deliberately, and studies it.*

LEWIS: 'Louis.'

MRS DELL: What do you mean, 'Louis?'

LEWIS (*sharply*): L.O.U.I.S., 'Louis.'

MRS DELL (*awed*): Louis! . . .

LEWIS: Show him in.

> FRANCIS *bows, puzzled, and goes into the hall.*
>
> MRS DELL *rises to her feet and crosses, twittering with nerves. The others follow suit.*
>
> SOPHY RAFFETY *enters from the hall. She is twenty-eight, well-dressed, of real but strikingly unusual beauty; her features are wild, her manners haughty and brusque, both the outward shows of a creature without fear and without rest. She looks like a noble peasant. She advances slowly and looks from one to the other.*

SOPHY: I am Sophy Raffety; who has been granted the honour to accompany to Dover, over dangerous roads, the exalted personage who is about to enter this room; preparing for the day when France will be free of the Corsican usurper Bonaparte, who calls himself Emperor, and he, the rightful King, can regain the heritage to which he was born, and of which he was so cruelly cheated. His wishes, for the moment, are that no mention be made of the name which in the eyes of truth is his, and that henceforth he is spoken of as . . . Mr Leroy. I would also crave the forbearance of you all; the unspeakable trials through which he has passed have left their mark on his spirit . . . and, alas, on his mind.

> *Her whole speech has been a quite impressive imitation of the grand manner. She steps aside. The hall doors open.*
> FRANCIS *appears.*

FRANCIS (*announcing*): Mr Leroy.

> SOPHY *curtsys. The others are too awed to move.* MR LEROY *comes in from the hall.*
> *He is inoffensive, but somehow mysteriously impressive in his shabby black, which he carries with a certain simple dignity; he might be any age from twenty-eight to forty.*
> LADY ATKYNS *goes to* MR LEROY, *and scrutinises his face. He stands immobile.*

LADY ATKYNS: Bourbon nose. Cheek-bones. Curve of the mouth. . . . Remarkable.

SOPHY: And there is the scar which was verified by the physicians, and the crescent-shaped vaccination-mark on the left arm, both of which Mr Leroy is more than willing to show.

LADY ATKYNS (*staring at him*): Uncanny.

> *She is obviously deeply impressed. The moment is a solemn one.*

SOPHY: It is the particular wish of Mr Leroy that his hand need not be kissed.

> SOPHY *seats* MR LEROY *in the Dante chair and stands behind him.* LEWIS *stands before the fireplace.* LADY ATKYNS *sits on the chaise-longue.*

LADY ATKYNS: I am Lady Atkyns.

SOPHY: Oh yes. We have heard of you, of course.

LADY ATKYNS: Did Mr Leroy have a not too unpleasant——

MRS DELL (*firm*): Speaking as Mr Leroy's hostess, may
I ask him ... if he had a pleasant journey——

LADY ATKYNS: Speaking as Lady Atkyns, who has
lived most of her life in France, may I ask Mr Leroy ...
if he would prefer that I speak to him in his native tongue?

MRS DELL: I feel sure that Mr Leroy would prefer
good English to bad French.

> *The kitchen door bursts open and* MASON *appears. He
> is a young man of dishevelled good looks but sensitive appear-
> ance; his clothes are unobtrusive. When his manner breaks
> through a considerable barrier of shyness, it is lively and
> natural; his high spirits are completely unself-conscious. He
> carries a small pile of shirts.*

MASON: Oh ... I beg your pardon. (*Confused.*) I thought
this was the linen-cupboard.

MRS DELL: Does it look like a linen-cupboard? (*To
MR LEROY.*) I beg your pardon. ...

MASON: The door misled me, madam.

LEWIS: Oh ... Mr Leroy, this is my sister's new music-
master.

MASON: Newly arrived from the country. In case you
have forgotten, the name is ... Mason. Common, but
eminently pronounceable. At your service.

MRS DELL: Have the goodness, Mr Mason, to go to
the servants' hall and tidy up Miss Priscilla's music. It's
there, on the table.

MASON (*taking the music, and bowing*): Madam, I thank
you.

> *He starts to go.*

MRS DELL: Mr Leroy, could I tempt you——

MASON (*turning, with an afterthought*): I crave your pardon for trying the pianoforte in the ballroom.

MRS DELL: Not at all. (*Annoyed.*) I trust it is to your liking?

MASON (*amiably*): The most beautiful tone. I was surprised.

 He goes back into the kitchen.

MRS DELL: He must be taught his place, Lewis. . . . Mr Leroy, may I tempt you to a glass of port-wine——

LADY ATKYNS (*with over-Continental vivacity*): Monsieur Leroy, voulez-vous prendre un verre de vin après votre voyage?

 MR LEROY *looks from her to* SOPHY, *polite and puzzled.*

MRS DELL: That was French.

SOPHY: I am afraid Mr Leroy does not understand French.

LADY ATKYNS: Oh.

SOPHY: Twenty years is a long time, and at the age of ten one forgets so easily.

MRS DELL: Of course.

SOPHY: Everything, that is, but the horrors of the past.

LADY ATKYNS: Ah, ma foi, that past! How painfully, for instance must Mr Leroy recall that famous incident of his mother . . . (*speaking quickly, with point*) . . . in the coach on the flight to Varennes on the night of 21st June 1791, which must be so indelibly printed even on the mind of a child?

 A pause. MR LEROY *looks from her to* SOPHY, *tentatively.*

Perhaps Mr Leroy does not understand English either?

SOPHY: Madam, he was not seven years old at the time you speak of.

LADY ATKYNS (*sweetly*): I said 'indelibly printed even on the mind of a child.' Well, Mr Leroy?

A pause.

MR LEROY (*to* MRS DELL, *timidly*): If there's anythin' I'd like better than anythin' else, it's a nice glass o' beer.

His accent is Cockney. SOPHY *flinches, but only for a moment. The others are a little taken aback.*

SOPHY: Mr Leroy has resided from the age of eleven, in London.

MRS DELL: Indeed. Lewis. . . .

LEWIS *goes up and turns the bell-handle.*

SOPHY: And has been subjected, I fear, to a cruel denial of the graces of education which mark a gentleman.

LEWIS (*to* SOPHY, *with an ingratiating smile*): And what, may one ask, is your relationship to Mr Leroy?

SOPHY (*tartly*): Not, sir, what you think.

MRS DELL (*confused*): Let me see, where were we?

SOPHY (*sitting on the sofa, grandly*): This gentleman was kind enough to cast doubts on the relationship between Mr Leroy and myself. I first encountered him two years ago, while visiting in Gray's Inn Hospital. With the Vicar of Spitalfields. Mr Leroy was destitute. I gave up my home to nurse him.

LEWIS (*quizzically*): Such affection!

SOPHY: Not affection, sir. Loyalty. In a great cause.

MRS DELL: You mentioned – er – destitution. Was he long in that regrettable state?

SOPHY: He has never been out of it.

MRS DELL: Oh.

SOPHY: Our friends in Maidstone were loyal to a degree; they opened their hearts to us, and their purses too; and tomorrow I am expecting a package from a certain titled gentleman in St James's Street, London.

LADY ATKYNS: Splendid. Oh yes, the flight from Varennes. (*Playful but insistent.*) Now, now, Mr Leroy, what was that incident?

> *A pause.* MR LEROY *closes his eyes, and his head falls slowly forward on to his chest. Confusion. All seem to move and speak at once.*

PRISSY: He has fainted! Oh dear . . .

SOPHY (*as the others help her to deposit* MR LEROY *on the chaise-longue*): I should have warned you——

> FRANCIS *enters from the hall.*

I am afraid you have upset him——

MRS DELL: Francis – salts – water——

SOPHY: No, indeed. I am the only one to deal with this – would you leave him alone with me for a moment.

MRS DELL: But of course——

> SOPHY *whispers to* FRANCIS, *who goes back into the hall.*

LADY ATKYNS: Why, what's the matter with him?

MRS DELL: You ought to be ashamed, you cruel creature—— Prissy, go up to your room and bathe your eyes, there's a dear. . . . Poor unfortunate. . . .

> *She bustles* PRISSY *into the hall, and follows her.*

LADY ATKYNS (*wandering after them*): Have no fear, Miss Raffety, I have taken Mr Leroy under my wing. (*Turning at the hall door.*) And once you're under my wing, you don't get out in a hurry.

> *She follows the others into the hall.* LEWIS *looks from* SOPHY *to* MR LEROY, *perplexed.*

SOPHY: Our coachman's boy is waiting at the door. Would you give him a shilling for me?

> LEWIS *colours, bows stiffly, and goes into the hall.* SOPHY *and* MR LEROY *are alone.*

MR LEROY (*sitting up dolefully*): I was never cut out for this sort o' thing. . . .

SOPHY: Don't be a fool, uncle. Where's that letter. . . . (*Taking a paper, quickly, from her under-skirt, and reading.*) '. . . This Mrs Dell is ignorant of the whole matter, but invite yourself to her house, for there you will find all details of *his* childhood, and the mementoes you need. . . .' What more d'you want?

> Her manner has changed completely; she is coarse, free and natural, almost like a barmaid.

MR LEROY: It isn't signed. Foreign-looking writing too. I don't like it at all. It's fishy.

SOPHY: It's got all about those mementoes in it. Just what they are. (*Going to the desk.*) I'll try this room first. . . .

MR LEROY: They're out of the room 'fore the questions 'ave sunk in, never mind the answers, and every time I open my mouth I think how common I sound. And when you're forty-one next birthday, it isn't easy to look thirty in a strong light when the dye on your hair comes off on everything you lean against. And——

SOPHY: Sh!

> FRANCIS *returns from the kitchen with a mug of beer, and hands it to* MR LEROY.

SOPHY: That will do.

> FRANCIS *bows and goes back into the kitchen.*

SOPHY: My dear uncle, I've told you what to do. Talk as little as you can, and leave everything to me. I'll do all the talking.

MR LEROY: I should think you will! The way you spit out them long words——

SOPHY: Oh, they come easy to me. Besides, I've rehearsed 'em enough. And don't say spit. The ladies don't like it. . . . Well, we're in for it now! It's exciting!

MR LEROY: And I wish you wouldn't tell people I'm out of my mind. I don't like it.

SOPHY: Well, it does help to account for you. (*Looking out of the smaller window, as he drinks.*) But I can't say that I like the look of those two men.

MR LEROY (*spluttering*): What two men?

SOPHY: Watching the house.

MR LEROY (*rising, panic-stricken*): I'm going. I'm going——

SOPHY: Sit down, uncle, and finish your drink——

MR LEROY (*collapsing again*): It's those questions, my dear – I can't go on fainting all the time! 'Ow am I going to answer 'em? . . . (*Picking up something on which he has sat.*) What's this?

SOPHY (*opening a drawer, and searching*): Lady Atkyns's purse.

MR LEROY: Oh. . . . There's two five shillin' pieces in it.

SOPHY: Well, leave 'em in it, we don't want your old tricks here. . . . I must say she gave me a bit of a shock.

MR LEROY (*wedging the five-shilling pieces into his pocket*): Wouldn't trust her an inch, meself.

SOPHY: But didn't you see how your likeness to the painting knocked her all of a heap?

MR LEROY: Oh, that painting. . . . (*As SOPHY pries into the desk.*) I wish to 'eaven that French feller had never stopped us in Cheapside and asked me if I was 'is king. That's what started you off. And me so obligin' and you so self-willed, just like your mother when we was children. Always hitting me, she was. When they ask me what I remember before I was ten, all I can think of is your mother hitting me. And when that mad doctor feller went an' scraped me arm when I was a little 'un, he never knew the trouble he was goin' to get *me* into.

SOPHY: Don't be a fool, it was the vaccination that made my mind up——

MR LEROY: Yes, but suppose the real one is alive? That Lady Atkyns said——

SOPHY: Of course he isn't alive, that's just her idea, poor old thing. . . . (*Walking restlessly across the room.*) We haven't made a bad beginning! You know how excited they were at Maidstone. My collection at the garden fête was exactly twenty pounds.

MR LEROY: And when that's gone there'll be nothing to live on. Except thin ice.

SOPHY: I love thin ice.

MR LEROY: Why couldn't we go on staying in Cheapside, in peace? You'd got your three gentlemen——

SOPHY (*in a burst of fury*): I've finished with my three gentlemen! They taught me to talk like a lady when I feel like it, and that's all. And I've finished with Cheapside lodging-houses. Stale perfume, bad wine, sniggering and tickling of the palm of the hand . . . (*laughing, caustically*) . . . cheap indeed. . . .

MR LEROY: I dunno where you get all these ideas from, I'm sure. You're not goin' to drag me to France, are you?

Sophy: I don't think even I could palm you off on your French subjects.

MR LEROY: What are we goin' to do, then?

SOPHY: You just keep your head, and go on reminding yourself that where there's a title, some folk will believe anything . . . and we'll make a fortune. Look at this Mrs Dell——

A knock at the hall door. MR LEROY *sits back again.* LEWIS *enters, puzzled, carrying a letter.*

LEWIS: I beg your pardon, I found this pushed under the door. Addressed to Mr Leroy.

He hands the letter to SOPHY. *She looks quickly at the letter, and looks at* LEWIS, *waiting. Reluctantly, he goes back into the hall. She runs to the smaller window and looks out.*

SOPHY: They've gone. . . . It was one of those men. This minute. The same writing.

MR LEROY: Foreign. I told you.

She tears out the letter, hastily, and reads. She seems unable to take in what she sees.

What does it say?

SOPHY (*reading, slowly*): '. . . We cannot put the name on paper. But he is in the house with you now.'

A pause. She stares at MR LEROY, *who stares back.* Then . . . she's right! (*Awed and excited.*) He didn't die. And the memories we're looking for, we shan't find them in Mrs Dell's desk. They're . . . in his mind! *He* is in the house with us now. . . .

MR LEROY: He?

SOPHY: The son, Lewis. . . . It must be. (*Considering, desperately.*) Wait . . . let me think——

A knock at the hall door. MRS DELL *peers round it, then comes into the room, followed by* LEWIS, PRISSY *and* LADY ATKYNS.

MRS DELL (*in a whisper*): We hear that he is quite recovered.

SOPHY (*mechanically*): Nearly.

She pilots MR LEROY *to the sofa.*

MRS DELL (*coming into the room*): May one ask what was in the letter?

SOPHY (*tearing it up*): Merely another declaration of allegiance to Mr Leroy.

MRS DELL: Well-wishers! Thank heaven, I might have known——

SOPHY: Lady Atkyns!

LADY ATKYNS: Yes?

SOPHY: Lady Atkyns, may I know one thing? It is very important to us. You believe in Mr Leroy?

LADY ATKYNS (*after a pause, shrugging, with a smile*): Mon Dieu, I see no reason why not, the resemblance is startling, and the vaccination too. . . . You have papers, of course? Little mementoes?

SOPHY: Of course.

LADY ATKYNS: Good. (*Producing sheets of paper and unfolding them.*) Well, now we're back in the land of the living, we'll continue, shall we? I have here a list of very useful questions which I am in the habit of putting to all the Pretenders I come across.

SOPHY (*coldly*): Pretenders? What do you mean?

LADY ATKYNS: Well, you never know. . . .

> *The kitchen door opens and* MASON *reappears. He carries a sheaf of manuscript.* LADY ATKYNS *wanders to the french windows, arranging her papers, and peering at them short-sightedly.*

LEWIS (*impatiently*): Well?

MASON: Sir, my pupil's music.

MRS DELL: Oh. (*As he crosses to the pianoforte.*) Is it sorted already?

MASON: Tabulated, madam, to the last crotchet. Poor old Bach is no longer sandwiched unhappily between 'The Village Maiden' and Mr Beethoven, but I fear I can do nothing for Mr Purcell, who is stuck to 'The Merry Cliffs of Dover' by an old piece of sweet.

MRS DELL: Oh. . . . (*Presenting, reluctantly.*) Mr Mason

. . . my son Lewis. . . . My daughter Priscilla . . . Miss
Raffety.

> SOPHY *rises, studying* MASON, *intent, quizzical. He*
> *bows pleasantly.*

MRS DELL: And . . . (*passing over* LADY ATKYNS, *with*
unction) . . . Mr Leroy.

MASON: I hope you are well, Mr Leroy.

MR LEROY: Nicely, thank you.

LADY ATKYNS: In case you should take me for a bit of
furniture, young man, I'm Lady Atkyns.

MASON: Madam, your servant. . . .

> LADY ATKYNS *goes back to her papers.*

MRS DELL: Mr Mason is here, Mr Leroy, to improve
my daughter's music.

MASON: Judging by your daughter's look, madam, I
shall find my task a difficult one.

> MRS DELL *does not quite know what to make of the*
> *compliment.*

LEWIS: You may go.

> MASON *bows to the company and begins to go.*

SOPHY (*calling, clearly*): Young man!

MASON: Madam?

> *He is startled. They look at each other.*

SOPHY (*to* MRS DELL): Mr Leroy is devoted to music.
Perhaps Mr – er——

MRS DELL: Mason——

SOPHY: Perhaps Mr Mason would stay and give him a
taste of his talents at the pianoforte?

MRS DELL: Certainly.

MASON: With pleasure. (*Sitting at the pianoforte.*) Mr
Leroy is taking the sea air for long?

LEWIS: Do let us know your favourite piece, Mr
Mason.

MASON: Your pardon, sir.

    MASON begins to play, softly. SOPHY crosses slowly till she is almost beside him. The others listen, all looking at MR LEROY; except SOPHY and LADY ATKYNS, who studies her papers.

SOPHY: You take your duties very lightly, sir.

MASON: I am very light of heart today.

PRISSY: Why?

MASON (*punctuating his recitative, lightly, with allegro music*): The music-master . . . is enjoying a change of air.

SOPHY: A change from what?

MASON: From living in the country, so long like a mouse . . . walking through the streets of Dover was like ploughing through a mill-race, in the sun. . . . So many new faces, so many new voices . . . are as exciting to the little music-master . . . as wine . . . And he has set eyes on the sea. . . . That has lifted his spirits too. . . .

    The tune comes neatly to an end with his words.

LADY ATKYNS (*applauding loudly and mechanically*): Bravissimo, quelle merveille. . . . Now!

    She rises, walks into the middle of the room, and leans against the pianoforte, paper in hand. The day begins to wane.

MRS DELL: What *is* she going to do?

LADY ATKYNS: Not going to sing. . . . Let me see. . . . Curse and dammit, my spectacles. . . . Looks like fly-paper——

SOPHY: Then perhaps it might be best to leave the catechism till——

MASON (*who is directly next to* LADY ATKYNS): Can I help you, madam?

LADY ATKYNS (*placing the paper over the music on the pianoforte*): Much obliged, young man. Just read these questions out.

MASON: With pleasure. (*Reading tentatively.*) 'Have you ever experienced any undue palpitation of the heart?'

LADY ATKYNS, MRS DELL *and* LEWIS *look at* MR LEROY. SOPHY *looks at* MASON *without his knowing it; he is amused. A pause;* MR LEROY *suffers inward agonies of indecision, and finally shakes his head.*

LADY ATKYNS: Good. That's to catch 'em out. Go on.

MASON: I like this game. . . . (*Reading and playing negligently.*) 'What was your pet name for your favourite uncle?'

They all look at MR LEROY. *A pause.*

MR LEROY: It's on the tip o' my tongue. . . . I've forgotten.

LADY ATKYNS: Oh. Well, that's possible. Though it would have been a good thing to have remembered. Now, I warn you, the next one I *shall* expect you to answer. (*To* MASON.) Next.

MASON (*reading*): 'What was the pet name given to you by . . .'

His voice trails away, and with the last soft chord of the music as his fingers are still.

LADY ATKYNS: Go on.

MASON (*motionless, in a smooth voice*): I beg your pardon. I cannot decipher the next word.

LADY ATKYNS: My writing, of course. . . . (*Pondering, as* SOPHY *takes the paper abruptly from* MASON.)

SOPHY: The question is . . . 'What was the pet name given to you by . . . Marie Antoinette?'

A pause. All except MASON *and* SOPHY *look at* MR LEROY. MASON'S *head is slowly lifted, the setting sun catches his face as he looks before him, a strange and haunted light in his eyes.* SOPHY *stares at him.*

MR LEROY *appears to consider. He is about to speak when* MASON'S *hands fall on the pianoforte with a crash of discords. They stare at him.*

A gong is heard beyond the hall.

MRS DELL (*rising, busily, with relief*): That means it is time to dress for our poor little dinner, Mr Leroy . . . (*to* LADY ATKYNS) . . . if we may defer the inquisition?

LADY ATKYNS: With pleasure. Put anything off for a square meal. Now, madam, if somebody would show me the smallest corner where I can patch up my battered old face——

MRS DELL: I regret deeply, madam, my inability to offer you a bed——

LADY ATKYNS: I will not *hear* of your putting yourself out, I can sleep . . . (*pointing vivaciously to the sofa*) . . . ici! (*Taking* PRISSY *by the arm and drawing her towards the hall.*) When I was in the Secret Service during the Revolution, dressed as a sailor, I once passed the night in a haystack with three marines, and nothing daunts me. . . . Come, Miss Dell!

She and PRISSY *disappear into the hall.*

MRS DELL: Mr Leroy, I beg your excuses. She is an eccentric.

MR LEROY (*meditative*): I thought she was funny meself.

MRS DELL: Most amusing. . . . And now, Mr Leroy, may I have the honour to accompany you to your room? It's very small, I fear. . . .

MR LEROY: I'm not puttin' anybody out, I hope?

MRS DELL: Oh, sir. . . .

She turns, starts to go towards the hall, remembers, and goes out of the room backwards, nearly knocking over the console table as she does so.

146

Mr LEROY *follows her into the hall.*

As if in a dream, MASON *walks on to the balcony and looks out.*

LEWIS: Miss Raffety?

SOPHY: Thank you, sir. I shall follow.

LEWIS: You must be tired.

SOPHY: I am never tired.

She looks quizzically, under her lids, from one to the other.

LEWIS (*stiffly*): A glass of wine, madam?

SOPHY: Thank you, sir; not before dinner, with two handsome young gentlemen in the house.

LEWIS (*without unbending*): And after dinner, madam?

SOPHY (*insolent, teasing*): A loving cup with you, sir, and a walk on the cliffs.

On his dignity, LEWIS *looks from her to* MASON, *bows stiffly, and goes back into the hall.* MASON *and* SOPHY *are alone. He is still on the balcony. The daylight is fading perceptibly.*

She watches him, without his knowing; he is fixed in preoccupation.

SOPHY (*calling*): What are you thinking of?

He comes back into the room. A pause.

MASON: I was actually wondering . . . who this Mr Leroy can be.

SOPHY: A visitor. He and that mad old woman were playing a game.

MASON: I see . . . (*Light, again.*) But it is stupid of me to be thinking of anything at the moment.

SOPHY: Why?

MASON: Would it surprise you to know that I have never before been alone with a beautiful young woman?

SOPHY: At the age of thirty?

147

MASON (*laughing*): Yes. . . . (*Puzzled.*) How did you know how old I was?

SOPHY: A guess. . . . But lord, what sort of a life have you had, then?

MASON: Alone with an older sister, over an inn, outside an English village; playing the church organ for a pittance. Talking to myself. Making up stories, for my own amusement.

SOPHY: Since when?

MASON: Since I was a child. (*After the flicker of a pause.*) Monastic, I think, is the word. That's why I'm in good spirits today. (*Half bantering.*) Do you wonder that I should feel in your company . . . the quickening of a virgin pulse?

SOPHY: You talk like a book. D'you mean that you've never had anything to do with a woman?

MASON: Yes. Is that a disappointment to you?

SOPHY: It's a novelty. And anyway, it's hard to believe. (*Going up to him, slowly.*) Those lips were made for love.

MASON (*an edge to his voice*): Are they so weak?

SOPHY: Soft, and full. I wonder how weak they are. . . . (*Her mouth almost on his, suddenly.*) Did you notice just now?

MASON: What?

SOPHY: Like a cold wind it was. Right through the room.

MASON: When?

SOPHY: When I spoke, out loud, the name of . . . a dead Queen.

A pause. MASON *rises abruptly.*

MASON: I noticed nothing.

SOPHY: I did. I noticed your face. It was frozen. With empty eyes. Like one of those death-masks.

She is describing him as he looks again now, for a moment; where the half-light catches them, his features are immobile and colourless.

SOPHY: The most secret face I had ever seen.

He moves away, without answering, and stands at the french windows.

SOPHY: Napoleon Bonaparte has left Paris. Had you heard?

MASON: They told me downstairs.

SOPHY: You asked me just now who Mr Leroy is. Ask me again.

MASON: As you please. (*Going to her.*) Who is . . . Mr Leroy?

They face each other.

SOPHY: Mr Leroy is the lost Dauphin of France. . .

Their eyes meet, in the half-light.

. . . Who is in search of the country that was taken away from him.

He is silent. PRISSY *comes in from the hall, followed by* FRANCIS, *who carries a lighted lamp, which he places on the console table.*

PRISSY (*to* SOPHY): Mamma says I must take you to your room.

SOPHY *goes abruptly into the hall, followed by* FRANCIS.

PRISSY *looks at* MASON, *shy and curious.*

SOPHY (*in the hall*): I am waiting, Miss Dell!

PRISSY *drops a quick curtsy, starts to go, then remembers.*

PRISSY: And she says she forgot to say that your sister is waiting to see you.

MASON *starts.* PRISSY *holds open the ante-room door.*

PRISSY: This way, madam.

MASON *collects himself.* MISS MASON *comes in from the ante-room.*

149

PRISSY *runs back into the hall. The two are alone.*

MISS MASON: It was unkind of you to leave home without saying good-bye.

MASON: I was afraid of tears. You found my message?

MISS MASON: Yes.

Her attitude is that of a teacher, his that of a sullen child.

MISS MASON: Why have you come here?

MASON: I saw in a gazette in Tonbridge that a Mrs Dell of Dover was looking for a music-teacher, and wrote offering my services.

MISS MASON: Why?

MASON: I was restless. Useless. I have been a hermit too long. Why have you followed me?

MISS MASON: To take you back to the country, to safety. I may have discovered nothing of your plans for coming here, but others may have been cleverer. (*Anxiety mounting in her voice.*) This house is already watched by two men – and this important visitor they have been expecting – who is he?

MASON (*after a pause*): I do not know.

MISS MASON (*collecting herself*): Every ship in that harbour carries a spy——

MASON: Yes . . . (*Looking out of the smaller window.*) Every face in Dover is turned towards the sea.

MISS MASON: It is dangerous. Come back.

MASON: Not yet. I came away to work, to earn my own living, to enjoy a new life. This is even more amusing than I expected. I am curious to see what is going to happen.

PRISSY *appears at the hall door.*

PRISSY: Mamma says they will be down to dinner in a moment. And will you finish with your business and kiss your brother good night.

She curtsys awkwardly and goes back into the hall. The noise of the cannon.

MISS MASON: For your own sake, if not for mine, come back!

MASON: I shall stay here.

MISS MASON: I command you!

He does not move. A pause. She turns to go.

He goes up to her, smiling, half-sad, half-tender.

MASON: 'Kiss your brother good night,' she said. . . You will not deny me the farewell kiss which God has favoured me to receive from you, every night for twenty years?

His demeanour is suddenly curiously distant, hers suddenly humble, as she was with the strangers; but it is a different humility. A smile steals sadly over her face.

MISS MASON: Good night . . . your Majesty.

She curtsys slowly to the ground, kissing his hand.

CURTAIN

ACT II

A week later. Night.

> *Before the curtain rises,* PRISSY'S *voice is heard singing, accompanied by the pianoforte, as at the beginning of the first act. She has changed her nostalgic chanson for a rousing English folk-song which suits her just as poorly.*

PRISSY: 'I'll race my love o'er hill and dale,
>> With a hey nonny nonny and a nay nay nay!'
> *The curtain rises.*

> *The evening is very fine. Candlelight; the curtains are closed.* LEWIS *and* MRS DELL *are seated at a small card table, playing picquet; she on the sofa, he on the chaise-longue.* FRANCIS *stands behind* PRISSY, *as he did at the beginning of the play. All four are noticeably more grandly dressed than before;* FRANCIS *is in resplendent red livery, with powdered hair;* PRISSY *and* MRS DELL *are dressed for a ball;* LEWIS *wears a dressing-gown. His coat, adorned with medals, lies before him on the chaise-longue. A glass of champagne in front of* MRS DELL. *A parcel of books, wrapped in sacking, on the end of the pianoforte.*

PRISSY (*singing*):
>> 'I'll chase my love through storm and gale,
>> With a hey nonny nonny –
>> – and a hey nonny nonny – and a hey,
>> nonny nonny – and a nay nay – nay!'

(*After banging out the final chord on a triumphant top note.*)
Would you like it again, Mamma?

LEWIS: Nay, nay nay.

FRANCIS *bows, takes up the music and retires into the hall.*

MRS DELL: I liked your French songs better, child.

LEWIS: So did I. At least the tunes were inaudible, and the words incomprehensible.

PRISSY: I liked them better too. But he made me give them up.

LEWIS: Who?

PRISSY: Mr Mason.

LEWIS (*dislike in his tone*): Oh.

A clock chimes. MRS DELL *starts and looks at it.*

MRS DELL: And the musicians haven't arrived. I knew they wouldn't.

LEWIS: Mother, you are fussing again.

MRS DELL (*with a sigh*): I know, my dear, but you know what I am before a ball. I keep on telling myself nobody can possibly be here for another hour, but it's no use. It *is* the night of nights, after all. . . . I'll have another mouthful, it'll steady my nerves. . . . (*After a sip.*) And now there's only the music——

A knock at the hall door.

(*Delighted.*) Ah, here they are——

FRANCIS *returns from the hall and hands* LEWIS *a note.*

MRS DELL (*peering*): It's another bulletin from the castle. . . . Bad news! I know it! (*Distraught, as* LEWIS *opens the letter and reads.*) The English have been defeated, dear heaven, and my ball is cancelled. . . . Well?

LEWIS (*reading*): 'Napoleon has captured twenty cannon. . . . A British regiment caught in line . . . overthrown, and lost a colour, but Napoleon driven back to . . . Frasnes. Another bulletin tomorrow morning; no further news.'

153

MRS DELL: Thank God, we are saved! (*To* FRANCIS.) You may go. My trick . . . Prissy, you're idling, finish sewing your brother's medals.

    PRISSY *takes up the coat, sits in the Dante chair, and tries to concentrate on her sewing.*

LEWIS (*folding up the letter*): A week since he left Paris. It's endless.

MRS DELL: I'll swear everybody's getting used to the suspense. There have been *so* many things to think about this week——

PRISSY (*loving, dreamy*): This morning he told me to keep my back straight when I walk to the pianoforte, and my mouth shut when I play. . . .

LEWIS: Are you sure he did not mean when you sing?

MRS DELL: Now now . . . Lewis, I do hope. . . . (*Casting her eyes towards the ceiling.*) . . . that he is thinking about changing. . . .

PRISSY: Who?

MRS DELL (*rebuking her, with grandeur*): Mr Leroy.

PRISSY: The last I saw of him was in the little dressing-room, trying on Lewis's rings.

LEWIS (*raising his eyebrows*): Oh? . . . Nowhere to write the score, damnation. . . . (*Taking up a book from a pile on the floor beside him.*)

PRISSY: That's Miss Raffety's.

LEWIS (*reading*): *History of France.* . . . Still? Miss Sophy will be a scholar by Sunday. . . . (*Tearing the flyleaf from another book and writing on it.*)

MRS DELL: Lewis, you know that is your sister's——

PRISSY (*still with her thoughts*): It doesn't matter, mamma, it's only Lord Byron. . . . When he is at the pianoforte, he looks right through me; but he does it so beautifully. He had the same far-away expression this morning, looking out of that window, for such a long time. And all he could see was the coast of France. . . . To think that he arrived only a week ago! (*With emotion.*) I feel that the house has never been empty of him.

LEWIS: I confess to having had that feeling myself.

MRS DELL: Lewis, you get worse-tempered every day. And Miss Raffety more restless. Mr Mason is courteous and spirited, and as clever as he can be while still keeping his place. . . . Is it my deal?

LEWIS: No.

PRISSY (*with spirit*): I know why you hate him, Lewis! Because Miss Raffety seeks his society more than yours! You see, I'm not as silly as all that.

LEWIS (*nettled*): Oh yes you are. Considerably sillier. Why has he made you give up your French songs?

PRISSY: He will not hear of anything French. Bad taste, he calls it.

LEWIS: Oh. Insular fellow.

MRS DELL: And, incidentally, a slight on Mr Leroy.

PRISSY (*puzzled, placing* LEWIS's *coat on the chaise-longue*): I think Mr Leroy must be one of the plainest kings who ever lived. And I'll never get used to going out of the room backwards without knocking something over.

> MASON *enters from the hall. He has acquired more self-confidence, but his manner shows from time to time a nervous edge. He is dressed as before. He lays his hat on the console table. He carries a small be-ribboned box.*

MRS DELL: Ah, Mr Mason! And how did *you* find Dover this evening?

MASON: Beside itself, madam. There is talk of nothing but your ball tonight; Napoleon Bonaparte is forgotten, and even the Lord Mayor's wife's little escapade with the

Town Clerk has sunk into the background of public events. The name of Mr Leroy trembles on the tip of every shopkeeper's tongue, as he gives generous measure to those who are invited, and short weight to those who are not. The schoolboys stand in the market-place holding history-books: and, for the first time in their lives, turning over their leaves. 'Here,' they say, 'every page is studded with royalty.' . . . And shading their eyes against the sun, they look up at this house and murmur, 'Behind those windows lives Mrs Dell, who is giving the ball tonight to which my mother has not been invited, which has vexed her so; behind those windows lives . . . a king!'

A pause. The word echoes strangely in the room.
(*Breaking the silence, lightly.*) Then I remembered that through her I had set eyes on this Mr Leroy; and in gratitude for my privilege——(*handing her the box with a flourish*) – went and bought her some sweets.

MRS DELL: Oh, Mr Mason, you are too kind! Lewis, out of his salary, too. . . .

LEWIS (*sarcastically*): Mr Mason has a nice turn for oratory.

MASON (*constrained*): My upbringing, sir, must excuse my flow of words; I fear I have had more communing with books than with people.

MRS DELL: And the lanterns all down the cliff?

MASON: The admiration of every passer-by. Seated under one of them, I espied the guest of honour himself.

MRS DELL: Oh dear, isn't he in yet? What is he doing?

MASON: Smoking a pipe. In what seemed like a brown study. I hope he doesn't fall into the sea.

MRS DELL: Lewis, that means he hasn't changed into his uniform!

PRISSY: I don't suppose Miss Raffety will be ready either——

MRS DELL (*sharply*): Well, they ought to be, their clothes have cost me enough. . . .

MASON (*going up to* PRISSY, *who stands up, confused*): Will my fair pupil accept a tribute to her talent and industry? I fear the flowers are young; but then so is she.

With charming simplicity, he hands her a corsage.

PRISSY (*overwhelmed*): Oh, Mr Mason. . . .

MRS DELL: Delightful, delightful. . . .

MASON *sits at the pianoforte and plays the tune* PRISSY *was attacking earlier in the evening.*

PRISSY (*singing away, delighted*):

'I'll race my love o'er hill and dale——'

MRS DELL: Now, Prissy, up to your room for that lotion, your elbows are getting red again. And then lie down for ten minutes.

PRISSY: Oh, Mamma——

MRS DELL: I don't want you falling asleep in the middle of a quadrille, you know what you are. (*As* PRISSY *goes disconsolately towards the hall.*) If you don't sparkle on the night of nights, you never will.

PRISSY (*to* MASON *as he holds open the hall door for her*): It's odd how easy it is to get used to a king in the house when he has hardly a tooth in his head. And lumbago.

She goes into the hall.

LEWIS: He hasn't got lumbago.

MASON: Well, he looks as if he had, and I think he's given it to me; I'm stiff with bowing.

He plays again.

MRS DELL: Come, come, let us finish our game, it will occupy our minds. . . . (*Dealing a hand.*) Ah! What a blessing we can gather for a moment or two like this, when we think of the multitude that will invade us within the hour! Here we are, our own cosy family group——

   The hall doors fly open and LADY ATKYNS *breezes in. She is in the same clothes as before, with feathers and jewels in her hair, and as irrepressible as ever.*

LADY ATKYNS: Cards! Hell, why did nobody wake me?

MRS DELL (*dealing in a measured tone*): Perhaps we thought you were dead.

LEWIS: Mamma, really. . . .

MRS DELL: I have failed to get this woman out of my house by the artifices of courtesy. From now on I am going to be rude. I shall conduct myself towards her like any of the fishwives who were her fellow-actresses at Drury Lane Theatre.

LADY ATKYNS: We behaved just as well as the gentlemen wanted us to, and no better.

MRS DELL: You look like a Christmas-tree.

LADY ATKYNS: Yes, but I'm going to look wonderful later on!

MRS DELL: She's going to sit on your medals, Lewis.

   LEWIS *picks up his coat from the chaise-longue.*

LADY ATKYNS (*pointing to the coat*): Shouldn't wear that one tonight.

MRS DELL (*to* LEWIS): Which one is it?

LADY ATKYNS: Republican Club Badge. . . .

   LEWIS *ignores her as he takes off his dressing-gown and his mother helps him into his coat.*

LADY ATKYNS (*taking the parcel from the pianoforte with a cry of pleasure*): Ah, rest of my library at last. . . . Anybody got a knife?

MASON: Permit me, madam.

He produces a knife and helps her to unwrap the books.

MRS DELL (*fussing with* LEWIS's *coat*): You know, my dear, that every single person accepted for tonight, except Prissy's officers who are abroad at the war? And they're not to be counted anyway.

LADY ATKYNS *curls up on the chaise-longue with one of her books.*

LEWIS: And judging by the present situation, they'll be abroad for a twelvemonth.

MRS DELL: Well, they can come next year. Lady Atkyns will be delighted to meet them.

SOPHY *enters from the hall door; she is in a magnificent ball dress, and carries herself with even more grandeur and assurance than before; her manner is restless and watchful. She carries a large parchment scroll.*

MRS DELL: Ah, Miss Raffety! Pretty as a picture!

SOPHY: Thank you, madam.

MRS DELL: Thank goodness you're ready. . . .

SOPHY (*looking at* MASON, *boldly*): How many L's in . . . Versailles?

A pause. Their eyes meet, in antagonism.

LEWIS: Two. And an S. . . . To whom, may one ask, is the letter?

SOPHY (*crossing to the desk*): It isn't a letter. It's Mr Leroy's address to the assembly tonight. I have been putting the finishing touches. Mr Mason should have set it to music.

LADY ATKYNS (*calling to* MASON): Young man, see those books?

MASON: Yes?

LADY ATKYNS (*pointing to herself*): Mentioned in every one of 'em.

MRS DELL: Lord, off again. . . .

LADY ATKYNS (*deep in her reading*): Not always favour-ably. But mentioned.

A pause. MASON *takes up one of the volumes slowly.*

SOPHY: What are the books, Mr Mason?

MASON (*reading in a clear voice*): 'The Mystery of Louis the Seventeenth; the Truth.' . . .

SOPHY: Yes?

MASON (*taking up another*): A translation by Sir Henry Cranshaw, of 'The Cause of the French Revolution.'

MRS DELL (*shuffling cards*): That, I take it, is the lady's own autobiography.

LADY ATKYNS *turns pages reminiscently, oblivious to her.*

MASON: From the *New York Gazette*. . . . (*Reading.*) 'An article by Cyrus S. Heuffer, Proving Conclusively that Louis the Seventeenth is still Alive, and an American.' . . . (*His tone more strained.*) 'The History of . . . the Phantom Orphan of the Temple Tower.' . . . (*After a pause, placing the books one on top of the other.*) What a pagoda of literature.

SOPHY: What a mountain of theories . . . when King Louis the Seventeenth of France, at this very moment, sheltered behind an anonymous name, lives with us in this house. (*After a pause.*) A glass of wine, Mr Mason?

LADY ATKYNS (*excited*): Ah, here is a record of a con-versation I had with the Queen. . . . (*To* MASON.) His mother, you know.

The others continue with their cards, and do not hear. Only SOPHY *listens.*

LADY ATKYNS (*reading*): ' "From the day of his birth," the Queen replied, "he was always in good spirits." '

MASON: Tell me what she was like.

LADY ATKYNS: But I'm always telling you what she was like!

MASON: Tell me again.

LADY ATKYNS: Thoughtless, but very kind. Always pretty. (*After consideration.*) And sometimes beautiful.

MASON: When?

LADY ATKYNS: Oh. . . . (*Pondering, still curled up on the sofa.*) Once . . . when I was standing in a crowd that was turning very unpleasant – wherever there was a bit of trouble in those days, sure to find old Charlotte, dressed up as something or other——

MASON: And where was she?

LADY ATKYNS: Standing at a window with her husband. Old and fat he looked, like Mr Leroy, not like a king at all. Held him up for the crowd to see. Not her husband, the little Dauphin. Waved to them, in his childish way, and shouted out. 'One day I shall be your king!' he shouted.

MASON: Did he?

LADY ATKYNS: 'Un jour je serai Roi!' (*To the others.*) French for it, you know. . . .

MASON: Oh yes.

LADY ATKYNS: Cheered their heads off. Of course that was before the Revolution; never dreamt of the horrors of the Temple prison. . . . (*Sadly.*) They used to give him mugfulls of wine, y'know, to make him drunk, and he was only ten, and then they used to make fun of him. Dear little boy. (*Loudly, at the others.*) D'you wonder I'm still looking for him?

LEWIS (*rising, irritated*): Oh, you've found him——

LADY ATKYNS: Yes, but *have* I?

MRS DELL(*putting away the card-table*): Pay no attention,

Lewis, it only makes her worse. . . . (*Bearing down on* LADY
ATKYNS.) What do you mean, *have I*?

MASON *stands looking out of the french windows.*

LADY ATKYNS: Well, sergeant, I still haven't my proof.
Every time I ask Mr Leroy a question about his childhood, he has to go to his room.

MRS DELL: That is because he is overcome by his
memories.

LADY ATKYNS: Wish he'd find time to tell me what they
are before being overcome by them. Only thing he ever
disclosed to me was what he said to a lady who died
fifteen years before he was born.

*She wanders to the desk, and immerses herself in one of
her books.*

LEWIS: Has it occurred to you, Lady Atkyns, that Mr
Leroy may be hiding intimacies from you, because he has
no wish as yet to put his position into black and white?

MASON: That, no doubt, is why you are to proclaim
him tonight, in your ballroom, as Louis the Seventeenth,
to three hundred people.

LEWIS: That is my mother's idea, not mine. My
revolutionary principles forbid me to take the slightest
public interest in a person of Mr Leroy's birth. I allow
him to stay here to please my mother.

There is a quarrel in the air at once.

MASON (*sitting at the pianoforte*): Would you walk up
and down the market square arm in arm with *me*, at the
busiest time of the day, to please your mother?

LEWIS (*nettled*): I am interested in Mr Leroy purely as
a phenomenon.

MASON: What sort of phenomenon?

LEWIS: One – one of debasement by reason of royal
origin.

MASON: Meaning that he ought to be ashamed of his exalted birth?

LEWIS (*taken aback*): Well – yes. Speaking as a republican——

MASON (*bantering*): Was it as a republican that you sent twelve special messengers to twelve old college friends of yours, asking them here tonight to meet 'a distinguished personage'?

LADY ATKYNS (*tickled*): Ha!

LEWIS (*angrily, going up to him*): Sir, you have been reading my letters!

SOPHY: I told him.

MASON (*smiling no longer*): Sir, you are hasty in your conclusions.

LEWIS (*suddenly infuriated*): So Miss Raffety has long talks with you, does she?

MRS DELL: Mr Mason is right, my dear. I think it would be kind of you to apologise——

LEWIS: I am not in the habit of apologising to servants.

MASON *starts, and rises passionately, as if stung; the others look at him apprehensively. As he stands looking* LEWIS *from head to foot, his anger gives way to an unfathomable contempt.* LEWIS *shrinks visibly; in a mysterious way, their rôles are suddenly reversed.* MASON *recovers with a start, and looks from one to the other, confused.* SOPHY *watches him intently.*

MRS DELL: Really! Mr Mason!

MASON *makes a desperate effort and collects himself.*

SOPHY: For one moment, sir, I thought you would strike Mr Dell!

MASON: It is for me to apologise, sir . . . and madam. I have a sharp——

He hesitates, smiles, and sits again at the pianoforte.

LEWIS: Well?

MASON: I was about to claim a temper; then I remembered that it is a luxury somewhat above my station. (*Smiling.*) I'll be humble, and call it a liver.

> FRANCIS *stands at the hall doors.*

FRANCIS (*announcing, ceremoniously*): His Majesty the King!

> *The six occupants of the room rise as one person, and bow or curtsy low.*
>
> MR LEROY *walks slowly in from the hall. He is finely dressed, and in one week he too has gained in self-confidence, though it is still on the tentative side. He advances, bows, and sits carefully, in the Dante chair.*

MR LEROY: Everyone may sit.

> *The others follow suit. The* DELL *family are very stiff. An awkward pause.*

MRS DELL: How pleasant to relax. . . . I trust his Majesty found the cliffs . . . agreeable?

> MR LEROY *considers, and nods.* FRANCIS *retires into the hall, backwards.*

LEWIS (*a statement, but an anxious one*): His Majesty will no doubt be going upstairs in a moment to change for the ball.

MRS DELL (*as there is no answer*): Our guests are due within the hour. . . .

> MR LEROY *nods slowly.*

MRS DELL: His Majesty has no doubt been considering his address for tonight.

MR LEROY: We dozed off.

> *His accent has improved, but is still unmistakable.*

MASON (*leaning over, suddenly*): Is your Majesty partial to dancing?

> MR LEROY *looks at him coldly. The others do the same.*

MRS DELL: Mr Mason, you are addressing a direct question.

MASON: I beg his Majesty's pardon.

MR LEROY (*with more weight than meaning*): You're welcome.

> FRANCIS *returns from the hall, plainly relieved, bows quickly to* MR LEROY, *and turns to* MRS DELL.

FRANCIS: The musicians are here, madam.

MRS DELL: Thank heaven. . . .

> *She half rises with excitement, remembers* MR LEROY, *half curtsys and rises again.*

FRANCIS: I have shown them into the ballroom, madam.

> *He bows and goes back into the hall.*

MRS DELL (*crossing to the pianoforte, in a flutter*): If your Majesty will permit me, I'll give them their music to try over, and their instructions. . . . (*Handing* MASON *a large pile of music from the pianoforte.*) Mr Mason, would you kindly carry these for me into the ballroom?

> MR LEROY *nods, and rises slowly.* MASON, SOPHY, LEWIS *and* LADY ATKYNS *rise.* MRS DELL *is already standing.* MR LEROY *bows. All bow or curtsy. Suddenly, ostentatiously,* SOPHY *sits. The others stare at her.* MR LEROY *is pained, but moves on.*

MRS DELL: Er . . . the music . . . His Majesty has perhaps a personal preference?

MR LEROY (*after thought*): Something with a tune in it.

> *He makes to go out into the hall.*

> *A knock at the kitchen door.* FRANCIS *enters, carrying an open message on a salver.*

FRANCIS (*timidly*): Er . . . Your Majesty. . . .

MRS DELL (*shocked*): Francis. . . .

FRANCIS: It is marked urgent, madam.

LADY ATKYNS patters across to the footman; with one hand she picks the note neatly from the salver, and with the other whips up her spectacles.

LADY ATKYNS (*reading*): 'Mr Jake the wine-merchant's compliments, but the Royal gentleman has been in again.'

A pause.

MRS DELL (*stiffly*): Francis.

FRANCIS bows and goes back into the kitchen.

LADY ATKYNS (*reading*): '. . . He has charged six bottles of hock to Mrs Dell's account, making fourteen in all, is Mrs Dell to settle for these as well or is the Royal gentleman liable which he says no?'

Dignity itself, MR LEROY goes into the hall. MRS DELL takes her letter from LADY ATKYNS.

MASON: As well as a fine sense of etiquette, Mr Leroy seems to have acquired a quite exceptional palate.

MRS DELL: His Majesty discusses his debts with me, and a great many other questions besides, frequently and freely.

MASON: So would I, after fourteen bottles of hock.

He goes into the hall, carrying the music. LEWIS watches SOPHY. The sound of the orchestra tuning up in the ball-room, intermittently.

MRS DELL (*looking at SOPHY*): Few people in this house seem to realise what his Majesty has been through. Life has cost him dear.

LADY ATKYNS: Not as dear as his wine account's going to cost you. . . . Well, don't want to miss the first arrivals. Must go upstairs and look for my other shoe.

She hurries into the hall.

MRS DELL: And now the music, and all will be ready. . . . (*Gathering up LEWIS's dressing-gown.*) Lewis, keep an

166

eye on him while you're dressing, there's a dear; last
night he had his stockings on inside out. . . .

 She hurries into the hall.

 Sophy *and* Lewis *are alone.*

Lewis: Your door was locked last night.

Sophy: I have a distaste for burglars.

Lewis: Your first night here, you had none.

Sophy: It is an acquired distaste.

 Lewis *stares at her, angrily.* Francis *stands at the
hall door.*

Francis (*announcing, as routine*): His Majesty the King.

 Mr Leroy *follows him, in his shirt-sleeves.* Francis
retires into the hall.

Lewis: What are his Majesty's wishes?

Mr Leroy (*grimly*): Just goin' to have an audience.
With this young lady.

 Lewis *bows, and goes out into the hall.*

Mr Leroy (*to* Sophy): I'm very annoyed with you, I
am really. Why did you sit down when I got up?

Sophy: Because I'm sick to death of this ridiculous
pretence.

Mr Leroy (*staggered*): Well, upon my word. . . . You
started it!

Sophy: Yes, and now I want to stop it.

Mr Leroy: Well, you're not goin' to. Just when I'm
beginning to enjoy meself. The idea. D'you know what
you are? You're a fraud! (*Sitting in the Dante chair, with
dignity.*) You've done nothing to help me, nothing at all.
You promised to get the truth, and you 'aven't.

Sophy: Out of who?

Mr Leroy: The real one. Whoever he is. Though I
don't think 'e's here at all. If you ask me, that foreign-
looking letter we got was a wicked pack of lies.

SOPHY: Indeed.

MR LEROY: You don't still think it's Mr Lewis Dell?

SOPHY: I made up my mind about him our first night here.

MR LEROY: Well, who else can it be?

SOPHY (*impatiently*): I don't know. Unless it's you all the time.

MR LEROY: Well, perhaps it is.

SOPHY: What?

MR LEROY: I mean it. (*Thoughtfully.*) After all, p'raps I was smuggled out of France long *before* I was ten, and that's the reason I can't remember anything. It's quite possible.

The sound of the music tuning, in the ballroom.

SOPHY (*losing her temper*): You were smuggled out not a day under ten, and if you take my advice you'll remember something in the next hour, and get hold of one or two of those mementoes we've talked so much about! I think you'll find the French guests tonight harder to fool than Mrs Dell. Or yourself.

He rises stiffly and walks towards the hall.

And I advise you to keep the royal fingers out of their purses.

He starts, looks at her with dignity, and stalks into the hall. The orchestra begins to play, in the ballroom, softly and insidiously.

SOPHY *stands a moment; then sighs impatiently, walks across the room, drinks a glass of champagne, walks to the pianoforte, takes up a book, looks at it curiously, sighs impatiently again, walks across as if to go into the hall, hears the noise of the kitchen door opening, and stands against the ante-room door so that she cannot be seen from the kitchen.*

MASON *comes in from the kitchen; he has his party manners, as if he expected there would be people in the room. He sees nobody, and slowly becomes himself; nervous and preoccupied. He is about to cross the room when his eye catches* LADY ATKYNS' *books on the pianoforte. He struggles an instant in his mind, but is drawn towards them; he takes the top book and begins to read.*

SOPHY *watches him. The music plays on. He lifts his head slowly, listening, his face rapt, torn between the delight and the torment of remembrance.*

SOPHY (*almost at his ear*): D'ye know the tune?

MASON (*involuntarily*): Mozart. . . . (*Turning to her, realising she is there.*) A little delicate for you, my dear.

He crosses and sits on the chaise-longue.

SOPHY: But not for you, I take it? . . . (*As he turns from her.*) They are playing the melodies most popular at the palace of Versailles during Mr Leroy's childhood there.

He tries not to listen. She watches, drumming her fingers. He stirs, impatient with her presence.

MASON: Our hostess has spared neither trouble nor expense for Mr Leroy's little rout.

SOPHY (*slowly, insistently*): You mean . . . the reception given to meet the august child that escaped from the Temple Tower?

MASON (*after a pause*): I beg his pardon. . . . Your language, my dear, grows more flowery every day.

The music stops, in the middle of a phrase.

SOPHY: It's from listening to you, I expect.

MASON: Do you know me so well?

SOPHY: Well enough. Have you forgotten last night?

MASON: Is that important?

SOPHY: It hardly slips even my memory.

MASON: It has slipped mine.

SOPHY: Does that mean that from now on, your door is locked against me?

MASON (*insolently, into her eyes*): No.

SOPHY: Your manner, sir, puzzles me.

MASON: I am sorry.

SOPHY: When I first made love to a raw country yokel, I didn't bargain for this.

MASON: For what?

SOPHY: For something so close to the patronage of . . . royalty.

> *A pause. The music starts again. He rises abruptly.*

MASON: I would thank you, Miss Raffety, to mind your own business.

SOPHY (*taunting*): Ah, so the country yokel's afraid of me, too? Afraid of where my talk may lead him? . . . (*As he sits on the sofa without answering.*) Another day in this house, and I'll be swearing like a trooper. . . . (*Again as he does not speak, angrily.*) Why, do you think?

MASON: Because you cannot put any leading questions to me, to find out if I am the winning candidate for the post of Louis the Seventeenth, without giving away your own poor Mr Leroy; and so, for the past week, matters have been at a deadlock.

SOPHY (*lying on the chaise-longue*): Go on.

MASON: In spite of the fact that I have hinted to you that I have a very shrewd idea that Mr Dell is the gentleman.

SOPHY (*impatiently*): His mother showed me a cameo of him when he was four years of age, in London. . . . (*Slowly.*) Could your mother do the same?

> *A pause. He starts, makes to speak, then controls himself. The music stops. She watches him; then continues.*

SOPHY: However, I have still the greatest admiration for Mr Dell's qualities.

MASON: Indeed.

SOPHY (*pointedly*): They are so much finer than a mere gift of the gab; the manly qualities of ambition and action.

He starts, offended by the challenge in her voice.

SOPHY: Give me some wine, please.

MASON (*changing the subject as he pours out wine for her*): May I ask precisely what you hoped for when you embarked on this adventure?

SOPHY (*after thought*): The gamble of making money. . . . The possibility of being in a position to order a great many people about in a great many ways. . . . (*As he listens, despite himself.*) Luxury; sensation; power. . . .

The music starts again.

MASON: I should have thought that the alcove and its secrets would have kept your mind occupied for some years to come.

SOPHY: I am one of those fortunate women who tire of men before most women begin to wonder if men are getting tired of them. They tell me I am good at making love . . . (*kissing him, boldly, passionately*) . . . and I know how to deal with my lovers; but I lose interest very soon in what you call the alcove and its secrets.

The music stops again, in the middle of a phrase.

MASON: You ought to have been a man.

SOPHY (*suddenly*): I ought to have been a man, if being a man means refusing to live any longer as a servant and a nobody. . . . (*As he starts up.*) How's that for plain speaking, Mr Mason?

He makes to go out to the kitchen. She goes up to him, impetuously.

SOPHY: Wait! I throw in my hand! Mr Leroy is not Louis the Seventeenth, but my uncle the pickpocket who had never seen the English Channel till a week ago! And a ball is being given tonight for three hundred people who will expect definite proof that he is what he pretends to be! We came to this house for that proof! He must have it . . . now!

MASON: You'll get no proof from me. (*Again making to go.*) Search my room, if you like——

SOPHY (*intercepting him*): I've done that already. And found nothing. . . . But your trunk is locked, and there is . . . a deed-box rattling about in the bottom of it . . . isn't there ? . . . (*As he stares at her, angrily.*) Isn't there ?

MASON (*again evading her*): Even a nobody has one or two private papers——

SOPHY (*fiercely, following him*): I do not believe that they are the private papers of a nobody.

A pause. They look challengingly at each other.

MASON: You are free to believe what you please.

SOPHY: I believe in that deed-box. All he needs to carry me to success is your papers and your memories——

MASON (*in a wild outburst, his first hysterical moment in the play*): Memories, memories! (*Sinking into the arm-chair, in a frightened whisper.*) I have no memories. . . .

SOPHY: Then why do you sleep with every light burning, and the door wide open?

He looks slowly at her, speechless.

SOPHY: And why, as you heard that music playing, was your face the same as that first day, frozen – with memory ? . . . And shall I tell you something more, my friend ? Every day for a week, I have been watching you; and with every hour of every day, slow but sure . . . you have changed. Since the day when you left your place of hiding and came to this house——

MASON: When I came to this house to earn my living, I knew nothing of what I would find here, and if I had known, I should never have come!

SOPHY: Then why have you stayed? (*Her voice with each phrase louder and more insistent.*) And why must you make fun of Mr Leroy and question Lady Atkyns, rubbing bitterness into your heart? And why does the servant of a week ago turn on the master of the house? Shall I tell you? Because you are not thinking only of the past. . . . There are other thoughts in that head of yours; and they are tearing, like smoke, towards the future!

MASON: They must not. They must not! . . . (*Quietly, insistently.*) Shall I tell you, my friend, why my candle burns all night? (*Explaining, like a child.*) Because in the dark my little room never stops changing. . . . (*Articulate at last.*) First it's a coach . . . and the horses' hoofs racing, racing through the night . . . and then it's a ditch . . . but the horses' hoofs are still racing, over my head this time, beating, beating, after me, after me . . . and then my pillow turns to straw, and I can hear the walls crackling as they move towards me . . . and then the horses again . . . like thunder . . . through the night . . . after me . . . after me!

> *He clings to her, like a terrified child. A pause. He gradually recovers. A knock at the hall door.* PRISSY *enters.*

PRISSY (*smiling, conspiratorial and shy*): I beg your pardon, dear Mr Mason. Somebody to see you. I saw her from my window walking up the hill and I wasn't going to have *your* visitor kept waiting in the hall a second time.

MASON: Thank you.

PRISSY: It is nothing in the world, dear Mr Mason. (*Calling through the hall door.*) This way, madam.

> MISS MASON *enters; she looks tired but composed.*
> MASON *looks at her, perturbed.*

Miss Raffety, this is dear Mr Mason's sister. (*As the two women survey each other.*) Please be kind to her. (*Curtsying awkwardly as the other two curtsy to her.*) I wonder if Mama is in the ballroom? (*Going.*) My shoes are too tight. . . .

> *She goes back into the hall.*

SOPHY: Your brother did not tell us, madam, that you were to visit us again?

MISS MASON: He is forgetful.

SOPHY: You look tired, madam. Have you been hurrying? (*Going to the wine-table, eager, as if a little intoxicated.*) A little of Mr Leroy's medicine!

MISS MASON: Mr Leroy?

SOPHY(*pouring out two glasses, one eye on* MASON, *ironically*): The visitor; a horrid plain man, we'll not talk of him! (*Handing* MISS MASON *a glass of wine.*) But we can drink his health!

MISS MASON: But who is this Mr Leroy?

SOPHY: Mr Leroy, madam, is the august child that escaped from the Temple Tower.

> *She waits for the other woman to answer;* MISS MASON *stares before her, without moving.*

And now a toast. . . . (*Raising her glass, solemnly.*) To the King!

> *She drinks, and hurries into the hall.*

> MISS MASON *stares at* MASON; *his attitude seems curiously impersonal.*

MISS MASON (*passionately*): I hated this house as soon as I saw it – it has brought us to what I have feared for

twenty years. . . . (*Controlling herself.*) I beg your pardon.
What she said is a shock to me.

MASON: It was a surprise to me too. (*Wearily.*) It seems
that he needs proofs to support his claim, and spies wrote
to him with instructions to come to this house——

MISS MASON (*agitated*): I told you they were watching
us. . . . So he knows?

MASON: They wrote, it seems, with an excess of
caution, and mentioned no names——

MISS MASON: You are sure that he does not suspect?

MASON: Apart from once asking me to open the door
for him, his Majesty has maintained towards me the
silence of the grave. (*As she gives a sigh of relief.*) His lady
just now occasionally fires an indirect question, but she
has no proof.

MISS MASON: Has he talked French in front of you?

MASON: He doesn't know any. The language which
you silenced so completely has lain entirely undisturbed.

The music starts again, in the ballroom.
They listen; she is moved by it.

The music-lessons are progressing too, if one can over-
look a distinct tendency to tone-deafness. It is all very
amusing.

MISS MASON: Then you are content?

MASON: The early mornings I spend at this window.
. . . The sign on the 'Bull and Lizard' swings and catches
the sun; the milliner perches on her doorstep and waves
to the dragoons in the barrack yard; a fisher-girl tickles
with her toes the feathery edge of the ocean; and the
sign on the 'Bull and Lizard' swings and catches the sun
again. (*After a pause.*) And far away . . . the coast of a
strange country.

MISS MASON: You are not content. . . . (*Smiling, but on*

the verge of tears.) Until this week, we had not spent a day
apart for twenty years.

> *She masters herself.*

> *He looks at her, and seems suddenly overwhelmed with
> tender contrition.*

MASON: Madame . . .

MISS MASON: Monsieur . . .

> *He falls impetuously at her feet, his head at her knee.*

MASON: Have you missed me?

> *The music stops, in the ballroom.*

MISS MASON (*slowly*): It has been the longest week in
the history of the Gregorian Calendar. . . . Mr and Mrs
Tawny send you their love.

MASON: And little Sandy?

MISS MASON: He misses his music-lesson, and cries;
I tell him Mr Mason has now to teach lessons to people
who give to him in exchange something more useful
than conkers, but he will not be comforted——

MASON: Has William finished painting the flagpole?

MISS MASON: Yes, and then the rain came and washed
away the paint, and the pole——

MASON: And you, Madame . . . what have you been
doing?

MISS MASON (*after a pause*): Nothing. . . . (*Changing the
subject, quickly.*) Where is this Pretender now?

MASON: Upstairs. Squeezing into the royal breeches.

MISS MASON (*smiling*): But what sort of man is he?

MASON: Beyond bearing a much more marked resemblance to me as a child than I do myself – which is
the ultimate irony – Mr Leroy does not make a very
good King. He possesses . . . (*enumerating on his finger-tips*)
. . . a pair of small eyes that challenge disbelief with the
bright courage of the canary; a pair of good-sized ears,

with as marked a dislike for leading questions as for water; a thirsty but courageous tongue that braves the cynical with lie after lie; and eight stalwart finger-nails which have, for some forty years, faithfully sheltered the good English soil from which they have sprung.

The music begins again in the ballroom; a quiet tune.

MISS MASON (*laughing*): I am glad. . . . (*Closing her eyes.*) Oh, Monsieur. . . . The last week is a nightmare, and I am awake at last. We are home over our inn, with the perfume of the hay and the children singing across the square in the schoolroom. Our dear English village. . . . And you on the rug, reading aloud to me. Miss Fanny Burney . . . *Clarissa Harlowe* . . . Miss Austen's *Sense and Sensibility, the Spectator* . . . and when I am feeling very strong, Mr Gibbon's *Decline and Fall of the Roman Empire.* (*Contented.*) Thousands of English words. Sweet English pages turning slowly, to the thin melody of our poor little pianoforte.

MASON (*looking before him, caught in her mood*): Words, falling on the air; and as the echo of each one dies away, one step further from . . . that first life. (*Brooding.*) One more wisp of vapour blown between us and that dim fantasy . . . (*as she places her hand instinctively on his arm*) . . . which must never be mentioned. Pages turning . . . (*his voice altering, sombrely*) . . . for months. For years. The calendar changes. Seventeen hundred and ninety-six . . . ninety-seven . . . and still it goes on, until the last book is read . . . and so comes to an end – our procession of triumphant ineffectuality.

The music stops. A pause. She studies him, troubled.

MISS MASON: You have never talked like this before, Monsieur.

MASON: Is it so startling, Madame, for a man to put

philosophically into words the life that is arranged for him every day until he dies?

MISS MASON (*stung*): Was it such a tedious business, those years with me? (*Calmer, but urgent.*) When we came to England twenty years ago, your old life was dead; unspeakably destroyed. . . . (*Quickly.*) I have never said this to you before, but I must now. . . . In body and in spirit you were wrecked. I cleared away the ruins; I built a new foundation. Do not . . . do not assail it with so much as a thought, for thoughts are for you the most dangerous weapons of all. . . . (*Pretending to make light of the situation.*) I am sorry, Monsieur, that your reading should appear so useless, when I was under the impression it had occupied your mind, filled your head with useful knowledge, and formed your character. I——

MASON (*in an outburst*): Character! What is my character, but a riddle?

MISS MASON (*entreating*): Monsieur——

MASON (*his eyes blazing*): I am speaking, Madame!

She bows her head submissively. He is transformed into a wilful child, stamping his foot, petulant and all-powerful. (*His voice rising, derisively.*) What is a man that speaks English perfectly, yet his native tongue is not English, and yet he has no native tongue? Whose home is an English inn, and whose title is 'Monsieur'? That comes of such a good family that we may never speak of it, and yet has no family? And what, in the name of God, is a creature that came into the world thirty years ago last March, and yet has had only twenty years of life? (*Calmer.*) Can you deny that the only moment of every day when I have been alive, was the moment when you said good night to me, and called me by my true title? Can you deny it?

MISS MASON: You must forget that moment, from now on and for ever——

MASON (*exultant*): Then why did you do it?

MISS MASON: How could I help a foolish promise, made a long time ago——

MASON: To whom? (*As she cannot answer.*) Who made you promise?

MISS MASON (*agonised*): Somebody who begged me to keep that one moment, untouched, for ever——

MASON: For ever? (*Triumphant.*) Then . . . the old life is not dead?

MISS MASON: It is – it is! It must be! . . . I am wiser than you, my child. . . . (*Taking his hands, with solemn intensity.*) In the name of God I beg you to come away with me . . . now. I killed your bad memories, that can drive you mad if you let them – in this house you bring them back to life——

MASON: I am earning my bread in this house——

MISS MASON (*quickly*): I have told you before that there is no reason for you to earn your bread – the money that I draw from Brussels is for you, and not for me——

MASON: A pension to keep my miserable mouth shut——

MISS MASON (*rising, urgently*): Listen to me. . . . I have some news for you.

They stand facing each other, taut with emotion.

You remember what I once told you of the summons we must fear more than all the others?

MASON: Yes?

MISS MASON: I have received a message. The first for twenty years. I am to tell you that if you do not return with me, at once . . . there can be no answering for the consequences – for either of us.

*He looks at her; the news has shaken him. The hall door
opens, and* SOPHY *comes between them. She looks inquiringly from one to the other.*

SOPHY: Well?

MISS MASON: Monsieur, I think that there is something
we should hand over to this lady.

MASON (*dully*): Yes?

MISS MASON: Something which I have always guarded
for you, and now is missing from my room. A box.

A pause. MASON *smiles, half-sadly, half-humorously,
and hurries smartly into the kitchen.*

The two women look at each other.
(*Addressing her inferior.*) You are in love with him.

SOPHY: You think so?

MISS MASON: I am willing to supplement these objects
which we are handing over to you with every single
detail of his childhood that can be remembered. With
such help you will make even your pretender triumphant.

SOPHY: I cannot help thinking, however, that there is
one pretender whom I could make even more triumphant. . . . (*After a pause.*) The . . . real King?

They look at each other.

MISS MASON *rises and moves towards* SOPHY.

MISS MASON: His heart is warm and alive, but you
must remember that he has not led an ordinary life. He
is not a strong character. He is easily swayed; and like
many so, once swayed, could be obstinate. He is, above
all . . . unstable. You are strong. I beg of you to leave him
alone.

SOPHY: Who are you?

MISS MASON (*after a pause*): A poor relation who was
once a Princess of the House of Bourbon. It was necessary
for his own peace of mind that every impression of the

past should be driven from his remembrance; since we set foot on English soil, no word of French has passed my lips. Beyond the gratitude of a very charming woman, who was on earth a Queen, and is now an angel in heaven . . . (*crossing herself*) . . . who left her child in my care, I have nothing. I have no language, and no love; being that object, mademoiselle, which weathers time even more ungracefully in your country than in mine: (*shrugging her shoulders, smiling*) I am a virgin. But he was born again, at the age of ten, and I have been useful. I beg you to leave him alone.

> MASON *returns from the kitchen, carrying a small deed-box. He stands between the two women.*

You are sure that nobody in this house has seen this?

MASON: Quite sure.

MISS MASON (*to* SOPHY): A ring. Two miniatures. A lock of fair hair. Four papers.

MASON: Precious papers, Miss Raffety, which will give your Mr Leroy unchallenged entry into every holy of holies. Beer-bottles and all. (*His voice rising, mock-oratorically.*) Lords and ladies of the French aristocracy will stretch attenuated hands to envelop his dumpy figure; and minor members of the French Royal Family will melt into inarticulate tears as they genuflect to the thrilling note of his Cockney voice. For there will stand, at last, the phoenix of the age: the king who rises from the ashes, the genuine article, ladies and gentlemen, the one and only . . . Louis the Seventeenth of France!

> *He ends on a posture, with a flourish; he looks down at the box.*

(*Soberly.*) To the last tangible glory of a dream . . . adieu.

> *It is the first French word he has spoken for many years.*

181

In spite of himself, he is moved. He hands the box to
SOPHY. *The music dies away in the ballroom. She looks*
at him with bitter and searching eyes. He moves towards the
pianoforte.

MISS MASON: You are brave, Monsieur. This house is
no place for us. Where is your room?

MASON: There in the passage. Next to the kitchen.

MISS MASON: I'll go and pack your things.

She hurries out into the kitchen.

MASON: She called me brave. I take it that I am
mistaken, Miss Raffety, in observing in your eyes a look
of . . . contempt?

SOPHY (*as she places the box on the pianoforte*): If you
should lose your post here, Mr Mason, you will always be
able to earn an honest penny as a thought-reader.

He winces; he sits at the pianoforte. LEWIS *comes in*
from the hall-doors. He is changed for the ball.

Ah! . . . Mine host! (*Going to him, feverishly, with an*
exaggerated air of admiration, for MASON's *benefit.*) Take
care, sir!

LEWIS (*stiffly*): Madam?

SOPHY: You may turn out to be the handsomest man
at your own mother's ball, my dear, and that would never
do!

LEWIS (*embarrassed and distrustful*): Upon my word.
. . . You women, my dear, are as fickle as barometers.
What have I done to deserve this sudden attention?

SOPHY: But who would deserve it more than you? Not
only handsome, but successful! (*As* MASON *turns away,*
angrily.) The envy of all Kent! . . . But, sir, I have important news for you!

LEWIS: Oh?

SOPHY: You remember, I have spoken to you of certain

private possessions, which would prove his Majesty's identity to the most hardened cynic?

LEWIS: I remember——

SOPHY: His Majesty has at last persuaded himself to disclose them, to you and to the world . . . tonight.

LEWIS: Indeed! (*Elated.*) But this is wonderful news! . . . Wonderful! I shall suggest to his Majesty that he holds them up to the crowd in the ballroom, at the end of his address. . . . Er . . . (*As* MASON *collects his music from the pianoforte.*) You remember you promised I might hear the address, beforehand?

SOPHY (*taking the scroll from the desk wearily, ironically*): As you please. Though I promise you my grammar won't disgrace you. (*Beginning to read.*) 'My story is . . .'

She stops, looking at the scroll. MASON *gets up, and crosses as if to go out by the kitchen door.*

SOPHY (*intercepting him, a new note in her voice*): Mr Mason speaks very passably. Perhaps he will read it.

MASON (*accepting a challenge he does not fully understand*): Certainly.

He looks at her, puzzled, puts down his music portfolio, takes the scroll from her, and begins to read, impersonally, in a clear voice, moving slowly into the middle of the room.

'My story is in all history one of the strangest and saddest. . . .'

He bows to SOPHY, *with an ironical smile, and continues.* 'Having dwelt for twenty years among strangers, speaking a stranger's tongue . . . (*his voice changing*) . . . eating the bread of humility and drinking the water of bitter remembrance, I hereby declare solemnly, before God and man . . .'

His manner is altering too; the impersonal note has dis-

183

appeared. He looks up, and sees SOPHY's *face intently upturned towards his; he has involved himself in a situation from which there is no retreat.*

(*Reading.*) '. . . that I am the one and only Louis-Charles, son of Louis the Sixteenth and the unhappy Marie Antoinette . . .'

He stumbles.

A pause. His eyes fill with tears.

(*Reading.*) '. . . that I was born on the twenty-seventh day of March, seventeen hundred and eighty-five, in the Grande Chambre de la Reine, in the palace of Versailles, to the title of Duc de Normandie . . .'

The French words roll nobly off his tongue.

(*Reading.*) '. . . with for godfather the very high and very mighty Prince Louis Stanislas Xavier of France, Monsieur, brother of the King, and for godmother the very high and very mighty Princess Marie Charlotte Louise of Lorraine, Archduchess of Austria, Queen of the Two Sicilies, sister of the Queen . . . and in honour of my birth, Paris was illuminated . . .'

Over his face, and through his voice, grows great pride.

(*Reading.*) '. . . and again I declare, solemnly before all men, that in the ante-chamber of the Temple Prison, at half-past ten on the morning of the twenty-first day of January, seventeen hundred and ninety-three, when I was aged seven years and ten months, in the presence of my mother the Queen, my aunt, Elizabeth Philippine Marie Hélène de France. . . .'

A pause. His eyes move from the paper. SOPHY *holds her breath.*

'And the kitchen boy . . . (*his eyes moving back to the paper, reading again*) . . . I became, and must continue for the rest of my life here on earth Louis the Seventeenth,

184

King of France by the grace of God, of Jesus Christ,
and of the Holy Ghost, amen. . . .'

    A pause.

(*Without raising his eyes from the paper, in a level voice, as
if he were still reading.*) They had stood me on the table,
and I had one foot in my soup-plate left over from breakfast. I could see the rain through the window-bars. 'It is
thundering as well as raining,' I said, '*j'entends la pluie, et
puis le tonnerre*' . . . 'That is not thunder,' my mother
answered, 'it is drums, and it means that your father has
just perished on the guillotine.' (*Looking up, slowly.*) I was
surprised to see no tears in her eyes. They were like
blue stones, washed clean and hard. She kissed my hand,
and said 'The King is Dead, Long Live the King. . . . *Le
Roi est Mort, Vive le Roi.* . . .' And then she said, 'That
can never be altered, never.' Jamais! I can hear her
now. . . . (*Muttering, in a paroxysm of memory.*) Jamais,
jamais, jamais. . . .

    A pause.

LEWIS: He's play-acting! (*Beside himself with anger.*)
Making a fool of us! (*Going up to* MASON, *seizing the scroll
and taking him furiously by the arm.*) Have you been
drinking?

MASON (*without looking at him, coldly*): Remove your
arm, my little man.

    Nonplussed, LEWIS *steps back.* MASON *looks beyond
him, entranced.* LEWIS *recovers his composure, and turns
on* MASON, *furiously.*

LEWIS: How dare you have the face to make a fool of
me like this in my own house, how *dare* you? If you do
not leave in two minutes, by the kitchen door, I'll have
have you horse-whipped before my guests! Have you
forgotten who I am?

MASON (*topping him, exultantly*): Yes! I have forgotten! Tell us who you are! Let's play it up to the hilt, this game of identities, it's a fine mad game! (*Wilder.*) Come, sir, you keep us waiting! *Who* are you?

SOPHY: Go on, Lewis! Tell him!

LEWIS (*beside himself with humiliation, derisively*): Very well, then, you good-for-nothing tinkler of ballads to love-sick schoolgirls; I'll tell you! I am a man who chose to make a career for himself without the aid of his rich father, and has made for himself in Westminster a name which will grow considerably as he gets older. . . . I can hardly offer to a mistress – (*with a swift look at* SOPHY) – the shallow graces of flippancy, but I *can* boast of more lasting qualities which will give me power in the world——

MASON: Power? (*Coming back to life, and turning to him with a low and scathing intonation.*) Power? (*Smiling.*) That, sir, is hardly a word to use in *my* hearing. (*With quiet and malignant triumph.*) You are now giving orders to twenty men in your domain of four fusty parliamentary rooms, and before you die you will be ruler over ten rooms, and giving orders to a hundred men; it is very interesting, my man, very interesting. . . .

SOPHY (*eagerly, passionately*): May I join in the game, and ask our music-master what is the extent of *his* domain?

MASON (*transported*): My kingdom . . . is bound by every horizon, and melts into the mountains and the sea.

SOPHY (*in a whisper*): Yes?

MASON: A great murmur of voices, in low concert, like the leaves of the forest under the wind, and all breathing one name. . . . Mine. . . . A million faces watching, as a coach is drawn by white horses through the cities and along the country roads . . . down the avenues of poplar trees . . . up the great steps . . . through the hall of a thousand mirrors . . . past the lackeys . . . past the regiment of proud faces staring from the frames in panoplies of gold . . . (*speaking faster, as the vision grows*) . . . past the panels, the dolphins and the eagles . . . (*moving forward, slowly*) . . . the tinkle of the little harpsichord, the gleam of the needle, the rustle of embroidery against the skirts, the scent of powder, mother, maman. . . .

> *He sinks down; his eyes are bright, his face is smiling; time and place are indeterminate and dissolved.*

That is my kingdom.

> *A pause,* LEWIS *goes to him, in fury. The clang of a tocsin bell, in the distance.*

LEWIS: If you do not leave this house, at once——

> *They hear the bell. They listen. A pause. The echo of the tocsin, deep and terrifying.*

SOPHY: What does it mean ? . . . What is that bell ?

LEWIS: From the castle. The tocsin. . . .

SOPHY: What does it mean ?

LEWIS: The last time it rang . . . was the night of the Romney floods.

SOPHY: Then there is news. Bad news. . . .

LEWIS: A catastrophe. God. . . .

> FRANCIS *runs in from the kitchen, dishevelled. He sees* LEWIS, *and stops, confused, but only for a moment.*

FRANCIS: I beg pardon, sir—— There must be news——

> *He runs into the hall. Gradually, far away, the murmur of an excited crowd.*

LEWIS: Stay here! Come back, sir, come back——

SOPHY: What can he do for us now——

187

MISS MASON *runs from the kitchen, through the french windows, and disappears into the garden.*

LEWIS: He must go up to the castle – this instant – we must know the worst – I'll dismiss him for this——

MRS DELL *runs in from the hall, distracted.*

MRS DELL: Lewis! The tocsin! Prissy says there's a fire! There must be! My plate! . . . my linen! . . . my jewels! . . . Lewis——

LEWIS: Contain yourself, mamma, it's no such thing——

PRISSY *runs in from the hall.*

PRISSY: Lewis! There's a fire! Lewis!

MRS DELL: I was right—— Oh Heaven . . . if it spreads – the Great Fire of London did – and here we are beyond defence. . . . Look!

> She points to where a flickering red light shows between the curtains of the french windows.

> SOPHY *runs to the curtains and pulls them aside. A glow, beyond. The rumble of the crowd shouting, miles away.*

LEWIS: But it's outside——

PRISSY: But I told you there was a fire——

SOPHY: It is not that kind of fire.

> She comes down, slowly, and looks out of the smaller window.

There are many more starting, miles away across the Channel! . . . (*Quietly.*) They are bonfires.

> A pause.

LEWIS: Bonfires? (*Going to the french windows.*) Yes! Look! There's another! Can you see it? It must be on Sharples Hill!

MRS DELL (*bewildered*): But it isn't November, it's the middle of June——

PRISSY (*at the french windows*): Look! There's another

starting over there! I can see the church steeple against it—— (*Calling, excitedly.*) And there is a ship at sea! Lit up from one end to the other! . . . It's the *Rover*!

MRS DELL (*collapsing*): My party is ruined – ruined.

SOPHY: Sh——!

> *They are all silent. The tocsin dies away, but the murmur of crowds seems to grow.* MISS MASON *comes slowly back from the garden, through the french windows. They turn and look at her.*

SOPHY: Have you heard?

MISS MASON: Yes.

LEWIS: What has happened?

MISS MASON: Bonaparte. . . .

> *They hold their breaths.*

. . . has been defeated by the English.

> *A gasp of incredulous delight from the others.*

The name sounded like . . . Waterloo.

> *A pause. Cries of joy from* MRS DELL *and* PRISSY; *the wild cheers of the crowds in Dover can be clearly distinguished in the distance.*

LEWIS: That means . . .

SOPHY: That means France waits for her King again. And all across England, without knowing it, they are lighting bonfires for the lost Dauphin——

LEWIS: The lost Dauphin . . . Yes, by God, it's our visitor's night, after all—— Mr Leroy——

> *He races into the hall.*

MRS DELL: You mean – you mean . . . (*Also beside herself.*) Mr Leroy . . . dear Mr Leroy . . . (*Serious, sublime.*) This means that my party tonight will go down in history. . . . I must tell the servants!

> *She runs into the hall.*

PRISSY (*tearing after her mother*): They're sending off

rockets all along the cliff edge! And there's a Catherine
wheel on the mast of the *Wainwright*! Oh, come and look,
Mamma!——

> FRANCIS *rushes in past her, as she disappears into the*
> *hall.* MASON *staggers to the pianoforte, and begins to play.*
> *It is the piece the musicians were playing. He seems*
> *exhausted and listless.*

MISS MASON (*to* FRANCIS): I wish for a coach, at
once——

FRANCIS: You'll have to walk across the field for one
if you want it tonight——

> *He runs into the kitchen. She stands irresolute. A pause.*

SOPHY: This is a moment when we cannot both stay
with him. You've had your chance for twenty years. Go
and fetch the coach. And then see if he needs it.

MISS MASON (*to* MASON): Your things are packed. You
must come with me . . . now!

> *She hurries into the hall.* MASON *continues to play.*
> SOPHY *moves towards him, her eyes savage, bright with*
> *purpose.*
>
> *Far away, muffled, a welter of singing and cheering. Out*
> *on the balcony the reflections of red flame.*

SOPHY: Why are you playing Mozart?

MASON: Because I remember a time like this; a palace
surrounded by fire and noise. My mother sat down and
played Mozart. Sweetly and well.

> *A burst of raucous cheering, far away.*

MASON: It is the only thing to do. . . .

SOPHY: You are doing now, my friend, what you have
been doing for twenty years; you are pretending! (*As he*
stops playing and stares at her.) Pretending that nothing
can be done against this noise outside our windows
because it is revolt and disaster; pretending that it is not

rejoicing and a challenge; and pretending that it is not you who are challenged. . . . (*Taking him fiercely by the shoulders, and shaking him violently.*) You . . . YOU!

A tumult of church bells, rejoicing in the distance.

MASON: You have dug my grave up with your naked hands and brought my rotting bones to the light. . . . Let me rest. . . .

SOPHY (*vehement, with passionate conviction*): Across that sea lies the kingdom of France. . . . Silent, because she is waiting for her king who is in exile, the little boy of the Temple Tower who has been mourned for twenty years. . . .

MASON: Tell me. . . . Wake me from the dead. . . .

SOPHY: A hundred French hilltops are bursting into flames like these, a million French throats are aching to rejoice like that crowd out there. . . . Napoleon is gone, and they are waiting for you . . . *you*!

MASON: Wake me with your strong voice and your strong hands. Wake me. . . . The blood of the Bourbons and the Hapsburgs is stirring again. . . .

SOPHY: And there's one old man, called Charles, the oldest of them all——

MASON (*his eyes shut, his voice embracing the sonorous name*): Charlemagne . . . Charlemagne. . . .

SOPHY: That's the name! He's calling to his child across the sea——

MASON: And across the centuries – they are his ghostly arms ringing those bells——

SOPHY: Calling to the foolish English music-master to leave his exile for ever——

MASON: To hail the shores of France at the prow of his ship, the young King claiming his heritage at last——

SOPHY: Is this a time to play Mozart?

MASON (*calm and fascinated*): No. (*Rising, closing the piano forte with a crash, and drawing her wildly to him.*) Look into my eyes, and tell me I am speaking the truth. . . . I am thirty years of age. . . . My life is hardly begun! A creature of healthy flesh and blood, with a kingdom to fight for which was taken brutally from me before I was old enough to know its worth. . . . The rocky fields of Brittany . . . the smiling meadows of Touraine . . . France is waiting! Every milestone on every road, every leaf on every tree, is mine! . . . In my heart I have always known this moment would come, always. . . . (*Clasping her arms, kissing her mouth, passionately.*) Make me strong enough. I can feel you breathing life into me. . . .

The cheers have died gradually away.

SOPHY (*kneeling by him, calm and secure*): I'll never leave your side. . . . I have been trying to say this to you ever since I first knew who you were. . . . And do you know when I knew for certain, for ever? Last night, when you stopped at the door, and turned to me where I lay like the harlot I was, and gave me a haughty stare; and then I knew myself to be the mistress of a king. . . . And swore to remain so until I die. . . .

She kisses his hand, solemnly.

(*Excited and happy.*) I'll teach you to be as hard as I am, to turn your memories of fear into – weapons of hate! . . . The horses you have feared so long, Louis . . . we'll ride them . . . together!

MASON: Tomorrow. . . .

SOPHY: Not even tomorrow. . . . (*Turning to him, her face glowing.*) Tonight!

A loud knock at the front door. MRS DELL *runs in from the hall, followed by* LEWIS *and* LADY ATKYNS. *All seem to be talking at once.*

192

MRS DELL: That was the first arrival! They are coming up the hill now to the hall – the first guests – they'll be pouring in now they've heard the news – Dover is going mad with rejoicing – his Majesty will never forget this experience—— What a night to celebrate our party——

LADY ATKYNS: That was the first arrival! I have instructed Timms to go into Dover for some rockets——

> SOPHY *stands behind* MASON'S *chair; both are immobile and smiling.*

LEWIS: The whole town will be trying to get into our garden—— Mamma, tie my 'kerchief——

MRS DELL: Oh, Miss Raffety, the joy of us all for – for our distinguished guest!

SOPHY: Wait!

MRS DELL: Yes?

SOPHY (*excited*): You remember I was about to show to you the absolute proofs of His Majesty's identity——

> *A loud cry in the hall; the hall door bursts open. It is* PRISSY, *breathless and bewildered. She shuts it fearfully behind her.*

PRISSY: Mamma! Lewis! Mamma!

MRS DELL: Good heavens. . . . My dear, what is it?

PRISSY (*collapsing in the arm-chair*): My head is going round and round——

MRS DELL: She looks as if she had seen a ghost – tell mamma, my precious, tell mamma——

PRISSY: There's a strange man! At the front door!

MRS DELL: Yes?

PRISSY: He – he – he is having words with the footman, and I heard him say——

> *The hall door opens.* FRANCIS *stands aside, looking a little dazed.*

FRANCIS (*announcing*): His Majesty . . . King Louis the Seventeenth . . . of France!

> *A pause. A man follows slowly from the hall, stands majestically in the middle of the room and surveys the company. Tableau.*

CURTAIN

ACT III

Immediately afterwards, with no lapse of time.

> *Tableau. The new arrival is* LAMBERT; *he is forty, but looks younger, suave, over-dressed, with a foppish air of pleasant self-confidence which hides great malignancy. He speaks academic English, with an occasional French flavour. A pause.*

SOPHY: If this is a joke, sir, you have poor taste.

LAMBERT: On the contrary, madame; this is a serious matter, and my taste is on all occasions . . . impeccable. (*Kissing her hand.*) I will even go as far as to apologise for being the first guest to arrive at the ball given to meet me.

MRS DELL: I . . . I . . . (*Waving her hands, helplessly.*) Lewis. . . .

LEWIS (*stepping forward, belligerently*): Where have you come from?

LAMBERT: From a visit to my loyal subject the Marquis de Dalcour-Vandon, who lives, in miserable exile, outside Folkestone.

> *He sweeps off his cloak, hands it to* FRANCIS, *and sits in the Dante chair.*

MRS DELL: Lewis . . . Francis, put that down!

> FRANCIS *drops the cloak on the pianoforte stool and retires into the hall, completely at a loss.*

Lewis . . . Oh . . .

LAMBERT: Madame looks surprised. . . . (*To* LEWIS.) Do not tell me, sir, that I arrive at an awkward moment?

LEWIS: Awkward, sir, is the word. I should welcome something in the nature of an explanation——

LAMBERT: But you shall have it, and concisely! I am the lost Dauphin! . . . (*As* MRS DELL *sinks on to the arm-chair in a daze.*) Who escaped from Paris, from the Prison du Temple, in a clothes-basket at the age of ten, and for twelve years wandered in vagabondage over the face of Europe, concealing under the name of Richard Lambert my true title of King of France; a title which I must consider, tonight of all nights, can be concealed no longer. (*To* MASON.) Do you not agree, sir?

MASON (*bowing*): Sir, we are as one. Will you not continue?

LAMBERT: For the last eight years, being now thirty years of age, I have travelled between London, Brussels and Rome, speaking every language like a native, interviewing royalists and collecting funds for my reinstatement on the French throne; my memoirs, consisting of seven hundred and two closely written pages, and proving conclusively to the whole world my claim to the royal status which is my birthright . . . are in my luggage.

SOPHY (*dryly*): In a deed-box?

LAMBERT (*bowing*): At the bottom of my trunk. . . .

MASON (*as* SOPHY *makes to fetch the deed-box*): No, one moment! This is too rare to miss. . . .

LAMBERT (*to* MRS DELL): And this week, madame, visiting the Marquis, I chanced to hear that, by a miracle, I was also a guest at this house; and hurried over to investigate the phenomenon.

MRS DELL: Lewis, watch the doors. . . .

LEWIS *stands before the hall door.*

LADY ATKYNS (*stepping forward*): I am Lady Atkyns——

LAMBERT: You need not present yourself, milady. We have met before.

LADY ATKYNS: Oh? Where?

LAMBERT: In prison.

LADY ATKYNS: Well, done everything in my time, but don't recall goin' to jail.

LAMBERT: You were ... on a visit?

LADY ATKYNS: Oh?

LAMBERT: To a sick child, at a time when you were making most gallant attempts to rescue it from a living death. (*Touching his heart.*) That child has never forgotten. (*Rising, bowing and sitting again.*) Milady, enchanté.

LADY ATKYNS (*impressed*): Oh. . . . (*Going to him.*) And what, sir, do you recall of that visit?

LAMBERT: You brought me ... a picture-book?

LADY ATKYNS: Yes. . . . A geography book——

LAMBERT: And you were wearing a cloak, of brown velvet——

LADY ATKYNS: Yes, yes! (*Excited.*) I still have it! I kept it——

    FRANCIS *opens the hall doors wide, and stands beside them.*

FRANCIS: His Maj——

    He is too speechless to go any further. He is followed by MR LEROY, *changed into uniform, with a purple sash arranged regally and diagonally across his middle. He is flushed and jaunty, and only seems to lack the crown. He looks at* LAMBERT, *who is the only one sitting.* LAMBERT *seems unconcerned. A pause.*

    FRANCIS *goes back into the hall.* MR LEROY *looks inquiringly at* MRS DELL, *and settles on the chaise-longue.*

MRS DELL: This is too much to ask of any hostess. . .

    MR LEROY *looks from one to the other.*

MR LEROY: Everyone may sit.

Nobody moves. He looks inquiringly from one to the other, a shadow of apprehension clouding his serenity.

Has anything happened? (*No answer.*) I'd be willin', madam, for this rude gentleman to be presented to me. (*To* LAMBERT.) Are you invited to the ball tonight, sir?

LAMBERT: Mais il est charmant, ce monsieur. . . . (*To* MR LEROY.) How generous of our hostess . . . to lend her house to such an unworthy cause!

MR LEROY: Unworthy?

LAMBERT: Modesty compels one to say so. . . . Are *you* invited?

MR LEROY *stares at him.*

MR LEROY (*to the others, smiling*): Ignorant. . . . We are Louis the Seventeenth of France.

LAMBERT: How odd. So are we.

MR LEROY *starts, looks at the others, then back at* LAMBERT *dumbfounded.*

LADY ATKYNS (*significantly*): Will you not tell the company, sir, how you escaped from the Temple Tower?

MR LEROY *gulps. Unable to contain himself any longer,* MASON *begins to laugh. His amusement grows, till he is in fits of uproarious mirth. The* DELLS *are scandalised. He finally controls himself.*

LEWIS: I fail to see anything ridiculous in this very painful situation.

MASON: I am sorry, sir, but to my perverted sense of humour, it is the most ridiculous that has ever existed. I congratulate his Majesty on his variety of aspects. . . . (*Solemnly.*) Surely it has come to a pretty pass when nobody in this house can turn their backs for two minutes without finding that yet another crowned head has popped round the door!

LEWIS: There is an important private conference in progress in this company at this moment——

MRS DELL: Of a very delicate nature——

MASON: I beg your pardon——

The next three speeches are all spoken almost at once.

LEWIS: And I feel that in spite of your histrionic prowess just now, it cannot concern you in the very least——

MRS DELL (*closing her eyes, in despair*): But my house is infested with undesirables!

LADY ATKYNS: One at a time, please——

MR LEROY (*on his mettle, clear as a bell*): Every one may sit!

LADY ATKYNS (*to* LAMBERT): You were about to tell us, sir, how you escaped from the Temple Tower?

LAMBERT: I have told it so often, it is like a lesson. . . . (*Rising, ceremoniously.*) Madame Simon, the wife of the janitor, smuggled into my prison a great toy hobby horse; a present for a good little prisoner. Out of the hobby horse she took another little prisoner, a creature afflicted with dumbness and rickets; laid him among my straw; laid me among some dirty linen in a clothes-basket; and wheeled the basket through the streets of Paris to the house of emissaries of the Prince de Condé. (*Sitting again.*) And so I escaped from the Temple Prison.

MASON: Indeed.

MR LEROY: Snatching things away from their rightful owner, the impudence!

LAMBERT (*to* MRS DELL): May I suggest, madame, that your ball will be more successful if your guests are not, on arrival, publicly insulted by your coachman?

MR LEROY: We may look like a coachman, but it was me in the clothes-basket. (*To* SOPHY, *furious and injured.*)

H   199

And you, you wicked disloyal girl, why can't *you* say something in the cause of truth?

SOPHY: Truth? (*Looking at* MASON, *exchanging a confident smile with him.*) I can, and will——

MASON: Not yet – not yet!

LADY ATKYNS (*to* LAMBERT): I saw the likeness the moment your Majesty entered the room——

MRS DELL (*pointedly, to* MR LEROY): Is your Majesty comfortable?

MR LEROY: As comfortable as can be expected.

MASON: Considering all they have in common, the two gentlemen seem to have singularly little to talk about.

MRS DELL: What do you mean, in common?

MASON: Surely, madam, you would have something friendly to say to a gentleman with whom you had shared a basket of dirty linen right across Paris?

LEWIS: Your jocularity is offensive.

MASON: My humble apologies. To both Majesties.

MR LEROY: There is one King in this room! One and one only!

LAMBERT: One, and one only!

MASON (*bowing, catching* SOPHY's *eye*): One, and one only. . . .

LEWIS: I have asked you once to go. Have I to ask again?

MASON: I shall leave presently, sir, but till that time I must insist – respectfully – that as the only disinterested spectator here, I be allowed to hold parley between the two separate halves of this unfortunate monarch.

> *He stands in the middle of the room.* LEWIS *withdraws helplessly.*

LADY ATKYNS (*at him, loudly, staring into* LAMBERT's *face*): It is uncanny.

MASON (*to* MRS DELL, *with a bow*): Lady Atkyns' compliments, and she positively identifies her gentleman as Louis the Seventeenth.

MRS DELL: My compliments to Lady Atkyns, and she is quite capable of identifying *me* as Louis the Seventeenth if it serves her purpose!

MASON *bows and returns to* LADY ATKYNS.

MASON: The lady is sceptical.

LADY ATKYNS: But Mr Lambert is the *image* of the portraits——

MRS DELL (*shouting across the room, unable to control herself any longer*): So was Mr Leroy when you first arrived!

LADY ATKYNS: They are both like the portraits, only in different ways.

MASON: What an odd-looking child he must have been.

MR LEROY (*calling across, suddenly*): Are you vaccinated?

LAMBERT (*to* LADY ATKYNS, *loftily*): The idea that as a child the Dauphin was vaccinated is an entirely erroneous one.

MASON: The gentleman is not vaccinated. . . .

    The orchestra begins to play, in the ballroom; a jaunty tune. FRANCIS *comes in from the hall, carrying a visiting-card. He is still at a loss.*

LEWIS: Yes?

MRS DELL (*anxiously*): Who is it?

    MASON *takes the card from* FRANCIS.

FRANCIS: The first guests are here, madam——

MRS DELL (*closing her eyes*): I knew it. . . .

LEWIS (*to* FRANCIS, *in a panic*): Tell the musicians to go and play . . . er . . . on the lawn . . . and as the guests arrive show them straight into the garden. Tell them his Majesty is holding a conference.

FRANCIS: Very good, sir——

MASON (*stopping him*): With himself.

FRANCIS looks at him bewildered, and goes back into the hall.

LADY ATKYNS (*peering at the card, and reading from it*): Congratulations to his Royal Majesty from Mademoiselle Clara Ann Tangercross and her aunt.

MASON: I should be careful of the aunt.

The others look at him, abruptly.

LEWIS: What do you mean?

MASON: In she will sail, seven foot tall; her hair on end with powder and her carcase stiff with stays; heirlooms rattling like eggs against her shoulder-blades . . . and then all of a sudden her perruque will entangle itself in the chandelier, whisk off from an imposing but bald head . . . and reveal her as yet another candidate for a sadly crowded clothes-basket!

MRS DELL: You vile creature, to joke at a time like this——

The front-door knocker, loudly.

MRS DELL (*distracted*): Another arrival. . . .

MR LEROY, beside himself, rises to his full height.

MR LEROY: You're a fraud.

He stalks out into the hall.

MRS DELL (*closing her eyes, slowly*): I shall remember the battle of Waterloo as long as I live.

The front-door knocker again.

PRISSY: Another one——

MRS DELL: In two minutes they'll be pouring in thick and fast——

MASON: Not as thick and fast as Louis the Seventeenth.

MRS DELL: Lewis, please. . . . You're a Member of Parliament, you ought to be able to do *something*!

LEWIS: My dear mother, short of blowing up my own house with gunpowder, I am as powerless as you——

MRS DELL: Will no one deliver us?

MASON: Out of the goodness of my heart, madam, I will!

They all look at him.

LEWIS: I should be obliged, Miss Raffety, if you would dissuade your friend from making another exhibition of himself in my house.

SOPHY: Mr Mason has my full approval, sir, in . . . making an exhibition of himself.

MASON (*joyfully*): The moment has arrived. And with a clear dawn tomorrow, the King will see once more the shores of France!

LEWIS: This is no time for drunken poetry. Which King, can you tell us that?

SOPHY: I can.

MRS DELL: You mean those mementoes you spoke of? Quickly——

MASON: Much more besides!

MRS DELL: Thank God – Mr Leroy is safe——

SOPHY *moves into the centre of the room, solemnly and in silence.*

SOPHY: Before I ask our Mr Mason to set all your minds at rest, I have the honour to announce to you now in private, as I shall later tonight in public, that the King of France, whom you have all been seeking, is at this instant——

LAMBERT (*quietly*): One moment!

They look at him. He rises.

A word of warning.

SOPHY: Yes?

LAMBERT: We are standing on the edge of a precipice. (*To* SOPHY, *whimsically*.) You will pardon me, Mademoiselle, if as you put forward one delicate foot, I place my hand gently on your arm?

MRS DELL: Take no notice of him——

> *The orchestra begins to play again, in the garden.*

LAMBERT (*unctuously*): May I assure madame that all will be put to rights by a word in private with Mademoiselle?

LEWIS: There has been too much privacy already, and I see no reason for it now. This is an occasion——

LAMBERT (*putting up one hand, politely*): If you please . . . a quiet corner of the garden, mademoiselle——

MRS DELL (*alarmed*): No, no – stay here——

LAMBERT: But your guests——

MRS DELL: *They* will be in every quiet corner of the garden, and not likely to intrude here for a moment. Lewis – Prissy——

LEWIS: But what is to happen when the moment comes to——

MRS DELL: Wait and see. (*Ushering them across the room.*) Come, my dears – Lewis, bring your sister into the garden——

> LEWIS *goes through the french windows, followed by* PRISSY.

LAMBERT (*smoothly to* LADY ATKYNS): This is private, chère milady . . . je regrette. . . .

> LADY ATKYNS *curtsies and follows the others into the garden, a little subdued.*

MRS DELL'S VOICE (*in the garden*): Ah . . . Lady Graistovy . . . delighted . . . Lady Merritt, so early!

> LAMBERT *is left with* MASON *and* SOPHY.

LAMBERT: That is better. (*With a smile.*) Now, made-moiselle——

MASON: What a game! One king is played! Another king is played, a little higher! – and the prize is won . . . by the joker! (*Laughing happily.*) What a game!

LAMBERT: Your Mr Mason, mademoiselle, is in good spirits today!

SOPHY: Mr Mason, no! That name has served its pur-pose . . . (*turning to* MASON, *aglow*) . . . and now it's dead and finished with!

LAMBERT: May I draw the attention of the company to the little interview which I so humbly requested?

SOPHY (*smiling*): I can serve you no purpose for your cause, sir! I am pledged, and not to Mr Leroy either!

LAMBERT (*gently*): I fear that I told just now the smallest of lies. The interview that I beg is not with mademoiselle. It is with . . . monsieur.

A pause. MASON *looks at him, surprised.*

MASON: With me?

The music dies away, in the garden.

LAMBERT (*to* SOPHY): I shall be pleased to call you, mademoiselle, when it is over. (*Going to the hall doors, opening one of them, and bowing.*) I shall not be long. . . . À bientôt!

SOPHY (*to* MASON): Shall I stay?

MASON (*smiling*): No.

SOPHY: Is your mind firm?

MASON: Of course!

SOPHY *goes out into the hall. The music begins again.*

LAMBERT (*coming back into the room*): Women, my dear sir, are charming in the garden; delightful in the boudoir; in the bedroom, delicious; and in the council-chamber, a thundering nuisance.

MASON (*with a laugh*): Indeed. . . .

LAMBERT (*moving to the fireplace*): Trailing clouds of sentiment, throwing the dust of prejudice in our eyes, and then pretending that all humanity is in tears over some artificial tragedy.

A burst of cheering, in Dover.

MASON: You arrive on a very opportune night, sir.

LAMBERT (*sitting on the sofa, taking snuff*): Oh, intentionally! There were confidential rumours from London this morning that things were coming to a head in Belgium, with Bonaparte. So I hurried over.

MASON: Let us come to the point, quickly——

LAMBERT: By all means——

MASON: You know who I am, and like the other one you want the information about my childhood which is contained in this box. I am afraid you cannot have it, as I intend to use it myself——

LAMBERT: Doucement, doucement! Everything in its turn!

MASON: But the first guests are in the garden——

LAMBERT (*smiling*): It is such a fine night?

MASON: Miraculous. The sea and land and sky are laid out under daylight by the bonfires. . . . (*Walking to the french windows, exhilarated.*) Thousands of people in the fields above Dover, all dancing and shouting and cheering, all looking towards France . . . all talking about France. . . .

> *While his back is turned,* LAMBERT *goes swiftly to the hall doors, locks them, and returns to his same position on the sofa.*

(*His eyes shining.*) It is the finest night there has ever been in the world.

He comes down again, surveys LAMBERT *with curiosity and sits on the chaise-longue.*

You are very different from the other pretender. . . . (*Puzzled.*) Who are you?

LAMBERT: First of all, I have private information that you are almost without doubt . . . (*looking towards the garden, lowering his voice, and getting up*) . . . the lost Dauphin of France.

The music dies away in the garden.

MASON *bows, and sits.*

MASON: How did you gain this information?

LAMBERT: We shall discuss that in a moment. . . . (*Rising in a business-like way.*) Now we must forget all this talk of portraits and vaccination and concentrate on the fact that the young Dauphin Louis-Charles had one distinguishing mark . . . (*as* MASON *looks at him, slowly*) . . . concerning which his parents were particularly sensitive, and which in consequence, hidden as it was behind a lock of hair, is almost unknown. It consisted of a malformation . . . (*after a pause, quickly*) . . . on the back of the lobe of the right ear, in the shape of a minute egg, called an accessory auricle, with across it a tiny birthmark in the shape of a diamond, and was therefore . . . unique. (*After a pause.*) Forgive my familiarity.

He crosses, stands smartly behind MASON, *and stoops.*

Pardon.

He turns over a lock of hair, and examines MASON'S *right ear closely from the back. He stands upright, walks round, and faces* MASON.

My trifling doubt is . . . removed . . . Monsieur.

He bows. MASON *inclines his head.* LAMBERT *stares at him from head to foot. With unconscious authority,* MASON *motions him to sit.* LAMBERT *sits in the armchair.*

MASON: I feel like something in a circus.

LAMBERT: You must excuse me. (*Laughing, good-naturedly.*) When one knows that a certain *rara avis* has been missing from Europe for twenty years, and one is suddenly confronted with the only specimen extant, you must forgive a passing emotion.

The following scene of cross-examination is played very quickly.

MASON: We can take it that now we understand each other. What is it you want to ask?

LAMBERT: Three simple questions. The first is this: What other proof have you of your identity?

MASON: The relics contained in that box——

LAMBERT: Oh! Is that the one retrieved from Versailles?

MASON: Yes——

LAMBERT: The locket worn at the Temple? Your father's geometry plan? Your aunt's letter?

MASON: Yes.

He is puzzled by LAMBERT'S *exact knowledge.*

LAMBERT: Good. . . . The second question is this. . . . Who, in this house knows who you are?

MASON: The girl, Sophy Raffety.

LAMBERT: Nobody else?

MISS MASON *hurries in from the kitchen, and crosses to* MASON; *she is breathless from running. She carries* MASON'S *cloak.*

MISS MASON: The coach is here. . . . Here is your cloak——

LAMBERT: Monsieur's sister, is it not?

She starts, and looks at him, with inquiry. He does not rise.

MASON: If you still care to call her so. . . . Well?

LAMBERT: It is a little embarrassing. . . . I am waiting for Madame to recognise me.

MASON: And I am waiting for Monsieur to remember his manners.

MISS MASON: Who is this man?

LAMBERT: Madame, I realise that twenty years is a long time, but my vanity must remain a little piqued. The name, madame, is . . . Lambert.

MISS MASON: Lambert. . . . (*Going to him, terrified.*) Qu'est-ce que vous venez faire dans cette maison——

LAMBERT: Ne vous inquiétez pas, madame, je vous en prie, je ne suis ici que pour vous servir——

MISS MASON: Vous allez lui faire du mal! Je vous en défends——

LAMBERT: Je m'en défends moi aussi! Soyons d'accord là-dessus——

MASON (*suddenly, clasping his head*): No . . . no! (*Collecting himself, apologetically.*) I beg your pardon. It is so long since I heard . . . my own language. . . spoken. . . .

MISS MASON (*to* LAMBERT): Monsieur, je vous. . . . (*Hesitating, remembering, then continuing in English.*) I have known the world enough not to ask too much of life. Leave me the little I ask for. (*As he does not move.*) I am a proud woman, monsieur; I was proud even for that age when pride was everything; and outside the church of God I have never bowed my knee, or begged. I do so now.

MASON: But Madame . . . what have you to beg from him?

MISS MASON (*silencing him*): All I wish for in the world, is his company with me, in our English village.

LAMBERT: Then you have no wish for Monsieur to cross the sea?

MISS MASON: I have never wished it, never——

LAMBERT: But neither have I, Madame! We are in perfect accord! (*Rising.*) Leave me alone with him a moment and all will be well. (*Whispering, good humouredly.*) He shall not cross the sea.

MISS MASON: You swear it?

LAMBERT (*kindly*): Of course!

He goes and stands at the kitchen door.

MISS MASON (*after hesitation, then reassured*): Very well, I shall wait. . . .

> *She goes into the kitchen. A loud burst of cheering; MASON walks to the smaller window, and looks out, fascinated. Again without his knowledge, LAMBERT locks the kitchen door softly. MASON goes up the steps to the balcony.*

LAMBERT (*calling*): Monsieur! . . . (*As MASON turns impatiently.*) Then, besides Madame, nobody knows who you are except this Miss Raffety?

MASON: No. . . . (*Suddenly, with a frown.*) Why should she ask favours of *you*?

LAMBERT: Does Miss Raffety know of our little identification mark?

MASON (*coming into the room, restlessly*): No.

LAMBERT: Has she seen the contents of this box?

MASON: No.

LAMBERT: Then she has no proof that you are not labouring under a delusion?

MASON (*smiling, uneasily*): I suppose not. Delusion! . . . (*Sharply.*) I dislike that word.

> *He makes to follow MISS MASON. LAMBERT takes one step forward and stands in his way.*

MASON: Let me pass——

LAMBERT (*good-humouredly*): You must take no offence.

Since the year seventeen hundred and ninety-eight, twelve young Frenchmen, besides the professional pretenders, have suffered under the genuine delusion that they were the lost Dauphin.

MASON: Who is lost no longer.

LAMBERT (*nodding, as if humouring him*): Who is lost no longer.

A pause.

MASON *turns as if to make for the garden.* LAMBERT *walks slowly behind the pianoforte, again barring his way.*

MASON: I fear, sir, that your attitude displeases me.

LAMBERT: I am sorry. How should I behave?

MASON: As a subject who is given audience by his king.

LAMBERT (*looking out of the french windows*): And how am I treating you?

MASON: Like a – like a miscreant interviewed by a constable. Or a patient by a doctor. . . . (*Crossing to the desk.*) Who *are* you?

LAMBERT (*coming down to him, smiling mysteriously*): One more question, and I have finished; and this is the most important. What——

He sees the title of one of the books on the pianoforte, takes it up, smiles ironically at MASON, *and turns over the leaves during the next passages.*

What are your present intentions?

MASON: I should have thought that was perfectly clear. I shall declare myself to these people tonight, and as soon as I have collected sufficient funds, sail for Calais as the King of France.

LAMBERT (*smiling, in a voice of steel*): That, I fear, is out of the question.

A pause.

MASON (*his voice rising*): It is not out of the question. I

211

am the lost Dauphin and neither you nor any other Pretender will stand——

LAMBERT (*turning over leaves*): You may be the lost Dauphin, but you are not the King of France.

MASON (*with a cry*): Louis the Seventeenth is King of France, and nothing can destroy that——

LAMBERT: You speak the truth, my friend, but with a slight and important error in the numeral. . . . (*Slamming down the book and going to him, swiftly.*) You asked me who I am; I will tell you. I am the most important secret agent at present in the service of his Majesty King Louis the *Eighteenth* of France.

> *A pause,* MASON *moves slowly to the middle of the room.*

MASON: A spy.

LAMBERT: Secret agent, if you please; every spy likes to be called a secret agent.

> MASON *again makes to pass him;* LAMBERT *plants the desk chair so as to cut off his retreat between the pianoforte and the desk and sits in it.*

(*Jovially.*) Been at it since I could walk. The first time I saw Madame there, I was spying something out for somebody. The Girondistes. Or the Jacobins. I really can't remember; I was eighteen at the time. We were watching your mother.

> *A pause.* MASON *looks at him.*

She was climbing the scaffold. Very slowly. She looked tired.

MASON: Why do you stare at me with such hate?

LAMBERT (*coldly*): I was born a peasant in France before the Revolution. . . . (*Jovial, again.*) It suits my purpose at the moment to be a faithful servant to your uncle, King Louis the Eighteenth of France.

MASON: My uncle, who is not Louis the Eighteenth, but old Louis-Stanislas-Xavier, Comte de Provence; and who can call himself Louis the Eighteenth only on my death!

LAMBERT: But you died . . . (*quietly*) . . . twenty years ago last week.

A pause. MASON *looks into his face; from this moment the flame which* SOPHY *kindled in him can be seen dwindling, slowly but surely.*

LAMBERT (*speaking from memory*): 'Section of the Temple, third year . . .' (*taking a paper from his breast-pocket*) . . . 'of the Republic' . . . (*reading from the paper*) . . . 'Louis-Charles Capet, aged ten years and two months . . . profession . . . domiciled, in the Temple Tower; son of Louis Capet, last king of the French. . . . Born at Versailles, and the day before yesterday, died . . . of a scrofulous disease. . . . Signed by Dusser and Lasne. . . .' (*Conversationally.*) I saw the gravestone only the other day. In the cemetery of Sainte Marguerite. Covered with moss. . . . (*Holding out another paper, pinned to the other.*) And here is something written by your sister. Your *real* sister, the Duchesse d'Angoulême. Now an ardent subject of King Louis the Eighteenth. . . . I shall translate it for you, as you know no French.

The music begins again, in the garden.

(*Reading from the paper.*) 'He had a great deal of character, and loved his country very much, and the idea of accomplishing great things . . . except for his imprisonment, he would have been a great man. . . . But he is dead. . . .' (*Contemptuously.*) Not a bad epitaph for a debauched little liar. . . . (*Rising, putting away the papers, breezily.*) Why, last year, in Notre Dame, there was even a Requiem Mass for you! Did you know that?

Suddenly MASON *runs to the hall door and tries to open it.*

LAMBERT, *with one swift movement, stands before the french windows, immobile, guarding them.* MASON *runs back, sees him, walks falteringly to the kitchen door, and finds it also locked; he turns, a sudden mad fear in his face.*

The music dies away, in the garden.

MASON (*dully*): They have locked me in. . . . What's that?

He lifts his head suddenly, and listens, in the silence, as if he can hear sounds far above his head. He falls quickly to his knees, and crouches against the arm-chair.

Horses. . . . Thousands of horses. Faster . . . faster . . . over my head. . . . (*Clasping his head, muttering and whispering, in an agony of terror.*) No air . . . the windows are painted over black. . . . The doors are sealed with mortar . . . I cannot breathe. . . . Let me out. . . . What is happening to the room? The windows are closing in on me! Let me out! Let me out, while there is time! In the name of God let me out. . . . (*In a scream, beating on the back of the arm-chair.*) Let me out!

LAMBERT (*coming down*): You see, my dear sir, we are dealing with facts.

He taps his fingers on the pianoforte, then motions MASON *to sit, like a doctor.*

MASON (*in a whisper, panting and submissive*): They have locked me in.

He recovers, panting, and sits, exhausted, in the arm-chair; LAMBERT *has sat, deliberately, on the Dante chair.*

LAMBERT (*loudly, as if issuing an edict*): I appreciate how difficult it must be for a simple romantic soul like yourself, sheltered behind a woman, to visualise the endless ramifications of European diplomacy at the present time.

The dozens of treaties, the hundreds of secret letters, the thousands of soldiers, the millions of francs; and all involved by this momentous victory won today at Waterloo. King Louis, at this moment, needs all the loyal support which he can command. He has enemies, and any breath of scandal, any suspicion of his throne being insecure, would be fatal; all is arranged; nothing must be disturbed. (*Conversationally, with a laugh.*) When you have been king for twenty years, you cannot suddenly be told you are an impostor – oh no, it is too embarrassing——

MASON (*in an outburst*): I will not listen! . . . It is a lie, to cheat me out of my birthright. . . . (*Rising.*) I am the King . . . it is the sacred truth before God! Nothing can stand in my way! Nothing!

LAMBERT (*loudly, again*): Everything will stand in your way; for this is an occasion, I fear, when the sacred truth before God . . . (*quiet, deadly*) . . . is inexpedient fraudulence before the secret archives of Europe. (*Going up to* MASON, *suddenly venomous and impassioned, almost hissing at his ear.*) Archives, my friend, are ugly places, with long corridors like a mausoleum, and papers covered with dust . . . and on those papers, secret and dark as the tomb, written again and again, with mysterious marks against it, like the hieroglyphics of the destructive spider . . . is your name.

MASON *stares at him, as if hypnotised.* LAMBERT *plays up deliberately to this fascination. He sits on the chaise-longue, quieter.*

LAMBERT: Everything will stand in your way. . . . (*Putting his feet up, comfortably and taking snuff.*) I've had you watched off and on, in your little country inn, for twelve years; and when you suddenly planned to take up duties in Dover, I must confess that for a moment my brow was crossed by a frown. The only thing to do was to put another little pretender quickly on your track – so that he could catechise you for his own benefit – and to put our famous Lady Atkyns on his; for as soon as I suspect that a pretender is a fancy-dress fraud, like our Mr Leroy here, I am careful to encourage him in his deception, so as to make action impossible for the real Dauphin . . . (*snapping shut his snuff-box, with finality*) . . . by planting the field with as many false ones as possible – including myself! – thoroughly confusing the issue, and reducing the whole of the Louis the Seventeenth legend to the level of . . . a farce.

He barks the last word out, mercilessly.

MASON (*his throat dry, nodding mechanically*): A farce. I see.

The music again, in the garden.

LAMBERT: It is simple but effective strategy.

MASON: And when the pretender turns out to be the real Dauphin?

A pause.

LAMBERT (*smiling, evasively*): There is no precedent for that.

He rises and goes to the french windows.

MASON (*insistent*): When the pretender turns out to be the real Dauphin?

A burst of applause again, in Dover. The music plays on; sweetly and insidiously, it surrounds the room.

LAMBERT: The night of Waterloo. . . , With his retinue, the King of France will be leaving Belgium to return to Paris, to sit victoriously once more on the throne which has been his for twenty years, and now waits for him again. The crowds already prepare to line the streets. A great night for his Majesty. . . .

A fresh burst of applause, far away.

(*Smiling.*) Mrs Dell said she will remember it too, did she not? Waterloo – she will say – was not that the night when three hundred guests walked my grounds by the light of bonfires, and cheered that Mr Leroy – who I still believe *was* the Dauphin . . . and was not that the night, my dears, when that unfortunate music-master, whose name escapes me, was found. . . .

> *His sentence is uncompleted. A pause. He turns and looks at* MASON. MASON *looks at him.*

(*Smiling, with cold emphasis.*) I regret to disappoint your . . . Miss Mason, but it is no longer convenient . . . that Louis the Seventeenth should still be alive.

> *The music finishes, in the garden.*

> MASON *continues to look at him. During the next speech* LAMBERT *goes briskly to the wine-table, pours out a glass of wine, and places it carefully on the pianoforte.*

I have been instructed to deliver to you – a small object; it is, I fear, a melodramatic one, but we live in hysterical times, and I have lived long enough out of France to realise how much we Frenchmen love . . . a gesture.

> *He takes something from his waistcoat pocket; it is an ornamented phial.*

It came from Versailles. Another charming touch?

> *He unscrews the top of the phial and pours a few drops of liquid from it into the glass of wine. He puts the phial carefully back into his pocket, crosses slowly and stands against the sofa.*

It is hardly painful, and practically instantaneous.

> *A pause.* MASON *rises, and walks slowly towards the pianoforte; with a sudden mad impulse, he seizes the deed-box and leaps towards the french windows.*

(*In a shout.*) Take care! (*As* MASON *turns, like a trapped creature.*) I have two men outside that balcony with instructions to shoot you as you pass. Or, if you prefer it, I have here a warrant for your arrest. Forged passport. Undesirable alien. Dover – Prison. The Fleet – Prison. Newgate – Prison. . . .

> MASON *puts his hands to his ears; then, slowly, he recovers, and comes forward. He looks dully at* LAMBERT, *then at the box; he moves forward, as if in a dream, and holds out the box.* LAMBERT *takes it, then goes quickly and unlocks first the kitchen door, then the hall door, comes down, takes up his cloak and drapes it over his arm, taking care to cover the box with it.* LEWIS *comes in through the french windows, beside himself with anxiety.*

LEWIS: We cannot keep the guests waiting any longer——

LAMBERT: But my dear sir, you need not!

LEWIS: But where is Miss Raffety? What have you decided?

LAMBERT: Mademoiselle and I, my dear sir, have come to the happiest of agreements!

LEWIS (*incredulous*): Oh?

LAMBERT: In deference to the regrettable partiality of our charming hostess for Mr Leroy, Mademoiselle has persuaded me to pursue my claims to the French throne, indisputable though they are, in a different part of the country; and so, Monsieur, I beg leave tonight to plough my way through your guests, unaided . . . and anonymous. (*Turning to* MASON, *and bowing low.*) Adieu. . . .

> He bows to LEWIS *and goes smartly out through the french windows.* LEWIS, *overjoyed, makes to go into the hall, then sees* MASON.

LEWIS (*a threat*): I take it that the militia will not be

necessary to eject the music-master? (*Hurrying into the hall, calling, urgently.*) Miss Raffety! . . . Your Majesty! . . .

> MASON *is alone. He sinks to the floor. In the last moments his mind has wandered far away; he is delirious.*

MASON (*whispering, like a child*): Monsieur!

> *He listens, as if for a reply, crouched against the arm-chair, his ear close to the side, as if against a wall.*

Monsieur Jailer! . . . Can you hear me? . . . Tu comprends, n'est-ce pas, when the little citizen Capet calls through the wall? Give me some more wine, it makes me feel ill, sir, but it makes me sleepy. More wine. . . . Even the rats go to bed, monsieur, only I am left, is it not sad, for I live in a well . . . (*looking up*) and I always hated wells. . . . No, here comes the little one . . . the friendly one. . . . (*Talking to a creature which he seems to manœuvre delicately into his hand.*) Comment ça va, mon petit vieux? You have not heard the little song I learnt from Monsieur the Jailer, have you? They sang it the day my father died. (*Half singing, half humming, in a broken voice, the 'Marseillaise'.*)

> 'Marchons, Marchons . . .
> Qu'un sang impur . . .'

My mother had a beautiful skin, and a pretty laugh, and more than all she had a perfect neck, like a swan. There was a man who held her head up to the crowd. . . . (*suddenly, loudly*) . . . by the hair. (*Quietly, again.*) There was dirt in his finger-nails. And the crowd laughed, because there were tears on her cheeks. Somebody told me; I had to know. . . . Tears for me, because I told lies about her. But I always liked making things up, and I always shall. . . . (*With a sigh, mechanically, as if it is something he has said so often that it has lost its meaning.*) Dear mother, I miss you, I miss you, I miss you. . . .

MRS DELL'S VOICE (*in the garden, loud and proud*): My lords, ladies and gentlemen . . . (MASON *listens*) . . . before you take your places for the minuet, I have the humble honour to present to you, as my guest, on the sacred night of Waterloo, his Royal Majesty . . . King Louis the Seventeenth of France!

The music strikes up in the garden – a minuet of Mozart.

As if in a sudden fit of lucidity, MASON *staggers to his feet, gulps the poisoned wine, and flings the empty glass into the fireplace, where it breaks to pieces. A pause; the corrosive poison tears at his vitals, he cries with sudden pain and staggers towards the kitchen door.*

MASON (*calling, moaning*): Madame . . . Madame . . .

MISS MASON runs in from the kitchen.

MISS MASON: What is it – what is the matter——

MASON (*in agony*): Poison – burning – burning——

MISS MASON: Poison – Dieu – a doctor – quickly——

MASON (*clutching her to him, as she makes frantic efforts to go*): No, no . . . stay with me . . . I knew if I did not do it now . . . I never would——

MISS MASON: A doctor——

MASON (*holding her to him, convulsively*): No. . . . (*Drawing himself up, with sudden supernatural calm.*) Seventeen people looked on when I was born, mother . . . but now only you.

He dies.

A pause. SOPHY *comes in from the hall, puzzled, insistent.*

SOPHY: But we cannot allow her to announce, him——

She sees the scene. She comes forward.

What has happened?

MISS MASON (*without looking at her*): He has killed himself.

> *A pause. She is holding* MASON'S *head, as if he were a babe in arms, smiling and far away.*

SOPHY: The fool . . . I would have been strong enough for the two of us. . . . I would have made him great! (*In tears.*) God, why must I weep. . . . (*Looking at the other woman, incredulously.*) What are you thinking of?

MISS MASON: A spring morning, when he was four weeks old. I was allowed to carry him, down the avenue of poplars leading to the lake. The sun caught his eyes; he opened them; and clearly, for the first time in his life, he looked at the sky. And then he laughed; unheard-of in a creature so young. But then, you see . . . he was born gay.

> *In the garden, the swell of the minuet.*

CURTAIN

THE CORN IS GREEN

To
S. G. C.

CHARACTERS

Mr John Goronwy Jones
Miss Ronberry
Idwal Morris
Sarah Pugh
A Groom
The Squire
Bessie Watty
Mrs Watty
Miss Moffat
Robbart Robbatch
Glyn Thomas
Will Hughes
John Owen
Morgan Evans
Old Tom
Boys, Girls and Parents

The action of the play takes place in the living-room of a house in Glansarno, a small village in a remote Welsh countryside.

The time is the latter part of the last century, and covers a period of three years

ACT ONE
Scene 1: An afternoon in June
Scene 2: A night in August, six weeks later

ACT TWO
Scene 1: An early evening in August, two years later
Scene 2: A morning in November, three months later

ACT THREE
An afternoon in July, seven months later

THE CORN IS GREEN *was first produced at the Duchess Theatre, London, on 20 September* 1938. *It was presented by Stephen Mitchell, with the following cast:*

MR JOHN GORONWY JONES	John Glyn-Jones
MISS RONBERRY	Christine Silver
IDWAL MORRIS	William John Davies
SARAH PUGH	Dorothy Langley
A GROOM	Albert Biddiscombe
THE SQUIRE	Frederick Lloyd
BESSIE WATTY	Betty Jardine
MRS WATTY	Kathleen Harrison
MISS MOFFAT	Sybil Thorndike
ROBBART ROBBATCH	Kenneth Evans
GLYN THOMAS	Wynford Morse
WILL HUGHES	Jack Glyn
JOHN OWEN	Glan Williams
MORGAN EVANS	Emlyn Williams
OLD TOM	Frank Dunlop

The play directed by
THE AUTHOR

ACT I

SCENE I

The living-room of a house in Glansarno, a small village in a remote Welsh countryside. A sunny afternoon in June, in the latter part of the last century.

The house is old, and the ceiling slants away from the audience. Facing the audience, on the right (throughout the play, 'left' and 'right' refer to the audience's left and right), narrow stairs lead up to a landing and then on the right to a passage to the bedrooms; we can just see, facing, the door of one bedroom which is later to be MISS MOFFAT'S. Under the landing, a low door leads to the kitchen; at the foot of the stairs, an alcove and a door lead to a little room which is later the study. In the back wall, to the left, the front door, with outside it a small stone porch faintly overgrown with ivy, and opening to the left on to a path; in the back wall, to the right, one step leads up to a large bay window with a seat round the recess. In the left wall, downstage, the garden door, with above it a small side window; when the door is open we can just see a trellised porch with a creeper. Through the thickish muslin curtains over the bay window we glimpse a jagged stone wall and the sky.

The floor is of stone flags, with two rugs, one in front of the sofa next the footlights, to mark the fireplace. Faded sprigged wallpaper.

The furniture is a curious jumble of old Welsh and Victorian pieces. A large serviceable flat-topped desk under the side window, a desk-chair in front of it; a round table with a small chair, near the middle of the room; an arm-chair, between the desk and the table; a sofa, down-stage, between the table and the foot of the stairs; in the right wall, above the kitchen door, an old Welsh dresser with plates and crockery; in the right wall, against the staircase, a settle; in the window recess, a small table; below the bay window, an old spinning-wheel. In the back wall, to the left of the front door, a small grandfather's clock. An oil lamp on the centre table, another on the desk.

The most distinctive feature of the room is the number of books on the walls, of all sorts and sizes; some in open book-cases, others on newly-built shelves, on practically every available space.

The kitchen door is open; there are books on the window-seat, several on the edge of the sofa.

As the curtain rises, MR JOHN GORONWY JONES *and* MISS RONBERRY *are arranging the last books in their places; she is sitting on a small stool taking books out of a large packing-case and fitting them on to narrow shelves between the garden door and the side window, flicking each one mechanically with a tiny lace handkerchief. She is a gentlewoman in her thirties, with the sort of pinched pretti-ness that tends to look sharp before that age, especially when it makes sporadic attempts at coquetry; she wears a hat. He is a shabby Welshman of forty, bespectacled, gloomy and intense; a volcano, harmless even in full eruption. He is perched on top of a step-ladder, arranging books on a high shelf between the front door and the bay window, dusting them vigorously before putting them in place.*

MR JONES (*singing in a resentful bass*):

'. . . Pechadur wyf, y dua'n fyw – "O Uffern!"
    yw fy nghri;
Gostwng dy glust, a'm llefain clyw . . .
    (*Booming to a final note.*)
So – so – so – la – so – so!'

MISS RONBERRY: Your voice has given me an agonis-
ing headache. And if you must indulge in music, will
you please not do it in Welsh?

MR JONES: I wasn't indulgin' in music, I was singin' a
hymn. (*Putting the last book on the shelf and climbing down.*)
And if a hymn gives you a headache, there is nothing
wrong with the hymn, there is something wrong with
your head.

    His accent is marked, but not exaggerated.

MISS RONBERRY: I still don't see the necessity for it.

MR JONES (*picking up the empty packing-case and moving
towards the kitchen*): I sing to cheer myself up.

MISS RONBERRY: What do the words mean?

MR JONES: 'The wicked shall burn in hell.'

    *He goes into the kitchen. MISS RONBERRY looks
    depressed, fits in the last of her books, and crosses to the
    books on the back of the sofa, as IDWAL MORRIS comes
    in from the garden, carrying a bunch of flowers. He is a
    thin, ragged boy of thirteen, very timid.*

MISS RONBERRY (*graciously, flicking the books one by one*):
Is the garden nice and ready?

IDWAL: 'Sgwelwchi'n dda, d'wi'di torri'r bloda.

MISS RONBERRY (*calling*): Translation!

    MR JONES *returns from the kitchen, slowly climbs the
    ladder again, and settles to his books once more.*

IDWAL (*to him, as he does so*): Os gwelwchi'n dda, Mistar
Jones, d'wi'di torri'r bloda, a mae'r domen yn hogla'n
ofnadwy.

MR JONES (*to* MISS RONBERRY): He says he cut the sweet peas and the rubbish-heap is smelling terrible.

MISS RONBERRY: Oh dear. . . . (*Taking the flowers from* IDWAL, *and crossing to the desk with them and the books.*) His father must put something on it.

MR JONES: That's the English all over. The devil is there, is he? Don't take him away, put a bit of scent on him! (*To* IDWAL.) Gofyn i dy dad i roi rwbeth arno am heddyw.

IDWAL: Diolch, syr.

He runs into the kitchen.

MISS RONBERRY (*arranging the sweet peas in a vase on the desk*): I hope he will have the sense to give the message.

MR JONES: It is terrible, isn't it, the people on these green fields and flowery hillsides bein' turned out of Heaven because they cannot answer Saint Peter when he asks them who they are in English? It is wicked, isn't it, the Welsh children not bein' *born* knowing English, isn't it? (*In a crescendo of ironic mimicry.*) Good heavens, God bless my soul, by Jove, this that and the other!

MISS RONBERRY: Anybody in Wales will tell you that the people in this part of the countryside are practically barbarians. Not a single caller for fifteen miles, and even then——

SARAH PUGH *comes out of the bedroom and down the stairs. She is a buxom peasant-woman, with a strong Welsh accent.*

SARAH: Please, miss, I made the bed lovely. And I dust——

MISS RONBERRY: That will be all, dear, the Colonel is bound to have his own manservant.

SARAH (*disappointed, going to the front door*): Then I bettar have another sit down in my post-office.

MR JONES (*sternly*): What is the matter with your post-office?

SARAH (*turning at the door*): It has not had a letter for seven weeks. Nobody but me can write, and no good *me* writin', because nobody but me can read. If I get a telegram I put him in the window and I die straight off.

She goes.

MISS RONBERRY: You see? I can't *think* why a Colonel should elect to come and live in this place. (*Patting the last flower into position.*) There . . . (*Coming into the middle of the room, and surveying it.*) I have never *seen* so many books! I do hope the curtains will not be too feminine. (*Sitting on the sofa.*) I chose them with such care——

MR JONES (*darkly*): Why are you taking so much trouble getting somebody else's house ready for them?

MISS RONBERRY (*flustered*): You need not have helped me if you did not wish! . . . (*Finishing sewing a rent in a cushion on the sofa.*) I am frightened of the spinning-wheel, too, and the china; his own furniture is *so* distinctive. The desk. And the waste-paper-basket. So . . . so virile.

MR JONES: Are you hoping that the Colonel will live up to his waste-paper basket?

MISS RONBERRY: That is horrid.

MR JONES: And then you will have two on a string: him and the Squire——

MISS RONBERRY (*pleasurably shocked*): Mr Jones——!

MR JONES (*implacable*): And if I was a bit more of a masher, there would be three. Worldly things, that is your trouble. 'Please, Mistar Jones, my life is as empty as a rotten nutshell, so get me a husband before it is too late, double quick!'

He has gone too far.

MISS RONBERRY: You insulting man——

A knock at the front door; it opens and a liveried GROOM *appears.*

THE GROOM (*announcing*): The Squire.

The SQUIRE *follows him. He is a handsome English country gentleman in his forties, wearing knickerbockers and gaiters; a hard drinker, very moustached, bluff, kind, immensely vain; and, when the time comes, obtusely obstinate. The* GROOM *goes out again and shuts the door.*

MISS RONBERRY (*fluttering eagerly into a handshake*): Squire . . .

THE SQUIRE (*with exuberant patronage, throwing his hat on the table*): Delicious lady, delicious surprise, and a merry afternoon to ye, as our forebears put it. . . . (*A cold nod.*) How are you, Jones, making the most of your half-day?

MR JONES (*sullenly, making an uncertain effort to rise from the ladder*): Good afternoon, sir——

THE SQUIRE: Squat, dear fellow, squat, no ceremony with me! . . . (*Bowing* MISS RONBERRY *on to the sofa, and sinking himself into the arm-chair.*) And why, dear lady, were you not at the Travers-Ellis wedding?

MISS RONBERRY (*dashed*): Naughty! I sat next to you at the breakfast.

THE SQUIRE: By Jingo, so you did! Deuced fine breakfast. . . .

MR JONES: Excuse me——

He goes into the study, carrying the step-ladder.

MISS RONBERRY: We had a talk about children.

THE SQUIRE: *Did* we? . . . Well, the next wedding we're at, there'll be *no* chance of my forgettin' you, eh?

MISS RONBERRY (*breath suspended, for a second*): Why?

THE SQUIRE: Because you'll be the stunning, blushing bride!

Miss Ronberry: And who – will be the——?

The Squire (*in a paroxysm of joviality*): Now that's what *I* want to know, because *I'm* going to give you away!

Miss Ronberry: Oh!

MR JONES *returns from the study.*

The Squire: Now who's it going to be?

Miss Ronberry: Squire, you are too impatient! (*Teasing.*) I am taking my time!

> *She laughs, catches the gleam of* MR JONES' *spectacles, and subsides quickly.* MR JONES *sits at the table in the window-seat and dusts the books there.*

The Squire: Too bad . . . No sign of the new inhabitant?

Miss Ronberry (*sewing*): Any moment now, I think! The pony and trap met the London train at a quarter to twelve!

The Squire: Hasn't the fellow got his own private conveyance?

Miss Ronberry: I think not.

The Squire: I hope he's all right.

Miss Ronberry: He wrote very civilly to Mr Jones about the house——

The Squire: Oh yes. Not a club, I remember, but not bad texture. (*Suspiciously.*) Funny sort of chap, though, eh?

Miss Ronberry: Why?

The Squire: All these books.

> *A timid knock at the front door.* IDWAL *enters, very frightened.*

Idwal (*to the* Squire): Os gwelwchi'n dda, syr, mae Mistar Tomos wedi 'ngyrru i yma ich gweld chi!

The Squire (*chuckling good-humouredly*): Y'know, it's as bad as being abroad . . . been among it half my life, and never get used to it.

Mr Jones (*rising, and coming down*): The groom told him, sir, that you wanted to see him.

The Squire: Oh yes – well, come here where I can see you, eh? . . . (*As* Idwal *advances fearfully round his chair.*) Now, boy, how old are you, or whatever the Chinese is for it?

Mr Jones: Just turned thirteen, sir.

The Squire: Thirteen? Well, why aren't you working in the mine over in the next valley? Don't like to see young fellows wasting their time, y'know.

Mr Jones: He has got one lung funny.

The Squire: Oh, I see. . . . Rough luck – here, laddy, there's a penny for you, and remember all work and no play makes Taffy a dull boy!

Idwal (*delighted, going*): Diolch yn fawr, syr——

The Squire: And tell your uncle I want Ranger shod——

Idwal (*going*): Diolch, syr——

The Squire: And a window mended——

Idwal: Diolch yn fawr, syr——

He runs out by the front door.

Miss Ronberry: But he hasn't understood your orders!

The Squire: Neither he has——

Mr Jones: He thought the Squire was havin' a chat. (*Going towards the window.*) I will tell his uncle——

Idwal (*calling shrilly to his friends, in the road*): Tomos – Aneurin – dyma'r cerbyd – dewch i wel'd – fe ddwedai wrth y Scweiar – brysiwch!

Miss Ronberry (*rising, excited*): That must be something——

Idwal *appears at the front door, panting with expectation.*

IDWAL (*to the* SQUIRE): Pliss, syr, dyma'r cerbyd!

> *He darts back, leaving the door open.*

MISS RONBERRY: He must mean the Colonel – how gratifying——

THE SQUIRE: Capital——

> *He rises and stands between the arm-chair and the garden door, while* MR JONES *shrinks back into the window-recess, as* BESSIE WATTY *wanders shyly in from the front door. She is an extremely pretty, plump little girl of fourteen; it is a moment before one realises that her demureness is too good to be true. She wears her hair over her shoulders, is dressed very plainly, in a shabby sailor suit and hat, and carries brown-paper parcels. She stands immobile near the table. She is followed by* MRS WATTY, *a middle-aged Cockney servant, dressed for travelling, carrying a hamper in her arms surmounted by several articles tied together with rope, including a kettle, a rolling-pin, and a pudding-basin. Her self-confidence is not so overwhelming as the* SQUIRE'S, *but it is quite as complete and as kindly. She looks round uncertainly, unable to dispose of her burden.*

MRS WATTY (*to the* SQUIRE) D'you speak English?

THE SQUIRE (*taken aback*): I do.

MRS WATTY: Be a dear an' 'old this!

> *She hands him the hamper, takes the rest, manœuvres them on to the table, and hurries out through the front door.*

THE SQUIRE: Crikey! A Colonel with an abigail! (*Catching* BESSIE'S *owl-like expression, and stopping short.*) Why don't *you* say something?

BESSIE: I never speak till I'm spoken to.

THE SQUIRE: Oh . . . Well, who was that?

BESSIE: My mummy. I never had no daddy.

Her accent is not as natural as her mother's; she some-
times strains to be ladylike, especially at moments like
this. MRS WATTY *returns carrying two large cloth-covered*
parcels.

MRS WATTY: My Gawd, they're heavy.

MISS RONBERRY: What are they?

MRS WATTY: Books.

She drops the parcels on the floor, takes the hamper from
the SQUIRE, *and places it on the table.*

THE SQUIRE: Is your employer with you, my good
woman?

MRS WATTY: No, followed be'ind, most of the way.
(*Hurrying back to the front door and peering down the street.*)
Ought to be 'ere by now, I'll 'ave a see.... (*Calling.*) 'Ere
we are! Tally-o! Thought we'd lost you!

A pause. MISS MOFFAT *comes in from the road, wheel-*
ing a bicycle. She is about forty, a healthy Englishwoman
with an honest face, clear, beautiful eyes, a humorous
mouth, a direct friendly manner, and unbounded vitality,
which is prevented from tiring the spectator by its capacity
for sudden silences and for listening. Her most prominent
characteristic is her complete unsentimentality. She wears
a straw hat, collar and tie, and a dark unexaggerated skirt;
a satchel hangs from her shoulder.

MISS MOFFAT: I was hoping to pass you, but that last
hill was too much for me. (*Displaying the bicycle.*) There's
a smallish crowd already, so I thought I'd better bring
Priscilla inside. Watty, can you find somewhere for her?

She gives the room a quick appraising look, peers out of
the side window, and nods pleasantly at the SQUIRE.

I think I'll have a look at the garden first.

She goes out into the garden. The SQUIRE *stares at her.*

MRS WATTY (*wheeling the bicycle gingerly towards the kitchen*): Dunno, I'm sure – that must be my kitchen in there, we'll 'ave to ang 'er with the bacon. (*To* BESSIE.) Come on, girl, give us a 'and, don't stand there gettin' into mischief!

BESSIE: I'm frightened of it.

MRS WATTY: It won't bite you! Most it can do is catch fire, and I'll 'ave a drop o' water ready for it. . . .

Her voice fades away into the kitchen.

BESSIE: Has anybody got a sweetie?

MISS RONBERRY: No.

BESSIE (*depressed*): Oh . . .

She trails after her mother into the kitchen. MISS MOFFAT *returns, very businesslike; not a movement of hers is wasted.*

MISS MOFFAT: It's bigger than I expected. . . . (*Shutting the front door, then unpinning her hat, pleasantly, as they stare at her.*) There! Good afternoon! (*Looking round the room, as she pitches her hat on to the desk.*) So this is my house. . . .

THE SQUIRE (*blustering*): No, it isn't!

MISS MOFFAT: Oh? Isn't this Pengarth? The name of the building, I mean?

MISS RONBERRY: Yes, it is——

MRS WATTY *returns from the kitchen, motions to* MR JONES *to unpack the books in the hamper, and takes the kettle and its appurtenances back into the kitchen.* MR JONES *unpacks. During this,* MISS MOFFAT *speaks.*

MISS MOFFAT (*relieved*): That's right, it was left me by my uncle, Doctor Moffat. I'm Miss Moffat. (*As she unstraps her satchel.*) I take it you're Miss Ronberry, who so kindly corresponded with me?

THE SQUIRE (*sternly*): But surely those letters were written by a man?

237

MISS MOFFAT: Well, if they were, I have been grossly deceiving myself for over forty years. . . . (*Addressing him as his equal and not as his inferior, for him a new experience with women.*) Now this is jolly interesting. Why did it never occur to you that I might be a woman?

THE SQUIRE: Well – the paper wasn't scented——

MISS RONBERRY: And such a bold hand——

THE SQUIRE: And that long piece about the lease being ninety-nine years, don't you know——

MISS MOFFAT (*concerned*): Was there anything wrong with it?

THE SQUIRE: No, there wasn't, that's the point.

MISS MOFFAT: I see.

MISS RONBERRY: And surely you signed your name very oddly?

MISS MOFFAT: My initials, L. C. Moffat? You see, I've never felt that Lily Christabel really suited me.

MISS RONBERRY (*sitting on the sofa*): And I thought it meant Lieutenant-Colonel . . . .But there *was* a military title after it!

MISS MOFFAT (*after thinking a second*): M.A., Master of Arts.

THE SQUIRE: Arts? D'ye mean the degree my father bought me when I came down from the Varsity?

MISS MOFFAT: The very same. Except that I was at Aberdeen, and had to work jolly hard for mine.

THE SQUIRE: A female M.A.? And how long's that going to last?

MISS MOFFAT (*placing her satchel next the desk*): Quite a long time, I hope, considering we've been waiting for it for two thousand years.

MR JONES (*who has been silent as the grave, since she entered*): Are you saved?

MISS MOFFAT (*starting, turning and taking him in for the first time*): I beg your pardon?

MR JONES: Are you Church or Chapel?

MISS MOFFAT: I really don't know. . . . (*To the* SQUIRE, *as she crosses to the table to fetch some books.*) And now you know all about me, what do *you* do?

THE SQUIRE (*distantly, moving towards the front door*): I'm afraid I don't do anything.

He extricates his hat angrily from the table.

MISS RONBERRY (*shocked*): Mr Treverby owns the Hall!

MISS MOFFAT (*frank and friendly*): Really. I've never had much to do with the landed gentry. Interesting.

THE SQUIRE (*to* MISS RONBERRY): Au revoir, dear lady. 'Day, Jones.

He goes frigidly out by the front door.

MISS MOFFAT: Well, nobody could say that I've made a conquest there. . . . (*Crossing towards the stairs.*) What's the matter with him?

MRS WATTY *comes in from the kitchen, carrying a small tray with three cups and saucers.*

MRS WATTY (*placing the tray on the table*): I found the tea, ma'am, it *looks* all right——

MISS MOFFAT: Good——

MRS WATTY: An' the big luggage is comin' after——

MISS MOFFAT (*opening the study door*): This isn't a bad little room——

MR JONES *crosses to the desk with books from the table.*

MISS WATTY (*to the others*): Where's his lordship?

MISS MOFFAT (*going upstairs*): Took offence and left.

She disappears down the passage.

MRS WATTY: Took offence? At 'er?

MISS RONBERRY: I am afraid so.

MRS WATTY: I'm jiggered! (*Arranging the cups and saucers.*) What d'*you* think of 'er, eh? Ain't she a clinker?

MISS RONBERRY: She is unusual, is she not?

MRS WATTY: She's a clinker, that's what. Terrible strong-willed, o' course, terrible. Get 'er into mischief, I keep tellin' 'er. Would bring me 'ere. I said no, I said, not with my past, I said.

MISS RONBERRY: Your past?

MRS WATTY: Before she took me up. But what with 'er, an now I've joined the Corpse, it's all blotted out.

MR JONES: The Corpse?

MRS WATTY: The Militant Righteous Corpse. Ran into 'em in the street I did, singin' and prayin' and collectin', full blast; and I been a different woman since. (*Turning to MR JONES.*) Are *you* saved?

MR JONES (*stiffening*): Yes, I am.

MRS WATTY: So'm I, ain't it lovely?

MISS RONBERRY: But what *was* . . . your past?

MRS WATTY (*sorrowfully*): Light fingers.

MISS RONBERRY: Light fingers? (*The truth dawning on her.*) You mean – stealing?

MRS WATTY: Everywhere I went. Terrible. Pennies, stockin's, brooches, spoons, tiddly, anything; and I always looked so pi! Every time there was a do, everything went; and I always knew it was me!

> MISS MOFFAT *comes downstairs.*

(*Moving towards the kitchen.*) I was just tellin' 'em about my trouble.

MISS MOFFAT: Well, don't tell them any more. Is your kitchen all right?

MRS WATTY: I ain't *seed* no mice yet.

> *She goes into the kitchen.* MISS MOFFAT *looks round again. Far away, softly, the sound of boys' voices, singing*

an old country song, in harmony, in Welsh: '*Yr Hufen Melyn*'.

MISS MOFFAT: I agree with the last tenant's taste. Though I don't see myself spinning very much. . . . (*Warmly.*) You have arranged my things quite splendidly, Miss Ronberry, I do thank you – both of you. . . . (*Savouring the atmosphere of the room.*) I like this house. . . . (*As the music grows imperceptibly, in the distance.*) What's that singing?

MR JONES: Boys coming home from the mine.

MISS RONBERRY: They burst into song on the slightest provocation. You mustn't take any notice——

MISS MOFFAT: I like it. . . . (*After listening a moment, looking out of the side window.*) And those mountains. That grand wild countryside . . . the foreign-looking people. . . . (*As the singing dies away.*) But business . . . I've heard about that mine. How far is it?

MR JONES: It is the Glasynglo coal mine, six miles over the hills.

MISS MOFFAT (*moving towards the bay window*): Hm . . .

MISS RONBERRY: We're hoping it will stay the only one, or our scenery will be ruined – such a pretty landscape——

MISS MOFFAT (*looking out, suddenly*): What is the large empty building next door?

MR JONES: Next door? The old barn belongin' to the Gwalia Farm, before the farm was burnt down——

MISS MOFFAT: So it's free?

MR JONES (*perplexed*): Free? Yes——

MISS RONBERRY (*losing interest, rising and crossing in front of the table*): I am over-staying my welcome – so very charming——

MR JONES (*taking the rest of the books to the desk*): I also – all the volumes are dusted——

MISS MOFFAT: I want you two people. Very specially. First you, Miss Ronberry. (*Coming down to her.*) I used to meet friends of yours at lectures in London. You live alone, you have just enough money, you're not badly educated, and time lies heavy on your hands.

MISS RONBERRY (*sitting again, suddenly, in the arm-chair*): The Wingroves! How mean – I should never have thought——

MISS MOFFAT: Isn't that so?

MISS RONBERRY: Not at all. When the right gentleman appears——

MISS MOFFAT: If you're a spinster well on in her thirties, he's lost his way and isn't coming. Why don't you face the fact and enjoy yourself, the same as I do?

MISS RONBERRY: But when did you give up hope – oh, what a horrid expression——

MISS MOFFAT: I can't recall ever having any hope. (*Sitting on the sofa.*) Visitors used to take a long look at my figure and say: '*She's* going to be the clever one.' I shall never forget what I looked like the night my mother put me on the market. A tub with pink ribbon in every hoop. And when the only young man who had spoken to me said I was the sort of girl he'd like for a sister, then I knew.

MISS RONBERRY: But a woman's only future is to marry and – and fulfil the duties of——

MISS MOFFAT: Skittles. I'd have made a shocking wife anyway.

MISS RONBERRY: But haven't you ever – been in love?

MISS MOFFAT: No.

MISS RONBERRY: How very odd.

MISS MOFFAT: I've never talked to a man for more than five minutes without wanting to box his ears.

MR JONES *looks apprehensive.*

MISS RONBERRY: But how have you passed your time since——

MISS MOFFAT: Since I had no hope? Very busily. In the East End, for years.

MISS RONBERRY (*politely*): Social service?

MISS MOFFAT: If you like; though there's nothing very social about washing invalids with every unmentionable ailment under the sun . . . I've read a lot, too. I'm afraid I'm what is known as an educated woman. Which brings me to Mr Jones; (*to him*) the Wingroves told me all about you, too.

MR JONES (*advancing stiffly*): My conscience is as clear as the snow.

MISS MOFFAT: I'm sure it is, but you're a disappointed man, aren't you?

MR JONES (*startled*): How can I be disappointed when I am saved?

MISS MOFFAT: Oh, but you can! You can't really enjoy sitting all by yourself on a raft, on a sea containing everybody you know. You're disappointed because you're between two stools.

MR JONES (*at a loss*): Between two stools? On a raft?

MISS MOFFAT: Exactly. Your father was a grocer with just enough money to send you to a grammar-school, with the result that you are educated beyond your sphere, and yet fail to qualify for the upper classes. You feel frustrated, and fall back on being saved. Am I right?

MR JONES (*turning away*): It is such a terrible thing you have said that I will have to think it over.

MISS MOFFAT: Do, but in the meantime would you two like to stop moping and be very useful to me?

MISS RONBERRY: Useful?

MISS MOFFAT (*walking about*): Tell me – within a radius of five miles, how many families are there round here?

MISS RONBERRY (*at home for a moment*): Families? There's the Squire, of course, and Mrs Gwent-Price in the little Plas Lodge, quite a dear thing——

MISS MOFFAT: I mean ordinary people.

MISS RONBERRY (*lost again*): The villagers?

MISS MOFFAT: Yes. How many families?

MISS RONBERRY: I really haven't the faint——

MR JONES: There are about twenty families in the village and fifteen in the farms around.

MISS MOFFAT: Many children?

MR JONES: What age?

MISS MOFFAT: Up to sixteen or seventeen.

MR JONES: Round here they are only children till they are twelve. Then they are sent away over the hills to the mine, and in one week they are old men.

MISS MOFFAT: I see. . . . How many can read or write?

MR JONES: Next to none.

MISS RONBERRY: Why do you ask?

MISS MOFFAT: Because I am going to start a school for them.

MISS RONBERRY: Start a school for them? (*Coldly.*) What for?

MISS MOFFAT: What for? You cheerfully contribute funds to send missionaries to African heathens, who are as happy as the day is long, and you ask me what for? See these books? Hundreds of 'em, and something wonderful to read in every single one – these nippers are to be cut off from all that, for ever, are they? Why?

Because they happen to be born penniless in an un-
civilised countryside, coining gold down there in that
stinking dungeon for some beef-headed old miser!

MR JONES (*roused*): That's right. . . .

MISS MOFFAT: The printed page, what is it? One of
the miracles of all time, that's what! And yet when these
poor babbies set eyes on it, they might just as well have
been struck by the miracle of sudden blindness; and that,
to my mind, is plain infamous!

MR JONES (*in an excited whisper*): My goodness, Miss,
that's right. . . .

MISS RONBERRY: The *ordinary* children, you mean?

MISS MOFFAT: Yes, my dear, the ordinary children,
that came into the world by the same process exactly as
you and I. When I heard that this part of the world was
a disgrace to a Christian country, I knew this house was
a godsend; I am going to start a school, immediately,
next door in the barn, and you are going to help me!

MISS RONBERRY: I?

The rest of the scene is played very quickly.

MISS MOFFAT (*settling again on the end of the sofa*): Yes,
you! You're going to fling away your parasol and your
kid gloves, and you're going to stain those tapering
fingers with a little honest toil!

MISS RONBERRY: I couldn't teach those children, I
couldn't! They – they smell!

MISS MOFFAT: If we'd never been taught to wash, so
would we; we'll put 'em under the pump. . . . Mr Jones,
d'ye know what I'm going to do with that obstinate old
head of yours?

MR JONES: My head?

MISS MOFFAT: I'm going to crack it open with a skewer.
And I'm going to excavate all those chunks of grammar-

school knowledge, give 'em a quick dust, and put 'em to some use at last——

MR JONES: I am a solicitor's clerk in Gwaenygam and I earn thirty-three shillings per week——

MISS MOFFAT: I'll give you thirty-four – and your lunch.

MISS RONBERRY: I have an enormous house to run, and the flowers to do——

MISS MOFFAT: Shut it up except one room, and leave the flowers to die a natural death – in their own beds. . . . (*Crossing excitedly to the foot of the stairs.*) I've been left a little money and I know exactly what I am going to do with it——

MR JONES: But those children are in the mine – earning money – how can they——

MISS MOFFAT: I'll pay their parents the few miserable pennies they get out of it. . . . And when I've finished with you, *you* won't have time to think about snapping up a husband, and *you* won't have time to be so pleased that you're saved! Well?

MR JONES (*after a pause, solemnly*): I do not care if you are not chapel, I am with you.

MISS MOFFAT: Good! (*Crossing swiftly to the desk, and taking her satchel.*) I have all the details worked out, I'll explain roughly. . . . Come along, my dears, gather round——

> *She takes the dazed* MISS RONBERRY *by the arm, sits her beside her on the sofa, beckons* MR JONES *to sit on her other side, opens the satchel and spills a sheaf of papers on to her knees.*

Of course we must go slowly at first, but if we put out backs into it . . . (*Aglow.*) Here we are, three stolid middle-aged folk, settled in our little groove and crammed with benefits; and *there* are those babbies scarcely out of the shell, that have no idea they are even breathing the air. . . . Only God can know how their life will end, but He will give us the chance to direct them a little of the way——

MR JONES (*intoning, seized with religious fervour*): We have the blessed opportunity to raise up the children from the bowels of the earth where the devil hath imprisoned them in the powers of darkness, and bring them to the light of knowledge——

MRS WATTY (*coming in from the kitchen, sailing round the table with an enormous steaming teapot, calling shrilly, as* MISS MOFFAT *displays her papers*): Tea!

Black out. The curtain falls, and rises immediately on

SCENE II

A night in August, six weeks later. The window-curtains are closed and the lamps lit. The arm-chair has been pushed above the desk, and a small bench put in its place, facing the audience. Red geraniums in pots across the window-sills. MISS MOFFAT'S *straw hat is slung over the knob at the foot of the stairs. The big desk, the desk-chair, the sofa and the settle are littered with books, exercise-books, and sheets of paper. Apart from these details the room is unchanged.*

Sitting on the bench are five black-faced miners, between twelve and sixteen years of age, wearing caps, mufflers, boots and corduroys embedded in coal; they look as if they had been commanded to wait. They all look alike under their black; the ringleader is MORGAN EVANS, *fifteen, quick and impudent; his second is* ROBBART ROBBATCH, *a big, slow boy, a year or two older; the others are* GLYN THOMAS, WILL HUGHES *and* JOHN OWEN.

247

      Mrs Watty comes downstairs, carrying a basket of washing.

Mrs Watty (*singing*): 'I'm saved, I am – I'm saved, I am – I'm S-A-V-E-D——' (*Seeing the boys, and halting.*) You 'ere again?

Robbart (*nudging* Morgan): Be mai'n ddeud?

Mrs Watty: I said, you 'ere again?

Morgan: No, miss.

Mrs Watty: What d'ye mean, no, miss?

Morgan (*a strong accent*): We issn't 'ere again, miss.

Mrs Watty: What are you, then?

Morgan: We issn't the same lot ass this mornin', miss.

Mrs Watty (*coming downstairs*): Ain't you?

Morgan: Miss Ronny-berry tell us to wait, miss.

Mrs Watty (*calling*): Ma'am!

Miss Moffat (*in the bedroom*): Yes?

Mrs Watty: Five more nigger-boys for you!

      She goes into the kitchen. Morgan *takes a bottle from his pocket and swigs at it; one of the others holds out his hand, takes the bottle, gulps, and gives it back, while another begins to hum, absent-mindedly, a snatch of the same song as before –* 'Yr Hufen Melyn'. *The rest (including* Morgan*) take up the harmony and sing it to the end.*

Robbart (*loudly, derisively*): Please, miss, can I have a kiss?

Morgan: No, you can't, you dirty Taffy, you dirty my nose!

Robbart: Get out o' my school, you dirty Taffies——

Morgan: Get out——

      He gives a hefty push and sends all the others sprawling to the floor. Pandemonium, involving a torrent of Welsh imprecations.

Glyn: Denna'r trydydd tro – be haru ti, diawl——

JOHN: Get out o' my school, cer gartra – mochyn budur gwaith glo – cer gartra——

WILL: Wtisho dy drwyn i waedu eto?

MORGAN: Sospon mawr, yn berwi ar y llawr – sospon bach – wtisho dy drwyn di i waedu?

> *In the middle of this* MRS WATTY *comes in from the kitchen, her arms covered in soapsuds.*

MRS WATTY: Now, now, you boys, me on me washin' night too!

MORGAN: Please, miss, can I have a kiss?

MRS WATTY (*shocked*): You naughty boy! You wait till you see Miss Moffat, she'll give you what for! (*On her way back to the kitchen.*) Can I 'ave a kiss, indeed, bad as the West End. . . .

> *She goes.*

ROBBART (*bored, singing raucously*): 'Boys and girls come out to play——'

> *He claps his hands to his knees, the others half take up the refrain.* MR JONES *comes in from the front door.*

MORGAN: Sh!

> *The boys are silent, turn, and watch* MR JONES. *He eyes them fearfully.*

MORGAN (*blandly*): Good evenin', sir.

MR JONES (*relieved, taking off his hat*): Good evening.

> *He moves towards the kitchen.*

MORGAN (*suddenly*): I seed you and the lady teacher be'ind the door!

> *A chorus of* 'Oooo!' *in mock horror from him and the others.*

MR JONES (*frightened and dignified*): You wait till you see Miss Moffat. She will give you what for.

MORGAN (*muttering, mimicking him*): You wait till you see Miss Moffat, she will give you what for!

The others join in as MR JONES *goes into the kitchen:*
'You wait till you see Miss Moffat, she will give you
what for!'

MORGAN: Sh!

The rest are silent, as MISS MOFFAT *comes downstairs
from the bedroom. She is dressed much the same, and carries
a roll of papers.*

MISS MOFFAT (*calling*): I told you, the shape of the bedroom doesn't allow for a door into the barn – oh, she
isn't here. . . . (*Picking up her hat from the knob and putting
it on.*) Sorry to keep you waiting, boys, but I have to go
across to Mr Rees, the carpenter, and then I'll be able
to talk to you. In the meantime, will you go to the pump
in the garden shed, and wash your hands. Through there.
You'll find a lantern.

They stare before them, immovable.

(*Smiling.*) Did you understand all that?

MORGAN (*with false submissiveness*): Yes, miss.

THE OTHERS (*taking his tone*): Thank you, miss.

MISS MOFFAT: Good.

MORGAN (*as she starts for the front door, loud and shrill*):
Please, miss, can I have a kiss?

A pause.

MISS MOFFAT (*turning*): What did you say?

MORGAN (*rising, leaping over the bench, and grinning at the
others*): Please, miss, can I have a kiss?

MISS MOFFAT (*after a pause, quietly*): Of course you can.

*She walks briskly down, puts one foot on the end of the
bench, seizes* MORGAN, *turns him over on her knee, spanks
him six times, hard, with the roll of papers, then releases
him.*

(*Looking coolly at the others.*) Can I oblige anybody
else?

She goes out by the front door. The others follow her with their eyes, aghast, in silence.

ROBBART (*imitating* MORGAN): Please, miss, can I 'ave a smack bottom?

An uproar of mirth, and a quick tangle of Welsh.

MORGAN: Cythral uffarn——

GLYN: Be hari hi – hi a'i molchi——

JOHN: Pwy sisho molchi——

WILL: Welso ti 'rioed wraig fel ene——

MORGAN: Mae'n lwcus na ddaru mi mo'i thrawo hi lawr a'i lladd hi——

ROBBART: Nawn i drio molchi – dewch hogia – mae'n well nag eistedd yma – dewch——

They lumber into the garden, MORGAN muttering furiously, the others talking and laughing. Their voices die away. MR JONES'S head appears timidly round from the kitchen. He sees they are gone, gives a sigh of relief, and comes into the room, carrying books. He sits at the desk, intoning a hymn. BESSIE comes in from the front door, dejected and sulky. She is munching a sweet; her hair is in curls, and one curl is turned round one finger, which she holds stiffly in the air. She lays her hat on the sofa, then decides MR JONES'S company is better than none.

BESSIE: Would you like a sweetie?

MR JONES: No thank you, my little dear. Have you had another walk?

BESSIE: Yes, Mr Jones. (*Perching on the edge of the sofa.*) All by myself.

MR JONES (*genially, for him*): Did you see anybody?

BESSIE: Only a lady and a gentleman in the lane, and mother told me never to look. . . . (*As he pretends not to have heard.*) I do miss the shops. London's full o' them, you know.

Mr Jones: Full of fancy rubbish, you mean.

Bessie: I'd like to be always shopping, I would. Sundays and all . . . Mr Jones, d'you remember sayin' everybody who don't go to chapel on Sundays will go to hell?

Mr Jones (*bravely*): Indeed I do.

Bessie: Last Sunday Miss Moffat was diggin' the garden all afternoon; she's in for it, then, isn't she?

Mr Jones: Miss Moffat is a good woman. If she went to chapel she would be a better one, but she is still a good woman.

Mrs Watty (*calling, in the kitchen*): Bessie!

Bessie (*shyly*): Mr Jones, is it true the school idea isn't going on that well?

Mr Jones (*after a pause*): Who told you that?

Bessie: Miss Ronberry was sayin' something to my mum – oh, I wasn't listenin'! . . . Besides, we've been here six weeks, and nothin's started yet.

Mr Jones: Everything is splendid.

Bessie (*disappointed*): Oh, I am glad. Miss Moffat's been cruel to me, but I don't bear no grudge.

Mr Jones: Cruel to you?

Bessie: She hides my sweets. (*Going.*) She's a liar too.

Mr Jones: A liar?

Bessie: Told me they're bad for me, and it says on the bag they're nourishin'. . . . (*Going, dipping her nose into her bag.*) And the idea of learnin' school with those children, ooh. . . .

Mr Jones: Why are you holding your hair like that?

Bessie: These are me curls. D'you think it's nice?

Mr Jones: It is nice, but it is wrong.

Mrs Watty (*calling shrilly, in the kitchen*): Bess-ie!

Bessie: I've been curlin' each one round me finger and

holdin' it tight till it was all right. (*Moving, dejectedly, still holding her hair.*) My finger's achin' something terrible.

> *She goes into the kitchen. A knock at the front door.*

MR JONES (*calling*): Dewch ifewn.

> IDWAL *appears, drawing a small wooden crate on tiny wheels which he pushes to the front of the sofa.* MISS RONBERRY *comes in from the study, poring over a book and looking harassed.*

IDWAL: Cloch yr ysgol, Mistar Jones.

MR JONES: Diolch, ymachgeni. Nos dawch.

IDWAL: Nos dawch, Mistar Jones.

> *He goes back through the front door.* MISS RONBERRY *sits on the settle.*

MISS RONBERRY: It says here that eight sevens are fifty-six. Then it says that seven eights are fifty-six – I can't see that at all.

> MISS MOFFAT *returns from the front door. Her cheerfulness is a little forced.*

Well?

MISS MOFFAT: No good.

MISS RONBERRY: Oh dear.

MISS MOFFAT (*throwing down her hat*): Mr Rees says he's had a strict order not to discuss lining the roof till the lease of the barn is signed.

MR JONES: Who gave the order?

MISS MOFFAT: That's what I want to know!

MISS RONBERRY: And when will the lease be signed?

MISS MOFFAT: Never, it seems to me. (*Anxiously, to* MR JONES.) Did you call at the solicitor's?

MR JONES (*unwillingly*): They have located Sir Herbert Vezey, but he is now doubtful about letting the barn and will give his decision by post.

MISS MOFFAT: But why? He'd already said it was no

use to him. And my references were impeccable. . . .
(*Flinging herself on the sofa, on top of papers and books*) *Why?*

MISS RONBERRY: You look tired.

MISS MOFFAT: It's been a bit of a day. A letter from the mine to say no child can be released above ground – that's all blethers, but still . . . A request from the public house not to start a school in case it interferes with beer-swilling and games of chance. A message from the chapel people to the effect that I am a foreign adventuress with cloven feet; and Priscilla's got a puncture. A bit of a day.

MRS WATTY *comes in from the kitchen, carrying a cup of tea.*

MRS WATTY: Drop o' tea, ma'am, I expect you've 'ad a bit of a day. . . .

MISS MOFFAT: Who was that at the back, anything important?

MRS WATTY (*handing* MISS MOFFAT *her tea, and stirring it for her*): Only the person that does for that Mrs Gwent-Price. Would you not 'ave your school opposite her lady because of her lady's 'eadaches.

MISS MOFFAT (*angry*): What did you say?

MRS WATTY: I pulverised 'er. (*Stirring, hard.*) I said it would be a shame, I said, if there was such a shindy over the way that the village couldn't hear Mrs Double-Barrel givin' her 'usband what for, I said. The person didn't know where to put 'erself.

She goes back into the kitchen.

MR JONES (*gathering books and making to cross towards the study*): That has not helped the peace in the community, neither.

MISS MOFFAT: I know, but she does make a tip-top cup of tea. . . . (*Seeing the crate, wearily.*) What's that?

MR JONES: It is the bell, for the school.

MISS MOFFAT (*sitting up, more cheerful*): Oh, is it?

MISS RONBERRY (*rising*): The bell? Do let us have a peep——

> MISS MOFFAT *unhinges the side of the crate and shows the bell. It is an old one, about a cubic foot in size.*

MR JONES: It was on Llantalon Monastery before it burnt down——

MISS MOFFAT: Look, it's got the rope, and everything. . . . (*Getting depressed again.*) Well, it's good to see it, anyway.

MISS RONBERRY: The mason finished the little tower for it yesterday – do let us tell those boys to put it up! It'll bring us luck!

MISS MOFFAT (*sitting on the sofa drinking her tea*): If it keeps them out of mischief till I'm ready——

MISS RONBERRY: Mr Jones, do go and tell them!

> MR JONES *gives her a doubtful look and goes towards the garden. A sudden noise of raucous abuse outside in the shed; he winces, and goes.*

MISS MOFFAT: Poor Jonesy, he's terrified of 'em.

MISS RONBERRY: So am I. They're so big. And so black——

> *A knock at the front door.* SARAH *runs in, excited, leaving the door open behind her.*

SARAH: A letter from a gentleman that owns the barn, I had a good look at the seal!

MISS MOFFAT: At last——

> *She hands her cup to* MISS RONBERRY, *takes the letter quickly from* SARAH *and reads it.*

MISS RONBERRY (*putting the cup on the settle*): What does it say?

MISS MOFFAT: Sir Herbert still cannot give a definite

decision until the seventeenth. (*Crushing the letter.*) Another week wasted. This is infuriating.

She rises and crosses towards the desk.

MISS RONBERRY: Does it mean he may not let you have it?

SARAH (*disappointed*): Oh . . .

She moves towards the front door.

MISS MOFFAT: He must – it would ruin everything——

MISS RONBERRY: Sarah, isn't there another empty building *anywhere* round here?

SARAH (*considering*): There is the pigstyes on the Maes Road, but they issn't big enough.

She goes. MISS MOFFAT *sits in the desk chair.*

MISS RONBERRY: Can't we start afresh somewhere else?

MISS MOFFAT: I've spent too much on preparations here – besides, I felt so right here from the start – I *can't* leave now. . . . I'm a Christian woman, but I could smack Sir Herbert's face till my arm dropped off.

The front door is opened unceremoniously and the SQUIRE *strides in; he is in full evening dress, without a hat, and smokes a cigar; he is a little flushed with port. He smiles foolishly at* MISS MOFFAT.

THE SQUIRE: Jolly good evenin', teacher. Remember me?

MISS MOFFAT: Would you mind going outside, knocking, and waiting quite a long time before I say 'Come in'?

THE SQUIRE: Jolly good! Parlour games, what?

MISS RONBERRY (*horrified*): But Miss Moffat, it's the *Squire*! Squire, you must forget you ever saw me in this dress – so ashamed – I shan't be a moment——

She runs upstairs into the bedroom.

THE SQUIRE: Rat tat tat, one two three four come in, one two three four, forward *march*! My dear madam, you're not in class now!

A knock at the garden door.

Come in!

ROBBART enters. His attitude is a little chastened, though he does not see the SQUIRE. He is followed by MR JONES and MORGAN, who carries a lantern.

ROBBART (*touching his forelock*): Please, miss, for the bell.

THE SQUIRE (*with jolly patronage*): Evening, Jones! Evening, boys!

The boys recognise him, and doff their caps, deeply impressed.

(*With mock solemnity.*) I am appalled to observe, my boys, that you are still soiling your fingers in that disgusting coal-mine!

An awkward pause.

MR JONES: Excuse me, please. . . .

He goes into the study. ROBBART makes an uncertain movement towards the bell.

THE SQUIRE: What's that you've got there?

ROBBART: Bell, syr, for the school.

THE SQUIRE (*laughing loudly*): Up with it, boys, up with it!

ROBBART lifts the crate and carries it out of the front door, which MORGAN has opened for him. MORGAN follows him, shutting the door.

THE SQUIRE (*during this*): Ding dong bell – teacher's in the well! . . . (*Pushing books off the sofa and sitting on it.*) Now, my dear madam——

MISS MOFFAT: I'm rather irritable this evening, so unless there's a reason for your visit——

THE SQUIRE: Oh, but there is! Very important message. Word of mouth. From a gent that's just been dining with me. Sir Herbert Vezey.

MISS MOFFAT (*with a start*): Yes? . . . Oh, do be quick . . . !

THE SQUIRE: He has definitely decided that he has no use for the barn – but . . . (*rising, and lifting a finger, playfully*) . . . he does not see it as a school, and under no circumstances will he let it as such, so he must regretfully decline, et cetera.

> *He sits down suddenly. A pause.* MISS MOFFAT *tries in vain to hide her chagrin.*

MISS MOFFAT: He implied in his first letter that he would be willing to sell.

THE SQUIRE: Then some bigwig must have made him change his mind, mustn't he?

MISS MOFFAT (*suddenly looking at him, incredulously*): You?

THE SQUIRE (*rising, serious, and taking the floor with a certain authority*): I have not called on you, madam, because I have been eyeing your activities very closely from afar—— (*Confused.*) It is with dis – disapproval and – er – dis——

MISS MOFFAT: It is unwise to embark on a speech with the vocabulary of a child of five.

THE SQUIRE (*suddenly aggressive*): I am not going to have any of this damned hanky-panky in my village!

MISS MOFFAT: *Your* village?

THE SQUIRE: *My* village! I am no braggart, but I'd have you know that everything you can see from that window – and you haven't got a bad view – *I own*! (*Heavily.*) Now, my dear madam——

MISS MOFFAT (*in an outburst*): And stop calling me your

dear madam, I'm not married, I'm not French, and you haven't the slightest affection for me!

THE SQUIRE: Oh . . . First of all, I'm not one to hit a woman below the belt. If you know what I mean. Always be fair – to the fair sex. . . . All my life I've done my level best for the villagers – they call me Squire, y'know, term of affection, jolly touching – I mean, a hamper every Christmas, the whole shoot, and a whopping tankard of beer on my birthday, and on my twenty-first they all got a mug——

MISS MOFFAT: Go on.

THE SQUIRE: They jabber away in that funny lingo, but bless their hearts, it's a free country! But puttin' 'em up to read English, and pothooks, and givin' 'em ideas – if there were more people like you, y'know, England'd be a jolly dangerous place to live in! (*With a chuckle.*) What d'ye want to do, turn 'em into gentlemen? What's the idea?

> *Raucous cat-calls from the garden.*

MISS MOFFAT: I am beginning to wonder myself.

THE SQUIRE (*sobering*): Anyway, this buyin' 'em out of the mine is a lot of gammon. I own a half-share in it.

MISS MOFFAT: That explains a good deal.

THE SQUIRE: Why don't you take up croquet? Keep your pecker up!

> MISS RONBERRY *comes out of the bedroom. She has put on a new dress, and is much prinked up.*

Well, dear lady, anything I can do to make your stay here a happier one——

MISS MOFFAT: Thank you.

THE SQUIRE: I must be getting back. If I know Sir Herbert my best old port will be no more——

259

Miss Moffat (*rising suddenly, and facing him*): Wait a minute.

> Miss Ronberry *pauses on the stairs, and looks inquiringly, from one to the other.*

The Squire: Yes?

Miss Moffat: I know I shall be sticking a pin into a whale, but here are just two words about yourself. You are the Squire Bountiful, are you? Adored by his contented subjects, intelligent and benignly understanding, are you? I should just like to point out that there is a considerable amount of dirt, ignorance, misery and discontent abroad in this world, and that a good deal of it is due to people like you, because you are a stupid, conceited, greedy, good-for-nothing, addle-headed nincompoop, and you can go to blue blazes. Good night!

> *She turns away. A frozen pause. The* Squire *walks to the front door, and turns.*

The Squire (*majestically*): I perceive that you have been drinking.

> *He goes.*

Miss Moffat: That was undignified, but I feel better for it.

> *She sits on the bench, intensely depressed.*

Miss Ronberry: I am glad, because it *was* plain-spoken, wasn't it? (*Coming down.*) Has he been nasty? So unlike the Squire——

Miss Moffat: He was kindness itself. He advised me to go and live in a hole in the ground with my knitting. He has persuaded the owner not to sell.

Miss Ronberry: Oh dear. . . . Of course. . . . (*Sitting beside her on the bench, after giving it a cautious flick with her handkerchief*) . . . I always think men know best, don't you?

MISS MOFFAT: Yes.

MISS RONBERRY: I'm wearing my mousseline de soie, and he never even noticed. . . . What will you do?

MISS MOFFAT (*rising, her back to the audience*): Sell the house; take this brain-child of a ridiculous spinster, and smother it. Have you got a handkerchief?

MISS RONBERRY: Yes, Miss Moffat. Why?

MISS MOFFAT: I want to blow my nose.

> *She holds her hand out;* MISS RONBERRY *hands her the handkerchief. She blows her nose, and hands the handkerchief back.*

MISS RONBERRY: You ought to have had a cry. (*As* MISS MOFFAT *crosses to the study.*) I love a cry when I'm depressed. Such an advantage over the gentlemen, I always think——

MISS MOFFAT (*opening the study door*): Mr Jones, will you write letters to the tradespeople and the mine? We are giving up the school. . . . (*Coming back to her desk and picking up the waste-paper basket.*) I suppose we'd better start putting some order into this chaos, and get the business over. . . . (*Sitting on the sofa, the basket beside her, picking up five grubby books lying open, one on top of the other.*) What are these filthy exercise books doing among my papers? . . .

MISS RONBERRY (*going to the desk and tidying papers*): Those hooligans just now. They said Mr Jones had picked them out because they could write English, and would I mind my own some-dreadful-word business.

> *She crosses and drops some papers in the basket.*

MISS MOFFAT (*glancing at the top book*): I set them an essay on 'How I would spend my holiday.' (*Throwing it into the basket.*) I must have been mad. . . .

Miss Ronberry *takes another of the exercise books from her and looks at it as she crosses back to the desk.*

Miss Ronberry (*reading, laboriously*): 'If – I has ever holiday – I has breakfast and talks then dinner and a rest, tea then nothing – then supper then I talk and I go sleep.'

Miss Moffat: From exhaustion, I suppose.

Bessie *comes in from the kitchen, advances to the sofa and takes up her hat.*

(*Tearing up pages.*) Where are you going?

Bessie: Just another walk, Miss Moffat.

Miss Ronberry (*as* Bessie *trails up to the front door, wiping an eye, ostentatiously*): What's the matter, little dear?

Bessie: Mum's hit me.

Miss Ronberry: Oh, naughty mum. Why?

Bessie: 'Cause I told her she was common.

She goes.

Miss Ronberry (*crossing to the table, and taking up papers*): That child *is* unhappy.

Miss Moffat: I can't be bothered with her. (*Glancing at another book.*) Another time I'd have been faintly amused by this one's idea of a holiday, judging by a rather crude drawing.

Miss Ronberry: What is it?

Miss Moffat: A bicycling tour with me in bloomers.

Miss Ronberry: Tch, tch. . . .

She crosses to the settle, where she collects more papers.

Miss Moffat (*reading from a third exercise-book*): ' "Holiday-time." That carefree magic word! What shall it be this year, tobogganing among the eternal snows or tasting the joys of Father Neptune?'

Miss Ronberry: But that's beautiful! Extraordinary!

Miss Moffat: I might think so too if I hadn't seen it in a book open on that desk.

She tears up the book and throws it away.

MISS RONBERRY: Oh!

MISS MOFFAT: No, your Squire was right. . . . (*Her eye resting casually and despondently on the last book.*) I have been a stupid and impractical ass, and I can't imagine how——

A pause. Her eyes have caught something on the paper. She begins to read, slowly, with difficulty.

'The mine is dark. . . . If a light come in the mine . . . the rivers in the mine will run fast with the voice of many women; the walls will fall in, and it will be the end of the world.'

MISS RONBERRY *is listening, inquiringly.* MORGAN *enters brusquely from the front door. He has made no attempt to wash, but now that he is alone he half-emerges as a truculent arresting boy, with, latent in him, a very strong personality which his immaturity and natural inclination make him shy to display.*

MORGAN: Please, miss, I help with the bell——

MISS RONBERRY: Shhh – the garden—— (*To* MISS MOFFAT.) Do go on——

MORGAN *moves sulkily towards the garden door.* MISS MOFFAT, *who has not looked up from the paper, begins to read again.*

MISS MOFFAT (*reading*): '. . . So the mine is dark . . .'

MORGAN *stops, turns, sees what she is holding, and stops abruptly. She continues without having noticed him.*

(*Reading.*) '. . . But when I walk through the Tan – something – shaft, in the dark, I can touch with my hands the leaves on the trees, and underneath . . . (*turning over a page*) . . . where the corn is green.'

A pause.

MORGAN: Go on readin'.

MISS MOFFAT *looks up at him, then back at the paper.*

MISS MOFFAT (*reading*): '... There is a wind in the shaft, not carbon monoxide they talk about, it smell like the sea, only like as if the sea had fresh flowers lying about ... and that is my holiday.'

A pause. She looks at the front of the book.

Are you Morgan Evans?

MORGAN: Yes, miss.

MISS MOFFAT: Did you write this?

MORGAN (*after hesitation, sullenly*): No, Miss.

MISS MOFFAT: But it's in your book.

MORGAN: Yes, Miss.

MISS MOFFAT: Then who wrote it?

MORGAN: I dunno, Miss.

> MISS MOFFAT *nods to* MISS RONBERRY, *who patters discreetly into the study.* MORGAN *makes for the garden.*

MISS MOFFAT: Did you write this?

> *It is difficult to tell from the crisp severity of her manner that she is expressing a growing inward excitement.* MORGAN *stops and looks at her, distrustfully.*

MORGAN: I dunno, Miss. . . . (*After hesitating, bursting out.*) What iss the matter with it?

MISS MOFFAT: Sit down.

> *He stares at her, looks uncertainly towards the garden door, and moves towards the bench.*

And take your cap off.

> *He stares at her again, on the brink of revolt, then doffs his cap and sits on the bench.*

Spelling's deplorable, of course. 'Mine' with two 'n's', and 'leaves' l, e, f, s.

MORGAN (*interested, against his will*): What wass it by rights?

MISS MOFFAT: A 'v', to start with.

MORGAN: I never 'eard o' no 'v's', Miss.

MISS MOFFAT: Don't call me Miss.

MORGAN: Are you not a Miss?

MISS MOFFAT: Yes I am, but it is not polite.

MORGAN (*uninterested*): Oh.

MISS MOFFAT: You say 'Yes, Miss Moffat', or 'No, Miss Moffat'. M, o, double f, a, t.

MORGAN (*after a pause*): No 'v's'?

MISS MOFFAT: No 'v's'. Where do you live?

MORGAN: Under the ground, Miss.

MISS MOFFAT: I mean your home.

MORGAN: Llyn-y-Mwyn, Miss . . . Moffat. Four miles from 'ere.

MISS MOFFAT: How big is it?

MORGAN: Four 'ouses and a beer-'ouse.

MISS MOFFAT: Have you any hobbies?

MORGAN: Oh yes.

MISS MOFFAT: What?

MORGAN: Rum.

MISS MOFFAT: Rum?

> *He takes his bottle from his pocket, holds it up, and puts it back.*

Do you live with your parents?

MORGAN: No, by me own self. Me mother iss dead, and me father and me four big brothers wass in the Big Shaft Accident when I wass ten.

MISS MOFFAT: Killed?

MORGAN: Oh yes, everybody wass.

MISS MOFFAT: What sort of man was your father?

MORGAN: 'E was a mongrel.

MISS MOFFAT: A what?

MORGAN: 'E had a dash of English. He learned it to me.

MISS MOFFAT: D'you go to chapel?

MORGAN: No thank you.

Miss Moffat: Who taught you to read and write?

Morgan: Tott?

Miss Moffat: Taught. The verb 'to teach'.

Morgan: Oh, teached.

Miss Moffat: Who taught you?

Morgan: I did.

Miss Moffat: Why?

Morgan: I dunno.

Miss Moffat: What books have you read?

Morgan: Books? A bit of the Bible and a book that a feller from the Plas kitchen nab for me.

Miss Moffat: What was it?

Morgan: *The Ladies' Companion.*

> *A pause. She rises, and walks thoughtfully up towards her desk, studying him. He sits uncomfortably, twirling his cap between grimy fingers.*

(*Rising, at last, making to don his cap.*) Can I go now, pliss——

Miss Moffat (*suddenly, decisively*): No.

> *He sits, taken aback. She walks round the bench and stands near the garden door, facing him.*

Miss Moffat: Do you want to learn any more?

Morgan: No thank you.

Miss Moffat: Why not?

Morgan: The other men would have a good laugh.

Miss Moffat: I see.

> *A pause. She crosses slowly to the sofa, turns, and faces him again.*

Have you ever written anything before this exercise?

Morgan: No.

Miss Moffat: Why not?

Morgan: Nobody never ask me to. (*After a pause,*

truculently, feeling her eyes on him.) What iss the matter with it?

MISS MOFFAT (*sitting, looking thoughtfully at the book*): Nothing's the matter with it. Whether it means anything is too early for me to say, but it shows exceptional talent for a boy in your circumstances.

MORGAN (*after blinking and hesitating*): Terrible long words, Miss Moffat.

MISS MOFFAT: This shows that you are very clever.

A pause. He looks up slowly, not sure if he has heard aright, looks at her searchingly, then away again. His mind is working, uncertainly, but swiftly.

MORGAN: Oh.

MISS MOFFAT: Have you ever been told that before?

MORGAN: It iss news to me.

MISS MOFFAT: What effect does the news have on you?

MORGAN: It iss a bit sudden. (*After a pause.*) It makes me that I—— (*Hesitating, then plunging.*) I want to get more clever still. (*Looking slowly, wonderingly round the room.*) I want to know what iss – behind of all them books. . . .

MISS MOFFAT (*after studying him a moment, calling suddenly*): Miss Ronberry! . . . (*To him.*) Can you come tomorrow?

MORGAN (*taken by surprise*): Tomorrow – no – I am workin' on the six till four shift——

MISS MOFFAT: Then can you be here at five?

MORGAN: Five – no, not before seven, Miss – six miles to walk——

MISS MOFFAT: Oh yes, of course – seven then. In the meantime I'll correct this for spelling and grammar.

MORGAN (*staring at her, fascinated, after a pause*): Yes, Miss Moffat.

She walks briskly towards the study. He has not moved.
She turns and looks at him.

MISS MOFFAT: That will be all. Good night.

MORGAN (*after a pause*): Good night, Miss Moffat.

He goes towards the front door, putting on his cap.

MISS MOFFAT: Are you the one I spanked?

He turns at the door, looks at her, blinks, and goes.
(*Calling, excitedly.*) Miss Ronberry! Mr Jones!

MISS RONBERRY runs in from the study.

MISS RONBERRY: Yes?

MISS MOFFAT: I have been a deuce of a fool. It doesn't matter about the barn; we are going to start the school, in a small way at first, in this room. . . . And I am going to get those youngsters out of that mine if I have to black my face and go down and fetch them myself! Get Jonesy before he posts those letters, and tell those others I'll be ready for them in five minutes. We are going on with the school!

MISS RONBERRY, who has punctuated this speech with a series of nods, scampers into the study, rather dazed. Her voice is heard, calling: 'We are going on with the school!'

The door shuts behind her.

MISS MOFFAT looks down at the exercise-book she is still carrying.

MISS MOFFAT (*reading*): '. . . and when I walk – in the dark . . . I can touch with my hands . . . where the corn is green . . .'

The fitful joyous clang of the school bell above.
She looks up, excited, listening.

CURTAIN

ACT II

SCENE I

An early evening in August, two years later; the sun is still bright.

The room is now a complete jumble of living-room and school-room, and there is every sign of cheerful over-crowding. The table in the window recess is replaced by two school-desks; the table and its small chair are pushed behind the sofa; the spinning-wheel has been removed; a school-desk stands isolated between the big open-top desk and the sofa; between the sofa and the bay window, two rows of four school-desks each, squeezed together and facing the audience at an angle. Charts, maps, an alphabet list and a slate with writing on it, are pinned up higgledy-piggledy over all the books; a large world globe on the shelf; hat-pegs have been fixed irregularly on the stair-banisters. Books over-flow everywhere, all over the dresser especially, in place of plates; the hat-pegs are loaded with caps and hats; MISS MOFFAT'S hat is still perched on the knob at the foot of the stairs; her cloak hangs on a hook on the back of the front door; an easel and blackboard lie against the sofa, with 'Constantinople is the capital of Turkey' written across in MISS RONBERRY'S tremulous handwriting; stuffed fish in a glass case on top of a book-case. The lamp on the table has been removed. Potted plants on the window-sills.

Before the curtain rises, voices are heard singing, in harmony, in Welsh, 'Bugeilio'r Gwenyth Gwyn': children, shrill, sweet and self-confident, reinforced by harmony from older boys and parents, especially SARAH.

The room seems full of people; MISS RONBERRY *stands perched on the tiny stool between the sofa and the foot of the stairs, her back to the audience, conducting stiffly with a ruler;* MR JONES *is crouched in the desk-chair, correcting exercises at the open desk.* SARAH, *two older peasant women in shawls, and three older men in their shabby best stand crowded behind the eight desks and in the window recess. In the front row of desks sit* ROBBART, IDWAL, *a little girl, and* GLYN THOMAS; *in the second sit another little boy, another little girl,* BESSIE, *and* WILL HUGHES. *In another desk pushed provisionally next the front row sits* JOHN OWEN, *and in the other isolated one sits* OLD TOM, *an elderly, distinguished-looking, grey-bearded peasant, his cap and stick before him, carried away by the music.*

BESSIE *is silent, bored, and prettier than ever, though still dressed as a sober little schoolgirl. The boys we saw before as miners are clean and almost spruce; the parents follow every movement of* MISS RONBERRY'S *with avid curiosity. The pupils have slates and slate-pencils in front of them.*

The song is sung through to the end.

MISS RONBERRY: Now that was quite better. Full of splendid feeling, and nice and precise as well. Have you all got my English translation?

THE PUPILS: Yes, Miss Ronberry.

MISS RONBERRY: Are you all quite sure of the meaning of 'Thou lovedest him, fair maid, that doth not love thee back'?

THE PUPILS (*as she climbs down from her stool*): Yes, Miss Ronberry.

OLD TOM (*singing stentoriously, in broken English*):
. . . 'That doth not luff thee . . . ba-a-ck!'

MISS RONBERRY: Capital, Mr Tom.

She takes a small handbell from a book beneath the stairs, rings it vigorously, and hangs it up again; nobody moves.

Home sweet home, children! . . . (*Gaily, as they all study her like owls.*) Boys and girls, come out to play!

IDWAL: Please, Miss Ronberry, can we have some more?

MISS RONBERRY: Well, just the tiniest lesson. (*Climbing on to her stool again.*) We must keep to the curriculum. Now what would you like?

IDWAL: Please, Miss Ronberry, how do you spell it?

MISS RONBERRY: What, dear?

OLD TOM: Curriculum!

MISS RONBERRY: What would you like? The rivers of Europe or King Alfred and the cakes?

OLD TOM (*ecstatically*): Multiplication table!

MISS RONBERRY: Twice six are twelve!

THE PUPILS: Twice seven are fourteen – twice eight are sixteen——

They continue up to 'Twice twelve are twenty-four', and stop.

OLD TOM: Twice thirteen are twenty-six!

MISS RONBERRY: Capital – school dismiss!

The children and grown-ups bustle and chatter. One or two scribble on their slates; another rubs out what he has written; others run over for hats and coats.

IDWAL (*after looking out of the open garden door, calling to the others*): Dyma'r fistress!

The whole room, except BESSIE, who remains seated, stand silent and respectful while MISS MOFFAT walks in

*from the garden. She is more alert and business-like than
ever, carries a tiny portable desk under one arm, and is
studying an exercise book. She nods pleasantly to the room,
goes upstairs and into her bedroom; as she sets foot on the
stairs the hubbub starts again abruptly, and the crowd
saunter or hurry chattily through the front door; during this*
ROBBART *takes the blackboard and easel, leans them
against the settle and puts away the stool, while* JOHN
OWEN *shuts the garden door and pushes his desk into the
corner near the grandfather's clock. The crowd finally trickle
out, shepherded by* MISS RONBERRY, *who shuts the door
after them. Besides* BESSIE, *there are left* OLD TOM,
standing immovable next to his desk, studying MISS
RONBERRY *as if she were a book, and* IDWAL, *who hovers
eagerly on the other side.*

   *The overlapping crowd dialogue in this scene could be
allotted roughly from the following:*

1. Be'di'r gloch, Merry?
   Chwarter i bump.

2. What iss the next thing in the multiplication?
   Wn i ddim yn wyr – gofyn iddi——

3. Why issn't there any geography now?
   Friday geography, Thursday today——
   Pnawn dydd iau, te, hanner awr wedi tri——

4. Mi ddylaswn fod yn pobi heddyw——
   A dwidi gadal y cig yn y popdy——
   Mi fydd eich cegin chi ar dan, Mrs Pugh——

5. IDWAL: 'Nhad, gai fynd i chwara yn nghae John
      Davies——

OLDER MAN (*answering him*): Ddim heddyw – dwisho
    ti gartre——

6. Yfory d'wi am drio sgwennu llythyr——
    Os gynnachi steel-pen golew?
    Mae'na gymaint o flots!
    Dwi wedi sgwennu llythyr at fy nain, wni ddim be
        ddidi'thi . . . Welsochi 'rioed eiriau fel ene?

7. Fedri'thi ddim canu fel Cymraes, digon siwr——
    Mae'r hen ddyn am ofyn rwbeth iddi eto – dry-
        chwch arno——
    Mi gollith'o ei Gymraeg cyn bo hir——

8. Idwal, what you looking so sorry – always wanting
    to know something——

9. Mae genni just ddigon o amser i gyrraedd at y
        llyn——
    Mae'r dŵr yn rhy oer i ymdrochi——
    Nag ydi – mae'r haul wedi bod yn rhy boeth
        heddyw——

10. Neidi ofyn i Morgan ddwad——
    Feder o ddim——
    Mae o'n gweithio'n rhy galed——

MISS RONBERRY *shuts the door on the crowd, with a
sigh of relief, and finds herself between* OLD TOM *and*
IDWAL.

IDWAL: Miss Ronberry, please, what is four times
fourteen?

MISS RONBERRY: Thank you so much for the flowers,
Idwal, dear.

IDWAL: Yes, Miss Ronberry.

He follows the others, calling after them by name.

MISS RONBERRY (*nervously*): Is there anything *you* would like to know, Mr Tom?

OLD TOM: Where iss Shakespeare?

MISS RONBERRY: Where? . . . Shakespeare, Mr Tom, was a very great writer.

OLD TOM: Writer? Like the Beibl?

MISS RONBERRY: Like the Bible.

OLD TOM (*looking at her doubtfully*): Dear me, and me thinkin' the man was a place. (*Following the others, muttering sadly.*) If I iss been born fifty years later, I iss been top of the class. . . .

MISS RONBERRY (*shutting the front door after him*): Oh dear. . . . (*Tidying the desks.*) Miss Moffat has been doing grammar with Form Two under the pear tree for an hour, she must be dead. . . . (*To* BESSIE, *who is climbing over the desks.*) Why did you not get up when she crossed?

BESSIE: My foot went to sleep.

Her manner is more impudent than when we last saw her.

MISS RONBERRY (*coming down to the sofa*): That, dear, is a naughty fib.

BESSIE (*subsiding into* OLD TOM'S *desk*): If you want to know, Miss Ronberry, I feel quite faint sometimes, as if my heart'd stopped and the world was coming to an end.

MISS MOFFAT *comes downstairs, still carrying her portable desk, and studying her exercise-book.*

MISS RONBERRY (*with guileless solicitude*): Bessie dear, how *horrid*!

MR JONES: It may be in the nature of a premonition.

MISS RONBERRY: A what?

She perches on the edge of a desk in the recess and tries to get ink off her knuckles with pumice-stone. MISS MOFFAT

274

lays her portable desk on the table, and paces slowly towards the front door, studying her exercise-book.

MR JONES: I had a premonition once. Like a wave of the ocean breakin' on a sea-shell. Something had said to me that morning: 'Walk, and think, and keep off the food, for thirteen hours.' So I ordered my supper, and I went. Towards the end of the day, I was sittin' on a stile in a cloak of meditation; and a voice roared at me: 'John Goronwy Jones, tomorrow morning is the end of the world!'

MISS MOFFAT: And was it?

MR JONES (*sadly*): It was eight years ago. It was a splendid experience.

He goes back to his correcting.

MISS MOFFAT: Which proves how much the gift of prophecy can owe to an empty stomach. . . . Anybody seen a Greek book? (*Picking up a tiny volume from under a pile of papers on the desk.*) Here it is. . . .

MISS RONBERRY: Greek, Miss Moffat?

MISS MOFFAT: Morgan Evans is starting Greek this month.

MISS RONBERRY: No! I didn't know you knew Greek?

MISS MOFFAT (*hurrying upstairs*): I don't; I've just got to keep one day ahead of him and trust to luck.

She disappears into her bedroom.

MISS RONBERRY: To think that two years ago he hardly knew English!

BESSIE: Stuck-up teacher's pet.

MISS RONBERRY: You must not think that, dear, Miss Moffat says he is clever.

BESSIE: He always looks right through me, so I don't know, I'm sure. Stuck-up teacher's pet. . . . I got some scent on my hands, Mr Jones, like to smell them?

MR JONES (*timidly*): No, thank you, Bessie, I can smell them from here, thank you.

BESSIE (*sniffing her hands, softly*): Ooh, it's lovely. . . .

MISS RONBERRY: She has some wonderful plans for him – I can tell by her manner. *I* think she is trying to send him to one of those Church schools to be a curate. Would not that be exciting?

BESSIE (*resting her head on her hands, indolently*): *I* think she's ridin' for a fall.

MISS RONBERRY: Bessie! Why?

BESSIE: All this orderin' 'im about. I've got eyes in my head, if she hasn't, and he's gettin' sick of it. *I* think a lady ought to be dainty. She's no idea.

> MISS MOFFAT *appears at the top of the stairs, wiping her hands with a towel.*

MISS MOFFAT: Evans!

> *A pause.* MORGAN *comes in from the study. He is now seventeen. He is dressed in a shabby country suit, and is at the moment the submissive schoolboy, very different from the first act. He carries a sheet of writing and a pen.* MISS MOFFAT'S *attitude to him seems purely impersonal. The others watch them.*

MISS MOFFAT: Finished?

MORGAN: Yes, Miss Moffat.

MISS MOFFAT: How many pages?

MORGAN: Nine.

MISS MOFFAT: Three too many. Boil down to six. Have you got those lines of Voltaire?

MORGAN (*showing the paper*): Yes, Miss Moffat.

MISS MOFFAT: It's just five – have your walk now, good and brisk . . . (*taking his cap from a peg and tossing it to him*) . . . here.

MORGAN (*starting for the front door, putting his pen behind his ear*): Yes, Miss Moffat.

MISS MOFFAT: But kill two birds and get the Voltaire by heart. If you can ever argue a point like that, you'll do. Back in twenty minutes – and take your pen from behind your ear.

> *She disappears into her bedroom. Her manner is too matter of fact to be unkind, but* MORGAN *is not taking it well. He throws his pen on to* BESSIE'S *desk; he has stopped close to her, and catches her eye.*

BESSIE: Now turn a somersault and beg.

> *He looks at her with contempt. She returns his stare brazenly; he is unwillingly attracted to her. She turns to see if the others are noticing.* MISS RONBERRY *is busy with her pumice-stone in the window recess and* MR JONES *is engrossed in his work.* BESSIE *looks away from them all, suddenly soft and mysterious.*

BESSIE: Can you smell scent?

MORGAN (*after a pause*): Yes.

BESSIE (*dreamily*): Nice, isn't it?

MORGAN: I don't know, I never come across scent before. (*Correcting himself unwillingly.*) I did never come across . . . scent before. . . .

BESSIE: Bright, aren't you? Don't you ever get tired of lessons?

> *She begins to sing, softly, at him. He goes to the front door, turns, arrested by her singing, then goes, banging the door. She flings down her slate with annoyance.*

BESSIE (*darkly*): There we go. And my mummy ought to be back soon, and then we'll know somethin'.

MR JONES: What is the matter? Where has she gone?

BESSIE: One of her prayer meetings. Twenty miles to shake a tambourine in the open air, I think it's wicked.

... She ought to be just in time, and then we'll know.

MR JONES: Know what?

BESSIE: About that horrid Morgan Evans. It's been lessons every night with teacher, hasn't it, since we left the mine? And long walks in between, to blow the cobwebs away? But the last week or two we've been breaking our journey, so we've heard.

MR JONES: How do you mean?

BESSIE (*triumphantly*): A glass of rum next door at the Gwesmor Arms and then another, and then another!

MR JONES (*perturbed*): Oh. . . . Whoever told you that?

BESSIE: A little bird. (*As he crosses and sits at the table.*) And if my mummy's sciatica's better she's going to jump up and look over the frosty part and then we'll *know*.

> MRS WATTY *hurries in through the front door, in high spirits. She wears an ill-fitting Militant Righteousness Corps uniform, and carries an umbrella and a brown-paper parcel.*

MRS WATTY: Guess what's 'appened to me!

BESSIE: What?

MRS WATTY: I'm a Sergeant-Major!

> MISS MOFFAT *has come out on to the landing; her hair is down and she is brushing it.*

MISS MOFFAT: Watty, you're not!

MRS WATTY: Oh, ma'am, I didn't see you——

MISS MOFFAT: Tell me more!

MRS WATTY: You remember Sergeant-Major 'Opkins desertin' in Cardiff and marryin' a sailor?

MISS MOFFAT: Yes.

MRS WATTY: Well, last week, not two months after she give up the Corpse, she was dead!

MISS MOFFAT: And you've stepped into her shoes?

MRS WATTY: They're a bit on the big side; but I can

put a bit of paper in. The uniform fits lovely, though. (*Moving towards the kitchen.*) I'll get you a cup o' tea and an egg, ma'am, you never 'ad that cold meat, ma'am, I'll be bound?

MISS MOFFAT: Folk eat too much anyway.

She goes back into her bedroom.

BESSIE: Did you jump?

MRS WATTY (*coming back into the room*): Just caught 'im. (*To* MR JONES, *sorrowfully.*) 'Avin' a good swig, sir. . . . (*To* BESSIE.) Don't you dare tell '*er*, you little dollymop, or I'll rattle your bones——

MISS MOFFAT *reappears and comes downstairs, finishing doing up her hair, her little book between her teeth.*

MISS MOFFAT: Was it a nice service, Watty?

MISS RONBERRY *walks round the desks and begins to take an interest.*

MRS WATTY: Beautiful, ma'am. They said they 'oped the late Sergeant-Major was gone where we all want to go, but with 'er having deserted they couldn't be sure. Then we saved three sinners. (*Prodding* MR JONES *with her umbrella.*) *You* ought to been there. . . . And the collection! (*Going.*) I 'adn't seed so much oof since the Great Liverpool Exhibition.

MISS RONBERRY: But they didn't make a collection at the Liverpool Exhibition, did they?

MRS WATTY: No, but I did.

She goes into the kitchen. MR JONES *erects the board on its easel next to the stairs, takes an old duster which is trailing from his pocket, rubs out what is written, takes out a chalk and copies a diagram carefully and indistinguishably on to the board from the paper in his hand.*

MISS MOFFAT *wanders towards the front door, studying.*

279

BESSIE: Please, Miss Moffat, can I have the money for my ticket?

MISS MOFFAT: What ticket?

BESSIE: For Tregarna Fair tomorrow. You said I could go.

MISS MOFFAT: On the contrary, I said you couldn't. Not in school hours.

She studies. BESSIE *sighs and tries to look ill.*

MISS RONBERRY: Are you feeling better, dear?

BESSIE: No, Miss Ronberry. It's all this sittin' down. It's been going on for two years now. I heard tell it ends in everythin' rottin' away.

MISS MOFFAT (*looking up*): What's rotting away?

MISS RONBERRY: Bessie says she's been sitting down for two years.

MISS MOFFAT: She's lucky. My feet feel as if I've been standing for the same length of time. (*Sitting at the open desk and looking at some papers on a book.*) What are these, Ron?

MISS RONBERRY: Two more accounts, I fear.

MISS MOFFAT: Oh yes. The Liddell and Scott and Evans's new suit—— (*seeing the amounts*) tch. . . . (*Cheerfully.*) I shall have to sell out a couple more shares, I expect.

MISS RONBERRY: Oh dear.

MISS MOFFAT: Not at all. (*Unlacing her boots.*) It's easy to squander money, and its easy to hoard it; the most difficult thing in the world is to use it. And if I've learnt to use it, I've *done* something. That's better. . . . (*Rubbing her hands.*) My plans are laid, Ron my dear, my plans are laid! But don't ask me what I'm hatching, because I can't tell you till tomorrow.

MISS RONBERRY: You are wonderful!

MISS MOFFAT: Go to Halifax. I'm enjoying myself.

> MISS RONBERRY *crosses, sits on the sofa, and peers at her papers.* MISS MOFFAT *puts her head in her hands and studies her Greek dictionary.* BESSIE *sighs again, ostentatiously.* MISS MOFFAT *looks at her.*

MISS MOFFAT: Bessie Watty, what is all this dying duck business?

BESSIE: Yes, Miss Moffat.

MISS MOFFAT: Don't 'yes, Miss Moffat' me. Explain yourself.

> *The instinctive hostility between them is strong.*

BESSIE: My mummy said all these lessons is bad for my inside.

MISS MOFFAT (*turning back to her book*): She told me they stop you eating sweets, but perhaps *I* am telling the lies.

BESSIE: Yes, Miss Moffat.

MISS MOFFAT: What's the matter with your inside?

BESSIE: It goes round and round through sittin' down. P'raps what I want is a change.

MISS MOFFAT: What you want is castor oil. (*Muttering.*) 'Adelphos, a brother' . . . There is nothing to prevent you going for walks between lessons. You can go for one now, as far as Sarah Pugh Postman, to see if my new chalks have arrived. (*Looking round at* BESSIE, *as the latter stares before her without moving, her inward rage mounting.*) Quick march.

> *She goes back to her book.* BESSIE *rises, moves sulkily towards the front door, stops, and turns. The only sound is the scratch of* MR JONES's *chalk on the blackboard.*

BESSIE: I'm not goin'.

> *The other three turn and look at her, astounded.*

MISS MOFFAT: What did you say?

BESSIE: I'm not goin'. Everybody's against me . . . I'm goin' to throw myself off of a cliff, an' kill myself. . . . It'll make a nice case in the papers, me in pieces at the bottom of a cliff! . . . I'm goin' mad, mad, and I'm goin' to kill myself, nothin's goin' to stop me – stone dead at the bottom of a cliff – ah – ah – ah——

> *She has gradually warmed up into a fit of hysteria, half natural, half induced; her paroxysm rises to a crescendo of screaming and wringing of hands: spoilt, unfortunately, by* MRS WATTY *striding in from the kitchen with a cupful of cold water which she throws into her daughter's face.* BESSIE *splutters, chokes, and subsides into inarticulate moans of self-pity.*

MRS WATTY (*to* MISS MOFFAT): I made a mess o' your rug, ma'am, but it's worth it. She's got bad blood, this girl, mark my word.

MISS RONBERRY: She'll catch her death!

MRS WATTY: Nothing like cold water, ma'am. I learnt that with her father. 'E was foreign, you know.

> *She goes back into the kitchen.* BESSIE *stands sniffing and gulping.* MISS MOFFAT *studies her with distaste.*

MISS MOFFAT: And how do you feel after that?

BESSIE: I can't remember anything. I'm in a comma.

MISS MOFFAT (*taking her by the arm and pushing her upstairs*): We'll sit on our bed for an hour with the door locked, shall we, and *try* to remember? And next week you go away into service – and see how we like that——

> *She pushes her out of sight into the passage; a door bangs; the noise of a lock turning.*

> MISS MOFFAT *comes downstairs, tucking the key into her petticoat pocket.* MR JONES *turns the blackboard round back to front on its easel.*

I must count her as one of my failures. Fish out of

water, of course. Guttersnipe species – if there is such a fish. She'll be more at home in service. . . . (*Muttering.*) 'Dendron, a tree——'

MISS RONBERRY: I beg your pardon? . . . Oh, Miss Moffat, I am bursting with curiosity – your plans for Morgan Evans . . . is it a curateship?

MISS MOFFAT (*slowly, amused*): No, it isn't a curateship.

> *She laughs happily, walks towards the desk, and takes up an exercise-book.*

MISS RONBERRY: I really don't see anything funny about curates. (*To* MR JONES.) I mean, there is nothing *wrong* with curates, is there?

MR JONES: No, except that they ought to go to chapel.

MISS MOFFAT: Who has been writing in here?

> MRS WATTY *appears at the kitchen door.*

MRS WATTY: Your egg, ma'am!

MISS MOFFAT: 'Bessie Watty has the face of an angel'!

MISS RONBERRY: What an extraordinary——

MISS MOFFAT: But I know the writing——

> *She looks again;* MR JONES *blinks behind his spectacles, takes his hat from a peg, and makes to pass her.*

MISS MOFFAT: John Goronwy Jones, I'm ashamed of you.

MR JONES: I shall see you tomorrow if we are spared.

MISS RONBERRY (*shocked*): Oh!

MR JONES: You all misjudge that little girl. She has the face of a good woman in the melting-pot.

MISS MOFFAT: I've got the face of a good woman too, and well out of the melting-pot, but I don't think I'd ever find it in writing.

> *She goes into the kitchen, chuckling, as* MISS RONBERRY *puts on her hat in a little mirror in front of the study door.*

MRS WATTY: I never thought I'd live to call *you* a dirty old man.

She follows MISS MOFFAT *into the kitchen.* MR JONES *goes out through the front door.* MISS RONBERRY *sighs a little disconsolately into the mirror, tries to look like an angel, fails, and sighs again. The front door opens abruptly and* MORGAN *appears. He is dishevelled, and it is fairly apparent that he has been drinking. His manner is defiant, and he does not remove his cap. The door bangs behind him.*

MISS RONBERRY: Oh, it's you, Morgan.... (*Back at the mirror.*) Miss Moffat is having something to eat.

MORGAN: And I have been having something to drink, so we are quits.

MISS RONBERRY (*looking round at him, sharply, the unpleasant truth dawning on her*): I will tell her that you are back——

MORGAN (*looking away, breathing hard*): I don't want to see no Miss Moffat.

MISS RONBERRY (*bravely*): You mean 'I don't want to see Miss Moffat'. The double negative——

MORGAN: Now don't you start! ... (*Bearing down on her.*) I like the double negative, it says what I want the way I like, and I am *not* goin' to stand *no* interferences from *nobody*! (*Taking his paper from his pocket and kicking it savagely into a corner of the room.*) Voltaire indeed. ...

MISS RONBERRY: Morgan! I've never seen you like this before!

MORGAN: You haven't, have you? (*In a rising torrent of invective, getting more Welsh as it goes on.*) Well, now I come to think of it, I haven't neither, not for two years, and I'm surprised by meself, and shocked by meself! Goin' inside one o' them public houses and puttin' me nice clean boots on that dirty rail, and me dainty lady-fingers on that detestable mucky counter! Pourin' poison rum down me nice clean teeth, and spittin' in a spittoon – what's come over you, Morgan Evans? You come back to your little cage, and if you comb hair and wash hands and get your grammar right and forget you was once the Middle-weight Champion of the Glasynglo Miners, we might give you a nice bit of sewin' to do.... (*Turning back to the front door, muttering.*) Where's that Bessie Watty, sendin' her mother to spy on me, I'll knock her bloody block off....

Miss Ronberry (*outraged*): Morgan Evans, *language*! Don't you dare use an expression like that to me again!

Morgan (*turning back on her*): I got plenty of others, thank you, and they are all comin' out. I am goin' to surprise quite a few——

> He stops short and pulls off his cap as Miss Moffat enters from the kitchen.

Miss Moffat (*pouring milk into a cup from a jug*): Have a good walk, Evans?

Morgan (*controlling himself, avoiding Miss Ronberry's eye*): Yes, Miss Moffat.

Miss Moffat (*sitting on the sofa, drinking*): Can you repeat the Voltaire?

Morgan: Not yet.

Miss Moffat: It's very short.

Morgan: Paper blowed away.

Miss Moffat: Oh. Copy it again, will you, and bring it to me.

Morgan (*muttering*): Yes, Miss Moffat.

> He goes towards the study.

Miss Moffat (*holding out the jug*): Would you like a drink?

> He starts, looks round at her and sees the milk.

285

MORGAN: No thank you.

He goes into the study. MISS MOFFAT *takes her little book again from her pocket and opens it.*

MISS MOFFAT: I hope he's not going to be slow at French. It'll make the Greek so much more difficult——

MISS RONBERRY (*timidly*): You don't think perhaps all this – in his situation – is rather sudden for him? I mean——

MISS MOFFAT: Not for him, my dear. He has the most brilliantly receptive brain I've ever come across. Don't tell him so, but he has.

MISS RONBERRY: I know his *brain* is all right——

MISS MOFFAT (*absently*): I'm very pleased with his progress, on the whole. . . .

A knock at the front door. MISS RONBERRY *looks at her uncertainly, then moves towards the door.* MISS MOFFAT *suddenly remembers something, and stops her.*

Wait a minute! (*Rising, hurrying to the bay window, and peering out towards the front door, and hurrying down again urgently.*) Yes, it is. . . .

MISS RONBERRY: Who?

MISS MOFFAT (*sitting on the sofa and doing up her boots, hastily*): Royalty, the Conservatives and all the Grand Lamas rolled into one. The Squire.

MISS RONBERRY: The Squire! (*In a panic.*) Oh, *my*!

MISS MOFFAT (*lacing*): It is indeed, oh my——

MISS RONBERRY: But he hasn't been here since that dreadful evening——

MISS MOFFAT: I behaved more stupidly that night than I ever have in my life, and that's saying something——

MISS RONBERRY: But why is he here now?

MISS MOFFAT (*placing the milk-jug and cup on the table*): Never you mind. . . . All I can tell you is that it is to do

286

with Morgan Evans, and that it is vital I make the right impression——

MISS RONBERRY (*as* MISS MOFFAT *runs upstairs*): What sort of impression?

MISS MOFFAT: Helpless and clinging, or as near as dammit——

> *She disappears into her room, as there is a second impatient knock at the front door.*

MISS RONBERRY (*timidly*): Come in!

> *The door opens and the* GROOM *appears.*

THE GROOM (*announcing*): The Squire.

> *The* SQUIRE *follows the* GROOM, *who retires and shuts the door.*

THE SQUIRE: Good afternoon.

> *His manner is stiff and careful. He is dressed in a summer lounge suit, and holds his hat in his hand. He looks round the room with cold disapproval.*

MISS RONBERRY: Your hat, Squire——

THE SQUIRE: No, thank you, I'm not staying.

MISS RONBERRY: Oh dear, I do look a sketch. . . .

THE SQUIRE: So this is the seat of learning.

MISS RONBERRY: We are always on the point of a good spring-clean. How dreadful that we have no refreshment to offer you!

THE SQUIRE: Has she given it up, then? . . . You can tell her from me that I am not here to be insulted again.

MISS RONBERRY: Oh, I'm sure you aren't! I mean——

THE SQUIRE (*ruminatively*): She called me an addle-headed nincompoop.

> MISS MOFFAT *comes downstairs, a lace shawl draped over her shoulders. She carries a bowl of flowers.*

MISS MOFFAT: Miss Ronberry, dear, my roses are dying – would you pour out a little water for them, I have such

287

a headache I don't think—— (*Feigning surprise.*) *Squire!*

THE SQUIRE (*as she crosses to him, hand outraised*): You wrote to me. Perhaps you have forgotten.

MISS MOFFAT: How could I forget! I only thought that after the overwrought fashion of my behaviour at our last meeting you must ignore my very nervous invitation—— Miss Ronberry, a chair, dear, for the Squire——

> *Startled,* MISS RONBERRY *looks for a chair, then back at her. Puzzled, and trying not to unbend, the* SQUIRE *stands examining* MISS MOFFAT.

THE SQUIRE: I have not a great deal of time to spare, I fear.

MISS MOFFAT (*sitting on the lower end of the sofa*): Of course you haven't, I was just saying to Miss Ronberry, he's so busy he'll *never* be able to fit it in! Miss Ronberry dear, would you get some water for them?

> *She hands the bowl to* MISS RONBERRY, *who passes the* SQUIRE *and goes into the garden, bewildered.*

Tell me, Squire, how did your prize-giving fare this afternoon?

THE SQUIRE: Rather a bore, y'know.

MISS MOFFAT: I had so hoped to see you judge. I love flowers.

THE SQUIRE: It wasn't flowers. It was cows.

MISS MOFFAT: Oh. It was your speech I wanted to hear, of course; I heard you made such an amusing one at the Croquet.

THE SQUIRE (*breaking into a smile*): Oh, did they tell you about that? Rather a good pun, eh? (*Laughing reminiscently*): Ha ha . . . I – may sit down?

MISS MOFFAT: Do!

THE SQUIRE (*after looking at* BESSIE'S *desk, and finally*

choosing the top end of the sofa): I thought Griffiths the butcher was going to laugh his napper off.

MISS MOFFAT: Indeed. . . . Do you know, Squire, that makes me rather proud?

THE SQUIRE (*stiffening again*): Proud? Why?

MISS MOFFAT (*innocently*): Because he would not have understood a word if his little girls hadn't learnt English at my school.

THE SQUIRE: Oh. Never thought of it like that. . . . (*As she puts her hand to her head.*) Headache?

MISS MOFFAT: Squire, you see before you a tired woman. We live and learn, and I have learnt how right you were that night. I have worked my fingers to the bone battering my head against a stone wall.

THE SQUIRE (*puzzled*): But I heard you were a spiffing success.

MISS MOFFAT: Oh no.

THE SQUIRE (*muttering*): It's fair of you to admit it, I must say.

MISS MOFFAT: You see, in one's womanly enthusiasm one forgets that the qualities vital to success in this sort of venture are completely lacking in one: intelligence, courage and authority. . . the qualities, in short, of a man.

THE SQUIRE: Come, come, you mustn't be too hard on yourself, y'know. After all, you've meant well.

MISS MOFFAT: It's kind of you to say that.

THE SQUIRE: What about this Jones chappie?

MISS MOFFAT: He's a dear creature, but . . . (*soberly*) . . . I have no wish to be fulsome, I mean a man like yourself.

THE SQUIRE: I see.

MISS MOFFAT: One gets into such muddles! You'd never believe!

THE SQUIRE: Well . . . I've never been on your side, but I'm sorry to hear you've come a cropper. When are you giving it up?

MISS MOFFAT (*taken aback*): Oh. . . . That again is difficult; I have all my widow's mite, as it were, in the venture——

> *A knock at the study door.* MORGAN *appears, carrying a paper. He has regained his self-control. He hesitates on seeing there is a visitor, and makes to go back.*

MORGAN: Please excuse me——

MISS MOFFAT (*hastily*): It's all right, Evans. Have you copied it? On my desk, will you?

MORGAN (*bowing, and crossing in front of the sofa*): Excuse me, sir. . . . (*Turning back his head.*) Good afternoon, sir.

THE SQUIRE (*eyeing him curiously as he places the paper on the desk*): Good afternoon, my boy.

MORGAN (*bowing, before crossing him again*): Excuse me, sir. . . . (*Turning at the study door, and bowing again.*) Thank you.

> *He goes.*

THE SQUIRE: Nice well-spoken lad. Relative?

MISS MOFFAT: No. A pupil. He used to be one of your miners.

THE SQUIRE: No!

MISS MOFFAT: I'm glad you thought he was a nice well-spoken boy.

THE SQUIRE (*vaguely*): Yes. . . . One of my miners, interesting. . . .

MISS MOFFAT: Because he is the problem I should like your advice about.

THE SQUIRE: What's he been up to, poaching?

MISS MOFFAT: No.

THE SQUIRE: A bit o' muslin?

MISS MOFFAT (*amused*): No, no. . . . There are none, anyway——

THE SQUIRE (*suddenly shrewd*): What about the little Cockney filly?

MISS MOFFAT: Bessie Watty? Oh no, I assure you—— (*amused*) – she's a schoolgirl——

THE SQUIRE: I dunno, all these young people growing up together, y'know – eh?

MISS MOFFAT: I think it's good for them. . . . No, there's nothing of that sort—— (*getting back to the point*) – but he's a problem just the same. And like a true woman I have to scream for help to a man. To you.

THE SQUIRE (*after a pause, completely won*): Scream away, dear lady, scream away!

MISS MOFFAT (*earnestly*): Well, he's . . . clever.

THE SQUIRE: Oh, is he? Good at figures, and all that? Because if he is, there's no reason why I shouldn't put him in my Mine Office, as junior office boy. (*Munificently.*) What d'ye think of that?

MISS MOFFAT: No. Figures aren't his strong point.

THE SQUIRE: Thought you said he was clever.

MISS MOFFAT: To begin with, he can write.

THE SQUIRE: Oh. Well?

MISS MOFFAT: Very well.

THE SQUIRE: Then he could make fair copies. Eh?

MISS MOFFAT (*patiently*): No. (*Choosing her words carefully*): This boy . . . is quite out of the ordinary.

THE SQUIRE: Sure?

MISS MOFFAT (*with great earnestness*): As sure as one of your miners would be, cutting through coal and striking a diamond without a flaw. He was born with very exceptional gifts. They must be – they ought to be given every chance.

291

THE SQUIRE: You mean he might turn into a literary bloke?

MISS MOFFAT: He might, yes.

THE SQUIRE: I'm blowed! How d'ye know?

MISS MOFFAT: By his work. It's very good.

THE SQUIRE: How d'ye know it's good?

MISS MOFFAT: How does one know Shakespeare's good?

THE SQUIRE: Shakespeare? What's he got to do with it?

MISS MOFFAT: He was a literary bloke.

THE SQUIRE: Ye-es. *He* was good, of course.

MISS MOFFAT: But how do you *know* he was?

THE SQUIRE (*after thought*): I've heard he was.

MISS MOFFAT: This little tenant of yours, Squire, has it in him to bring great credit to you.

THE SQUIRE: Yes, he *is* a tenant of mine, isn't he?

MISS MOFFAT: Imagine if you could say that you had known – well, say Lord Tennyson, as a boy on your estate!

THE SQUIRE: Rather a lark, what? (*Sobering.*) Though it's a bit different, y'know, Tennyson was at Cambridge. My old college.

MISS MOFFAT (*damped*): Oh . . . (*Rising and crossing towards her desk.*) Poor Evans. What a pity he was not born at the beginning of the eighteenth century!

THE SQUIRE (*pondering*): Beginning of the eighteenth century – now when was that . . .

MISS MOFFAT (*wandering to the bookshelves between the side window and the garden door*): He would have had a protector.

THE SQUIRE: What against?

MISS MOFFAT: A patron. (*Taking down two books and coming back to him.*) Pope, you recall, dedicated the famous

292

'Essay on Man' to his protector. (*Showing him the fly-leaf of the first book.*)

THE SQUIRE (*reading*): 'To H. St John Lord Boling-broke.' Mmm . . . I *have* heard of it, now I remember——

MISS MOFFAT: Isn't it wonderful to think that that inscription is handed down to posterity? (*Reading from the other book.*) 'To the Right Honourable Earl of South-ampton. . . . Your Honour's in all duty, William Shake-speare.'

THE SQUIRE: Oh.

MISS MOFFAT: I often think of the pride that surged in the Earl's bosom when his encouragement gave birth to the masterpiece of a poor and humble writer!

THE SQUIRE: Funny, I never thought of Shakespeare being poor, somehow.

MISS MOFFAT: Some say his father was a butcher. The Earl realised he had genius, and fostered it.

THE SQUIRE: Mmm!

> *She takes the books and places them on the table, studying him anxiously behind his back.*

(*Following her reasoning with surprising quickness.*) If this boy really is clever, it seems a pity for *me* not to do something about it, doesn't it?

MISS MOFFAT (*eagerly*): A great pity. (*Sitting beside him, on his right this time, and mustering for the offensive.*) And I can tell you exactly how you can do something about it.

THE SQUIRE: How?

MISS MOFFAT: There's a scholarship going.

THE SQUIRE: Scholarship? Where?

MISS MOFFAT: To Oxford.

THE SQUIRE (*staggered*): Oxford?

MISS MOFFAT (*attacking hard*): A scholarship to Trinity College, Oxford, open to boys of secondary education in the British Isles. My school hardly comes under the heading of secondary education, and I wrote to your brother at Magdalen, he pulled some strings for me, and they have agreed to make a special case of this boy, on one condition. That you vouch for him. Will you?

THE SQUIRE: My dear lady, you take the cake. . . . Can't he be just as clever at home?

MISS MOFFAT: No, he can't. For the sort of future he ought to have, he must have polish – he has everything else. The background of a university would be invaluable to him. . . . Will you?

The SQUIRE *blinks and rises. He is almost thinking.*

THE SQUIRE: Well, the 'Varsity, y'know, hang it all . . . mind you, he'll never get it.

MISS MOFFAT: I know, but he *must* have the chance——

THE SQUIRE: Still, y'know, even the mere prospect of one o' my miners——

MISS MOFFAT (*desperately*): Think of Shakespeare!

THE SQUIRE (*after a pause*): All serene. (*As she rises.*) I'll drop a line to Henry next week. Rather a lark, what? I must be off——

MISS MOFFAT: I should be most obliged if the letter could be posted tomorrow. Would you like me to draft out a recommendation and send it over to the Hall? You must be so busy with the estate——

THE SQUIRE: I am rather. Polka supper tomorrow night. . . . Yes, do do that. (*Moving towards the front door.*) Good-bye, dear lady!

MISS MOFFAT (*seeing him out*): Thank you so very much, Squire——

THE SQUIRE: Happier conditions, and all that! Glad you've come to your senses!

MISS MOFFAT: Thank you so very much, Squire!

THE SQUIRE: Not at all, I'm all for giving a writer-fellow a helping hand. Tell my brother that, if you like. . . . (*At the front door.*) Y'know, I can never get over Henry bein' a Don, though I always said he'd end up as something funny. . . .

> *He goes, chuckling. She shuts the door after him and walks down, relieved and excited.* MISS RONBERRY *hurries in from the garden, carrying the bowl of roses.*

MISS RONBERRY: Well?

MISS MOFFAT: That man is so stupid it sits on him like a halo.

MISS RONBERRY (*putting the bowl down on the desk, hurriedly*): What happened?

MISS MOFFAT: In ten minutes I have given the Squire the impression that he spends his whole time fostering genius in the illiterate.

MISS RONBERRY: But how?

MISS MOFFAT: Soft soap and curtseying; with my brain, my heart and my soul. I've beaten you at your own game, my dear – at my age and with my looks, I flirted with him! And he is going to write to Oxford; at least, I am going to write to Oxford for him. Hurray, hip, hip, hip, hip, hurray!

MISS RONBERRY: Oxford?

MISS MOFFAT (*shaking her, happily*): I am entering my little pit-pony for a scholarship to Oxford, child, Oxford University!

MISS RONBERRY (*incredulous*): But they don't have miners at Oxford University!

MISS MOFFAT: Well, they're going to. (*Haranguing her.*) The lad is on this earth for eighty years at the most out of a few millions, let the proud silly ones grovel and be useful for a change, so he can step up on their backs

L   295

to something better! I was bursting to say that to the Lord of the Manor, so I must vent it on you. . . . Thank you for your shawl, my dear – (*wrapping it round the helpless* MISS RONBERRY *and piloting her to the front door*) – and now you've served your purpose, you can go home – but you'd better watch out, I may race you to the altar yet——

> *She shuts the front door on her, and comes back into the room. She looks round, with a sigh of pleasure, then calls:*

Evans!

> *She pulls the table round the sofa to the centre of the room, takes the milk-jug and cup from the table to the desk, pulls the desk-chair up to the table, and sits at it, studying the exercise-book she has been correcting earlier. She holds her eyes a moment; it is obvious that she could be tired if she allowed herself to be.*

> MORGAN *comes in from the study, carrying a pen, books and papers; his mantle of reserve has descended on him again; his inward rebellion is only to be guessed at from his eyes, which she does not see. He pulls the table-chair up to the table and sits opposite her, half behind the sofa; it is apparent that this is a daily procedure at this hour. He makes fitful notes of her ensuing comments. The daylight begins to wane.*

Is this your essay on the Wealth of Nations?

MORGAN: Yes.

MISS MOFFAT (*reading briskly*): Say so and underline it. Nothing irritates examiners more than that sort of vagueness.

> *She crosses out three lines with a flourish, reads further, then hands him the exercise-book.*

I couldn't work this sentence out.

MORGAN (*reading*): 'The eighteenth century was a

296

cauldron. Vice and elegance boiled to a simmer until the kitchen of society reeked fulminously, and the smell percolated to the marble halls above.'

MISS MOFFAT (*as he hands the book back to her*): D'ye know what that means?

MORGAN: Yes, Miss Moffat.

MISS MOFFAT: Because I don't. Clarify, my boy, clarify, and leave the rest to Mrs Henry Wood. . . . 'Water' with two t's . . . (*scoring heavily*) . . . that's a bad lapse. . . . (*After reading quickly to herself while he broods.*) The Adam Smith sentence was good. Original, and clear as well. (*Writing.*) Seven out of ten, not bad but not good – you *must* avoid long words until you know exactly what they mean. Otherwise domino. . . . (*Handing the essay back to him.*) Your reading?

MORGAN (*concentrating with an effort*): Burke 'Cause of the Present Discontents'.

MISS MOFFAT: Style?

MORGAN: His style appears to me . . . as if there was too much of it.

MISS MOFFAT (*mechanically*): His style struck me as florid.

MORGAN (*repeating*): 'His style struck me as florid.'

MISS MOFFAT: Again.

MORGAN (*mumbling*): 'His style struck me as florid.'

MISS MOFFAT: Subject matter?

MORGAN: A sound argument, falsified by – by the high colour of the sentiments.

MISS MOFFAT: Mmmm. 'The high colour of the sentiments' . . . odd but not too odd, good and stylish. . . . For next time. (*Dictating, as* MORGAN *writes.*) Walpole and Sheridan as representatives of their age; and no smelly cauldrons. (*Opening another book.*) By the way, next Tuesday I'm starting you on Greek.

MORGAN (*looking up, feigning interest*): Oh yes?

He writes again.

MISS MOFFAT (*subduing her excitement*): I am going to put you in for a scholarship to Oxford.

A pause. He looks up at her, arrested.

MORGAN: Oxford? Where the lords go?

MISS MOFFAT (*amused*): The same. (*Rising happily, and crossing to the desk with the two books with which she wooed the* SQUIRE.) I've made a simplified alphabet to begin with. It's jolly interesting after Latin. . . .

She searches among her papers. The matter-of-factness with which she is (typically) controlling her excitement over the scholarship seems to gall him more and more; he watches her, bitterly.

Have a look at it by Tuesday, so we can make a good start – oh, and before we go on with the lesson, I've found the nail-file I mentioned——

In his mood, this is the last straw. He flings his pen savagely down on the table.

(*Without noticing, rummaging briskly.*) I'll show you how to use it. I had them both here somewhere——

MORGAN (*quietly*): I shall not need a nail-file in the coal-mine.

MISS MOFFAT (*mechanically, still intent at the desk*): In the what?

MORGAN: I am going back to the coal-mine.

She turns and looks at him. He rises, breathing fast. They look at each other. A pause.

MISS MOFFAT (*perplexed*): I don't understand you. Explain yourself.

MORGAN: I do not want to learn Greek, nor to pronounce any long English words, nor to keep my hands clean.

MISS MOFFAT (*staggered*): What's the matter with you? Why not?

MORGAN: Because ... (*plunging*) ... because I was born in a Welsh hayfield when my mother was helpin' with the harvest – and I always lived in a little house with no stairs only a ladder – and no water – and until my brothers was killed I never sleep except three in a bed. I know that is terrible grammar but it is true.

MISS MOFFAT: What on earth has three in a bed got to do with learning Greek?

MORGAN: It has – a lot! The last two years I have not had no proper talk with English chaps in the mine because I was so busy keepin' this old grammar in its place. Tryin' to better myself ... (*his voice rising*) ... tryin' to better myself, the day and the night! ... You cannot take a nail-file into the 'Gwesmor Arms' public bar!

MISS MOFFAT: My dear boy, file your nails at home! I never heard anything so ridiculous. Besides, you don't go to the Gwesmor Arms!

MORGAN: Yes, I do, I have been there every afternoon for a week, spendin' your pocket-money, and I have been there now, and that is why I can speak my mind!

She looks at him, alarmed and puzzled.

MISS MOFFAT: I had no idea that you felt like this.

MORGAN: Because you are not interested in me.

MISS MOFFAT (*incredulously*): Not interested in you?

MORGAN (*losing control*): How can you be interested in a machine that you put a penny in and if nothing comes out you give it a good shake? 'Evans, write me an essay, Evans, get up and bow, Evans, what is a subjunctive'! My name is Morgan Evans, and all my friends call me

Morgan, and if there is anything gets on the wrong side of me it is callin' me Evans! . . . And do you know what they call me in the village? Ci bach yr ysgol! The school-mistress's little dog. What has it got to do with you if my nails are dirty? Mind your own business!

He bursts into sobs and buries his head in his hands on the end of the sofa.

She turns away from him, instinctively shying from the spectacle of his grief. A pause. She is extremely upset, but tries hard not to show it. She waits for him to recover, and takes a step towards him.

MISS MOFFAT: I never meant you to know this. I have spent money on you – (*as he winces quickly*) – I don't mind that, money ought to be spent. But time is different. Your life has not yet begun, mine is half over. And when you're a middle-aged spinster, some folk say it's pretty near finished. Two years is valuable currency. I have spent two years on you. (*As he raises his head and stares before him, trying not to listen to her.*) Ever since that first day, the main-spring of this school has been your career. Sometimes, in the middle of the night, when I have been desperately tired, I have lain awake, making plans. Large and small. Sensible and silly. Plans for you. And you tell me I have no interest in you. If I say any more I shall start to cry; and I haven't cried since I was younger than you are, and I'd never forgive you for that. (*Walking brusquely to the front door and throwing on her cloak.*) I am going for a walk. I don't like this sort of conversation, please never mention it again. If you want to go on, be at school tomorrow. (*Going.*) If not, don't.

MORGAN (*muttering, fiercely*): I don't want your money, and I don't want your time! . . . I don't want to be thank-ful to no strange woman – for anything!

A pause.

MISS MOFFAT (*shaking her head, helplessly*): I don't understand you. I don't understand you at all.

She goes out by the front door.

*He sits up and folds his arms, with a deep breath; he feels
something in his breast pocket, roots out a little rum bottle;
takes a pull at it, lifts an exercise-book, crashes it viciously
on the table, and relapses into moody thought. The daylight
has faded perceptibly. Without his hearing her,* BESSIE
*comes in from the garden. She has put her hair half up and
wears ear-rings.*

BESSIE: Hello!

*He stares at her coldly, plants the bottle on the table and
stares away again.*

(*She clutches her leg, ostentatiously.*) Caught my knee climb-
in' down the rainpipe, ooh. . . . (*As he takes no notice.*)
P'r'aps I'm invisible. . . .

*She tosses her head, marches into the kitchen, singing
raucously, and bangs the door behind her. Far away, the
sound of singing: men returning from the mine, harmonising
their familiar melody, 'Yr Hufen Melyn'.* MORGAN
*brushes a tear angrily from his cheek, but unhappy thoughts
assail him; his mood is fed by the music. A pause.* BESSIE
*returns from the kitchen. She is suddenly changed, subdued
and almost timid.*

BESSIE: Mum's gone out. (*After a pause, advancing
slowly towards the foot of the stairs.*) Expect she's gone to tell
Mrs Roberts about her meetin'. Though how she
manages with Mrs Roberts knowin' no English an' deaf
as well . . . (*After a pause.*) Talking a lot, aren't I?

MORGAN: Yes.

BESSIE: Well, I'm not deaf.

MORGAN (*looking up at her*): Been spyin'?

BESSIE (*pointing upstairs*): If people lock me in and take the key out of the key-hole, they can't blame me for listenin' at it. (*As he turns away.*) Oo, I think she's wicked.

MORGAN (*stung*): Mind your own business!

BESSIE: I won't. (*Gaining confidence.*) I like to know about everything. I like doin' all the things I like, I like sweets, I don't care if it does make me fat, and I *love* ear-rings. I like to shake my head like a lady. . . .

She stands, hands on hips, transformed from the sullen child into something crafty, mischievous and attractive.

The singing stops. A pause.

It's funny. . . . We never been by ourselves before.

He looks at her. She returns the look. He turns away, disconsolate. A pause. She wanders up towards the bay window, and begins to sing in Welsh, in a voice surprisingly pure and pleasing. The tune is 'Lliw Gwyn Rhosyn yr Haf'. He raises his head and listens, arrested. She leans against one of the desks in the window recess, and looks out towards the setting sun; her voice ends softly on a phrase. A pause. She turns her head and looks at him. She smiles, begins to sing again, more sure of herself, and walks slowly between the desks to his right, where she rests her elbows deliberately on the table; she looks dreamily before her as her voice dies away. He looks sharply round at her. Slowly her head turns towards him; slowly she smiles at him; subtle, and quite self-confident now.

BESSIE: Didn't know I knew Welsh, did you? . . . You like that song, don't you? That's why I learnt it.

MORGAN: You are different when you sing.

BESSIE: Am I? . . . (*Picking the bottle from the table.*) What's this, medicine? (*Taking a gulp, and choking.*) Tastes like rubber. Nice though. . . . (*As he takes it roughly from her, rises, drains the bottle, and puts it back in his pocket.*) You

302

know, you was quite right to put her in her place. Clever chap like you learnin' lessons off a woman!

MORGAN: That's right. . . .

BESSIE (*soft, persuasive*): You don't 'ave to go to Oxford! Clever chap like you!

MORGAN (*in a whisper*): That's right. . . .

> *He turns slowly and looks at her. She crosses behind him and sits on the back of the sofa.*

BESSIE: What a man wants is a bit o' sympathy!

> *He looks at her, his hand on the back of the chair. It is growing faintly darker. She laughs, and begins to sing again; she turns, still singing, looks up at him, and smiles. He pushes away the chair, seizes her with violence, and kisses her passionately. Their arms entwine and the chair crashes to the floor.*

> *Black out. The curtain falls, and rises immediately on*

SCENE II

> *A morning in November, three months later. The room is much as it was; the potted plants have been removed; the daylight is so poor that the lamps are lit.*

> MRS WATTY *is carrying in from the kitchen a small table, new and light, with on it blotter, ink, pens, pencil, a duster and a cup of tea.* MISS RONBERRY *is pushing the arm-chair in from the study past the sofa into its old place, next to the isolated desk.*

MRS WATTY (*singing*): I'm saved I am, I'm saved I am. . . .

> *She puts down the small table, pushes the desk-chair back against the desk, drags the large table and its chair to*

its old place behind the sofa, then sets the small table well
downstage, between the arm-chair and the sofa. She fetches
a loose seat attached to one of the desks and places it below
the small table, its back to the audience.

(*During this.*) What would the arm-chair be for, miss?

MISS RONBERRY: The Squire's coming. He's invigilating.

MRS WATTY: *What* was that, please, miss?

MISS RONBERRY (*taking a parcel tied with string from a*
drawer in the desk, and unpacking papers from it): The Oxford
people have appointed him and Miss Moffat to watch
Morgan Evans while he is sitting the scholarship, so that
he cannot cheat.

MRS WATTY: What a shame.... (*Still arranging furniture*).
You'd never think it was nearly nine in the morning,
would you?

MISS RONBERRY (*peering out of the side window*): It's
stopped snowing.

MRS WATTY: Only just. The milkman said the road was
blocked down by the bridge.

MISS RONBERRY: How terrible if Morgan couldn't get
through!

MRS WATTY: Countin' sheep all night, I was. She didn't
'ave a wink neither. (*Picking up two envelopes from the floor,*
near the front door.) I could 'ear her thinkin'.

MISS RONBERRY: It is a very important day for her.

MRS WATTY (*handing the envelopes to her*): Looks like that
one's Bessie. Would you mind?

MISS RONBERRY (*opening it*): That means Sarah the Post
got through——

MRS WATTY: She'd come the other way, down the
'ill——

MISS RONBERRY: That's true. . . . (*Reading.*) 'Dear

Mum' – to think I taught her to write – 'Cheltenham is terrible. Can I have a shilling. I do the steps. Madam is terrible. Your obedient girl.'

MRS WATTY (*taking back the letter, as* MISS RONBERRY *glances at the other and tucks it into her belt*): Obedient, I like that. . . . (*Throwing the letter into the waste-paper-basket.*) She's been away three months now, she ought to be gettin' used to it.

MISS RONBERRY (*busy at the desk*): But do you not miss her?

MRS WATTY (*emphatically, dusting the little table*): No! I don't like 'er, you know, never 'ave.

MISS RONBERRY: But Mrs Watty, your own daughter!

MRS WATTY: I know, but I've never been able to take to 'er. First time I saw 'er, I said 'No'. (*Going.*) With 'er dad being foreign, you see.

MISS RONBERRY: But couldn't your husband have taken her abroad to his own family?

MRS WATTY: Oh, my 'usband was quite different. British to the core.

> *She goes into the kitchen.* MISS RONBERRY *blinks after her, and places foolscap paper on the little table.* MISS MOFFAT *comes slowly downstairs. She is alert, but more subdued than the audience has yet seen her.* MISS RON-BERRY *takes up the cup of tea, and watches her, appre-hensively, as she crosses her.*

MISS MOFFAT: It's stopped snowing.

MISS RONBERRY (*sitting on the sofa, and sipping*): It's a white world, as they say. . . . (*Watching* MISS MOFFAT *as she looks out of the side window.*) Do you think he will get through the snow?

MISS MOFFAT: This morning he would get through anything.

MISS RONBERRY: I am so glad. I thought perhaps he – he had not been working satisfactorily——

MISS MOFFAT: At ten o'clock last night I had to take his books away from him.

MISS RONBERRY: I *am* glad.

MISS MOFFAT (*still looking out*): I hope he won't get wet – he must not be upset in any way. . . . (*Playing nervously with the string* MISS RONBERRY *has left on the desk.*) What made you think he wasn't working well?

MISS RONBERRY (*flustered*): Nothing, only . . . you remember the night you went for that long walk, when he might be going back to the mine?

MISS MOFFAT (*after a pause*): Yes?

MISS RONBERRY: The next morning he started studying again, and yet it seemed so different.

MISS MOFFAT: How?

MISS RONBERRY: Almost strained . . . what a silly thing to say . . . I mean, as you did not say anything more about the mine——

MISS MOFFAT (*playing with the string*): He didn't say any more himself. He just turned up. I didn't embrace him on both cheeks, but I said 'righto'. Since which time, he has never stopped working.

MISS RONBERRY: I *am* so glad. . . . (*Taking the other envelope from her belt, relieved to be changing the subject.*) Oh, this arrived from the Penlan Town Hall! It must be his birth certificate——

MISS MOFFAT: Good. . . . (*Crossing, taking it from her briskly, and taking it back to her desk.*) I must send it off to the President of Trinity. Rather a nervous post-mortem from him last night; two pages to ask if the youngster's legitimate; thank heaven he is. And no convictions for drunkenness; references have been spotless. That will help, I hope.

MISS RONBERRY: Would it not be splendid if he . . . won!

MISS MOFFAT (*after a pause*): Not very likely, I am afraid. (*Moving about, nervously.*) The syllabus rather attaches importance to general knowledge of the academic sort. His is bound to be patchy – on the exuberant side – I have had to force it; two years is not enough even for him. If he checks himself, and does not start telling them what they ought to think of Milton, with fair luck he might stand a chance. He will have some pretty strong public-school candidates against him, of course. Bound to. It depends on how much the examiners will appreciate a highly original intelligence.

MISS RONBERRY: But wouldn't it be *exciting*!

MISS MOFFAT (*after a pause, in a measured voice*): Yes, it would. People run down the Universities, and always will, but it would be a wonderful thing for him. It would be a wonderful thing for rural education all over the country.

MISS RONBERRY: And most of all, it would be a wonderful thing for you!

MISS MOFFAT: I suppose so. . . . (*After a pause, almost soliloquising.*) It is odd to have spent so many hours with another human being, in the closest intellectual communion – because it has been that, I know every trick and twist of that brain of his, exactly where it will falter and where it will gallop ahead of me – and yet not to know him at all. (*Realising the other woman's presence, and breaking her mood.*) I woke up in the middle of the night thinking of Henry the Eighth. I have a feeling there may be a question about the old boy and the Papacy. (*At one*

307

of the bookshelves between the side window and the garden door.)
I'll cram one or two facts into him, the last minute. . . .
*(Suddenly, in a sob, with all the inward strength of which she is
capable.)* Oh God, he must win it. . . .

> Mrs Watty *comes in from the kitchen, carrying a
> steaming cup and saucer.*

(Leaning her head against the bookcase; brokenly): He
must. . . .

> Mrs Watty *stops short, and exchanges a distressed
> look with* Miss Ronberry. *She goes over to* Miss
> Moffat.

Mrs Watty *(coaxingly)*: Tea!

> Miss Moffat *turns and looks at her, trying to pull
> herself together.*

*(Giving her the tea-cup and stirring the tea for her, with an
attempt at jauntiness.)* Now, ma'am, don't get in a pucker!
Six more Saturday mornin's like this in the next 'alf-year,
remember!

Miss Moffat *(recovering quickly, and making a note at the
desk, from a book)*: The first paper is the important one –
I expect we'll get more used to the others——

Miss Ronberry *(chatty again, as* Mrs Watty *takes the
empty cup)*: Suppose the Squire doesn't come!

Miss Moffat: He will. He has got to the point of looking on the lad as a race-horse.

Miss Ronberry: You don't think the snow might
deter him?

Mrs Watty: I just seed 'is nibs' gardener clearin' a
way from the gates. Shame the red carpet gettin' so wet.

> *She goes back into the kitchen.* Miss Ronberry *rises
> and looks out of the side window.*

Miss Ronberry: Surely it is getting brighter this side.
. . . Oh, I can see him! Morgan, I mean!

MISS MOFFAT (*looking past her*): Can you?

MISS RONBERRY: Coming up the Nant, do you see? Ploughing through!

MISS MOFFAT: What is the time?

MISS RONBERRY: Ten minutes to!

MISS MOFFAT (*sitting at her desk and searching again in her book*): He will have just two minutes——

A knock at the front door.

MISS MOFFAT: Good. There's the Squire——

MISS RONBERRY (*running to the front door*): He is as excited as any of us——

She opens the front door. BESSIE *stands in the porch, in the drifted snow. She enters the room, followed by* MR JONES, *heavily muffled and looking very sheepish.* MISS RONBERRY *shuts the door and follows them into the room in wonderment. They are faintly powdered with snow.*

Bessie! . . . But it cannot be you, your mother has just received——

BESSIE: I left the same day I posted it.

She is shabbily dressed, in semi-grown up fashion, and wears a cloak. Her manner is staccato, nervy and defiant; she is bursting with news, which might be good or bad. Her hands twitching over her Gladstone bag, she faces MISS MOFFAT, *who stares at her, puzzled.*

MISS MOFFAT (*without rising*): This is unexpected.

BESSIE: Isn't it just? I have been travellin' all night, quite a wreck. I woke Mr Jones up and he got the station-master to drive us over in his trap, in the snow, nice, wasn't it?

She is trying not to be frightened, and not succeeding. The conversation from now on quickens and grows more nervous.

MISS MOFFAT: You have arrived at an inconvenient time.

BESSIE: Fancy.

She plucks up courage and sits suddenly in the arm-chair. MISS MOFFAT frowns and rises. MISS RONBERRY is near the kitchen door; MR JONES hovers round the front door.

MISS MOFFAT: Have you come to see your mother?

BESSIE: No.

MISS MOFFAT: Then why are you here?

BESSIE: Questions and answers, just like school again!

MISS MOFFAT (*to* MR JONES): Why have you brought this girl here this morning?

MR JONES: I did not bring her, Miss Moffat, she brought me——

MISS MOFFAT (*to* BESSIE): Whom have you come to see?

BESSIE: You.

MISS MOFFAT: Me?

BESSIE does not speak. Undecided, MISS MOFFAT crosses above the arm-chair, looks at the clock, then quickly out of the side window.

I can give you exactly one minute of my time. Is it money? (*As* BESSIE *does not answer, impatiently to the others.*) Will you wait in the study?

MR JONES follows MISS RONBERRY into the study; she is perplexed, he is very worried.

MISS MOFFAT (*before they are out of the room*): One minute. . . . Quickly!

BESSIE: Why?

MISS MOFFAT: Morgan Evans is sitting for his Oxford examination here this morning.

BESSIE: Well, 'e needn't.

MISS MOFFAT: What do you mean?

BESSIE: Because he won't ever be goin' to Oxford.

MISS MOFFAT: Why not?

BESSIE: Because there's goin' to be a little stranger.
A pause.
I'm going to have a little stranger.
*She begins to whimper into her handkerchief: half acting,
half nerves and excitement. MISS MOFFAT stares at her.*
MISS MOFFAT: You're lying.

BESSIE (*looking up, suddenly*): Doctor Brett, The Firs,
Cheltenham. . . . And if you don't believe it's Morgan
Evans, you ask 'im about that night you locked me up –
the night you had the words with him!
A pause.
MISS MOFFAT: I see. . . . (*With a sudden cry.*) Why
couldn't I have seen before! . . .
*Her eyes rest on the examination table. She collects her-
self, desperately.*
Does he know?

BESSIE: I've come to tell 'im! I was ever so upset, of
course, and now I've lost me place – ooh, she was artful
– he'll have to marry me, or I'll show him up, 'cause I
must give the little stranger a name——

MISS MOFFAT (*exasperated beyond endurance*): Stop saying
'little stranger' – if you must have a baby, then call it a
baby! . . . Have you told anybody?

BESSIE: Mr Jones, that's all——
MISS RONBERRY peers timidly round the study door.
MISS RONBERRY: The Squire is coming up the road!
*She looks anxiously from one to the other and goes back
into the study.*
BESSIE: I'll wait here for him.

MISS MOFFAT (*panting*): For the next three hours, he
must not be disturbed. You are not going to see him——

BESSIE (*almost triumphantly*): You can't bully me, the
way I am! (*Rising, and facing her across the examination table,*

311

the resentment of two years pouring out, real hysteria this time.)
'Asn't sunk in yet, 'as it? I'm teaching *you* something, am
I? You didn't know things like that went on, did you?
Why? You couldn't see what was goin' on under your
nose, 'cause you're too busy managin' everythin'! Well,
you can't manage him any longer, 'cause he's got to
manage me now, the way I am, he's got to——

> Mr Jones *pokes his head round the study door; he is in*
> *a state of panic.* Miss Ronberry *hovers behind him.*

Mr Jones: Morgan Evans has turned the corner up
the hill——

Miss Ronberry: So there isn't much time!

> Mr Jones *gives the others a desperate look and follows*
> Miss Ronberry *back into the study.*

Miss Moffat: I'm afraid I am going to do a little
managing now. You are going into the kitchen, where
your mother will make you breakfast; you will then lie
down, and as soon as this session is finished we will go
upstairs and talk it all over when we are a little calmer.

> *A knock at the front door.*

Bessie: He's here! (*Rising.*) I got to see him!

Miss Moffat (*seizing her by the arm, suddenly*): If you try
and disobey me, I shall not answer for the consequences.

Bessie (*cowed*): You wouldn't dare lay a finger on
me——

Miss Moffat: Oh yes, I would.

> *They face each other, panting; deadly enemies.*

Miss Moffat: If you attempt to stay in this room, or to
blab to anybody about this before we have had that talk
– even your mother – I am in a pretty nervous state myself,
this morning, and I shall strike you so hard that I shall
probably kill you, and be hanged as a thwarted spinster
... I mean every word of that.

Another knock, more impatient. She quells BESSIE *with her look; crosses, and holds open the kitchen door.*

BESSIE: I don't mind. (*Following her, and turning at the door.*) Three hours'll go soon enough.

She goes into the kitchen, her head high. MISS MOFFAT *shuts the door after her, straightens herself, and opens the front door. The* SQUIRE *enters, in Inverness cape and hat, stamping the snow from his boots; he carries several periodicals, chiefly 'Sporting and Dramatic'. The rest of the scene is played very quickly.*

MISS MOFFAT (*shutting the door*): So very sorry – how kind of you – such a dreadful day——

THE SQUIRE: Not at all, Mistress Pedagogue, anything for a lark. . . . (*Looking at the little table.*) Glad it isn't me, what? . . .(*Settling on the sofa, as she takes his overcoat.*) I've got a spiffy bit of news for you.

MISS MOFFAT: Yes?

THE SQUIRE: I've bought the barn from Sir Herbert, and we can move the whole shoot next door by March. What d'ye think?

MISS MOFFAT (*abstracted, hanging the coat behind the front door*): Wonderful——

THE SQUIRE (*showing the study as he settles on the sofa*): We can knock a door straight through here to the barn——

A knock at the front door.

Aren't ye pleased about it?

MISS MOFFAT (*crossing to the desk, hardly aware of what she is doing, as* MISS RONBERRY *runs in from the study*): Yes, but you know, this examination, rather worrying——

MISS RONBERRY (*crossing*): Good morning, Squire! Terrible weather——

THE SQUIRE (*half rising*): Beastly——

MISS RONBERRY *opens the front door and lets* MORGAN

313

*in. His overcoat, cap and muffler are sprinkled with snow.
He has been hurrying, but he is quiet and calm. His eyes
rest immediately on the little examination table.*

MISS MOFFAT: Wet?

MORGAN (*taking off his overcoat*): No, thank you – good-
day, sir——

MISS RONBERRY: Let me take your things——

MORGAN: Thank you——

MISS MOFFAT: Before I open the papers, I have a feeling they may bring up Henry the Eighth. (*Holding out the
paper on which she has been scribbling.*) Memorise these two
facts, will you?

    MORGAN *takes the paper and studies it, brushing stray
flakes of snow out of his hair as he does so.*

MISS RONBERRY (*taking a spray from her blouse and laying
it on the small table*): White heather – just a thought!

    She runs into the study with MORGAN's *coat, scarf and
cap.*

MORGAN: Thank you——

THE SQUIRE: Good luck, my boy.

MORGAN: Thank you, sir——

THE SQUIRE: Glad it isn't me!

    MR JONES *pops his head round the study door.*

MR JONES: Pob llwyddiant, ymachgeni!

MORGAN: Diolch——

    MR JONES *goes back into the study.* MORGAN *hands
the paper back to* MISS MOFFAT, *who crumples it and
throws it in the waste-paper basket. He sits at the little
table, his back to the audience.*

MISS MOFFAT: Name and particulars, to save time.
And don't get exuberant.

MORGAN: No.

MISS MOFFAT: Or illegible.

MORGAN: No.

> *He writes. She takes up an official envelope from the desk.*

THE SQUIRE: But aren't *you* going to wish my little protégé good fortune?

MISS MOFFAT (*after a pause, to* MORGAN): Good luck.

MORGAN (*looking up at her, after a pause*): Thank you.

> *The clock begins to strike nine.*

MISS MOFFAT: Ready?

> MORGAN *nods. She cuts the envelope and places the examination paper in front of him. He studies it anxiously. She looks at the duplicate.*

(*Involuntarily, gratified.*) Henry the Eighth!

> *She sits in the arm-chair. The* SQUIRE *embarks on his periodical.* MORGAN *begins to write.* MISS MOFFAT *raises her head, looks anxiously towards the kitchen, then steadfastly at* MORGAN, *her lip trembling. A pause. The only sound is the scratch of a pen.*

THE CURTAIN FALLS SLOWLY

ACT III

An afternoon in July. Seven months later.

> *The school has been moved next door, and the room is much less crowded; the small table is back in the window recess, the arm-chair is in its old position; the large table, however, is no longer behind the sofa with its chair, its place being taken by three small school-desks facing the front door; between the front door and the bay window a black-board on its easel faces the audience at an angle, with 'Elizabeth, known as Good Q. Bess' written on it in block letters.*

> MR JONES *stands in command beside the blackboard. In two of the school-desks sit* IDWAL *and* ROBBART, *each poring over his slate. On the settle sit the* SQUIRE, *down-stage, his arms folded like a pupil, his eyes fixed on* MR JONES, *and next to him* OLD TOM, *upstage, laboriously copying the inscription on to his slate.*

OLD TOM (*muttering, as he writes*): Elissabeth . . . known . . . as . . . what in goodness is a 'k' doin' there, that iss a pussell for me——

MR JONES (*suddenly*): 'I wandered lonely as a cloud.' From the Daffodils, by Wordsworth.

> *The boys scratch busily. The* SQUIRE *begins to nod sleepily.* MISS RONBERRY *hurries in from the garden.*

MISS RONBERRY (*to* MR JONES, *in an urgent whisper*): What is the capital of Sweden?

MR JONES: Stockholm.

MISS RONBERRY: Thank you.

316

She hurries back into the garden.

OLD TOM (*after pondering anxiously, to the* SQUIRE): Please, sir, how many l's in 'daffodils'?

THE SQUIRE: Blest if I know.

He closes his eyes again. JOHN OWEN *comes in by the study door.*

JOHN: Please, Mistar Jones, Form Two Arithmetic Report – Miss Moffat says will you come in school with it.

He goes back. MR JONES *takes some papers hastily from the dresser and follows him through the study. A mild snore from the* SQUIRE.

ROBBART (*looking at him*): Mae o'n cysgu. Tyd. Idwal——

OLD TOM (*in a passion*): Plenty Welsh at home, not in the class please by request scoundrels and notty boys!

IDWAL (*to him*): Squire iss 'avin' a snore. Nai ddangos rwbeth ichi——

He rises, runs to the blackboard, takes the chalk and the duster, and swiftly rubs out and adds to the inscription till it reads: 'NO . . . GOOD . . . BESSIE.' *The* SQUIRE *grunts.* IDWAL *throws the duster under the open desk, darts back to his desk and buries his head in his slate.* MR JONES *returns.*

MR JONES: Now history. (*Crossing* THE SQUIRE, *waking him.*) Excuse me. . . . (*Going to the blackboard.*) Elizabeth——

He sees the inscription and stops short. He turns on the others, grave and perturbed. OLD TOM *watches, missing nothing.*

Who did this?

IDWAL: Please, Mr Jones, perhaps it iss some terrible dunce that want to know what iss Bessie Watty been doin' the last few months.

A pause.

MR JONES: Whoever it was . . . I am going to cane him! (*To* THE SQUIRE, *timidly, as the latter rises and walks up.*) It was not you, sir, by any chance?

THE SQUIRE: Not guilty . . . (*Going to the bay window and peering out towards the left.*) Bessie Watty? Little Cockney thing? Nice ankles?

MR JONES: I do not know, sir. . . . (*As* IDWAL *giggles.*) Silence, boys! Where is my duster?

THE SQUIRE (*coming back with a sigh*): Still no sign of him.

MR JONES: You mean Morgan Evans, sir?

The boys sober suddenly and look round at THE SQUIRE. He is not expected before the train leaving Oxford half-past one——

THE SQUIRE: There's a sporting chance the Viva finished yesterday, and I sent the wagonette to meet the one-ten.

He sits again on the settle. The boys watch him.

MR JONES: Do you think that he may know the result when he arrives?

THE SQUIRE: I doubt it, Miss Moffat said we'll hear by letter in a day or two. . . . (*Rising restlessly, and going towards the front door.*) Think I'll propel the old pins down the highway, just in case. . . .

IDWAL: Please, sir, what sort of a place is Oxford?

THE SQUIRE (*turning at the door*): Dunno, I'm sure. Cambridge myself.

He goes.

MR JONES (*standing in front of the blackboard*): Now history. Repeat after me——

IDWAL (*in a piping voice*): Please, Mr Jones, tell us about Bessie Watty!

Mr Jones (*after a pause, cornered*): If you are kept in to-morrow, I will give you religion. Repeat after me——

The school bell rings.

Dismiss!

> *He goes to the dresser and tidies papers in his satchel.*
> Idwal *and* Robbart *breathe on their slates and wipe them, gathering their books hurriedly together and tie them with a strap.* Sarah *hurries in from the front door. She is dressed in her best, in the traditional Welsh peasant costume with a steeple hat.*

Sarah: Please, sir, have you got my father—— (*Seeing* Old Tom.) – tiddona, n'had, ma'dy frwas di'n oeri——

Old Tom (*furious*): English, daughter, in the class, pliss!

Sarah (*pulling at his sleeve*): You are an old soft, your porridge it iss gettin' cold and you have not got your sleep——

Old Tom: But I got my Queen Elizabeth——

Sarah (*helping him towards the front door*): And in the mornin' you got your rheumatics – come on!

> Miss Ronberry *comes in from the garden and places her papers on the open desk.*

Robbart: Sarah Pugh, what you all clobbered up for?

Sarah: Because for Morgan Evans.

Mr Jones (*starting forward*): Is there some news?

Miss Ronberry: About Morgan? Oh, quickly!

Sarah: Not yet, Mistar Jones. (*As they sigh impatiently.*) But when it comes, I know it iss good news, so what do I do? I open the dresser, out the lavendar bags and into my Sundays! Home, dada, for Sundays——

Mr Jones: Before we have definite news, that is un-wise——

Sarah: John Goronwy Jones pliss sir, you are an old

soft. Everybody is ready to meet him by the Nant! The grocer got his fiddle——

IDWAL: And William Williams the public got his cornet!

ROBBART: And with me on me mouth-organ——

SARAH: And me singin'!

ROBBART: Tyd, Idwal——

He runs out by the front door, followed by IDWAL.

MR JONES (*calling after them*): Jack Rhys Policeman will be after you with his breach of the peace!

MISS RONBERRY: Perhaps preparing for news to be good means that it will be.

MR JONES: Everything is pre-ordained. Morgan Evans has either won the scholarship, or lost it.

MISS RONBERRY: Let us all say together, 'Morgan Evans has won the scholarship'!

ALL (*except* MR JONES, *lustily*): 'Morgan Evans has won the scholarship!'

SARAH (*to* OLD TOM): Tiddona, 'nhad——

She stands arranging her shawl.

OLD TOM (*wistfully*): I never got a lettar yet, and nobody never put Sundays on for me. . . .

He goes out by the front door. MISS RONBERRY *is about to cross into the school when her eye catches the blackboard;* SARAH *is about to follow her father when* MISS RONBERRY'S *voice arrests her.*

MISS RONBERRY: 'No . . . good . . . Bessie.' Good gracious!

MR JONES (*trying to hide the board from* SARAH, *but too late*): Where *is* my duster?

MISS RONBERRY: What does that mean?

SARAH: Bessie Watty. Miss Ronberry, where is she?

320

Miss Ronberry (*after a stifled look at* Mr Jones): I don't know, dear.

Sarah: Miss Moffat she hears from her, in my post-office. We wass all wonderin'.

She goes out by the front door.

Miss Ronberry (*turning on* Mr Jones): Well, *I* have been wondering too! (*Sitting on the sofa, as he crosses to the desk.*) She came back that morning and just went away again – Morgan Evans was telling me only the day he left for Oxford that he didn't even *see* her. Where is she?

Mr Jones (*pouring ink from a bottle in a drawer into a rack of ink-wells on the desk*): It is more important to know if Morgan Evans has won or not.

Miss Ronberry: I know. . . . If he hasn't, it will break her heart.

Mr Jones: Would she feel it so keen as all that?

Miss Ronberry: I used not to think so, but since that day they have been so much better friends, it has been a pleasure to hear them conversing – perhaps it is the strain of all these examinations——

She stops guiltily as Miss Moffat *comes in from the study, reading an exercise-book and chuckling; she wanders up towards the blackboard.*

Miss Moffat: Gwyneth Thomas the plasterer's eldest: essay on Knowledge. 'Be good, sweet maid, and let who will be clever' – I wonder if the reverend Kingsley had any idea what a smack in the eye that was for lady teachers? And then Gwyneth Thomas starts (*reading*) 'It is not nice to know too much, I wish to be like Miss Ronberry, Miss Moffat is different, she knows everything.' Ha! Not bad for a youngster! Hit the nail—— (*Suddenly, apprehensively, catching* Miss Ronberry's *face.*) Any news?

MR JONES: Not yet.

MISS MOFFAT (*relieved*): I thought not. . . .

> *She sees the blackboard and stops short. A pause. She takes out her handkerchief and with a swift movement wipes the board clean. The others watch her.*

Where is the Squire?

MR JONES: Gone to see if there is any sign.

MISS MOFFAT: Thank the Lord, that man is really becoming a nuisance. (*Sitting on the top end of the sofa.*) He gave up Henley to be here this week – did you know?

MR JONES (*coming down towards her*): You do not appear nervous?

MISS MOFFAT: I am past being nervous. If he has won, I shan't believe it. Flatly.

MISS RONBERRY: And if he has lost?

MISS MOFFAT: If he has lost . . . (*after a pause*) . . . we must proceed as if nothing had happened. The sun rises and sets every day, and while it does we have jolly well got to revolve round it; the time to sit up and take notice will be the day it decides not to appear. (*Rising briskly.*) In the meantime, Mr Jones, your report is on your desk; Miss Ronberry, Form Two are waiting for your music like a jungle of hungry parakeets.

MISS RONBERRY: Yes, Miss Moffat.

> *They retire meekly through the study.* MISS MOFFAT *is alone. She looks at her watch; her armour loosens perceptibly; she is on edge and apprehensive. She goes towards the stairs, but before she reaches them, the garden door opens suddenly, and* MORGAN *appears. He wears a new dark suit, carries a travelling bag and his cap, and looks dusty and tired. His manner is excited and unstable; he is alternately eager and intensely depressed. She stares at him, not daring to speak.*

322

MORGAN: I caught the early train. I knew they would all be watching for me, so I got out at Llanmorfedd and got a lift to Gwaenygam.

MISS MOFFAT (*fearfully*): Does that mean——

MORGAN: Oh, no news.

He puts down his bag and cap next to the arm-chair; she relaxes, comes down, and sits on the lower end of the sofa.

MORGAN: Except that I am not hopeful.

MISS MOFFAT: Why not?

MORGAN (*sitting in the arm-chair*): They talked to me for one hour at the Viva——

MISS MOFFAT: That doesn't mean anything. Go on.

MORGAN: They jumped down hard on the New Testament question. As you said they would – you are very pale.

MISS MOFFAT: Better than a raging fever. Go on.

MORGAN: I spent five minutes explaining why Saint Paul sailed from a town three hundred miles inland.

MISS MOFFAT: Oh dear.

Their manner together has changed since we last saw them together; they are hardly at all teacher and pupil, superior and inferior, adult and child; they are more like two friends held solidly by a bond unsentimental and unself-conscious. MORGAN'S *English has immensely improved, and he expresses himself with ease.*

MISS MOFFAT: Parnell?

MORGAN: Parnell. . . . Oh yes – I was going to stick up for the old chap, but when they started off with 'that fellow Parnell', I told the tale against him for half an hour, I wasn't born a Welshman for nothing.

MISS MOFFAT: Ha . . . And the French?

MORGAN: Not good. I said 'naturellement' to everything, but it didn't fit every time.

MISS MOFFAT: And the Greek verbs?

MORGAN: They were sarcastic.

MISS MOFFAT: Did the President send for you?

MORGAN: I had half an hour with him——

MISS MOFFAT: You did?

MORGAN: Yes, but so did the other nine candidates! He was a very kind and grand old gentleman sitting in a drawing-room the size of Penlan Town Hall. I talked about religion, the same as you said——

MISS MOFFAT (*correcting him, mechanically*): Just as you advised——

MORGAN: Just as you advised. He asked me if I had ever had strong drink, and I looked him straight in the eye and said 'No'.

MISS MOFFAT: Oh.

MORGAN: I was terrible – terribly nervous. My collar stud flew off and I had to hold on to my collar with one hand, and he did not seem impressed with me at all. . . . He was very curious about you. Did you know there was an article in the *Morning Post* about the school?

MISS MOFFAT (*waving aside the news*): Was there? . . . But what else makes you despondent?

MORGAN: The other candidates. They appeared to me brilliant – I had never thought they would be, somehow! Two from Eton and one from Harrow, one of them very rich. I had never thought a scholarship man might be rich. He had his own servant.

MISS MOFFAT: Gosh!

MORGAN: And the servant looked so like my father I thought it was at first. . . . And as I was leaving the examiners appeared to be sorry for me in some way, and I received the impression that I had failed. I——

He is suddenly depressed, rises and wanders towards the stairs. She catches his mood.

MISS MOFFAT: When shall we know?

MORGAN: The day after tomorrow. They are writing to you.

MISS MOFFAT (*rising and pacing towards the desk*): The villagers are all in their best, and talking about a holiday tomorrow. It is very stupid of them, because if you have failed it will make you still more sick at heart——

MORGAN: If I have failed? (*In sudden desperation.*) Don't speak about it!

MISS MOFFAT (*turning to him, surprised*): But we must! You faced the idea the day you left for Oxford——

MORGAN: I know, but I have *been* to Oxford, and come back, since then! (*Sitting on the lower end of the sofa, facing her.*) I have come back – from the world! Since the day I was born, I have been a prisoner behind a stone wall, and now somebody has given me a leg-up to have a look at the other side ... (*vehement*) ... they cannot drag me back again, they cannot, they *must* give me a push and send me over!

MISS MOFFAT (*sitting beside him, half-touched, half-amused*): I've never heard you talk so much since I've known you.

MORGAN: That is just it! I *can* talk, now! The three days I have been there, I have been talking my head off!

MISS MOFFAT: Ha! If three days at Oxford can do that to you, what would you be like at the end of three years?

MORGAN: That's just it again – it would be everything I need, everything! Starling and I spent three hours one night discussin' the law – Starling, you know, the brilliant one.... The words came pouring out of me – all the words that I had learnt and written down and never spoken – I suppose I was talking nonsense, but I was at least holding a conversation! I suddenly realised that I had never done it before – I had never been *able* to do it. (*With a strong Welsh accent.*) 'How are you, Morgan? Nice day, Mr Jones! Not bad for the harvest!' – a vocabulary of twenty words; all the thoughts that you have given to me were being stored away as if they were always going to be useless – locked up and rotting away – a lot of questions with nobody to answer them, a lot of statements with nobody to contradict them . . . and there I was with Starling, nineteen to the dozen. (*Suddenly quieter.*) I came out of his rooms that night, and I walked down the High. That's their High Street, you know.

Miss Moffat (*nodding, drinking in the torrent with the most intense pleasure*): Yes, yes. . . .

Morgan (*looking before him*): I looked up, and there was a moon behind Magd – Maudlin. Not the same moon I have seen over the Nant, a different face altogether. Everybody seemed to be walking very fast, with their gowns on, in the moonlight; the bells were ringing, and I was walking faster than anybody and I felt – well, the same as on the rum in the old days!

Miss Moffat: Go on.

Morgan: All of a sudden, with one big rush, against that moon, and against that High Street . . . I saw this room; you and me sitting here studying, and all those books – and everything I have ever learnt from those books, and from you, was lighted up – like a magic lantern – ancient Rome, Greece, Shakespeare, Carlyle, Milton . . . everything had a meaning, because I was in a new world – my world! And so it came to me why you worked like a slave to make me ready for this scholarship. . . . (*Lamely.*) I've finished.

326

MISS MOFFAT (*smiling, dreamily*): I didn't want you to stop.

MORGAN: I had not been drinking.

MISS MOFFAT: I know.

MORGAN: I can talk to you too, now.

MISS MOFFAT: Yes. I'm glad.

> THE SQUIRE *comes in from the front door, leaving it open behind him.* MORGAN *rises.*

THE SQUIRE (*coming down*): No sign of the feller-me-lad, dang it – Evans! There you are! . . . Well?

MORGAN: Good-day, sir, they are sending the result through the post.

THE SQUIRE: The devil they are. (*To* MISS MOFFAT, *as he sits in the arm-chair.*) D'ye know I am finding this waiting a definite strain? . . .

> MR JONES *runs in from the study, in a state of excite-ment, as* MISS MOFFAT *rises and walks round the room.*

MR JONES: Somebody said they had seen Morgan——

MORGAN: Day after tomorrow.

> *He sits, abruptly, on the settle.*

MR JONES: Oh. . . .

> *He wanders sheepishly towards the open front door.*

THE SQUIRE: Examiners all right, my boy?

MORGAN: Rather sticky, sir.

THE SQUIRE: Lot of old fogies, I expect. Miss Moffat, I told you you ought to have made inquiries at the other place. However . . .

> MISS RONBERRY *runs in from the study, excited, carry-ing a sheet of music.*

MISS RONBERRY: Somebody said they had seen——

THE SQUIRE and MR JONES (*in irritated chorus*): The day after tomorrow!

MISS RONBERRY (*dashed*): Oh . . . How are you, Morgan, dear. . . .

> MORGAN *half rises to greet her. She crosses to the desk.*
> MORGAN *looks thoughtfully before him.* MISS MOFFAT
> *tries to busy herself with a book at the dresser.*

MR JONES (*wandering out into the porch*): The suspense is terrible.

THE SQUIRE: I know.

MR JONES: Even the little children are worrying about——

> *He stops short; he has seen somebody coming down the
> village street; he looks again, doubtfully, starts, then peers
> anxiously into the room; everybody is preoccupied. He
> comes into the room, shuts the door, and stands a moment
> with his back to it.*

MR JONES: Morgan, my boy . . . are you not exhausted after your journey – would you not like something to eat?

MORGAN (*rousing himself from his thoughts*): I am rather hungry, yes——

MISS MOFFAT: But how stupid of me – Watty will boil you an egg – (*moving towards the kitchen*) – come along——

MORGAN (*rising*): Thank you – (*to the others*) – excuse me——

MISS MOFFAT (*as she goes into the kitchen*): Did they spot the Dryden howler?

MORGAN (*following her*): No.

> MR JONES *crosses quickly and shuts the door after them.*

THE SQUIRE: You seemed very anxious to get 'em out of the room. What's the matter——

> *The front door opens suddenly, and* BESSIE *walks in. She
> has completely changed; she might be ten years older. Her
> hair is up; she wears a cheaply smart costume, with a cape,*

and looks dazzlingly pretty in a loose opulent style. Her whole personality has blossomed.

A pause. They stare at her. She is perfectly self-possessed.

BESSIE: Hallo!

THE SQUIRE (*mechanically*): How d'ye do. . . .

BESSIE: I'm very well indeed, thanks, and how are you, blooming?

Her accent is nearer the ladylike than it has been yet.

THE SQUIRE: Yes, thanks. . . . (*To the others.*) What *is* this?

MISS RONBERRY: I really couldn't say. . . . Good gracious, it's Bessie W——

BESSIE: Right first time. Hello, Miss Ronberry, how's geography, the world still goin' round in circles? Hello, Mr Jones, flirty as ever?

She sits on the sofa, completely at home.

THE SQUIRE: And to what do we owe this honour?

BESSIE: Well, it's like this——

MR JONES (*to* MISS RONBERRY, *desperately*): Miss Ronberry, will you please return to your class——

MISS RONBERRY (*agog, shutting the front door*): They are quite safe, I left Mary Davies in charge——

BESSIE (*to* MR JONES): No, you don't. We've had too many secrets as it is——

MR JONES: Three days ago she sent money to you – did you not receive the letter——

BESSIE: Yes I did, and all the others, till I was sick of 'em.

THE SQUIRE: What *is* all this?

BESSIE (*taking off her cape*): Last week I was glancing through the *Mid-Wales Gazette*, and I'm here to congratulate a certain young gent in case he has won that scholarship.

329

Mr Jones: Oh!

Miss Ronberry: But what has that got to do with you?

Bessie: You see, Miss, it's like this——

Mr Jones (*in a last effort to stop her*): Don't say it – don't say it!

Bessie: Four weeks yesterday, I had a baby.

A pause. Miss Ronberry *and the* Squire *stare at her.* Mr Jones *gives a sigh of impotent despair.*

The Squire: You had a what?

Bessie: A baby. Seven pounds thirteen ounces.

The Squire: Good God, how ghastly.

Mr Jones (*moving up, as* Miss Ronberry *sinks into the desk-chair*): It is a disgustin' subject and——

Bessie: It isn't disgusting at all, if I had a wedding-ring you'd think it was sweet.

Mrs Watty *hurries in from the kitchen.*

Mrs Watty: Morgan Evans's luggage. Excuse me, sir——

She crosses, picks up the bag and cap, and is about to take them back to the kitchen when she catches sight of the Squire's *serious face.*

Mrs Watty: Oh! . . . (*Fearfully.*) Any news?

The Squire (*rising*): Well, yes. . . .

He goes towards the front door, turning to watch the scene; Mrs Watty *looks from* Miss Ronberry *to* Bessie, *then back, not having recognised her daughter the first time.*

Mrs Watty: Bessie! (*Dropping what she is carrying, in her excitement.*) My, you do look a dollymop! Excuse me, sir. . . .

The Squire: Say anything you like——

Mrs Watty: Where d'you get them bracelets?

Bessie: Present.

MRS WATTY: Oh, that's all right. . . . Where 'ave you been, you madam?

BESSIE: Turnin' you into a granny.

MRS WATTY: A gra . . . (*Delighted.*) Well, *fancy!*

MISS MOFFAT comes in from the kitchen.

MISS MOFFAT (*calling back into the kitchen*): And I should try and have a sleep if I were you——

MRS WATTY (*as MISS MOFFAT comes down and begins to go upstairs*): You could 'ave knocked me down with a feather!

BESSIE: Hello.

MISS MOFFAT stops short, turns and looks at her.
I've just been telling them you-know-what.

It is plain she is no longer afraid of MISS MOFFAT. The latter looks from one to the other, helplessly.

THE SQUIRE: And now I think it's time you told us who the fellow is. I am going to take drastic proceedings——

MRS WATTY: That's right, dear – who is it——

BESSIE: Well, as a matter of fact——

MISS MOFFAT (*with a cry, coming down*): No! I'll pay you anything . . . anything!

BESSIE (*kindly*): It's no good, Miss. (*To the others, quickly.*) It's Morgan Evans.

A pause. MISS MOFFAT puts her clenched fist to her eyes in despair.

THE SQUIRE: What!

MISS RONBERRY (*dazed*): I don't believe it. . . .

MRS WATTY (*really upset, to MISS MOFFAT*): Oh, ma'am. . . .

MISS MOFFAT: I've been dreading this, for months. In a terrible way it's a relief.

BESSIE: Bamboozlin' me every week he was in the gutter!

MISS MOFFAT: Lies, all lies, and I was glad to be telling them——

MISS RONBERRY (*suddenly articulate*): I can't go on listening! I can't bear it! (*Wringing her hands.*) It all comes of meddling with this teaching – she was in my class – what *would* Papa have said! (*Collapsing in the arm-chair.*) This horrible unnatural happening——

MISS MOFFAT (*exasperated beyond endurance*): Don't talk nonsense, it isn't horrible, and it isn't unnatural! On the contrary, it's nature giving civilisation a nasty tweak of the nose. All we can say is that she led him on, but even she was only obeying her instincts – what is at the bottom of the whole thing, actually, is my own crass stupidity for allowing not one jot for humanity. (*Clinging wearily to the banister.*) I should have tried to understand and forestall, instead of riding rough-shod like a mare with blinkers. Her own mother begged me not to bring her here in the first place – even the Squire gave me a hint – even *he* knew more about human nature than I did——

THE SQUIRE: I say, you know——

MISS MOFFAT: But I must do a little reforming, if you please, and this is where it has landed us. (*Sitting listlessly on the settle, her head turned away.*) The schoolmistress has learnt a lesson, but it's a little late now.

BESSIE (*rising*): Where is he?

MRS WATTY (*defending the kitchen door, trying not to shout*): Over my dead body, my girl——

BESSIE (*standing with her back to the audience, hands on hips*): She's right, mum, it's too late, I got a four weeks old baby, kickin' healthy and hungry, and I haven't got a husband to keep him, so his father's got to turn *into* my husband. That's only fair, isn't it?

THE SQUIRE: I'm sorry, Miss Moffat, but I'm inclined to agree——

BESSIE: I'll call him——

MR JONES (*blinking*): There is no need to call him!

THE SQUIRE: What's the matter with you?

MR JONES (*coming forward*): I am sorry to say that I have a strong feeling of affection for this young woman.

BESSIE (*sitting again on the sofa, amused*): Oh yes – I've got the face of an angel, haven't I?

MR JONES: And I am willing to do my duty by re-habilitating her in wedlock, and bestowing on the infant every advantage by bringing it up a Baptist.

MISS MOFFAT (*suddenly turning to him*): Are you serious?

MR JONES: I am always serious.

MISS MOFFAT (*rising, to* BESSIE, *entreatingly*): I know it sounds cold-blooded, but . . . will you agree?

BESSIE: No, I won't. (*Good-humouredly.*) I don't want to hurt anybody's feelings, but I do draw the line.

MISS MOFFAT: Oh, please think again!

MRS WATTY (*coming down round the sofa to* BESSIE): We're not pretendin' it's a windfall, but for a girl who's took the wrong turnin' it's a present! And you'd 'ave your own way in everything – wouldn't she, sir?

MR JONES (*eagerly*): Of course——

MISS MOFFAT: Watty's put it perfectly. . . . (*Sitting beside* BESSIE *on the sofa.*) I can't expect you to realise how much this means to me . . . except that I'm begging you, and begging doesn't come easily to me . . . Will you?

BESSIE: I'd like to oblige . . . (*looking at* MR JONES *and giggling in spite of herself*) . . . but really I couldn't! (*As he retreats despondently.*) Besides, my friend would be furious.

MRS WATTY (*clutching at straws*): Your friend?

BESSIE: Ever such a nice gentleman, sporting, quite a swell, owns a racecourse. (*Catching her mother's eye.*) You needn't look like that, I only met him ten weeks ago. I'd started servin' behind a bar for fun, I was the picture of health and ever so lucky in the counter bein' very high.

THE SQUIRE: I have never heard such a conversation outside a police-court. I am seeking the safety of my own quarters – anything I can do, Miss Moffat——

He goes towards the front door.

BESSIE (*to him*): I suppose *you* wouldn't care to stake a claim?

THE SQUIRE: Good gracious——

He gives a startled look and goes.

MISS MOFFAT: Doesn't this man of yours want to marry you?

BESSIE: 'E won't talk of anything else, but he won't have the baby. He says it would be different if the father'd been a pal of his – you can understand it, really, can't you? So I've got to give up my friend and marry Morgan Evans. (*As* MISS MOFFAT *rises and moves despairingly up to the bay window.*) Pity, 'cos my friend worships me. Ever since I left he keeps on sending me telegrams. I just got two at the station, and I expect I'll get some more tonight, isn't it rich? Mr Jones wouldn't consider the baby without me?

MISS RONBERRY: The baby without you! Your child! What about your – your mother-love?

BESSIE: I expect you'll think I'm a wicked girl, but d'you know, I haven't got any!

MISS RONBERRY: Oh, what a vile thing to say, vile——

BESSIE (*rising*): Now listen, dear . . . (*going to her*) . . .

334

you're seeing this baby as if it was yours, aren't you –
you'd think the world of it, wouldn't you?

MISS RONBERRY: It would mean everything to me . . .
(*suddenly pathetic*) . . . my whole life. . . .

BESSIE: I have a pretty near idea how old you are; well,
my 'rithmetic was never very good, but quite a year or
two ago you were twice as old as I am now. When I'm
your age I'll love the idea of a baby, but life hasn't begun
yet for me – I'm just getting a taste for it – what do *I*
want with a baby?

MRS WATTY: That's what we all want to know!

BESSIE: Yes, mum, but you know what it is——

MISS RONBERRY (*rising*): You're inhuman, that's what
you are! To think you don't want it. . . .

> *She is on the point of bursting into foolish tears, and runs
> into the study.*

BESSIE: I didn't mean to be nasty – but inhuman indeed!
I didn't want the baby, nobody would have, but I was
careful so it'd be all right, and now it is all right I want
it to have a good time – but *I* want a good time too! I
could have left it on a doorstep, couldn't I? But I must see
it's in good hands – (*turning up to* MISS MOFFAT) – and
that's why I've come to Morgan Evans.

MISS MOFFAT (*turning to her*): You want to make him
marry you, on the chance he will become fond enough
of the child to ensure its future – (*her voice rising*) – your
conscience will be clear and later you can go off on your
own?

> MRS WATTY *tries to silence them, pointing to the
> kitchen.*

BESSIE: I shouldn't be surprised——

MISS MOFFAT: In the meantime, it's worth while to
ruin a boy on – on the threshold of——

BESSIE: I don't know anything about that, I'm sure. (*Calling.*) Morgan!

MISS MOFFAT: Ssh! (*Intercepting her, desperately.*) Wait a minute, wait. . . . There may be a way out – there must be——

MRS WATTY: Gawd bless us, ma'am – I got it!

MISS MOFFAT: What?

MRS WATTY: Why can't you adopt it?

    BESSIE *and* MR JONES *stare from her to* MISS MOFFAT.

MISS MOFFAT (*turning away*): Don't be ridiculous.

MRS WATTY: Would that do you, Bessie?

BESSIE (*impressed*): Well! I never thought . . .

MRS WATTY: Would it, though?

BESSIE (*after consideration*): Yes, it would.

MISS MOFFAT (*really taken aback, for the first time*): It *would*? . . . But . . . but what would *I* do with a baby? I – I don't even know what they look like!

MRS WATTY: They're lovely little things – now it's all arranged——

MISS MOFFAT: But it would be fantastic——

BESSIE (*going up to her, eagerly*): Oh, do, please, it'd put *everything* to rights! I would know the baby was safe, Morgan Evans need never know a thing about it, I can marry my friend, and it will all be beautiful! He might grow like his father and turn out quite nice, and anyway I'm not really so bad, you know – and he's on the bottle now – and I could give all the instructions before I go – and you could have it straight away, see, because if it's going I don't want to have it with me longer than I can help, see, because I'd only start gettin' fond of it, see——

MRS WATTY (*to* MISS MOFFAT): Come on, ma'am,

you've been pushin' us about for three years, now we'll give *you* a shove!

MISS MOFFAT: But it's mad – I tell you――

MRS WATTY: Not as mad as takin' *me* in was, with my trouble! You've allus been like that, you might as well go on – where's that old gumption of yours?

MISS MOFFAT: But I was never meant to be a mother – I'm not like Miss Ronberry – why, *she* is the one to do it――

MR JONES (*hastily*): She would never agree – we were discussin' Marged Hopkins going to the workhouse – and she said she could never hold with any child born like that.

MISS MOFFAT: Oh . . . I suppose it would worry some folk. . . . But, Watty, you're the grandmother, and surely you――

MRS WATTY: Oh, I couldn't! I don't bear it no ill-will, but every penny I get goes to the Corpse. You're the one, dear, reelly you are.

MISS MOFFAT (*after thought, decisively*): Bessie Watty, do you mean that if I do not adopt this child, you――

BESSIE: I will have to tell Morgan Evans, and he will have to marry me, I swear that.

MISS MOFFAT: And do you swear that you would never let Morgan Evans know the truth?

BESSIE: I swear. If there are any questions, I'll say it was my friend's.

A pause.

MISS MOFFAT: Then . . . (*sitting in one of the desks*) . . . I give in.

BESSIE (*elated*): That's lovely. My friend *will* be pleased. I'll·pop back to the public-house for his telegram and send him a nice one back. (*Taking her cape from the sofa.*)

Good-bye all, we'll arrange details later, shall we? (*Showing them a clasp on her cape.*) My friend gave me this buckle, isn't it nice? He offered me a tiny one, real, but I think the false is prettier, don't you?

MR JONES (*as she turns to go*): Are you going to take up a life of sin?

BESSIE (*smiling*): I shouldn't be surprised. I'm only really meself with a lot of gentlemen round me, y'know, and a nice glass o' port will never come amiss, neither. (*To* MRS WATTY.) That cold water didn't really do the trick, mum, did it? . . . (*To* MISS MOFFAT, *serious for a moment.*) Good-bye . . . I only did it to spite you, y'know.

MR JONES: You are not fit to touch the hem of her garment.

BESSIE (*rounding on him, good-humouredly*): Oh yes, I am! Just because she's read a lot o' books. Books, books! . . . (*Embracing the room with a magnificent gesture.*) Look at 'em all! I got more out of life at my age than she has out o' them all her days – and I'll get a lot more yet! What d'you bet me?

She goes out by the front door.

MRS WATTY (*shutting the door after her, with a deep sigh*): That's settled. . . .

The voices of children, in the barn; singing 'Dacw 'nghariad'.

MR JONES (*making for the study door*): For which we must be truly thankful. . . .

MORGAN *walks in quickly from the kitchen. He goes straight to* MISS MOFFAT; *his face is white and shocked; they stare at him, instinctively silent.*

MORGAN: I have been waiting for her to go.

MISS MOFFAT: Why?

MORGAN: The Squire just came in to see me.

MISS MOFFAT: The fool! The clumsy idiotic fool——
MORGAN: Then it's true! . . .

A pause. The singing stops in the barn.
(*Looking at the others mechanically.*) He thought I knew.
Then he said it was for the best – that I ought to be told.
. . . It is funny. She and I, we do not know each other at
all – it was a long time ago, and I never thought again
about it – and neither did she, I know she didn't . . . and
here we are. . . . (*To* MISS MOFFAT, *dully.*) It is funny,
too, because if you and I had not made that bad quarrel,
it would never have happened. . . . It ought to make me
feel older . . . but I feel more – young than I have ever
done before. . . . (*Almost collapsing, suddenly.*) Oh God,
why should this happen to me. . . .

MISS MOFFAT: Steady. . . .

MR JONES: There is no need for you to upset yourself,
my boy. Miss Moffat is going to take care of – of——

MORGAN: What?

MISS MOFFAT: I am going to adopt it.

MORGAN (*to* MISS MOFFAT, *his old truculent self emerging*):
What in hell do you take me for?

MR JONES: Morgan, swearing! Be haru ti——

MORGAN (*in a rage*): I will swear some more too, if
people talk to me like that! (*To* MISS MOFFAT.) What do
you take me for?

MR JONES: Then what would you like to do, my
boy——

MORGAN: What would I like to do? (*Getting more and
more Welsh.*) It is not a question of what I would like to
do, or what I might be allowed, but what I am *going* to
do – what any fellow with any guts in him must do!
(*Crossing, impetuously.*) I am going to marry her!

339

MISS MOFFAT (*with a cry*): I knew this would happen, I knew——

MORGAN: What else is there, when I have made a fool of myself and of her, and of the poor – the poor – I am not going to talk about any of it to anybody, all I will say is that Bessie Watty and I are going to get married as soon as we can, and that is final!

He flings himself into the arm-chair, closing his eyes.

MISS MOFFAT (*crossing and sitting on the sofa, hopelessly*): I see.

> *A knock at the front door.* SARAH *hurries in, agog with excitement. She runs to* MRS WATTY.

SARAH: Bessie's telegram from her friend, they send it from Penlan— (*to the others gleegully, as* MRS WATTY *opens the envelope*) – I never seed one before!

MRS WATTY (*sniffing*): Poor chap, 'e'll be disappointed again. . . . (*Placing the telegram on* MISS MOFFAT's *lap.*) What does it say, ma'am? . . . (*As* MISS MOFFAT *does not move, almost tearfully.*) Read it, ma'am, take your mind off things. . . .

> MISS MOFFAT *glances half-heartedly at the telegram. A pause. She looks up at* MORGAN.

MISS MOFFAT: You have won the scholarship. (*Reading.*) 'First, Evans, Second Fayver-Iles, Third Starling. Congratulations.'

> SARAH *claps her hands and runs out by the front door.*
> MORGAN *laughs bitterly and turns away.*

(*Folding up the telegram carefully, tucking it into her belt, still quiet, burning with a slow-mounting and deliberate fever.*) Lock the school door, Watty, will you?

MRS WATTY (*to* MR JONES, *tremulously*): Go in there, sir, I'll make you a cup of tea. . . .

MR JONES *goes into the kitchen.* MRS WATTY *locks the study door and follows him.*

MISS MOFFAT: Look at me, Morgan.

MORGAN *faces her in the arm-chair, defiantly.*
For the first time, we are together. Our hearts are face to face, naked and unashamed, because there's no time to lose, my boy; the clock is ticking and there's no time to lose. If ever anybody has been at the crossroads, you are now——

MORGAN (*rising, and pacing restlessly up to the side window*): It is no good. I am going to marry her.

MISS MOFFAT: And I am going to speak to you very simply. I want you to change suddenly from a boy to a man. I understand that this is a great shock to you, but I want you to throw off this passionate obstinacy to do the right thing, which is natural at your age, and try to assume the sober judgment of somebody more *my* age. . . . Did you promise her marriage?

MORGAN: No, never——

MISS MOFFAT: Did you even tell her that you were in love with her?

MORGAN (*repelled*): No, never——

MISS MOFFAT: Then your situation now is the purest accident; it is to be regretted, but it has happened before and it will happen again. So cheer up, you are not the central figure of such a tragedy as you think——

MORGAN: That does not alter the fact that I have a duty to – to them both——

MISS MOFFAT: She has her own plans, and she doesn't want the child, and I am willing to look after it if you behave as I want you to behave. If you marry her, you know what will happen, don't you? You will go back to the mine. In a year she will have left you – both. You will

341

be drinking again, and this time you will not stop. And you will enjoy being this besotted and uncouth village genius who once showed such promise; but it will not be worth it, you know.

MORGAN (*moving to her, fighting*): There is a child, living and breathing on this earth, and living and breathing because of me——

MISS MOFFAT (*turning on him, with her old snap*): I don't care if there are fifty children on this earth because of you! . . . (*As he sits again, wearily in the arm-chair.*) You mentioned the word 'duty' did you? Yes, you have a duty, but it is not to this loose little lady, or to her offspring either.

MORGAN: You mean a duty to you?

MISS MOFFAT (*shaking her head, with a smile*): No. (*As he looks at her, arrested.*) A year ago I should have said a duty to me, yes; but that night you showed your teeth . . . you gave me a lot to think about, you know. You caught me unawares, and I gave you the worst possible answer back; I turned sorry for myself and taunted you with ingratitude. I was a dolt not to realise that a debt of gratitude is the most humiliating debt of all, and that a little show of affection would have wiped it out. I offer that affection to you, today.

MORGAN: Why are you saying this to me now?

MISS MOFFAT: Because, as the moments are passing, and I am going to get my way, I know that I am never going to see you again.

A pause.

MORGAN (*incredulously*): Never again? (*Rising.*) But why?

MISS MOFFAT: If you are not to marry her, it would be madness for you to come into contact with the child; so if I am adopting the child, you can never come to see me; it is common sense. Actually there is no reason why you should ever come to Glansarno again; you have been given the push over the wall that you asked for, and you have grown out of this already.

MORGAN: But you ... will be staying here –how can I never come back – after everything you have done for me?

MISS MOFFAT (*after a pause, smiling*): D'you remember, the last six months, I've gone for a long walk over Moel Hiraeth, every morning at eight, like clock-work, for my health?

MORGAN (*sitting*): Yes?

MISS MOFFAT: There's one bit of the road, round a boulder – and there's an oak tree, and under it the valley suddenly drops sheer. Every morning regularly, as I was turning that corner, by some trick of the mind, I found myself thinking of you working for this scholarship, and winning it. And I experienced something which must after all be comparatively rare: a feeling ... of complete happiness.

> She is suddenly moved. He looks away slowly. She recovers.

I shall experience it again. No, Morgan Evans, you have no duty to me. Your only duty – is to the world.

MORGAN (*turning to her*): To the world?

MISS MOFFAT: Now you are going, there is no harm in telling you something. I don't think you realise quite how exceptional you are, or what your future can become if you give it the chance. I have always been very definite about the things I wanted, and I have always had everything worked out to a T – p'raps that's the trouble with me, I dunno. . . . I've got *you* worked out, and it's up to you whether it will come right or not——

MORGAN (*eagerly*): Go on.

MISS MOFFAT: I rather made out to the Squire that I wanted you to be a writer – the truth might have sounded ridiculous; but stranger things have happened. You have brains, shrewdness, eloquence, imagination and enough personality; and Oxford will give you enough of the graces.

MORGAN: For what?

MISS MOFFAT (*simply*): Enough to become a great statesman of our country. (*After a pause, as he stares at her.*) It needn't be just politics – it could be more, much, much more – it could be . . . for a future nation to be proud of. . . . P'raps I'm mad, I dunno. We'll see. I know you're absurdly young for such an idea, and that so far you've only got the groundwork – I know all that; but I've got the measure of your intellect better than you have yourself. It's up to you. . . . (*After a pause.*) And now doesn't Bessie Watty and her baby seem a little unimportant?

    She hangs on his answer. A pause. He is looking straight before him.

MORGAN (*quietly*): Yes.

    MR JONES *appears timidly from the kitchen.*

MR JONES: Is it all right to ring the bell to say holiday tomorrow?

MISS MOFFAT: Yes.

    MR JONES's *face lights up; he hurries to the study door, unlocks it, and disappears.*

MISS MOFFAT (*rising, suddenly*): I think that's all.

    She goes to the back of the sofa and picks up MORGAN's *bag and cap.*

344

MORGAN (*rising, and facing her*): But – I – I do not know what to say.

MISS MOFFAT (*smiling*): Then don't say it.

MORGAN (*looking round*): I have been . . . so much time in this room.

MISS MOFFAT: And the lessons are over.

MORGAN (*turning to her, impulsively*): I shall – always remember.

MISS MOFFAT (*shaking her head, with a smile*): Will you? Well, I'm glad you think you will.

> *She presses the bag and cap into his unwilling hands.*
> IDWAL *runs in from the study, very excited.*

IDWAL: Please, Miss Moffat, the band is out, and they say Morgan got to come down to Penlan Town Hall for Wales to see a real toff!

> ROBBART *appears behind him.*

MORGAN (*unwillingly*): Na, ddim diolch——

ROBBART: Tyd, man, tyd, they never forgive you! (*An afterthought.*) And please, Miss Moffat, Mr Jones say is he to say school day after tomorrow, nine o'clock same as usual?

MISS MOFFAT (*turning to him, slowly*): Nine o'clock. The same as usual. . . .

ROBBART: Yes, Miss Moffat.

> *He runs back into the study, followed by* IDWAL. MISS
> MOFFAT *holds out her hand, smiling.*

MISS MOFFAT: Good-bye.

> *They shake hands.* MORGAN *is too near tears to speak.*

And I had my heart set on coming up to London and having tea on the Terrace.

IDWAL (*putting his head round the barn door, and disappearing again*): Brysia, Morgan Evans, brysia!

> MORGAN *tries to say something, fails, and hurries into*

345

the study. As he shuts the door, the kitchen door opens, and
MRS WATTY *appears cautiously.*

MRS WATTY (*whispering*): Has he gone?

MISS MOFFAT: Yes. (*Crossing to the desk.*) It's all over.

MRS WATTY: Oh no, it isn't all over, ma'am! Because you're wanted in the kitchen – Bessie's sent a gentleman over to see you from the public house——

MISS MOFFAT: Tell him I can't see anybody——

MRS WATTY: 'E wouldn't understand, ma'am; you see, he's only four weeks old.

> MISS MOFFAT *turns and looks at her. A pause.*

MISS MOFFAT (*quietly*): I had forgotten – all about that.

MRS WATTY: Poor little feller, nobody wants 'im! (*In a conspiratorial whisper.*) I only hope nobody'll put two and two together, ma'am, 'e's the spit of 'is father! (*Pressing a paper into her hand.*) This is 'is birth certificate she sent over . . . (*moving to the kitchen door*) . . . and I got everything else in there, and I'll see to the bottle. (*As* MISS MOFFAT *does not move.*) Come on, ma'am, you got to start some time!

MISS MOFFAT: Just coming.

> MRS WATTY *goes into the kitchen. The sound of the village people singing and cheering down the road. A pause.*
> MISS MOFFAT *looks down at the birth certificate. The singing and cheering die down. A pause.*

MISS MOFFAT: Moffat my girl, you mustn't be clumsy this time. You mustn't be clumsy. . . .

> *The school bell begins to ring, clear and confident. She looks up, as she did once before, listening, smiling faintly. A vociferous burst of cheering in the village. She turns and walks towards the kitchen.*

CURTAIN

THE LIGHT OF HEART

To
My Wife

CHARACTERS

MRS BANNER
BARTY
FAN
BEVAN
MADDOC THOMAS
CATTRIN
ROBERT
MRS LOTHIAN

The action of the play takes place in a room at the top of a house in Long Acre, London W.C.2.

The time is the present, and covers a period of eleven months.

ACT ONE
Scene 1: A morning in December
Scene 2: Nine hours later. Evening

ACT TWO
Scene 1: Five months later. A night in May
Scene 2: Six months later. An early afternoon in November

ACT THREE
Scene 1: Three hours later. Early evening
Scene 2: Twenty-four hours later. Early evening

THE LIGHT OF HEART *was first produced at the Apollo Theatre, London, on 21 February* 1940. *It was presented by* H. M. Tennent Ltd *and Stephen Mitchell, with the following cast:*

MRS BANNER	Gladys Henson
BARTY	Arthur Powell
FAN	Megs Jenkins
BEVAN	Edward Rees
MADDOC THOMAS	Godfrey Tearle
CATTRIN	Angela Baddeley
ROBERT	Anthony Ireland
MRS LOTHIAN	Elliot Mason

The play directed by
THE AUTHOR

ACT I

SCENE I

*A room at the top of a house in Long Acre, London, W.C.2.
A morning in December.*

*In the back wall, to the right (throughout the play 'left'
and 'right' refer to the audience's left and right) the door of
the room, set in a wooden partition and facing the audience.
From it the narrow stairway can be seen leading round
under the room (out of sight) to the left; at night, a dim
light is thrown up from downstairs. More centre, in the
same partition and also facing the audience, the door of a
small kitchenette. Two windows in the left wall, overlooking a back yard; in the right wall, downstage, another
window, overlooking Long Acre; outside the door, on the
stairs, to the right and almost out of sight, a third window.*

*During the first act, the room looks like thousands of
others in London; the cheapest kind of furnished lodgings,
redeemed from the sordid by an indefinable air of cheerful-
ness, and having been lived in a long time by the same people.*

*In the alcove between the partition wall of the kitchenette
and the left wall, a single bed (MADDOC'S) set in the
corner against the back and left walls, the top upstage;
beside it, a rickety night-table: both are half-hidden by a
tattered screen with scraps pasted over it. Against the right
wall, downstage under the window, its top downstage,
another single bed (CATTRIN'S). Both have brass bedsteads
and sagging middles.*

Against the bottom left window, an old chest of drawers;

between the windows, a wash-stand with basin, jug, and
towel. In the corner by MADDOC'S *bed, an improvised*
wardrobe, consisting of a triangular piece of wood studded
with pegs, and stuffed with clothes. Facing the audience,
between the kitchenette door and the front door, a deal
wardrobe with battered cardboard boxes piled on top of it.
Above CATTRIN'S *bed, a card-table and a tiny occasional*
table; below the bed, a weather-beaten trunk; beside the
bed, a pouf covered in greasy chintz. Downstage left, its
back to the audience, directly against the footlights, a low
sofa, its roll-top to the left; between this and the chest of
drawers, a low Moorish tabouret table; upstage, to the left,
an oblong kitchen table covered by a worn cloth, a kitchen
chair behind it and a cane chair (the cane bursting) beside
it on the right, a spare chair beside it on the left. Near the
middle of the room, an old swivel office-chair.

Worn linoleum on the floor, with two antediluvian rugs.
Faded wallpaper, dingy brown plush and lace window-
curtains. On the pouf, a roulette wheel. On the walls, pinned
between hideous oils in battered frames, photographs of
country scenes cut from journals. A narrow shelf carrying
a miscellany of old books. One naked electric-light bulb on
a bracket between the left windows. Old suitcases and junk
piled on top of the kitchenette, where a stove-pipe is also
seen, cut into the ceiling. An oil stove (unlit) between the
office chair and CATTRIN'S *bed.*

When the kitchenette door is open, one can see that it is
little more than a long cupboard, stacked with parapher-
nalia for the most elementary meals; a glimpse of a small
dust-bin; it has no window, only a feeble electric light.

Many cigarette-stubs, in and out of ash-trays; empty
packets; the remains of a desultory meal on the table, with
dirty crockery, tumblers, and an empty salmon tin; on the

floor above the sofa, a beer bottle and a tumbler; on the chest of drawers, a half-full whisky bottle, a jug of water and tumblers.

The kitchenette door is shut, and the curtains over all three windows are closed; the front door, however, is wide open, and from the window on the stairs filters the dismal light of a winter's morning.

A pause. MRS BANNER *is seen toiling upstairs and into the room; she leaves the door open. She carries a half-pint bottle of milk, a newspaper and a steaming kettle. She looks round vaguely, a little breathless, places the milk and the newspaper on the table, and opens the kitchenette door. She sees that the light inside has been left on, says a faint 'ttt' to herself, and disappears inside. We hear her pouring water into a teapot. She re-emerges, leaving the light on, pulls the curtains back from the top left window, then from the lower left window. She is revealed as an elderly woman with a large immovable face, masses of grey hair draped and looped over her head (but otherwise resembling a bird's nest) great tender feet and a permanently toneless voice; she is dressed in a blouse and skirt which have seen better days, and an old cardigan.*

She is about to cross when she sees something on the sofa, lifts an old dressing-gown from it, looks underneath, drops it again, impassively, crosses to the right window, opens the curtain, and peers motionlessly out.

BARTY'S *head rises slowly over the back of the sofa, and he sits up. He is a little man of forty, with the round ingenuous face (moustached) and the mentality of a public-schoolboy of fifteen. He wears a jacket, but no collar or tie, and looks the worse for wear; he is half asleep.*

BARTY: A lovely London morning, would you say?

MRS BANNER: The worst since my chest.

BARTY: Oh, don't say that. Rain?

MRS BANNER: An' fog. Very close. An' yet it's windy, some'ow.

BARTY: No hail?

MRS BANNER: My Rosie said you wasn't down in your own room, bless 'er——

BARTY: I came up here to wait for Maddoc.

MRS BANNER: And you done a flop up 'ere, I said to Rosie——

BARTY: Why aren't you behind your counter?

MRS BANNER: Rosie's very good with the change, bless 'er, if it's one of 'er good days. An' Cattrin asked me to come up 'ere an' see to 'er dad's cup o' tea in 'er absence, sort o' thing. As he ain't 'ere, we better 'ave it. You left the front door open all night, right on top o' Covent Garden. (*Crossing.*) My shop might 'a' been burgled.

BARTY: What, those chocolates go at last?

MRS BANNER: You 'aven't got no trousers on, you are a piece.

She disappears into the kitchenette.

BARTY (*murmuring*): I expect I meant to go to bed and it slipped my mind. Suppose I'd better go down to my own quarters. . . .

MRS BANNER *returns carrying two cups and saucers, with sugar.*

MRS BANNER: There's a bowler hat in the sink. Where was you brought up, you dirty thing?

BARTY: Bognor, Charterhouse, Corpus Christi and the gutter.

MRS BANNER (*pouring out milk*): Where's 'is lordship, on the tiles?

BARTY: Maddoc? God knows, I left him in the Cross-bones about three.

MRS BANNER: 'E's a bad lad while 'is little girl's away. (*Going back to the right window.*) I've made the tea. Is your grandmother dead yet?

BARTY (*despondently*): No.

MRS BANNER: '*Ow* much a year will it be?

BARTY: Four hundred.

MRS BANNER (*dashed*): Oh. (*Peering out again.*) The post-man told my Rosie two thousand. When you've found your trousers, the milk's three-haypence.

> *Through the open doorway* FAN *is seen coming upstairs; she shuts the door below her. She is a stout woman of forty, common, healthy and high-spirited, still pretty, though at the moment a slut. She wears an old dressing-gown, and very high-heeled feathered mules; her hair (dyed blonde) is in curlers; she is smoking, and carries a pillow, a crumpled garment, and a comb, with an unfolded 'Daily Sketch' and a small book in the other hand.*

FAN: My room's like an ice-box, must get that window-pane seen to. . . . (*Putting the book and newspaper down on the sofa.*) Hello, Barty, I saw your bed hadn't been slept in, where's Maddoc?

MRS BANNER: On the tiles.

FAN: Oh dear. . . . (*Sitting in the office chair and settling the pillow over her feet.*) I feel a bit down this morning. Woke up counting who'd come to my funeral. I could only think of Aunty Mill, an' she's been gone herself seven years. (*Sticking the comb in her hair, and beginning to take out curlers.*) Five weeks behind with my rent an' three months since I heard from Penang.

BARTY: Put not your trust in Empire-builders. Didn't

somebody see you having grub at the Cri? With a dark romantic bloke?

FAN: In two minutes I knew about his wife, three little girls and a mortgage in Palmer's Green. (*Holding out the crumpled garment, which has collapsed on her knee.*) Anybody missed a pair o' trousers?

BARTY: Oh lord. . . . Thank you.

FAN (*throwing them*): They were on the banisters——

BARTY: I don't want to hear.

FAN (*shivering*): Brrr. . . . (*Rising and striking a match.*) Let's light the stove an' get in a nice fug, shall us? . . . (*Lighting the stove.*) Is your grandmother dead yet?

BARTY: No.

FAN: Oh. How old is she?

BARTY (*half rising, pulling on his trousers*): Ninety-two.

FAN: I saw in the paper about a Turk that lived to a hundred and forty.

MRS BANNER: 'Uman bein's is different.

BARTY: Isn't a Turk a human being?

MRS BANNER: I thought she said a turkey.

FAN (*sitting again, in the office chair*): Pass my book, dear, will you. . . . There, cheer us up, eh? Fog any better, Mrs B.?

MRS BANNER: The other side o' the street's gone again.

BARTY (*picking up the book, and reading*): 'How to be a success, in twelve chapters, with a sex-appeal appendix.'

FAN (*undoing curlers*): Got it with some coupons.

BARTY (*reading*): 'The human body is an automobile. If in trim you do fifty miles, if not you wake up one morning and where is your self-starter?'

FAN (*seeing the cup and saucer*): Somebody made tea?

MRS BANNER: Me.

FAN: Goody! (*Going into the kitchenette.*) Penny for 'em, Barty!

BARTY (*his eyes closed*): I'm wondering what my inside'd fetch at the Motor Show.

> MRS BANNER *crosses and takes the cup and saucer from the table.*

MRS BANNER: 'Ope it clears up for this afternoon.

BARTY (*eating*): Why, what are *you* going to?

MRS BANNER: Society wedding.

BARTY (*incredulous*): Society wedding? Where?

MRS BANNER: Outside St Margaret's.

> FAN *returns carrying a tray with steaming teapot, one cup and loose lumps of sugar; she places the tray on the table, and pours out.* MRS BANNER *goes to the table for her cup and saucer.*

FAN: Got anything tomorrow, Mrs B.? I might come.

MRS BANNER: Waterloo Station. My Rosie's lookin' forward to that, bless 'er. (*Holding out her cup.*) Shirley Temple's father an' mother.

BARTY (*his mouth full*): Fan, a lollipop?

FAN (*pouring*): No ta, and they say drunkards never have a sweet tooth, my feet on this lino, goes right through you, worse'n *my* room——

> *She takes her pillow, climbs into the foot of* CATTRIN's *bed with her own tea and the newspaper from the table, and tucks the bedclothes round her. At the same time* BARTY *climbs into the head of the bed, with his tea and newspaper; this is obviously a procedure in cold weather. They sip their tea.*

That's better. Now, up boys and at 'em——

MRS BANNER (*extracting a 'Daily Mirror' from inside her jacket*): Just one go, then I must see to Rosie, sort o' thing——

357

She drifts above CATTRIN's *bed.*

FAN *puts her tea on the card-table, takes up the roulette ball, and throws it. All three hold their newspapers before them, deep in thought.*

BARTY: Not strong enough, Fan——

FAN: No, gentle's best——

The ball clicks into place. FAN *peers at it.*

FAN: Twenty, black, even.

BARTY: Huddersfield, Derby, Blackburn——

FAN: Burnley, West Ham, Blackburn——

MRS BANNER: Arsenal, Spurs, Wolves.

They whip pencil-stubs from nowhere and mark their choice.

FAN: Some woman I know's charwoman would ha' won three thousand if Newcastle hadn't let her down.

MRS BANNER (*going, tucking away her paper*): Wait for me for the next throw——

FAN (*combing her hair*): I rather like fog. Somebody wonderful looming out o' the void.

MRS BANNER: Lot of accidents, I expect.

She goes, leaving the door open, taking her tea with her.

FAN: Fancy old Maddoc. Cattrin'll give him sleeping out.

BARTY: It's her being away that's done it.

FAN: Well, you can't blame her, she's never been away before, and it has been to go to a wedding, catch me missing a wedding . . . I only hope he got to his new job this morning.

BARTY: Peter Robinson's, is it?

FAN: Selfridge's. Christmas toys. Very good, y'know, for Mad. My feet are lovely now, I could sit here all day.

MRS BANNER *returns, impassive as ever.*

MRS BANNER: I felt I ought to tell you.

BARTY: What?

MRS BANNER (*drinking her tea*): There's a p'liceman on the stairs.

> FAN *and* BARTY *leap from the bed; she sits on the cane chair, he on the spare chair. They drink their tea.*

FAN (*to* BARTY): Is it you?

BARTY: No. Isn't it you?

> *Through the open doorway,* BEVAN *the policeman is seen coming upstairs; he enters. He is young, Welsh, and on the pompous side; he is in uniform.*

BEVAN: Any person here by the name o' Fan?

FAN (*cowed*): Frances. Mrs Frances – (*haughty*) – Mrs Colonel Wharton. Living apart——

BEVAN: I have got a chap here that says he was on the stage with Sarah Siddons.

FAN (*puzzled, then relieved*): That's right, this is his room. (*Ingratiating.*) He used to be on the stage, y'see——

BEVAN (*going to the stairs; calling*): Come on up. (*Louder.*) Come on up!

MADDOC'S VOICE (*down the stairs, bawling*): Speak up, sir, two inches from your nose and can't hear a word!

BEVAN: If you took that rubbish off of your face you might 'ave a chance – come on up!

MADDOC'S VOICE: Not before the way is clear, sir, for my entrance!

> BEVAN *looks at the others in despair, comes into the room and stands aside.* MADDOC *comes upstairs and walks slowly into the room. He wears the long scarlet hooded robe of Father Christmas (muddy and torn) and his face is hidden by cotton-wool moustache and beard. He is still a little drunk, and in a devilish mood. He looks at* BEVAN.

MADDOC: 'You do look, my son, as if you were dismayed, be cheerful, sir, our revels now are ended. . . .'

(*Coming down.*) After which impersonation of the old actor which is expected of us, 'our little life is rounded' – (*sinking on* CATTRIN's *bed and curling up*) – 'with a sleep'.

> MRS BANNER *looks at him sadly and goes, taking her tea, and leaving the door still open.*

BEVAN (*advancing, patiently*): Take that rubbish off of your face.

MADDOC (*sitting up*): How do I *know* you're a fellow-Welshman? Prove it!

BEVAN: Take it off of your face, there is a good boy——

MADDOC: Prove it, come on! I've got you, boy! (*Standing, and singing from 'The Bells of Aberdovey'.*) 'Un dau, tri pedwar, pump chwech. . . .'

BEVAN (*after a struggle with himself, singing quickly*): 'Un dau, tri pedwar, pump chwech, meddau clychau Aber-dofi!'

MADDOC: That's the boy!

> *He whisks off beard and moustache. He is a big man in his fifties, with the remains of fine looks and physique, both considerably ravaged; he is running to fat and there are deep pouches under his eyes. He looks particularly battered at the moment; his suit under the robe is dirty as well as old, and he has two days' growth of beard. Except that he has a fine voice which he is now using to play the fool, he is not the traditional idea of an actor; he looks more like a seedy general practitioner with charm. His natural reserve is now completely obscured by the childish wilfulness of the drunkard.*
>
> *Only in moments of excitement does his accent become a little Welsh*

FAN: How long has this been going on?

BEVAN: All down Regent Street. Couldn't get him past the B.B.C. for love nor money, wanted to pop in

and say a bad Welsh word on the West Regional. . . .
(*To him.*) I take it these persons are your friends?

MADDOC: Never set eyes on 'em, who are they, rabbits?
London's full o' rabbits, y'know, all down Regent Street,
down Haymarket, flip flop the rubber soles, clippety
clop the high heels, scurrying through the miasma –
rabbits!

> *He sits on the sofa abruptly, tossing the beard on to the
> floor.*

BEVAN: What are you to do with a codger that is worse
than a preacher——

MADDOC: I would remind you, sir, that while I was
receiving praise from Edward the Seventh, you were
being photographed in a state of nature on a moulting
rug.

> *He espies the bottle of beer and the glass on the floor
> beside him, and pours out a drink.*

BEVAN (*discomposed*): I charge you with abusive
language. Come along, please!

MADDOC: What part of Wales are ye from?

BEVAN (*implacable*): Never mind what part——

MADDOC (*more and more Welsh*): Flintshire, by any
chance?

BEVAN: Tryddyn. (*On his dignity.*) Come along,
please——

MADDOC: And I'm from Rhoslan.

BEVAN (*transformed*): Rhoslan! (*Sitting beside* MADDOC
on the sofa.) You would not have heard of my Aunty
Blodwen Bevan, Church House?

MADDOC: I must have been at school with her, have a
bottle o' Bass.

BEVAN (*excited, as* MADDOC *forces the glass on him*): At
school with her, man, well – thank you, Temperance

really – you were acquainted with her, doubtless, when she——

   Mrs Banner *comes upstairs, and into the room.*

Mrs Banner: I felt I ought to tell you——

Barty: Oh lord. . . .

Mrs Banner: Selfridge's on the phone.

Fan: What'd they say?

Mrs Banner (*to* Maddoc): Will you keep your whiskers clean an' send 'em back registered. An' they said what you done wi' the presents.

Fan: Presents?

Maddoc (*crossing to the chest of drawers and taking a tumbler*): Parcels festooned over my body in the hope that women would purchase the same. (*Subsiding, mumbling.*) The parcels, not the body.

Bevan (*drinking*): What did you do with 'em?

Maddoc: Gave 'em away to the passers-by. (*Drinking.*) Hwyl!

Bevan (*rising, perturbed*): You mean what you was distributin' all down Regent Street——

Maddoc: Exactly. (*To* Mrs Banner.) Report unto Mr Selfridge that one at least has heeded the inscription across his front 'Christmas is Near, GIVE'! And I've never seen such black looks either – people never give you a nice cosy smile in the street, do they, ye know why? 'Cause they're rabbits. (*Sitting on the table.*) Tell Mr Selfridge, will you?

Mrs Banner (*going, memorising*): 'Christmas is Near . . . Give . . .'

   She goes out.

Maddoc: The ten-bob note was mine though.

Barty: Ten bob?

Fan: And who d'you give that to, you big stiff?

MADDOC: A woman on the pavement. I pressed it into her hand, she looked so wretched.

FAN: You're a nice one to be giving to beggars——

MADDOC: She wasn't begging, she was stepping into her car. (*Thoughtfully*.) Looked a little surprised.

BARTY: Golly, what a jape.

BEVAN (*going towards the door, putting his glass down on the card-table*): Better for me to talk to them——

MADDOC (*to* BEVAN, *pointing to* BARTY): Officer, arrest the only middle-aged schoolboy extant! Remove him, sir, for accosting police-women under age!

FAN: Mad, he is a bobby, do be careful——

MADDOC: And for setting fire to petticoats in the rain. ... Baa baa black sheep have you any wool ... baa baa. ... (*Trailing away into a giggling mumble*.)

BARTY: Come on, old boy, what about a spot of bed——

BEVAN (*taking out notebook and pencil*): One moment. (*To* MADDOC.) Kindly repeat what you said of your friend here.

FAN: Mad, I told you, we're all for it now——

BEVAN (*pencil poised*): 'The only middle-aged school-boy intact' was it?

MADDOC: 'Extant,' surely?

BEVAN (*writing, carefully, and putting the notebook away*): Thank you. 'Avin' missed my higher education, I am broadenin' myself in a night class.

> *He hurries out. A pause.* FAN *shuts the door behind him, shakes her head, takes* BEVAN'S *beer, and settles at the foot of* CATTRIN'S *bed;* BARTY *follows suit at the top.*

MADDOC: I'm suddenly very depressed.

FAN: You always are after 'olding forth.

MADDOC (*as if asking for a cigarette, as he gets out of the robe*): Will ye marry me, Fan?

FAN (*as if accepting one*): Yes, dear.

MADDOC: When?

FAN: When you win the pools, dear ... I would, Mad!

MADDOC: So would I – jolly good thing.

> *He throws aside the robe, crosses with his beer and packs
> himself beside* BARTY.

Is there a postcard from my daughter?

FAN: You got one last night, and another tomorrow, didn't she say? She won't like this, y'know——

BARTY: I wish you'd left the Crossbones when I gave the word.

MADDOC: I didn't fancy up here by myself, night before was bad enough, give us a fag, will ye? (*As* BARTY *obeys*.) And what, mates, is the programme for today?

BARTY (*lighting a match, for them both*): Aren't you due back at Selfridge's?

MADDOC: I'll find out for you—— (*He leans over, gives the roulette wheel a slight twist, and spins the ball. Languidly.*) I back ... red ... Rien ne va plus. ...

> *The ball clicks into position.*

(*Looking at it, then at* BARTY.) No.

FAN: But who's going to replace those parcels?

MADDOC: Time, the great healer. The question, musketeers, is what we propose to do with this wonderful day scarce begun, this endless miracle of new hope for the fallen. Eh?

BARTY (*drinking*): Well, up to the club for any letters.

MADDOC: Y'know, Barty, you're a r'markable little chap.

BARTY (*suspiciously*): Remarkable?

MADDOC: One absolutely sees that club, Regency

portico – flunkeys. . . . You make it hard to recall the
Soho basement, the smell of stale beer, and the two fruit
machines. (*Imitating* BARTY.) Up to the club for any
letters. . . .

BARTY: It's the way I always talk.

MADDOC: Delightful, my dear fellow, don't change it.
And next?

BARTY: A round of short ones at the local——

MADDOC: While you, Barty, sweat over the *Evening
Standard* children's crossword. Cold sausage and crisps
off the counter——

BARTY: Down to the Tivoli——

MADDOC: Before one o'clock, in time for fifty thousand
seats at threepence. If we stay the course, with a nap, that
takes us till five. . . .

BARTY: A quick one when they open half-past——

MADDOC: Which takes us till ten to eight. . . . Yes?

BARTY: Then the club——

MADDOC: For any letters. Which takes us till bed-
time, and by that hour . . . (*his voice trailing away mock-
ingly*) . . . the precious day will have dropped like a heavy
fruit into the lap of eternity. It's my birthday tomorrow.
Cheers. . . .

    A pause.

FAN: Snap out of it, just 'cause we're all down on our
luck. The pools may surprise us Saturday, my horoscope
said quite definitely——

    The door opens, and CATTRIN *hurries in, leaving it open;
she is twenty-eight, but looks younger, in spite of an un-
gainly appearance caused by one (pronouncedly) crippled
foot, in a boot, which she manages with cheerful address.
Her hair is done simply, her face hardly made up; her effect
of being pretty seems to come mostly from the frank*

365

pleasantness of her manner. In moments of stillness and contemplation, she is beautiful. During the next moments, out of breath and excited, she is like an awkward puppy stumping round the room. She carries a suitcase, packages, and her hat. Like her father, in moments of stress, she betrays a slight Welsh accent.

CATTRIN: Hello—

MADDOC (*overjoyed*): Cattrin!

FAN (*as* CATTRIN *kisses her father and deposits her suitcase and parcel next to the screen*): But you weren't coming back till the day after tomorrow——

CATTRIN: What d'you think!

BARTY: What?

CATTRIN: I've got a new job!

FAN: You haven't!

CATTRIN (*taking a portfolio from the table drawer and sorting some music*): I was making shorthand notes of the music, playing the fool in the middle of the service, when Mrs Hollis leant over – the one who got me this thing for father at Selfridge's – and said 'Could you play the piano in the music department, my brother wants somebody' – just like that!

    She hurries into the kitchenette.

FAN: Would that be in Selfridge's too?

CATTRIN: Yes, isn't it wonderful – how long has this light been on? – so it's as good as settled, I've just got to go along and play to him now – you haven't washed up since I went, you are a slack lot. . . .

    She returns, leaving the door open, carrying a shoebrush.
    She sits on the sofa.

CATTRIN: I tore from Charing Cross – (*holding up her lame foot*) – look at the mud, never do for Selfridge's——

FAN: How much will you get?

CATTRIN: Three pounds five, every time I go through the toys I shall cut Father Christmas dead. (*Brushing vigorously, rattling on.*) It's in music too! Do you realise, Tadda, between this and your wages we'll get half out of the muddle, and I can really do something to this room at last – I worked it all out in the train. And if she hadn't noticed my boot she'd never have seen me at all, so the poor little lame girl gets there just the same, like the tortoise. Though I can't have looked very pathetic wolfing the wedding breakfast – I wish I weren't so greedy, it doesn't go a bit. (*Laughing happily.*) I haven't felt like this since the summer. . . . (*Suddenly placid and thoughtful, a characteristic of hers.*) It's very pleasant.

> She rises, and goes back to the table; out of the corner of her eye she sees MADDOC, who is feasting his eyes on her, like a surprised and delighted child. She crosses to him.

(*Smiling.*) All right, love?

MADDOC: Fine.

> He looks at her, smiling, without moving.

CATTRIN: What's the matter with me?

MADDOC: Nothing. Just making sure you're back.

CATTRIN: Fan, what d'you think I've brought you? (*Searching in a pocket.*) The menu!

FAN (*taking it*): Oh joy, I love menus——

> BEVAN comes back, very worried.

MADDOC: Another Bass, sir, my daughter's found a job!

BEVAN (*soberly*): I am glad to hear it, because you have lost one.

> The others look at him.

CATTRIN: Not the Father Christmas job?

BEVAN: Quite right.

CATTRIN: Why?

BEVAN: For distributin' merchandise gratis to the populace.

CATTRIN looks at MADDOC. He subsides slowly till he is completely hidden under bedclothes.

I tried 'em with soft soap, but no go. We don't hold with Santa Claus, they said, breathin' whisky on the kiddies.

CATTRIN: And there was a permanent job to follow. Ah well——

She crosses to the table again, and fastens up the portfolio.

BEVAN: Then another bit that I failed to assimilate. About some music, would it be?

CATTRIN (*anxiously*): Yes?

BEVAN: That the post is already filled, would it be?

A pause. She is deeply disappointed.

CATTRIN: They *must* have been furious. And we're back where we were. Further back . . .

She replaces the portfolio in the drawer and bangs it to; a pause; mechanically, she takes the salmon-tin, puts it in the dust-bin, and comes back.

FAN: We're all in the same boat, dear, down on our luck——

CATTRIN (*realising that she is showing her feelings, and making an effort*): Never mind. Come on, I want to tidy the bed——

She peels off her mackintosh and hangs it behind the kitchenette door with her hat; puts some crockery and glasses from the table on the tray, which she carries into the kitchenette, together with her parcels. FAN and BARTY exchange a depressed look.

It grows imperceptibly darker outside.

BEVAN (*official*): Let this be a warning to you. Good morning.

368

BARTY ⎫
FAN   ⎭ (*submissive, as he goes*): Good morning.

BEVAN (*turning at the door, melting*): Tell him I'm writing to my Aunty Blodwen tonight.

He goes.

CATTRIN *returns, fastening on an overall.*

CATTRIN (*placing* BARTY'S *bowler hat on the table*): What a nice bobby——

FAN: Tell us about the wedding. What did your friend look like?

CATTRIN (*clearing the chest of drawers*): Perfect. And I felt it was partly me, because her mother'd wanted pink and I had to fight for the grey. And the groom looked a dream.

FAN: Are they very in love?

CATTRIN: Very. I thoroughly enjoyed the whole thing. A room to myself – come on, I want to tidy the bed——

She goes into the kitchenette, carrying various tumblers, and the basin of water.

FAN: Her only chum's wedding, too. She's a funny one.

BARTY: Why funny?

FAN (*clambering from the bed*): I once read a book where a lame girl went to a wedding and felt so out of it she poisoned the cake and all the guests died in a terrible state, a translation it was. After all, it's nature——

CATTRIN *returns with a piece of cake, the empty basin and a dishcloth.*

CATTRIN: Who'd like some wedding-cake? I begged it for you – catch.

FAN (*sitting on the bed, clasping the piece*): Oh joy, will it go with Bass, never mind. . . . You *really* enjoyed it?

CATTRIN(*putting back the empty basin, and wiping the chest of drawers with the cloth*): Of course I did, just because I've always known I can't get married is no reason to gnash my teeth at people who can! Will you be up for tea?

FAN (*taking the hint, as* BARTY *climbs out over* MADDOC): You bet your life, dear. Be a duck, Barty, come an' look under my bed for the tweezers, between my eyebrows is gettin' terrible again.

> *She goes, taking her newspaper and book.*

BARTY (*yawning*): Wish I could say the same for the back of my head.

> *He takes his hat and follows* FAN, *closing the door.* CATTRIN *sees something on the floor by the sofa and picks it up, puzzled. It is the Father Christmas beard. She is about to put it away in the chest of drawers when she hooks it round her ears.*

CATTRIN: Tadda!

> *The heap under the bedclothes remains inanimate.*

Are you awake?

MADDOC (*muffled*): Not if I'm going to be lectured, I'm not.

CATTRIN: All's well.

> MADDOC *sits up, sees her, stares, and laughs uproariously; he climbs out of bed, childishly relieved. She takes brown paper from the drawer, wraps the beard in it, puts it away, and lays the red robe on* MADDOC's *bed*

CATTRIN: I'll give Rosie something to take it back, save postage. . . . This fog's getting too much of a good thing – and this light is so awful – we'll have one of the oil lamps, shall we, eleven in the morning and hang the expense——

> *She goes into the kitchenette, taking the dishcloth. Still chuckling, he crosses uncertainly, takes off his jacket, and puts on his dressing-gown, which has been trailing over the sofa. He sighs with relief, and sits on the sofa; he settles a*

moment with his eyes shut. CATTRIN *switches off the kitchenette light, returns with an oil lamp lit, shuts the kitchenette door, and places the lamp on the tabouret. She turns up the wick; the soft light glows in the room, transforming it.*

CATTRIN: That's better. . . . (*Taking his jacket, sitting on the end of the sofa, and brushing marks from it.*) Did you pay the fishmonger the ten bob?

MADDOC (*sheepishly*): I gave it to a woman in Regent Street who was getting into her car.

CATTRIN (*vexed*): You really are the limit. . . . When did you wash your neck last?

MADDOC: Er – the day before yesterday.

CATTRIN: I thought so.

She thinks of something, and bursts out laughing.

MADDOC: What's the matter?

CATTRIN: I'd have given anything to see her face. . . . (*Recovering, hanging the jacket in the wardrobe, going to her bed and turning back the clothes.*) Now, you bad lad, what's the programme for today?

During the following he is in a comfortable haze; she treats him exactly like a child.

MADDOC: A quick shave——

CATTRIN (*tidying the bed*): And then a quick spring-clean, I don't like the look of this lino at all. Lunch – I brought in some baked beans——

MADDOC: Not very hungry——

CATTRIN: You'd better be. You'll sleep till four, tea with the gang, work till seven, a brisk walk to Queen's Hall, fog or no fog – because what d'you think?

MADDOC: What?

CATTRIN: Janet gave me two six-bobs for Toscanini.

MADDOC: Toscanini! What a bit of luck!

CATTRIN: Isn't it? And home to catch up on your late nights. . . . You put the pistol to the gas for washing up, will you, while I turn out——

MADDOC (*suddenly*): Cattrin . . . let's work now and clean up's afternoon, eh?

CATTRIN: It's got to be done——

MADDOC: I'd like to sit for a bit. (*Coaxing.*) Come on, I want to work!

CATTRIN (*humouring him*): All right. I'll roll you some cigarettes, at the same time.

> *She goes to the corner of the room, takes two books, an exercise book, a pencil, and some tobacco and cigarette-papers from the drawer in the tiny occasional table, and brings them down on the card-table, which she places against the foot of the sofa; she brings down the cane chair and sits at the card-table.*

CATTRIN: Number twenty-three we'd got to – d'you realise that four more, and it'll be a real book?

MADDOC: What'll we call it?

CATTRIN: What d'you think of 'New Songs of Old Wales'? Because they *are* new, you know, Chappells were telling me the words of eight of them will never have been printed before – all due to your memory, isn't that good?

MADDOC: Might turn into a best seller, eh?

CATTRIN: Well, they can only count on selling five hundred copies at most.

MADDOC: And how much would we make?

CATTRIN: About four pounds ten.

MADDOC (*lying back, disappointed*): Oh . . .

CATTRIN: But a lot of kudos. Now . . . you remembered the words of the third line, and gave up.

MADDOC: Give me the first three lines again.

CATTRIN (*singing, the old Welsh folk-song, 'Tra Bo Dau'*):
　　　　'Mae'r feinwen fwyn a garaf fi
　　　　Ymhell oddi yma'n byw . . .
　　　　Ac nid oes harddach un imi . . .'
It is part of the day's work, but she sings freshly and with simplicity.
　　A pause.

MADDOC: Sorry about Father Christmas.

CATTRIN: Never mind.

MADDOC: I'll get one of those club dinners – you know, recitation and jokes. Eh?

CATTRIN: Yes, lovely. . . . (*Studying her paper, singing again.*) 'Ac nid oes harddach un imi . . .'

MADDOC (*half-singing, his eyes closed, as she looks at him, her pencil ready*): 'Un imi . . .' Damn. And Taid used to sing it for years, when I was a boy, not your grandmother's father, your grandfather's. When he put the sheep away. Y'know, when I'm with the gang you'd never think I'd ever opened a book ,and now, sittin' here, I'd like to be reading Trollope again, George Moore – 'Brook Kerith', got through that in the trenches. . . .
　　A pause.

CATTRIN (*singing*): 'Cyfoeth nid yw ond oferedd,
　　　　　　　Glendid nid yw yn parhau . . .'

MADDOC (*murmuring, reminiscently*): It was a summer song. Standing on the farm wall, and listening to him down the valley, seventy-seven and wouldn't be helped. Right till I was fifteen, the year I ran away to come to London.
　　A pause. There is sadness in the room.

CATTRIN (*singing*): 'Ond cariad pur
　　　　　　Sydd fel y dur,
　　　　　　Yn para tra bo dau . . .'

373

MADDOC: It's that fourth line, gone right away. . . .

CATTRIN (*rousing herself, and turning pages of a book*): There might be something in the back of this about it—— (*Coming upon a faded piece of paper, and reading from it.*) '5 February 1905.' What a long time ago. (*Reading.*) 'Dear Mr Thomas, your *Hamlet* is undistinguished.'

MADDOC (*sitting up*): And who was that impertinent puppy. . . .

CATTRIN (*laughing*): What a smack! (*Reading.*) 'Allowing for your extreme youth, however, you have deportment, voice, and imagination. With hard work you should end on the heights, Henry Irving.'

A pause. He lies back, abruptly. She puts the letter away.

MADDOC: I'm thirsty. (*Shamefaced.*) D'ye think——

CATTRIN (*rising*): A very small hair of the dog, eh?

MADDOC (*sitting up, pleased*): That's right. . . .

CATTRIN (*going to the chest of drawers and pouring out a weak whisky and water*): And then we'll get on to the next. . . .

MADDOC (*drowsy*): This room's miles away from anywhere. . . . Just you an' me, a li'l place where the rest can't get at us, back in the old days when I was a li'l chap, with the old songs. . . .

She sits again. He drinks.

CATTRIN: That's right, Tadda. They keep the cold out, and the fog. . . . (*Singing*):

'Mae'r feinwen fwyn a garaf fi
Ymhell oddi yma'n byw . . .'

MADDOC: They keep everything out, do the old songs.

A knock at the door, gentle but peremptory. She looks up, the lamplight catching her face.

CATTRIN: Come in.

*The lights fade slowly into darkness. The curtain falls,
and rises immediately on*

SCENE II

Nine hours later. Evening.

*The oil lamp and oil-stove are both lit, and there is
another oil lamp also (lit) on the occasional table. The
curtains are closed.*

CATTRIN *is sitting in the same place, mending a nightdress;* FAN *is reclined in* MADDOC'S *position on the sofa;
her light fawn coat on the table; she is transformed, in a
cheap showy evening dress, her hair curled, her face made
up; she is wearing sandals, has one foot on the other edge of
the sofa and is laboriously painting her toe-nails from a
little bottle in the other hand.* CATTRIN *finishes her
mending.*

FAN: It's no good, I can't reach, Cat, be a duck and
finish me off.

CATTRIN: All right. . . .

A knock at the door; the same knock as before.

(*Looking up.*) Come in.

ROBERT *opens the door and leans round it. He is in
shirt-sleeves, and his face is partly obscured by lather: he
carries a shaving-brush and smokes a cigarette. He is a
well-bred man in his thirties, whose dark good looks (a little
worn) help his rather over-flippant manner to suggest the
ladies' man fallen on bad times. But there is nervous defiance
in his flippancy, and behind it a serious and sensitive mind.*

ROBERT: Your father hasn't got a new Gillette blade,
has he?

CATTRIN: Well, I——

375

ROBERT (*coming down*): Sorry, I forgot this muck on my face – I'm the nuisance who called this morning and asked for a hammer.

CATTRIN (*recognising him*): Oh yes. (*Sitting on the sofa and taking the brush from* FAN.) I'm almost sure his razor's a different sort.

ROBERT: Oh. (*Going.*) I'll have to go on hacking with the old blade, I suppose——

FAN: Are you the new unfurnished over the yard?

ROBERT: Moved in yesterday. I'm afraid they made a bit of a shindy getting my piano up.

FAN: Not at all, I'm musical myself. Sit in the Corner House for hours——

CATTRIN: Don't wriggle, Fan, there's a good girl.

ROBERT (*going*): I'll be seeing you——

FAN: Are you a pianist?

ROBERT: In a way. I write music.

CATTRIN *looks up, interested for the first time.*

CATTRIN: Symphonies and things, do you mean?

ROBERT: No, songs.

CATTRIN (*losing interest*): Oh.

ROBERT: Sorry.

FAN (*as he goes*): 'Body and Soul' or 'A Monastery Garden'?

ROBERT: 'Body and Soul.'

FAN: That's all right.

MRS BANNER *comes upstairs.*

MRS BANNER (*to* ROBERT): There's a middle-age lady for you.

ROBERT: Oh, thank you. Won't find me exactly at my best—— What was the wedding like?

MRS BANNER: I was as near the bride as I am to you. I've put 'er in your room.

She goes.

ROBERT *follows casually, shutting the door.*

FAN: My horoscope *said* a dark musical man.

CATTRIN: A bit of a cad, I should say; careful, Fan, you know what you are. And I hope he isn't a cadger as well. Haven't *you* got a Gillette?

FAN: Yes, but I wasn't going to tell *him*. Ooh. . . . (*Getting up on the sofa end.*) That's better, d'you like my feet like that?

CATTRIN: They look terrible.

FAN: I know, but my Burton-on-Trent friend says a woman's no good to him unless she's sophisticated.

CATTRIN: Where are you meeting him?

FAN: Joey's Snack Bar.

CATTRIN: Isn't *he* musical and dark?

FAN: Ginger.

CATTRIN: Nice teeth?

FAN: Not sure about the top. But a *very* nice wit.

CATTRIN: What sort of wit?

FAN: Well, there was the waitress in the milk-bar. 'Don't get in an 'uff,' she said – y'know, Cockney – what d'you think *he* said?

CATTRIN: What?

FAN: 'Enough's as good as a feast,' I nearly burst. . . . What's your dad up to, I wonder?

CATTRIN: Prowling. Woke up at five with a coal-black hangover. I hope he's back for Toscanini.

FAN: Last I saw of him was outside the Garrick Club – oh, I wasn't going to tell you——

CATTRIN (*alarmed*): He wasn't trying to go in, was he?

FAN: He was sittin' on the step eatin' a Bath bun.

CATTRIN: Isn't he naughty. . . .

FAN: What are you goin' to do, money, I mean?

377

CATTRIN: Don't. . . . Heard from Penang?

FAN: No, don't suppose I ever will. (*Thoughtfully.*) Wouldn't it be nice if your dad won the pools and could marry again?

CATTRIN: Yes, wouldn't it?

FAN: D'you know, he's never mentioned your mother to me?

CATTRIN: He never has to me either.

FAN: Not to *you*?

CATTRIN: She died when I was born. I can understand him, really.

FAN: Was he very fond of her?

CATTRIN: I don't know. I imagine so – there!

FAN: Thank you, dear. (*Standing on the sofa.*) Now if the rain keeps off I'll look lovely– (*jumping down and looking at her wrist-watch*) – ten past, oh law – (*taking her coat*) last dinner date we had, I was four minutes late and he'd been at the fruit machine and we had sandwiches – but he *is* funny – ta, ta——

> *She goes downstairs, and is seen squeezing past* ROBERT, *who is on his way up; they are heard saying 'Hello' to each other.* CATTRIN *puts the varnish-bottle and brush on the card-table, takes a sock from under the nightdress, and begins to darn it.* ROBERT *enters. He has finished his shave and carries a hammer. He is still smoking.*

ROBERT: You haven't such a thing as a rawl-plug?

CATTRIN: I'm afraid not. Have you finished with the hammer?

ROBERT: I wish I'd thought of shaving with it.

CATTRIN (*as he closes the door, her manner polite and impersonal*): Haven't you got a visitor?

ROBERT: She's all right. What's a good grocer round here?

CATTRIN (*darning*): Murdoch in Rose Street's the cheapest.

ROBERT: Thank you. (*Suddenly.*) Are you a frank person?

CATTRIN (*looking up*): What did you say?

ROBERT: Are you a frank person? Yes or no?

CATTRIN (*at a loss*): Why . . . yes——

ROBERT: Good. (*Leaning against the top of* CATTRIN'S *bed, as if giving an interview*.) I'm frank too. And have been for some years, since my twenty-eighth birthday.

CATTRIN: What made you start then?

ROBERT (*playing with the hammer*): Waking up in Buenos Aires and realising that for seven years I'd been kept by a woman – oh, I'd been married to her for four, she made an honest man of me, I will say that for her.

CATTRIN: She was as far gone as that, was she?

ROBERT: She was set on Spaniards, and my Castilian grandmother was my downfall. Seven years with my foot planted on the bottom rung of the ladder.

CATTRIN: And when you realised all this?

ROBERT: It was the first rainy day for months, and there was a clock ticking. I suddenly walked to the stairs and shouted, quite ordinarily but rather loud, 'You remember asking about the flowers in your hair? Well, you looked bloody awful.' I haven't seen her since.

CATTRIN: What did you do?

ROBERT: Took my foot off the bottom rung and stepped into space. She divorced me soon after.

CATTRIN *rises and crosses to the chest of drawers*.

CATTRIN: And why all this to me?

ROBERT: Because I want you to be frank too.

CATTRIN: What about?

ROBERT: Your father.

CATTRIN (*startled*): My father? Is anything wrong?

ROBERT: How much does he drink these days?

A pause. He throws the hammer on the bed and looks at her.

CATTRIN (*coldly*): I think you'd better go, don't you?

ROBERT: The question has never been put to you before, even wrapped in tissue-paper, because you've always pretended he hasn't got any failings – so the only cure is to shock you with a direct hit: how much does he drink these days?

She looks at him, at a loss, puts away the sock in a drawer and takes out another.

CATTRIN: Do you talk to everybody like this?

ROBERT: No. How did you sum me up when I came in this morning?

CATTRIN: There wasn't anything to sum up, you just asked for a hammer and took it.

ROBERT: Well, just now?

CATTRIN (*putting back the cane chair*): You asked for a razor-blade, I've not seen you when you weren't wanting something.

ROBERT (*crossing to the office chair, and sitting*): How do I compare with other men you know?

CATTRIN: I don't know any except my father, and we're not going to discuss him——

She carries the card-table up to its old place at the foot of the bed.

ROBERT: Oh yes we are, but how would you sum me up?

CATTRIN: Conceited, superficial, and pushing.

ROBERT: Exactly, and if I were all that, I'd have got further than I have. I'm abnormally sensitive and oppressively shy. (*As she turns and looks at him.*) I smoke fifty cigarettes a day, in the presence of more than two people my palms are never quite dry, and each of the three times I've come in here I've had to stop outside and work up a jaunty manner. I've still got it. It's either getting the bull by the horns or running for my life, and people don't take to me. It's a pity, because I'm all right.

CATTRIN: But why are you able to talk to me like this?

ROBERT: Because you're a cripple.

She turns to him, startled but not upset.

CATTRIN (*after a pause*): I've never heard that word spoken before. (*Coming down with the nightdress and putting it under her pillow.*)

ROBERT: You don't mind?

CATTRIN: No. (*Turning to him.*) I'm assuming you're not being sorry for me?

ROBERT: Why should I, with people so much more unfortunate about, eaten away, deranged, heart-broken?

CATTRIN (*sitting on the bed*): I've been wanting to hear that for a long time.

ROBERT: Good for you——

CATTRIN: But why should my being as I am, make it easier for you to talk?

ROBERT: Fellow-feeling, I suppose. I have a little trouble too, not so definite, because it's in the mind; but it's probably made my character what it is. I'm illegitimate.

CATTRIN (*after a pause*): I see.

ROBERT: Once a week I was allowed to share toys with the legal offspring. . . . (*Rising and walking.*) I know it wasn't my fault, and I'm as good as anybody else – but there it is at the back of my mind, sitting pretty.

CATTRIN (*smiling*): How d'you know I'm not illegitimate too?

381

ROBERT: People who live with their fathers rarely are. How much does he drink these days?

CATTRIN (*without thinking*): Quite a lot. . . . Your shock tactics certainly have their effect.

ROBERT: Does he drink——

> MADDOC *shambles in, and they are silent.*
>
> *He wears the same clothes, with mackintosh and shabby soft hat; he carries a bottle of beer and a newspaper. He still has not shaved, and looks more disreputable than ever. His mood is different; his exhilaration has given way to sullen bad temper. He puts the bottle and newspaper on the table, crosses to the chest of drawers and takes up a tumbler and an opener.*

ROBERT: How are you, sir?

> MADDOC *turns, sees him, blinks, walks up to the table, takes up his beer and newspaper, opens the kitchenette door, turns on the light, and goes inside, banging the door behind him.*

CATTRIN: I'm afraid that's his way of asking you to go.

ROBERT: Does he drink enough to interfere with work?

CATTRIN: He doesn't work – I mean, he's – retired. He collects Welsh folk-songs.

ROBERT (*sitting again in the office chair*): A hobby you've engineered for him, I take it. . . . But if he did work?

CATTRIN (*darning*): He'd be all right while I was here, and as I'm always here – he'd be all right.

ROBERT: What was his last job?

CATTRIN: Father Christmas at Selfridge's. He gave notice. It wasn't what he was used to.

ROBERT: And what *was* he used to? What was the job before?

CATTRIN: An announcer. At the Ideal Homes Exhibition.

ROBERT: What did he announce?

CATTRIN (*with difficulty*): 'Move along please.'

ROBERT: Was he good?

CATTRIN (*darning*): Till he got bored and took to announcing 'There is a small fire in the basement.'

ROBERT: Then he gave notice?

CATTRIN (*catching his eye*): Ye'es.

ROBERT: But he'd be all right if he got interested?

CATTRIN: I'd see that he was. (*Suddenly getting his drift.*) You mean——

ROBERT (*rising*): Pity he's retired.

CATTRIN (*putting aside her work, confused and eager*): If it was something clerical and quiet – even copying out, he's wonderful at copper-plate – you know of something? – I didn't mean he drinks as much as all that——

ROBERT: It isn't clerical, and it isn't quiet.

CATTRIN: What is it then?

ROBERT: The stage.

> *She stares at him.*

CATTRIN: The stage? But . . . he hasn't acted for eight years——

ROBERT: All the more reason for starting now.

CATTRIN: But – I don't know if he'd want to – he's never breathed a word about it – since——

> *The door opens, and* MRS LOTHIAN *appears. She is a stout Scotswoman of fifty, blunt and irascible, expensively and tastelessly dressed.*

MRS LOTHIAN (*to* ROBERT): I'm not young and I've never been pretty, but I've got ten thousand in the bank and what's the meaning o' keeping me waiting?

ROBERT: I've been paving the way.

MRS LOTHIAN: Oh.

ROBERT (*proffering the office chair*): Sit down—— (*To* CATTRIN.) May I?

MRS LOTHIAN (*to* CATTRIN): Recognise me?

CATTRIN: No.

MRS LOTHIAN: Your father will.

CATTRIN: Were you a friend of his . . . when——

MRS LOTHIAN: He couldn't stand me, I was what I believe in these days they call a fan. It was his *Romeo* that started me off, when he was nineteen and I was the plainest schoolgirl in the pit. (*Sitting.*) I never left him alone after that. Remember Twelve A?

CATTRIN: You mean – Cumberland——

MRS LOTHIAN: Twelve A Cumberland Terrace, Regent's Park. Your house.

CATTRIN (*fascinated*): Yes . . . our house. . . . It's so long ago I'd given up remembering it. . . .

ROBERT: Was it a famous address?

CATTRIN: Everybody in London knew it. . . . (*To* MRS LOTHIAN, *eagerly*.) Didn't they?

MRS LOTHIAN: The suppers he gave were as talked-about as Beerbohm Tree's.

CATTRIN (*nodding, excited*): Yes, they were, weren't they?

MRS LOTHIAN (*smiling*): Had ye forgotten that ye had a celebrated man for a father?

CATTRIN: Almost . . . but not quite. . . . Did you ever go there? To Twelve A?

MRS LOTHIAN: Remember the Red Cross Tea, nineteen seventeen? A woman reciting 'Boots boots' in a tango skirt? That was me. You were seven, dressed as a nurse.

CATTRIN: Was he there?

MRS LOTHIAN: Yes, on leave – and a famous actor

384

even then . . . and I went pestering him right till he started on the down grade. Then I came into my bit of money and went abroad.

CATTRIN: And when you got back——?

MRS LOTHIAN: Kind folk were only too anxious to tell me how he'd sunk lower and lower, and I soon shut 'em up; but he was finished, just disappeared. So when my friend here told me last night he'd moved into the same house as Maddoc Thomas, there was no holding me.

CATTRIN: Is this your idea, for him to go back to the stage?

MRS LOTHIAN: Mine, and Robert's here – he'll tell you. I'm just here to bring pressure to bear——

    MADDOC *returns from the kitchenette, turning off the light and closing the door; his newspaper under his arm, he carries a glass of beer and the bottle, sucking his thumb; he has taken off his overcoat and collar and tie, and he looks like a disgruntled tramp.*

MADDOC (*shuffling down to the chest of drawers*): What the hell's the matter with that opener——

    He puts down the bottle, and his hat, sees MRS LOTHIAN *and stops short. She rises; she is shocked by his appearance.*

ROBERT: Do you know her?

MADDOC (*sourly, to* CATTRIN): She the one who got me to Selfridge's?

MRS LOTHIAN (*to the others*): It's this daft hat, they change so. (*To him.*) Mrs Lothian.

    He is taken aback. A pause. He looks a sorry sight.

MRS LOTHIAN: We haven't set eyes on each other for eleven years. (*As he does not stir.*) The last night of *Peer Gynt*, Drury Lane. (*To the others, who are watching anxiously.*) I waited nine hours. And at the stage door after I was top o' the poll; looking pretty witless with a great bunch of roses, but I was there. Drury Lane, just down the road. (*After a pause, simply, as she sits.*) I'm very moved.

MADDOC (*coldly*): I am not, I fear. (*Walking above the table, and leaning over it, a glimpse of the famous actor's public manner, for the first time, and frightening it is, too.*) Merely embarrassed. Having cut myself off from a profession which I detested——

MRS LOTHIAN: Have a nice sit-down, ye're not addressing the Critics' Circle now.

MADDOC: I have no wish to be reminded of the past by a lachrymose and ageing gallery-girl. (*Sitting heavily, in the kitchen chair.*)

MRS LOTHIAN (*to the others*): He's always talked to me like that, I used to love it. Getting into his cab once he kissed my hand – och, to make folk laugh, I knew. And what d'ye think I did? Had it in a glove for two days, and kept on taking it out and looking at it. . . . (*Sternly, over her shoulder.*) Not moved, but embarrassed, are ye? I'll embarrass you a bit more, shall I?

MADDOC (*spreading his newspaper*): Kindly take your leave.

MRS LOTHIAN (*swinging round on him*): Not before I've embarrassed ye, I don't. That speech had more lies to the square inch than one of my board meetings. For twenty years, Maddoc Thomas, I loved the ground ye trod. Not for your looks, but because ye were an actor. I thought your *Hamlet* at the Lyceum was pretty wonderful; but I wrote ye pages of criticism which ye heeded, so I am not lachrymose.

MADDOC (*muttering into his newspaper, marking*): Aston Villa . . .

MRS LOTHIAN: *And* ye didn't cut yourself from the stage, the stage cut itself from you. That last night of

Peer Gynt was pretty teasing, ye know; ye were the star of the piece, and in that last scene they were supporting ye all right. *And* it was not a profession ye detested; ye liked the applause, but ye loved the speaking and the moving more; because in them ye lived, brilliant and complete. And ye've been dead ever since.

She swings round in the chair towards the others.

MADDOC: Mind your own business.

MRS LOTHIAN: I've made it my business, and ye can't humbug me. Remember the first performance of *Vasco da Gama*?

CATTRIN: Was it a great night?

MRS LOTHIAN: It was worth while being alive. When he stood at the prow, and the cabin-boy played the lute. . . . (*To* MADDOC, *over her shoulder.*) Remember?

MADDOC (*marking*): Millwall, Tottenham Hotspurs. . . .

MRS LOTHIAN: He'd been joking with the crew to make them forget. Then he was alone, and the moon came out; the lute died away, and that vast place was so quiet ye could hear people catching their breath with pleasure. Then he prayed.

MADDOC *stops writing.*

'If in this peril, o God, the fish in the sea are dearer to thee than these men of mine, so that the men must rot in tomorrow's sun and the fish have more warmth than they, I shall in obedience love the fish both large and small. . . .'

MADDOC *looks before him. The room is filled with memories.*

MRS LOTHIAN: 'But more than ever, o Lord'——

MADDOC (*sharply*): No no – 'still more, o God.'

MRS LOTHIAN: 'But still more, o God, I shall love my men, and weep for them.' Then, far away, the violins, and just him standing there, and the light fading over the sea. (*Rising, abruptly, embarrassed by herself.*) There's a slight smell of cats on the stairs, but as it's the perfect life, you know best.

 She goes.

 MADDOC *looks at his paper, mechanically.*

ROBERT (*at the door, calling*): I'll see you down – are you sure? Mind, it's pretty dark——

 He comes back, shutting the door. He and CATTRIN
 look at MADDOC.

MADDOC: Have that woman locked up and bring me the key.

ROBERT: As a matter of fact, I asked her to come.

MADDOC: Asked her?

ROBERT: To get you in the right frame of mind.

MADDOC: A raging temper? Because you've suc-ceeded——

ROBERT: I have a proposition.

MADDOC (*looking from one to the other*): Are you on to this?

CATTRIN: Not yet. (*To* ROBERT, *rising.*) Yes?

ROBERT (*to* MADDOC): You know I write music?

MADDOC: You walk the tight-rope for all I care——

ROBERT: I've written three numbers for the new musical play at the Shaftesbury – a big chance for me, but that's neither here nor there. There's a part in the second act – quite short, with no singing – that they thought they'd got C. V. France for, but he's tied up with a film – it's important, and they're in a jam. Then I realised yesterday you were living in the same house, and got this idea from talking to Mrs Lothian about you. If you were keen and everything was all right, I know they'd jump at it——

MADDOC: What do you mean, all right?

ROBERT: If you behaved yourself.

MADDOC: I should like you to go.

ROBERT (*rising*): I know, but life's very short, and shorter for you than for me – I've got the part here, I'll fetch it.

MADDOC: I shouldn't trouble yourself——

CATTRIN: What would they pay him?

ROBERT: They mentioned fifteen pounds a week.

> *He goes, shutting the door.* MADDOC *continues to mark his newspaper.* CATTRIN *goes up and watches him, anxious and excited.*

MADDOC: Fresh, they call that sort, don't they? A fresh young fellow.... (*After a pause.*) I think I'll pop round to the Bird in Hand, Barty said he'd be in half-past eight. (*He rises, goes to the sofa, takes his hat, puts it on, turns to go and sees her steadfast look.*) What's the matter?

CATTRIN: Once, when I was very young, you told me about half-past eight, I've never forgotten. (*Rising.*) We're in the heart of London – theatres all round us. . . . The orchestras tuning up, the lights dimming, the curtains rising . . . half-past eight! For years after we came here, I watched you about this time, getting restless, drinking, looking out of the window . . . longing to be in the theatre. You woke up once and swore I was crying, remember? (*Nearer.*) I'd been dreaming about Twelve A, after a first night, with the chandelier lit and Mrs Patrick Campbell in the red dress she wore when she was really there; the front door sailed up like a curtain and you rode in on a horse and they all applauded, then I woke up and had a good cry and pretended it was the cistern.

MADDOC: I haven't been inside a theatre for eight years. It was another life, and it's finished with. You've never talked like that before! We're all right here, you said so yourself——

CATTRIN (*up to him*): We were all right till this minute, because there was nothing else – but now, there's this! We were making do, you know we were, muddling along – but I *would* like a hot bath just once, and there *is* a smell of cats on the stairs! Fifteen pounds a week. . . .

MADDOC: I'd never be able to learn it.

CATTRIN: He said it was a short part——

MADDOC: I couldn't stand the rehearsals – all the blasted politeness– clean collar every morning – kowtowing to some silly young woman who sings flat – and all of them wondering if I'm on the wagon or off it – no, give me Barty and Co. every time——

FAN runs in, bedraggled.

FAN: Lend me five bob, there's a duck.

CATTRIN: What for?

FAN: He'd had his pocket picked in the tube, isn't it wicked?

CATTRIN: Wicked. (*With meaning, as she gets the money from the drawer in the table.*) What d'you think, my father's got the chance of a job on the stage!

FAN: Mad, you haven't! Thank you, dear. . . . Of course you used to be on the stage properly, didn't you, when I was in India—— What're you going to be, hind legs in the panto? What a scream! . . .

She hurries out.

CATTRIN: Let's show them, Tadda. Let's go into partnership. It's a gamble, but just a bit better than the pools!

ROBERT returns, carrying a script.

ROBERT: It's about the Empress Eugénie, and the part
is the Duke of Alva. He arrives at a ball with bad news of
Paca. The music is playing in the ballroom – a waltz of
mine——

CATTRIN: And who's Paca?

ROBERT: His wife. She's just died.

> *He sits on the sofa. A pause.* CATTRIN *looks anxiously*
> *at her father.*

MADDOC (*muttering*): It's too late.

ROBERT (*reading, laboriously and brightly, on purpose*): 'In
the midst of this gaiety, my lords, ladies and gentlemen,
I am sad, for this hall has memories for me.' Countess –
'what memories, my lord, memories of love or of laughter,
or of both?' Duke – 'of love, my lady. There she
stood'——

MADDOC (*his teeth on edge*): What are you reading, a
boxing commentary?

ROBERT: I'm sorry, isn't that the way——

MADDOC: Of course it isn't the way.

> *A pause. They wait for him to speak; he does not.*

ROBERT: Well, in case you think twice, I'll be in my
room.

> *He goes, shutting the door, leaving the script on the sofa.*
> CATTRIN *crosses, sits on her bed, and watches* MADDOC,
> *who walks round the table, whistling defiantly. He sinks*
> *on the sofa, on the script, takes it, sees what it is, and tosses*
> *it on the sofa-end; his back square to the audience, his hat*
> *on the back of his head, he finishes his glass, and sits,*
> *elbows on knees.* CATTRIN *tries to go on with her darning.*
>
> *The sudden sound of music; in his room,* ROBERT *is*
> *playing the waltz on his piano. They both look slowly up;*
> CATTRIN *catches* MADDOC'S *eye, and goes back to her*
> *work. His look travels to the script beside him. He looks*

away, drums his fingers, takes off his hat and places it beside him, drums his fingers again, and looks again at the script; takes it up, looks at it casually, then turns his face to the audience to get a better light on the paper. He looks slowly round to see if CATTRIN *is watching; but just in time she is deep in her work. The music dies away; he begins to read, stiffly at first. She watches, breathless.*

MADDOC: 'There she stood, poised like a bird. "To the world," I said, "you have given beauty, and happiness to me; you are the light of heart" . . . "Next summer will be happier still," she said, and was gone.' (*He looks before him.*) 'The toast.' (*Raising an imaginary glass, slowly.*) 'My lords, ladies and gentlemen, to my . . .'

The waltz begins again, softly.

MADDOC (*sharply*): Tell that fellow to stop that row!

CATTRIN *watches him, her eyes bright with excitement.* (*Casually, as he lies thoughtfully on the sofa.*) I want a word with him. . . .

The waltz swells and echoes through the room as

THE CURTAIN FALLS

ACT II

SCENE I

Five months later. A night in May.

A few pounds have been spent on the room with the greatest skill, and it looks entirely different. The junk is replaced by unpretentious but good-looking pieces of furniture. The only objects remaining are the sofa, the beds and the trunk; the beds are camouflaged with designed quilts, and the trunk is hidden by a loose cover, while the sofa now faces the audience at an angle, downstage left. Also facing the audience, at an angle, downstage right, a comfortable arm-chair; both sofa and arm-chair are loose-covered. Between sofa and arm-chair, a middle chair. New chintz curtains. In place of the chest of drawers, a low ornamental chest; the wardrobe is in where the wash-stand was, and newly painted; a new screen in front of MADDOC'S bed, hiding it almost completely; in place of the wardrobe, a desk with a waste-paper basket and a wheel-back chair before it; a corner cupboard just above CATTRIN'S bed; a small table on the right edge of the arm-chair, with books. In the middle of the room, behind the sofa, a large round table with three wheel-backed chairs; at the head of CATTRIN'S bed, a low table with a telephone.

A second-hand carpet, not cut to measure; several prints; many more books, mostly on shelves over the desk; a small wireless set on the desk; three electric table lamps (the hanging bracket has gone) on the chest, the desk, and the telephone table. On the desk, a small clock. A small hang-

393

ing mirror above the right window. The kitchenette door is closed; but when it is open one can see that the light inside is a brighter one and the kitchenette seems cleaner and more orderly. Flowers; the window-curtains are closed, the lamps are lit. Newspapers; a copy of 'Ideal Home' on the chest.

When the curtain rises CATTRIN *is sitting on a low stool in the middle of the stage, on the edge of the footlights; her back to the audience, a paint-brush in one hand, a paint-pot in the other, she is surveying the room. She wears a patterned dressing-gown.*

A pause. ROBERT *enters, leaving the door open. He is in lounge suit, wears a hat, and smokes a cigarette. His mood is restless; this becomes more marked later. He puts his hat on the desk.*

ROBERT: How's it getting on?

CATTRIN: My back's broken, but I've finished. Mind the bookshelf, it's wet . . .

ROBERT: Looks pretty good.

CATTRIN: It's the most wonderful room I've ever seen.

ROBERT: How much has it cost?

CATTRIN: Sixteen pounds eight and five. Carpet, from a sale; curtains, sevenpence a yard, remnants; a clock, property man at the theatre; arm-chair, fifteen bob Caledonian Market – with any encouragement I'll tell you what I paid for the drawing-pins.

ROBERT (*sitting on* CATTRIN'S *bed*): How d'you feel?

CATTRIN: An exquisite sense of achievement. (*Rising.*) And now I'm going to forget all about it. . . . You won't tell my father it cost sixteen pounds, will you?

She places the stool next to the top end of the sofa.

ROBERT: Why?

CATTRIN: I told him fifty-four.

She places the paint and brush beside the desk, and begins to tidy it, sorting papers, tearing some and putting them in the waste-paper basket.

ROBERT: Why?

CATTRIN: Because I tell him there's less in the bank than there really is. It isn't that I'm deceiving him.

ROBERT: Oh no.

BEVAN comes in from the kitchenette. He is in uniform and helmet, wears an apron of CATTRIN'S, *and carries a large distemper brush and pot. He crosses to the trunk, taking* CATTRIN'S *paint-pot with him.*

BEVAN: Good evening. I regret to 'ave missed Mr Maddoc Thomas.

He packs his distemper and brushes into the trunk.

ROBERT (*to* CATTRIN): Has he gone out to supper?

CATTRIN: He's having what he calls a yarn after the show with an old pal. The pal's a rabid abstainer, so I was all for father being seen in the Green Room Club with a soft drink.

ROBERT (*to* BEVAN): I hear you haven't been to see him in our show.

BEVAN: I do not care for musical plays. (*Turning to him.*) No offence?

ROBERT: No offence.

BEVAN shuts the trunk.

BEVAN (*going*): And now back to the section house——

ROBERT: Not in that apron.

BEVAN: Oh.

He takes off his apron and hangs it behind the kitchenette door, turning off the light and shutting it.

CATTRIN: Bevan, I did appreciate your giving up your lecture.

BEVAN: Not at all, Miss Thomas, it was on Chinese Philosophy, with which I am out of sympathy.

He goes, shutting the door.

CATTRIN: When are you moving to your flat?

A pause. ROBERT *rises.*

ROBERT: Friday, why?

CATTRIN: I'm taking over your room as mine, and later on turning the Black Hole here into a bathroom.

ROBERT: But you were looking forward to leaving yourself.

CATTRIN: I could tell he hated the idea – it's been eight years, you see, and it's so cheap and central.

A pause. He crosses restlessly to the chest.

MRS BANNER *enters, leaving the door open.*

MRS BANNER (*coming down, to* ROBERT): Gentleman rang up twice. A Mr Rabbit.

ROBERT: You mean Robertson?

MRS BANNER: That's right.

ROBERT: Damn.

MRS BANNER: Said 'e'd be out late but 'e'd ring again.

ROBERT (*opening a journal*): Thank you, Mrs B.

MRS BANNER *advances slowly to the footlights and surveys the room.*

ROBERT: What d'you think of it?

MRS BANNER (*flatly*): It's different, isn't it . . . I must tell my Rosie.

ROBERT: D'you know I've never yet seen Rosie?

MRS BANNER (*going*): She don't go out much.

CATTRIN: How is she, Mrs Banner?

MRS BANNER: Sharp as a needle, bless 'er. Got 'er birthday next week.

ROBERT: Good, we must get her something – how old will she be?

MRS BANNER: Thirty-seven.

She goes, shutting the door. ROBERT *stares after her.*

CATTRIN: Is this Robertson to do with your New York thing?

ROBERT: Yes.

CATTRIN: Did you see them today about it?

ROBERT (*moodily*): It's to go to Radio City, composing and playing, forty pounds a week, for two years.

CATTRIN: Gosh! You didn't boast or get on the defensive?

ROBERT: Orders were obeyed to the letter.

CATTRIN: Wouldn't it be marvellous if you got it——

The telephone rings.

(*Eagerly.*) Ah . . . (*Putting down what she is holding, and running to it.*) Hello. . . . He's not back, I'm afraid. . . . Tonight they finish, yes, at the Shaftesbury . . . seventeen weeks, they were very pleased. . . . (*Whispering hurriedly to* ROBERT.) It's an offer! . . . I'm so glad you liked him, I thought he was jolly good too. . . . (*As* ROBERT *smiles.*) He is sort of free, yes, though I'm expecting a call about another engagement this very minute, what would it be for? . . . What was that? . . . Oh. It isn't quite what he wants to do, I'm so sorry. Good-bye.

ROBERT: What was it for?

CATTRIN: You know father's memory isn't what it might be? It was to play the lead in a new play every week, twice nightly, for forty-two weeks at Leighton Buzzard.

ROBERT: Phew. . . . This call you're expecting, was that eyewash?

CATTRIN (*leaning over the arm-chair*): Not this time, that's why I'm not at the theatre. This would be really good – a bigger part, five pounds more, going to the Lyric with

397

Edith Evans, and a straight play after this would be just right.

ROBERT: Have you had a lot of offers this week?

CATTRIN: Heaps – well, several very . . . it's the only one. I know he's made a big impression, but – there just have not been any others.

ROBERT: Except, of course, the windfall from Leighton Buzzard.

CATTRIN: That's why this Edith Evans thing is rather important.

ROBERT: Do you tell many lies?

CATTRIN: All the time. (*Collecting objects at the desk.*) Somebody rang up to ask if he'd ever made a film, and I said he'd played the Duke of Wellington and the negative was destroyed in a fire.

ROBERT: What did they say?

CATTRIN: They said that by a happy chance it must have been retrieved, as they'd seen the film and never realised the amazing resemblance between my father and George Arliss.

> *She takes the objects from the desk and packs them into the corner cupboard.*

RBOERT: How far would you go to get him where you want him? Stealing?

CATTRIN: Oh yes. (*Taking out a half-full bottle of whisky and studying it.*) Anything short of murder.

ROBERT (*as she puts the bottle on the cupboard*): I wouldn't put that past you.

> BARTY *knocks and enters, in a grubby dressing-gown, the same bleary cheery figure. He is smoking a cigarette. He leaves the door open.* CATTRIN *tidies the cupboard.*

BARTY: Sorry I'm late.

CATTRIN: Hello, Barty!

398

ROBERT: Been to the club?

BARTY: No fear, end o' the month. I went out to dinner.

CATTRIN: But, Barty, how chic! Who with?

BARTY: My aunt. She's off to the Bahamas tomorrow.

ROBERT: And who's taking *her* to the Bahamas?

BARTY (*despondently*): My grandmother.

    He sits on the top end of the sofa. FAN *enters. She is as she was on her first appearance, in dressing-gown and curlers.*

FAN: Sorry I'm late, my room's like an oven, must get that catch seen to. . . . A little housewarmer, dear, make the place look lived in, there!

    From inside her dressing-gown she whips a large doll covered in satin and beads, and seats her in the arm-chair.

CATTRIN (*summoning enthusiasm*): Oh, Fan, that is nice of you. . . .

FAN: A chap bought it me at the Wiggle Club, years ago, when that boom was on. . . . (*To* ROBERT, *sitting next to* BARTY.) Heard your waltz at the Corner House tonight, what a thrill, eh? The girl that touches up my hair went to a matinée. (*To* CATTRIN.) Said what a short part your dad'd got.

CATTRIN (*crossing*): It was a good part, that's the great thing.

FAN: Ever so sad, she said, but she was waitin' for him to sing and dance.

CATTRIN: She sounds awfully silly.

    She goes into the kitchenette, turning on the light.

FAN: Wonderful with hair, though.

ROBERT: Heard from Penang?

FAN: You would, wouldn't you! Yes, I have.

ROBERT: What does he say?

FAN: 'Rubber's terrible, yours to a cinder.'

ROBERT: Oh lord. . . .

FAN: I was all packed. You don't know of anybody wanting a shop-soiled topee?

BARTY: Not a soul.

ROBERT: Just the thing for the opera, I'd have thought.

CATTRIN (*in the kitchenette doorway, holding a bottle*): What about some beer, you two? Robert, I want to talk to them, do you mind?

ROBERT (*as she goes back*): Oh, sorry. (*Going.*) May see you later——

> *He goes, shutting the door.* BARTY *and* FAN *are seated side by side on the sofa, both sensing trouble, looking like two guilty and dissipated schoolchildren.*

FAN: A touch o' the step-in-the-office, if you ask me.

BARTY: Y'know, Queen Victoria must have been rather like her——

> CATTRIN *returns, closing the kitchenette door and switching off the light. She carries a small tray down, holding two glasses of beer;* BARTY *helps her place it on the stool. She sits on the edge of the arm-chair. An embarrassed pause.*

It was so rainy at the Oval they drew stumps.

FAN: Fancy.

CATTRIN (*suddenly, as they both drink*): How would you describe my father?

BARTY (*taken aback*): Your father? A damn fine chap——

FAN: A sport, is your dad. Have a drink with anybody!

CATTRIN: That's just it. He'd have several drinks with anybody. My father is exactly like a child.

BARTY: Well, you told me once I was fourteen last birthday.

CATTRIN: He's a different sort. He's a child with a touch of genius. And I've heard genius is a rare and elusive thing, Barty; when it's been starved for eight years, it's got to be heart-massage all the time. That's my job now.

FAN: Don't quite see where we come in, dear.

BARTY: Moi aussi.

CATTRIN (*disliking her task more and more*): Well . . . he's all right so long as he's not at a loose end. Then, like a child, he gets bored and silly. And now that his evenings are going to be free again, I've *got* to keep him away from people who – lead him on.

She looks anxiously from one to the other.

FAN: But I understand perfectly.

BARTY: Moi aussi.

CATTRIN: You do? (*Incredulous.*) You mean you'll help?

FAN: Of course, dear. He's got to give up galli-vantin'——

BARTY: Case of can't have your cake and eat it, eh?

CATTRIN: I'm so glad – it's just that when I can't be there, I must feel he's – in good hands——

FAN: Of course you must. And any time he's on his own——

BARTY: Just call out on your way down——

BARTY
FAN } (*together*): And we'll come straight up!

They drink. CATTRIN *rises and braces herself.*

CATTRIN: Here goes, even if I do sound like the Salvation Army. Since he's gone back to acting, the three times he's been really pickled were twice with you, Barty, and once with you, Fan. The first two, he missed rehearsal, and I said it was the dentist; the last was before a matinee – black coffee and angostura, and not so funny. You're both dears, but I want you to drop him – gently, not so as he'll notice – but to . . . drop him.

A pause. They are offended.

FAN: Are you insinuating that I drink?

CATTRIN: Oh, Fan——

FAN: Just because I'm jolly and good on parties——

BARTY: What's a hang-over once in a while? Doesn't interfere with me——

CATTRIN: It hasn't got much to interfere with, Barty dear, and Fan, I like you too much to get rude to you – only it's different for you, you're drifting – no, that's the wrong word——

BARTY: Make it cruising, old thing, make it cruising. . . .

CATTRIN (*patting him*): Thank you, Barty. Well, my father's been on a cruise for years, and he isn't any more. (*Behind the sofa, her arms on their shoulders.*) Now both of you, be honest. You're not very good for him, are you?

FAN (*truculent*): If you're turning into a kill-joy——

CATTRIN (*insistent*): Are you?

FAN: No.

BARTY: No.

CATTRIN (*walking round again*): You like him because when he's warmed up he plays the fool and tells wonderful rude stories, but if he'd gone to China this morning it wouldn't break your heart, would it?

BARTY: N-no.

CATTRIN (*with entreaty*): Barty, call me a priggish little madam, but pretend he went to China this morning!

BARTY: I'd miss our yarns, y'know. . . . (*Rising.*) All right.

CATTRIN: Thank you, Barty. And – I'm afraid I read his letters.

BARTY: You mean the loan?

CATTRIN: He wants to do it, but he's not out of the wood himself by any means. I've got to say no.

BARTY: I'll have to try the old lady again . . . I could pop up sometimes early-morningish, if I'm awake, eh?

CATTRIN: Of course you can. . . . Don't look so sad!

He goes to the door, like a scolded dunce.

(*Calling after him.*) You haven't finished your beer.

He turns, gives her a rueful look, and goes, leaving the door open.

CATTRIN: I feel a beast.

FAN: You're all right.

She rises, starts to follow, turns and comes down. For the first time, we see her embarrassed.

About your dad. He likes me, y'know.

CATTRIN: That's no news, Fan.

FAN: Did you guess?

CATTRIN (*smiling*): I never imagined his slippers got into your room all by themselves.

FAN (*her lip trembling*): He's fond o' me, Cat.

CATTRIN: Of course he is. He's not an old man, and you give him something I can't, and I'd sooner it was you than anybody else.

FAN: You know about me being separated from the Colonel?

CATTRIN: Yes?

FAN: I'm not. I made him up.

CATTRIN: What a shame, Fan, I'd got to like him.

FAN: And now Penang's off, I . . . (*in a rush*) . . . your dad said once he wouldn't mind marryin' me, well, if you got sick of it, I might take over.

CATTRIN: Thank you, Fan.

FAN: Anyway, until then you don't mind——

CATTRIN: Of course not, only in case he starts rehearsing, don't let him have too much to drink.

FAN (*brightening*): No, no. (*Going.*) I've got a tin of Ovaltine Mrs Banner gave me Christmas, they say it's delicious. . . .

> *She goes, shutting the door.* CATTRIN *smiles, and sighs with relief. She rises, looks at the doll, picks her up, and walks down to the trunk.* ROBERT *peers round the door.*

ROBERT: Sentence passed, all back in their cells?

CATTRIN (*holding out the doll*): I'm afraid in this case it's solitary confinement for life. (*Stowing her in the trunk and closing the lid.*) Aren't you rather depressed, Robert?

ROBERT (*falling on the arm of the arm-chair*): The evening might be described as a fiasco.

CATTRIN (*taking a small bottle of turpentine and some cotton wool from the side of the telephone*): Oh, of course, it was tonight, I'd forgotten. . . . (*Sitting on the trunk, and cleaning her hands.*) But you were madly in love with her! Where did you go?

ROBERT: Café de Paris balcony.

CATTRIN: Was the cabaret good?

ROBERT: She'd seen it in New York.

CATTRIN: Oh dear. Was she bad-tempered?

ROBERT: Never stopped smiling. At the band, the tablecloth, me, thin air, anything. *And* she talked French to the waiter.

CATTRIN: What's her French like?

ROBERT: Imperfect. She's got poise though. Oh yes. One arm supporting the oval chin, tapering fingers toying with a curl at the nape of the neck – a maddening and recurring gesture.

CATTRIN: Did she talk about the theatre?

ROBERT: Once. Said there's enough sorrow without paying to see it, you know the sort.

CATTRIN: I'd have slapped her.

ROBERT: I did.

CATTRIN: You didn't!

ROBERT: In the taxi. Over the knuckles, like a gentleman. I have an idea it hurts more.

CATTRIN: Robert, you *must* control that temper. . . . What was it about?

ROBERT: She said you must have a heart of gold.

CATTRIN: Me?

ROBERT: She thought we were having an affair.

CATTRIN: You and me? Oh, Robert, how funny! But didn't you tell her about me?

ROBERT: Yes, and that's when she said about the heart of gold.

CATTRIN (*without rancour*): I'm glad you slapped her. . . . But don't give up; if you married her, she might stop smiling and leave her hair alone and become quite sensible.

ROBERT: The trouble is I dance the tango. As soon as these women get wise to that sort of thing, it's paid to any fun as we understand it. (*As the clock chimes the half-hour.*) I feel I'm back in Buenos Aires, drifting, like Barty——

CATTRIN: They said they'd ring at eleven——

ROBERT (*suddenly*): What about you, are you drifting?

CATTRIN: No. (*Smiling.*) Steaming ahead on a shiny railroad track. Slow, but no stops.

ROBERT: Where to?

CATTRIN: Success. Not silly fame in a night, but

money in the bank, and clean shirts and self-respect. No, I'm not drifting. . . .

> *The telephone rings. She scrambles for it. He rises, and walks. His restlessness becomes more apparent.*

Hello. . . . Yes. . . . (*To* ROBERT, *hastily.*) It's them . . . I'm so glad, I thought he was jolly good too. . . . (*Her face lighting.*) He wouldn't mind it being a longer part, a bit . . . (*Puzzled.*) But why a delicate matter? . . . (*After another pause, flatly.*) How do you mean, 'unreliable in the past'? I should be careful, you know, there's such a thing as the law of defamation of——

> *The other end has rung off. She puts down the telephone.*

CATTRIN (*turning away in a sudden rage*): What a fool he's been, what an idiotic fool. . . . (*Recovering.*) I'm not going to cry, because it's just put me on my mettle. It's bound to get round he behaved himself in this last play – it's got to, if I have to give out handbills in the Savoy Grill. No, you can do the bills, I'm sticking to him, like a limpet. All that didn't happen, I just told them the part wasn't good enough, and that's that. (*Pacing across, desperately.*) A child with a touch of genius . . . and I'm jolly lucky to have a genius to look after. It's all worked out, like a chart.

ROBERT: Except for one little item.

CATTRIN (*at the back of the sofa*): And what's that?

ROBERT: Yourself. Where are you going to end up?

CATTRIN: Why . . . (*nonplussed*) . . . looking after him.

ROBERT: Is that right?

CATTRIN: Quite right. Why have you suddenly turned into a magistrate?

ROBERT: Isn't there anything in the world you've ever wanted, beyond trotting through life by his side?

CATTRIN: I don't think so.

ROBERT: Are you sure?

CATTRIN: Well, hardly anything.

ROBERT: And what's the exception?

CATTRIN: Oh, nothing. . . .

ROBERT: Have you ever been in love?

CATTRIN: When I was nineteen, in digs at Waltham-stow. (*Walking, and sitting on the sofa, reminiscent.*) He was very kind to me. I don't quite know how I expected it to end. Then one day I heard him on the phone saying he had a date and couldn't get out of it because she was lame.

ROBERT: What did you do?

CATTRIN: Told my father there were bugs and we were out next day. (*Back to her cleaning.*) Luckily I don't think I'm what Fan would call highly sexed, and I've never thought about that sort of thing since.

ROBERT: But you implied just now there was something you'd missed.

His manner is more eager than it should be, but she does not notice.

CATTRIN (*after a pause*): It doesn't matter – would you like Barty's beer——?

ROBERT: I've told you enough about me, God knows – what is the one thing you want?

CATTRIN (*cleaning her hands*): As I've always known it was out of the question, it isn't really such a tragedy. It's just that by nature I'm meant to . . . have children.

ROBERT (*after a pause*): I guessed right, then.

CATTRIN: I've never told anybody before. (*Smiling.*) It's odd that when I do, it should be a man.

ROBERT: And you can never have a child?

CATTRIN (*without looking up*): I could, I suppose – but I could never risk it. Not for myself. . . . You see, I once

407

got a medical book, and the bits about inherited disease have stuck in my mind. I don't feel terrible about myself, as you know, but anything wrong with a child – no, thank you. . . . Have a drink, Robert, do——

ROBERT: And you still – have this longing——

CATTRIN (*quickly*): It isn't a longing.

ROBERT: What is it then?

She has forgotten he is there, and speaks now as if thinking aloud.

CATTRIN: It isn't really from the heart at all. It's from the stomach, a sort of . . . hunger. It isn't sentimental and it isn't pretty. Hungry to be sitting about being what one was born for; fat, placid, and uncomfortable – that isn't very pretty either. But it's the only thing I want. And I can never have it.

Her hands are suddenly to her face, and she has broken down. He half rises in distress, not knowing what to do.

MADDOC'S VOICE: Will somebody open the door?

CATTRIN (*recovering, quickly*): I'm so sorry, Robert – you shouldn't have led me on——

She runs to the door and opens it. MADDOC *comes upstairs and in, carrying two suitcases and a small bunch of roses. He looks quite different, and ten years younger; his hair is cut, his suit is new, and he wears horn-rimmed spectacles. Now that he is neither drunk nor suffering from after-effects, his true manner emerges for the first time – shy, good-humoured and unpretentious.*

(*Shutting the door as* ROBERT *takes the smaller suitcase and puts it behind the screen.*) The taxi-man should have helped you – the big one goes under the sink——

MADDOC: I gave him a piece of my mind, I can tell you.

CATTRIN: What had he done?

MADDOC: Well, I rather thought he was drunk.

He leaves the larger suitcase in the kitchenette, returns immediately, and holds out the flowers.

To my daughter, whom I love.

CATTRIN: Tadda, diolch o'nghalon——

She hurries into the kitchenette.

ROBERT: Did you see your friend, sir?

MADDOC (*hanging up his hat*): He was boring about our young days, you know, but well meant. (*With a twinkle.*) And the Vichy was delicious. I think the future's so much more to the point, don't you—which reminds me—(*handing* ROBERT *a lighter*)—to go with your new suit, my dear Robert, with my thanks.

ROBERT: How very kind of you, sir – I'm delighted.

MRS BANNER *trundles upstairs, and comes in.* CATTRIN *returns and crosses to the wardrobe.*

MRS BANNER (*to* ROBERT): The phone, same gentleman.

ROBERT *goes out, abruptly.* MRS BANNER *sidles down.*

MADDOC (*taking off his jacket*): Looks a bit het up.

CATTRIN: It's that girl of his, I think.

MADDOC: Too bad——

She helps him into his dressing-gown, a new one.

MRS BANNER: Did the performance come to a good end?

MADDOC (*sitting in the arm-chair, absently*): Very healthy, thank you, Mrs Banner.

MRS BANNER: Last time I was in a theatre was the Boer War.

MADDOC: Really.

MRS BANNER: A catherine wheel went off in the upper circle.

MADDOC: Why?

MRS BANNER: I dunno, I never asked.

409

She goes, shutting the door. CATTRIN *puts the jacket on a hanger in the wardrobe.*

CATTRIN: That lighter was just what he wanted, it was nice of you. How much?

MADDOC: It's all right, it's out of my pocket-money——

CATTRIN (*taking a notebook from the desk*): No it isn't, it's general expenses and I'll give it to you tomorrow.

MADDOC (*looking round him*): Thank you, love, thirty-two bob.

CATTRIN (*coming down for the tray of beer*): You like the room, don't you?

MADDOC: Oh yes, I'll get used to it . . . I wonder if Barty went to the Oval today – shall we go Monday?

CATTRIN: Yes, indeed – oh, Barty said his grandmother's given him a cheque and for you not to bother, whatever that means.

She goes into the kitchenette.

MADDOC: Oh, thank you.

CATTRIN: They were nice at the theatre, were they?

MADDOC: Very. Sent you messages, the call-boy said the piece didn't seem the same. Young Fielding gave me a cigar. (*As* CATTRIN *returns, pulls out the stool and sits on it.*) Said it was for dressing with him seventeen weeks without mentioning Tree or Irving, wasn't it good of him? (*Lighting the cigar.*) And he said that off the stage he'd take me for a country doctor who's not going to be roped in for any theatricals, which pleased me still more. . . . Different from Stevens, he said. I had a dose of Stevens while I was making up.

CATTRIN: You know you haven't had your supper, yet?

MADDOC: Neither I have. Never mind, I've started it now.

At atmosphere of intimacy, warm and leisurely, grows in the room.

CATTRIN: Do Stevens for me.

MADDOC (*lisping pompously*): 'I woth ath near to him, Maddoc Thomath, ath I am to you, when he hithed in my ear roughly ath followth. . . .'

CATTRIN (*laughing*): It's so exactly like him. I wish you'd done it for the others that day.

MADDOC: My dear girl, I'd rather die, you know I could only do it for you – where's *David Copperfield* – (*taking up a book from the little table beside him*) – ah. . . .

CATTRIN: Tadda . . .

MADDOC: What?

CATTRIN: The smell of the cigar. . . . Are you thinking the same as I am?

MADDOC: Wait a minute. . . .

CATTRIN: Somebody coming to lunch?

MADDOC: Ellen Terry? (*As she nods.*) Good lord, yes . . . I don't think I've smoked one since.

CATTRIN: She was in grey, rather fluttery, against a big picture in a gold frame.

MADDOC: The Orpen.

CATTRIN: What became of it?

MADDOC: Sold, I suppose.

CATTRIN: We might find out and buy it back.

MADDOC: Good idea. How much have we got in the bank?

CATTRIN: Not as much as I thought. Twenty-five pounds.

MADDOC: Marvellous, we could offer twenty-four!

CATTRIN: You're good at your job, darling, but you'll

never be Chancellor of the Exchequer. . . . How was Mrs Turby?

MADDOC: Elsie wardrobe-mistress, you mean? Much better. She's having a baby, did you know?

CATTRIN: Is she?

MADDOC: Her fifth. She's been trying to get rid of it, that's why she's been *ill*, *she'll* tell you all about it when you see her.

A pause.

CATTRIN: I'll get your night-cap. . . . (*Shaking off her mood, going to the cupboard and pouring out a whisky and water.*) Was she funny about her troubles?

MADDOC: Very. I asked her if she'd wanted the baby, and she said nothing could have been further from her thoughts.

CATTRIN (*smiling*): Poor old thing. . . .

She gives him his drink and walks slowly about; she hums the Welsh tune, absently.

MADDOC: It's weeks since we did the old folk-songs.

CATTRIN: Yes. . . .

She stops at the left window, and listens.

If you stand here you can hear Covent Garden.

MADDOC: The porters, you mean?

CATTRIN: No, Tristan and Isolde.

MADDOC: Still at it?

CATTRIN: They won't be long now. We heard them once before, three summers ago. . . . That was Melchior just now. . . .

She listens, rapt. He savours his drink.

It's funny to think of that great place so near . . .

Very faintly, for a moment, the music.

Those rows of faces. . . .

MADDOC: Piles of white hair and diamonds and glassy eyes marking time – give me Betsey Trotwood.

CATTRIN (*as the music grows, imperceptibly*): One of these nights, they'll be sitting in rows watching you. Not a small part in a musical comedy, but getting your teeth into something. And being so wonderful that even Mrs Banner will come and see you.

MADDOC: Ah . . . Did they ring up about the Edith Evans play?

CATTRIN (*constrained*): Not yet.

MADDOC: Oh. I expect they'll clinch it in the morning.

The music dies away. She walks back behind him. ROBERT is playing the waltz on his piano; she listens.

All sorts and sizes of music tonight. I shall miss old Empress Eugénie. . . .

The phrase ends. Without warning, CATTRIN runs behind him, clasps her arms impetuously round his neck, and holds his head to her breast. Her lips are trembling.

MADDOC: What on earth – yngenathi, you're choking me! What is it?

CATTRIN: Just a burst of affection.

MADDOC (*kissing her hand*): Rare, and much appreciated.

CATTRIN: I'll get your supper – it's all on the tray——

She is at the kitchenette when the door opens abruptly and MRS LOTHIAN enters. She is in a dowdy but expensive evening dress and wears a turban. She shuts the door behind her.

MRS LOTHIAN: Hello.

CATTRIN (*cordially*): Hello, Mrs Lothian!

MRS LOTHIAN: Mrs Banner let me in

MADDOC (*coldly, taking off his spectacles*): We must have a key cut for you. Don't you ever knock?

413

MRS LOTHIAN: Never, the whole thing's a waste of time; I could write a book on it.

CATTRIN: You'll sit down, won't you——

MRS LOTHIAN (*to* MADDOC): Did ye miss me at the stage door tonight?

MADDOC: No.

CATTRIN: You must try and be polite——

MRS LOTHIAN: Don't care if he's polite or not, too old for that rubbish. (*Sitting on the sofa.*) Forget I've got this on my head, I knew in the shop it was a mistake. . . . Ask me why I couldn't be at the stage door.

CATTRIN (*leaning on* MADDOC's *chair*): Why?

MRS LOTHIAN: Had to meet somebody at the Savoy Grill. Ask me who.

CATTRIN: Who?

MRS LOTHIAN: C. B. Cochran. That's all.

CATTRIN: But how exciting——

MRS LOTHIAN (*to* MADDOC): He went to your musical tosh twice this week.

MADDOC (*rising, and going above the table*): I'm sorry to drive you out, but I'm going to take my trousers off.

MRS LOTHIAN: Take more'n that. Remember *Henry the Fifth*, when I walked in and the dresser sprang in front o' ye with a shield? . . . Now ask me why Cochran went twice.

CATTRIN: Why?

MRS LOTHIAN (*nodding at* MADDOC): To see him. He saw all the things in the old days. Talked a lot about *Vasco da Gama*.

MADDOC: Well?

MRS LOTHIAN: He's taken a long lease on Covent Garden.

CATTRIN: The Opera House?

414

MRS LOTHIAN: Opening in three months with the Ballet, to get it warmed up, and in the autumn, with a little financial co-operation from me – I insisted on that, it's my little gamble – he's got John Gielgud to do a production for him, and he's thinking of presenting you in the play.

MADDOC: Me?

MRS LOTHIAN (*to* CATTRIN): He said when your father came on the other night, the stage lit up slowly and the leading lady looked rather in the way. (*Rising, and going.*) I left him at his club, he's sending the car up for me. In case ye could be bothered to come to his house and say how-d'ye-do, chauffeur'll hoot up. Mind ye, it's not definite——

CATTRIN: But you haven't told us what the play is!

MRS LOTHIAN (*stopping, and turning to* MADDOC): Ever heard of a trifle called *King Lear*?

MADDOC: Lear?

MRS LOTHIAN (*taking a small Temple Shakespeare, very new, from her bag and slapping it on the table*): They say it's unactable, ye know. Good night.

> *She goes, shutting the door behind her. A pause.*

MADDOC: Did *you* hear her say *King Lear*?

CATTRIN: Yes. Did you?

> *He puts down drink and cigar, makes to take up the Shakespeare, refrains, walks a step, and stops, excited, thoughtful.*

MADDOC: And it *is* unactable. D'you know it?

CATTRIN: No. Do you?

MADDOC: No. (*Walking down.*) I knew it was the toughest pill of the lot and left it alone.

> *He sits on the sofa; she sits at the other end. A great burst of music, from the Opera House.*

MADDOC (*his excitement mounting*): Gielgud producing
. . . Covent Garden. . . . It would be back to the old days
– Kean played there, and Kemble. . . .

CATTRIN (*darting across and sitting by his side*): They'll
help – they'll be there – in and out of your dressing-room,
rather like me——

MADDOC: You'd never get the public to come to
it——

CATTRIN: The public will come to anything if it's true
and exciting! And people remember you more than you
think——

MADDOC: But would I remember *King Lear*? (*Rising,
hurrying to the table, sitting at it, and turning over the leaves.*)
Isn't it one of the longest – oh, God, don't let it be like
Hamlet – it'll fall through, I expect. . . .

    The music dies away.

CATTRIN: Rows of faces, in the dark. Music, like that,
and then silence, and then . . . the stage lighting up
slowly, and you in a great cloak . . . long white hair – that
flowing beard . . . speaking . . . speaking. . . .

MADDOC: It *is* like *Hamlet*. I'm sunk.

CATTRIN (*going to the table*): Oh no, you're not sunk. . . .
If this is settled tonight, we start tomorrow – go to the
sea for a week, to get you in training – then a clear two
months before you even think of rehearsals——

    They are sitting at the table, talking across to each other.

MADDOC: I'd have to do a lot of reading for it –
Bradley – Dover Wilson——

CATTRIN: I'll sneak them all out of the British Museum
for you. And then we'll get down to learning – over and
over again, like a parrot, right through meals – and we'll
do our old memory game – 'suffer the arm-in-a-slings
and arrows of outrageous fortune' and all that – they'll

think we're mad on the tops of buses, they'll turn us out of the pictures, but by the time we've finished, you'll know it backwards in your sleep. . . . We got away with last time, and we're going to have a shot at this – (*taking his glass from the table*) – we'll turn your nightcap into a toast – (*standing up and holding out the glass*) – 'From Father Christmas . . . to King Lear'!

> *She drinks. He rises. She puts the glass in his hand; he looks before him.*

MADDOC (*quietly*): It's unactable, is it?

> *He raises the glass, and is about to drink when a car hoots in the street, far below the right window. He puts down the glass in great haste, and starts for the door.*

CATTRIN: Your jacket——

> *He remembers he is still wearing his dressing-gown, and takes it off, while she fetches his jacket from the wardrobe. She helps him into it, and adjusts his tie.*

Finger-nails.

> *He holds out his hands.*

(*Nodding, as he takes his hat.*) Mind the stairs – good luck——(*Calling after him.*) Lemon squash, and don't talk salary!

> *She shuts the door, and stands a moment in a glow. A faint burst of music, far away.*
>
> *She takes a small mirror and some cleaning tissues from a drawer under the corner cupboard and turns off the switch at the door; the desk and bedside lights are extinguished, leaving a pool of light round the sofa. She comes down, sits on the lower end of the sofa, tucks her hair behind her ears and begins to clean her face. The music grows.*
>
> ROBERT *enters abruptly, closing the door behind him. He is in a state of deep inward excitement.*

CATTRIN (*looking up*): Hello, Robert.

417

She turns away again. He seems about to say something of great moment to him, then lacks the courage.

ROBERT: What was that about salary?

CATTRIN: Just – something in the offing – it mightn't be lucky to talk about it till he's back—— (*Casually, as he sits on the edge of the arm-chair, looking at her.*) What's the matter?

ROBERT: First time I've seen a woman without any lip-stick.

CATTRIN: What about Buenos Aires, did she always keep hers on?

ROBERT: To the last ditch.

CATTRIN (*without coquetry*): Does it look awful?

ROBERT (*without gallantry*): No. Like a schoolgirl. Why don't you go about like that?

CATTRIN: I couldn't, in public without lip-stick, I'd feel quite naked – tell me about your phone call.

A pause. He rises and wanders across to the left window.

ROBERT: What's that music?

CATTRIN: *Tristan.* It's nearly over.

ROBERT *listens.*

ROBERT: Isn't it supposed to be the most wonderful love music ever written?

CATTRIN (*abstracted*): So they say. . . . What did this Robertson have to say about New York?

ROBERT (*without turning round, suddenly strained*): Why do you think you're crippled?

She looks at him sharply.

CATTRIN: I'm not in the mood for your frank stunt, Robert, and I think you'd better go to bed.

He turns to her, breathing fast. The music fades away.

ROBERT: Why do you think you're crippled?

418

CATTRIN: Because I was born crippled. (*Angry, as he walks across, tormented, undecided.*) And if you want to know why, any doctor will give you the choice of several answers all equally unattractive. . . . *Why* did you make me tell you all that just now, how I wish I hadn't——

ROBERT: Shall I tell you why? Because this Mr Robertson who's been ringing up isn't anything to do with New York at all. He's a doctor.

CATTRIN (*alarmed*): Robert, are you ill?

ROBERT: He isn't my doctor, he's yours.

CATTRIN: I haven't got a doctor, what is all this? Who is he?

ROBERT: The man who brought you into the world. I'd been trying to trace him for weeks, and this morning got his address from the Medical Association – after a good deal of red tape, he's just told me you were one of the most perfect babies he ever saw.

A pause.

CATTRIN (*completely at a loss*): But . . . he told my father I was born crippled. Why should he have lied about it?

ROBERT: Because when you were a year old, your father had a bad fall. With you in his arms. When they found something was wrong, the doctor made out you'd been born like that, to save your father's feelings. You see, when he fell he – wasn't sober.

A pause.

CATTRIN: He was still missing her. Poor old Tadda. . . .

ROBERT (*nervous, exasperated*): Can't you think of yourself for one little minute? D'you realise this means that you can have a perfectly healthy child?

CATTRIN (*philosophically*): You mean I could have had – one might as well face the facts; I don't see any husbands suddenly rushing at me from nowhere——

ROBERT: Can't you see that I'm asking you to marry me?

She sits still, looking before her. A pause.

CATTRIN: Did you really say that, Robert?

ROBERT: I'll say it again. Will you marry me?

CATTRIN (*without moving*): Of course I will. (*Looking before her, again, in a far away voice.*) The thought of this has never crossed my mind. I've never been in love with you – not a bit – and yet, as you were saying that, I knew I was going to marry you. I'm in love with you, too, suddenly; now and for ever. I've been sleep-walking all my life. . . . Was it really now you asked me, Robert? It seems days ago . . . I feel as if I'd just gone over Niagara in a barrel. . . . (*Recovering, looking at him.*) Why do you want to marry me?

His strain over, ROBERT stands at the top of the sofa, and speaks, choosing his words with measured simplicity; she looks at him.

ROBERT: I'll work up quickly from the bottom of the list. Because I want a family, because you'll stop me being tactless and a fool over women, because when I'm depressed you'll tell me it doesn't matter about my parents, and I'm a genius and not a gigolo. Then again, I want to marry you because you're an exceptional person.

CATTRIN (*looking out, weakly*): I haven't got any lipstick on. . . .

ROBERT: You think you're ordinary, but you're not. You have a physical handicap which anybody else in a million would have made sentimental and oppressive; you've dealt with that. You're a fastidious creature, but you have a charming affection for dirty people. You have a deep and loving spirit, but a tongue to go with it and the teeth of a bull-dog. You're serious and you see

420

straight, but you're fun. . . . That's the thing about you, I think – you're great fun.

CATTRIN (*almost to herself*): I've never had anything like this said to me before.

ROBERT: Then again . . . (*sitting beside her*) . . . I want to marry you because your eyes are wide apart and your ears grow where they ought to. Because you have lovely breasts, perfect hands – chapped from washing up, but perfect – and a mouth that, when it isn't made up, looks like a child's. You have one very twisted foot, my darling wife . . . but the Venus de Milo is mutilated too.

She is too happy to stir or speak.

You've got tears in your eyes. . . .

The lights fade slowly into darkness. The curtain falls, and rises immediately on

SCENE II

Six months later. An early afternoon in November. The room is unchanged; pressed beech-leaves instead of flowers. Cold autumn sun filters through the net curtains.

MADDOC *is sitting on the edge of the table in his shirt-sleeves, an open copy of* The Times *on his knee. He is wearing his spectacles.* BEVAN *is sitting in the arm-chair, still in uniform, holding the copy of* King Lear, *now dog-eared and battered, and in the other hand a tumbler; beside him is a half-finished bottle of beer.* MADDOC *looks well; alert but serene.*

MADDOC: Now the last bit.

BEVAN: Act Four, Scene Six. (*Reading.*) 'O thou side-piercing sight.' (*Drinking.*)

MADDOC (*reeling off under his breath, at an unintelligible speed*): Nature is above art in that respect there's your press-money that fellow handles his bow like a crow-keeper draw me a clothier's yard look look a mouse peace peace this toasted cheese will do it there's my gauntlet I'll prove it on a giant bring up the brown bills o well flown bird in the air ha give the word.

BEVAN (*puzzled*): Oh. (*Reading, laboriously.*) 'I know that voice.'

MADDOC (*as before*): Ha Goneril ha Regan they flattered me like a dog and told me I had white hairs in my beard ere the black ones were there et cetera. Diolch, Bevan, my weak spot, and that's put it right.

The clock chimes the half-hour.

(*Drumming his fingers, with a smile.*) Six more hours. . . . (*Looking at the newspaper.*) There it is for you. 'Tonight . . . at Eight.'

BEVAN: As an academic point, Mr Thomas, would you say it was like waitin' to be hanged?

MADDOC: Having been denied that privilege, Bevan bach, I really don't know.

BEVAN: That is how it affected *me*.

MADDOC: When was that, Bevan?

BEVAN (*reading, thoughtfully*): Competin' in an Eisteddfod for the adult recitation.

MADDOC: Did you win?

BEVAN: I was sick twice and come in third. . . . (*Rising, and taking him the book, carrying bottle and glass with him.*) But you would at least say you were nervous, Mr Thomas?

MADDOC: Very. (*Taking the book.*) And yet I feel calm.

BEVAN: A bit the worse for wear, isn't it?

MADDOC (*addressing the book*): I've lived with you, my boy, eaten with you and slept with you every day and night for six months. Tonight, at eight . . . You'd never think such a little fellow could hold such a lot, would you? (*Taking the bottle from* BEVAN *and holding it out.*) Dyferin bach o gwrw, Bevan——

BEVAN: Ddim diolch, Mr Thomas – won't you finish it?

MADDOC: Not today, thank you. Come on, it'll be wasted——

> BARTY *enters, wearing the same old suit and bowler, carrying a basket covered with tissue paper, and an umbrella.* (*Seeing him.*) No, it won't.

BARTY: Cattrin said would I call and wish you luck——

> *The telephone rings.* MADDOC *starts* (*his nerves are not far below the surface*) *and controls himself. He gives* BEVAN *the book, places the bottle on the table, and crosses to the telephone.*

> BEVAN *sits in the arm-chair and becomes engrossed in* King Lear *again.*

MADDOC: Hello. . . . Hello, yes?

BARTY: Cattrin?

MADDOC: The management. . . . (*Into the receiver, as* BARTY *takes up the bottle and goes into the kitchenette, switching on the light.*) Yes, in bed by two. . . . Like a top. . . . Clear as a bell, touch wood . . . I am glad. . . . Oh yes. . . . The crown itself, you mean? Yes. . . . Oh, I agree, it's a detail, but it's important. . . . Yes, I will. . . . Very kind of you to ring me. . . . Do, I'll be in my dressing-room by seven. . . . Good-bye. . . .

> *During this,* BARTY *has wandered back from the kitchenette, leaving on the light, drinking his beer, still carrying his basket, which he now deposits on the small table next to the arm-chair.*

BARTY (*whisking off the tissue paper*): I thought I'd say it with fruit.

MADDOC (*crossing to the sofa*): My dear Barty, how very kind of you.

BARTY (*settling in the arm-chair*): I won a jack-pot last night. Fag?

MADDOC: No thanks – (*sitting*) – well, officer, what d'you think of *King Lear*?

BEVAN: So far, disappointing.

MADDOC: I'm sorry to hear that.

BEVAN: Thunder and lightning is all very well, but a dramatist should convince without the aid of emoluments. No offence?

MADDOC: None at all.

BEVAN: *Hamlet*, in my opinion, is an improvement.

MADDOC: I am glad.

BEVAN (*to* BARTY): What is the theme of *Hamlet* in one sentence?

BARTY: Oh. Well, it's about a fellow who – gets run down——

MADDOC: Ha!

BEVAN (*triumphantly*): It is about a fellow who is in love with his father.

BARTY: Crumbs! (*Finishing his beer.*)

MADDOC: Go on, officer.

BEVAN (*rising, and shutting his book*): Is there anything in *King Lear* as subtle as that?

MADDOC: I doubt it. But how do you account for Hazlitt's lecture on Ophelia?

BEVAN: I am not an admirer of the essayists, Mr Thomas, and it was Coleridge.

    He leaves the book on the table and takes the beer bottle into the kitchenette.

BARTY: I never knew the Welsh were swots.

CATTRIN *enters, carrying several packages and an opened newspaper; she shuts the door. She wears the same clothes as on her first appearance, the mackintosh being replaced by a hooded light coat. Behind the bustle of the next minute, there is the strain of the impending first night.*

CATTRIN: All right?

MADDOC: Fine. I've been hearing the plot of *Hamlet*.

CATTRIN (*taking off her coat and hanging it up on the kitchenette door*): Sounds good – public schools versus Welsh Metropolitan Police – (*affectionately*) – hello, Barty!

BARTY (*rising*): I just popped in, Catters. Just off——

CATTRIN (*undoing packages on the table*): It's all right, Barty . . . anybody ring up?

MADDOC: The management itself, no less. They've sold the last seat in the house.

CATTRIN: Lovely.

MADDOC (*rising, crossing, and looking absent-mindedly out of the right window*): And he said the crown in the first act wants to be wider after all – what you said, you remember. It's being done at Nathan's now, I'll just go round for it——

CATTRIN: You know you've got Gustave's as well – and I do want you to have your rest——

BARTY (*rising, his eyes shining*): Can't I fetch it?

CATTRIN: Oh, Barty, do you think you could? I mean, if you lost it——

BARTY: No jolly fear – Nathan's the costumiers, Panton Street, eh!——

CATTRIN: And leave it at the stage door——

MADDOC: That's fine. Haven't seen you for weeks, Barty.

BARTY: No – (*catching* CATTRIN's *eye*) – I've been busy.

425

MADDOC: You don't mean work?

BARTY: In a way. I'll pop along there now——

MADDOC: You're not being kept, Barty? Out with it!

BARTY: The old lady's companion's down with 'flu and I go along in the mornings and do the flowers.

He goes, shutting the door.

CATTRIN: I brought you the lunch *Star*, there's a photograph – and look!

She unfurls a poster and hangs it from the clock over the desk. It is a Covent Garden Opera House poster of 'MADDOC THOMAS *in* KING LEAR,' *with details.*

MADDOC: They're not exactly hiding me under a bushel, are they?

BEVAN stands in the kitchenette doorway, drying a glass jug with a cloth.

BEVAN: I cleared the dinner——

CATTRIN: Thank you so much, Bevan. (*Taking out another poster.*) I've got another here for Robert – d'you see his name? Not very big, but he'll be jolly pleased——

BEVAN (*standing back near the chest, to see better*): I didn't know Robert had to do with it!

CATTRIN: He's composed the incidental music, didn't I tell you? His first serious stuff, isn't it exciting——

MADDOC: I'll tack it up on his wall, as a surprise, eh——

He takes the poster and goes, leaving the door open.

BEVAN: Were you satisfied with the rehearsal last night, Miss Thomas?

CATTRIN (*coming down, smiling*): Oh, very difficult to answer, Bevan, I was so nervous. . . . Anyway, he's going to look absolutely marvellous . . . (*sitting on the sofa*) . . . and all I know is I heard the powers that be saying 'It'll

be something this generation won't have seen at all.'
That kept me awake a long time.

BEVAN (*going*): Splendid, Miss Thomas——

CATTRIN (*quickly*): Oh, and Bevan – could you get off
on Friday afternoon?

BEVAN: I might, Miss Thomas, what for?

CATTRIN: To be a witness. Robert and I are getting
married.

BEVAN: No! (*Coming down to her, delighted.*) This is
wonderfully unexpected, Miss Thomas!

CATTRIN (*back to her best*): It's all in rather a hurry –
he's sailing for New York on Saturday.

BEVAN: Oh yes, to be sure. . . .

> *A pause. He looks at the poster. She looks up at him.*
You are not sailing with him?

CATTRIN: No, following in a few weeks.

BEVAN: May I ask, Miss Thomas, how long will you
be away?

CATTRIN (*after a pause*): Well, you see, Bevan, it's the
most marvellous job, and means we'll be there about two
years——

BEVAN (*impassive*): Oh.

CATTRIN (*sensing vague reproach*): Coming over for
vacations in between, of course.

BEVAN: I see, Miss Thomas . . . I could inform you
this afternoon if I will be free.

CATTRIN: Thank you, Bevan – you won't tell a soul,
will you?

BEVAN: Not a creature.

CATTRINE: You see, I don't want – anybody to know
till after tonight.

BEVAN (*impassive*): Yes, indeed.

MRS BANNER *enters, leaving the door open. She carries a package.*

MRS BANNER: My Rosie says this 'as been left.

CATTRIN (*rising, and taking it from her*): Good, it's the throat-spray——

MRS BANNER *starts to go, then turns, her face working.*

MRS BANNER: I went last night.

CATTRIN: Oh, the dress rehearsal – (*at the table, undoing the parcel*) – of course you did, Mrs Banner.

MRS BANNER: I spotted your dad.

CATTRIN: I am glad.

MRS BANNER (*suddenly inwardly convulsed*): What *about* 'im, eh?

BEVAN: What about him?

MRS BANNER: What about that beard, eh?

She puts her hand to her mouth and goes into a paroxysm of silent giggling. CATTRIN *and* BEVAN *exchange astonished looks.*

CATTRIN: Well, what about it?

MRS BANNER: Mr Thomas in a beard down to 'is waist. I said to Rosie, talk about Charley's Aunt! (*Going.*) I did laugh, it was lovely.

CATTRIN: That's what comes of not having been inside a theatre since the Boer War.

MRS BANNER *backs into the room as* MADDOC *returns. She eyes him with a new vision.* BEVAN *goes into the kitchenette.*

MADDOC: You were longer than you expected, weren't you?

CATTRIN: I went a bit out of my way to have another look at the queue. I nearly went down the line and kissed them all. (*Going behind the screen.*) I'll get out the eiderdown for your rest——

428

MADDOC (*sitting in the arm-chair*): Did you enjoy the dress rehearsal, Mrs Banner?

> MRS BANNER *puts her hand to her mouth, giggles again, and goes.*

First time I've ever seen her smile. Extraordinary woman. . . .

BEVAN (*returning from the kitchenette, turning out the light and putting on overcoat and helmet*): That she will not be there tonight is a blessing. Pob llwyddiant, Mr Thomas, and Miss Thomas.

MADDOC (*taking his hand*): Thank you, Bevan bach, and for everything else.

CATTRIN (*to* BEVAN *as she brings down* MADDOC's *eider-down to the sofa*): Did the London Welsh Club get their seats all right?

BEVAN: They did indeed! Sixty-four in the upper circle they will be, so if you hear any applause, Mr Thomas, you will know where it is comin' from.

> *He goes, shutting the door.* MADDOC *sits, thoughtful, smiling.*

CATTRIN (*at the table, checking on a list from her bag*): Darker face powder – throat-spray——

MADDOC: The dresser could have done that——

CATTRIN: I know, but he doesn't quite take everything in——

> ROBERT *is playing the piano in his room. She raises her head, and listens, happily.*

MADDOC: Did you say there's a music rehearsal this afternoon? . . . (*As she does not hear.*) Is there?

CATTRIN: Sorry – yes, there is, and Robert wants me there for the timing, as I know exactly how long you take saying everything – and then, my boy, something

I've never run to in my life – I'm going to have my hair done! Oh, here's your first wire.

> *She takes it to him, opening it.*

MADDOC (*reading*): 'Warm good wishes, Green Room Club.'

CATTRIN (*back at the table*): How nice of them.

MADDOC: Isn't it? . . . So many people are being nice. Robert, for instance – played that march at least twenty times last night for me to get used to it. He's been a brick, all the way.

CATTRIN (*casually*): He has, hasn't he?

MADDOC: When does he sail, Saturday? We'll miss him, y'know, won't we?

> *The music stops. A pause.*

CATTRIN (*checking*): Spirit-gum – mend sandal strap – oh yes. . . .

> *She takes a sandal from a package, gets needle and thread from her bag, sits on the stool, and repairs briskly.*

MADDOC (*thoughtfully*): On a day like this, it's strange the things that become a matter of life and death. Sandal strap – wig a quarter of an inch too tight – powder a shade wrong – most essential. . . .

CATTRIN: And it's strange what they're all leading up to. There you sit, Tadda, in this most ordinary room, and – if you don't mind my saying so – looking most ordinary too——

MADDOC: I was thinking the same. (*Taking off his spectacles, reflectively.*) And there's that great empty place over the way, echoing with hammers and hoovers, hoovers and hammers, just a shabby factory. There's this most ordinary day; people are doing their jobs, or doing nothing, rushing about London exchanging all those worn pennies of speech we know so well – 'thought it was going to rain, must phone up so-and-so, didn't quite catch the name' – over and over again. And in a few hours they'll all be in that factory, waiting for the curtain to go up. And behind that curtain, in the wings, leaning on a grimy drum, a little man in dirty plimsolls will be waiting too. He hears them all, sitting out there like a lot of magpies – 'thought it was going to rain, must phone up' . . . and then the signal. The lights fade, the voices die into sudden silence, the pulse of the world is still . . . and then the drum. And like a cloud shaken from a sack, something spreads through the place from end to end. I don't know what it is, but it's magic, and there's nothing like it in the world. (*Unexpectedly, with a sob.*) Oh my dear, why have I wasted all those years – why. . . .

> *Startled, she runs behind him, and holds his head to her breast. She talks to him as she used to, as if he were a child.*

CATTRIN: It's like wine, you see, Tadda, the more dust there is the better it is——

MADDOC (*recovering quickly, sniffing, and laughing again like a child*): So long as the dust is off before they taste it——

CATTRIN: Well, we've given the old vintage a good spit and polish, and it's all ready——

> ROBERT *enters, still in his overcoat. He sees them and stops;* CATTRIN *signals to him reassuringly.*

ROBERT: I may tell you, sir, your first night's costing me a pretty penny; my new tails have arrived. But I must say when I saw that poster it was worth while. (*Seeing the one in the room.*) Ah. . . .

CATTRIN (*takes* MADDOC'S *overcoat from the wardrobe, and helping him into it*): And now actions, old boy, not words – down the road to Gustave's, they've got the wig all ready – and straight back for your rest – (*bundling him out of the door*) allay oop – (*calling after him*) mind the stairs, and don't get run over on the corner!

> *She shuts the door. A pause. She comes down, and finishes her repairing.*

ROBERT: How is he?

CATTRIN: Oh, wonderful – just nerves, for a minute, you know . . . I'm longing to see those tails.

ROBERT: I wish you were going to sit beside them. (*Sitting on the sofa end.*) Will you stay in his dressing-room all through the play?

CATTRIN: Only for his changes. It's a bit hard on his dresser, but he'll get panicky if I'm not there. And in between they're letting me watch from a cubby-hole. I hope he'll be careful, there's quite a bit of traffic – now is there anything I've forgotten – oh, the hand-mirror – the magnifying one——

ROBERT: I took one to the theatre this morning. I'm making him a present of it, with the cigars.

CATTRIN: He will be pleased . . . Robert, you really think – he may bring it off?

ROBERT: I'm sure of it. It was extraordinary to watch him last night. The others were saying the same. Like a race-horse on his last canter before the race. At the beginning he seemed quite lost in front of that great void – he was so obviously trying to get something from our anxious faces and not succeeding – and then, suddenly, it would happen; you heard a sizzle and a spurt, and he was off . . . twice the height, twice the breadth, and one got a glimpse of what he will do tonight with a real audience. . . . When that 'cello dies away, and he comes over the hill with the wind catching his white hair, and stands there——

CATTRIN: Yes, I wanted to tell the queue about that——

ROBERT: It seemed as if time was standing too. They were saying they wouldn't miss tonight for anything.

CATTRIN (*rising*): If only he remembers it all. He will, won't he?

ROBERT: Of course he will, he was as firm as a rock——

CATTRIN: We've been through it often enough. I could play it myself.

ROBERT: I'd pay money to see that. Tripping over that beard, the oldest dwarf of them all.

She laughs, and sits suddenly on the edge of the arm-chair, catching her breath.

ROBERT (*rising, and going up to her*): You're pretty whacked.

CATTRIN: Nerves, you know. We've all got them. For years I seem to have been getting ready for today – plotting, coaxing, scolding – and it's here at last. And tomorrow you and I'll be able to say we've done what we swore that night we must do – stick to the job and see it through.

ROBERT: And then . . . (*Sitting in the middle chair.*) You start on your real job – your own.

CATTRIN: Yes. . . . (*After a pause.*) I'll be glad when he knows, Robert.

ROBERT: So will I.

CATTRIN: I've never kept anything from him before about myself. It's not very pleasant.

ROBERT: Believe me, darling, we've done the right thing. We couldn't have told him before tonight – with all this on his mind it would have been pretty tactless, even I can see that – after the play, when the shouting

433

and the what-d'you-call-it's done, and he'll be a success, that'll be the moment to break the news.

CATTRIN: I know – it was my idea, anyway. I'm just being silly. . . . Oh, Bevan thinks he may get off on Friday.

ROBERT: Good. Have you thought much about – Friday?

CATTRIN: I've tried not to. Once or twice it's caught me unawares.

ROBERT: Same here – and then it was like trying to keep the sea out by pushing a door against it. But I managed. With old King Lear pushing as well.

CATTRIN: It got me at the oddest moments too. On the moving-staircase, washing up, hearing barrel-organs, listening to Mrs Banner——

ROBERT: Like a gust of wind, smack in the face, and your breath's gone and you miss a cylinder.

CATTRIN: That's it! And it all comes pouring in, all the new plans, just as complicated as the ones for him, only this time they're for us.

ROBERT (*rising and going towards the left window*): Then up pops old King Lear again——

CATTRIN: And he's going to be a success. Dear annwyl, I do feel excited——

MRS LOTHIAN *enters, closing the door behind her*.

MRS LOTHIAN: I saw him going into Gustave's down the road, so here I am.

ROBERT: D'you mean to say you're avoiding him?

MRS LOTHIAN: Well, we don't want him in a temper today, do we? I walked round from the theatre, they're expecting ye for some music or something.

CATTRIN: Are you excited?

MRS LOTHIAN: No.

She sits in the middle chair.

ROBERT: What did you think of the dress rehearsal?

MRS LOTHIAN: I didn't see it.

ROBERT: You didn't see it?

MRS LOTHIAN: I went to the pictures. An organ recital, and a tour through Lapland with the November Handicap and the King and Queen thrown in.

ROBERT: And what is it this evening, folk dancing at the Albert Hall?

MRS LOTHIAN: No, *King Lear* tonight. I wasn't going to take the edge off with any rehearsal.

CATTRIN: Where will you be, stalls or a box?

MRS LOTHIAN: I've got a stool.

ROBERT: You're not in the pit?

MRS LOTHIAN: I've been in the pit for thirty years, why should I go gadding in the stalls just because I've got some cash invested in the play?

ROBERT: Why indeed?

CATTRIN: Don't you even want to hear how it went?

MRS LOTHIAN: No.

ROBERT: You're an infuriating woman, you know.

MRS LOTHIAN: I know.

ROBERT: Suppose the scenery falls down?

MRS LOTHIAN: I'll push it up again.

ROBERT: I believe she would, too.

MRS LOTHIAN: What's the matter with the lot of ye? What d'ye think I was pinning my faith to before either of ye were born, standing in a queue once a week all the year round, eating nine hundred odd sandwiches? The man's a genius, I've said so from the start, so why not sit back and let William Shakespeare do the rest? – *(rising)* – come on, ye're late——

CATTRIN *(rising)*: She's right, of course.

435

MRS LOTHIAN: I'll see ye tomorrow forenoon——

CATTRIN (*putting on her coat,* ROBERT *helping her*): I can't believe there is a tomorrow.

MRS LOTHIAN: Oh, what I came up all those stairs for – I'm making you two a present.

They look at her, startled, then at each other.

CATTRIN: Us?

MRS LOTHIAN: Did ye know I was moving back to Scotland? Well, I've still got the wee house in Chelsea, and you're both welcome to it – (*routing in her bag*) – I've got a snap of it somewhere——

CATTRIN: But who told you we might be – wanting——

MRS LOTHIAN: I just thought this is a bit poky for your father now he's going to be a success, and there's just room for you and him and a maid, and for a sure twelve years. Here it is – what d'ye say?

A pause.

CATTRIN: It looks lovely – it's wonderfully kind of you, Mrs Lothian——

MRS LOTHIAN (*taking the snap*): I'm doing it for myself, don't want any strange folk paying to guy my ornaments – want it?

MADDOC *comes in, leaving the door open.*

MADDOC: They were on the doorstep waiting for me – (*seeing* MRS LOTHIAN) – oh——

MRS LOTHIAN: It's all right, I'm just going.

MADDOC (*polite*): I trust you are well.

MRS LOTHIAN: Fine, fine, and you? . . . Good-bye – oh, Cattrin, you haven't told me what you feel about my wee offer.

CATTRIN: Can I let you know tomorrow – while we've got tonight on our hands, you see——

MRS LOTHIAN: No hurry, dear, no hurry. Good-bye

... good-bye.... (*Turning to* MADDOC *at the door, off-hand, but very direct.*) My heart will be with you.

She goes, leaving the door open.

CATTRIN: You've got some grease-paint on your forehead.

MADDOC: Thank you – from the wig – (*going into the kitchenette, calling*) – like the poster, Robert?

ROBERT: Most impressed——

CATTRIN *closes the curtains over the right window. She crosses to the lower left window, half-closes the curtain, and stops, thoughtful.*

What's the matter?

CATTRIN: Just thinking.

ROBERT: I'll get those notes for the orchestra——

He goes, leaving the door open. The room is in twilight, with shafts of light cutting across.

MADDOC *comes back from the kitchenette, wiping his forehead. She takes his dressing-gown from the wardrobe and helps him into it. He puts one foot against the chest and loosens the laces of his shoes.* CATTRIN *turns out the kitchenette light and closes the door.*

ROBERT'S VOICE: Ready!

CATTRIN (*putting the cushion in place on the sofa*): Even if you don't sleep, you'll relax. I'll call you at six.

MADDOC: Right.

CATTRIN (*patting his shoulder*): And no bad dreams.

MADDOC: No.

She takes up parcels from the table, and hurries out, closing the door softly. He draws several breaths, and tests his throat. One shaft of light shines like a spotlight on the poster; he looks at it a moment, then away, smiling, and contented. He listens to the silence.

MADDOC: 'The pulse of the world is still ...'

He lies on the sofa, under the eiderdown, and settles under it.

A pause. The door opens. It is FAN, very excited.

FAN: Mad – oh, sorry, dear, if I woke you――

MADDOC: I'm all right for a minute――

FAN: Just to wish you the best of luck――

MADDOC: Thank you, Fan.

FAN: And you *are* three sly things, not to have told me!

MADDOC: Told you what?

FAN (*leaning over him*): About Cattrin! The registrar man just rang up downstairs and I took the message – could they come earlier as he's got two other weddings, he said – 'weddings!' I said, and got the whole thing out of him――

MADDOC: Weddings? What are you talking about?

FAN: Cattrin getting married! You sly things!

MADDOC: Cattrin . . . getting married?

FAN (*playful*): Now don't pretend you didn't know!

MADDOC: But I don't know. (*Half sitting up, and looking at her.*) You're joking, Fan.

FAN: Cattrin and Robert are getting married on Friday, three-thirty, Romilly Street Registry Office, twenty-four hours before he leaves for New York, and she's joining him in three weeks!

A pause.

MADDOC: You're making it up.

FAN: The man just told me – mean to say they've kept it from you? That's why they didn't give him this number here, o' course – and I *thought* it was funny that new suitcase comin' up for her, while you were at the theatre – my dear, I do wish them luck! Fancy keeping it from *you*, though, the sly pair!

438

He is looking before him. A pause.

MADDOC: It's thoughtful of them, really. So as not to worry me before tonight. I can see that. . . .

FAN (*sitting on the edge of the middle chair*): Oh yes, of course, natural really – but fancy——

MADDOC: So long, Fan.

He lies down, suddenly, as if settling down again to sleep.

FAN: Well, I'll push off, got to call at the box-office for my upper circles – see you, dear, but you won't see me – good luck, and ta ta——

She goes. The door bangs behind her, and the noise dies away. MADDOC lies without moving. Silence; not the same silence as before; oppressive, threatening.

A pause. He sits up, slowly, his face puzzled and worried, pale in a shaft of light.

MADDOC (*muttering*): Thoughtful of them . . . really . . . so as not to worry me . . . thoughtful, really. . . .

He makes an effort, and lies back. A pause. Silence. Suddenly, as if the wall between him and his thoughts had broken and swept away, and they had fallen upon him, he sits up again, abruptly this time; in growing panic, he throws back the eiderdown, staggers across the room to the right window, and pulls aside the curtains.

He sits on CATTRIN's bed, and looks before him, his breath coming and going heavily. We see his self-confidence oozing before our eyes. He looks round wildly, goes to the wardrobe, wrenches it open, does not find what he wants, looks at CATTRIN's bed, comes down to it again, kneels on the floor, and pulls objects from under it – cardboard boxes, the roulette wheel, old magazines, and a large suitcase, brand new. He tears it open; it contains several layers of new boxes and parcels (all ready for a long journey) which he lifts up and lets fall. He sits, looking before him, dazed.

439

*He rises, sees the poster again. He pulls himself together,
crosses to the table, sits at it, and opens his copy of* King
Lear; *it is no longer something that he loves, but something to be afraid of. He puts his head between his hands,
like a schoolboy doing homework.*

MADDOC (*muttering, without looking at the book*): 'We will
express our darker purposes . . . know we have . . .' (*after
a pause*) . . . what's next? . . . I can't remember. . . .
(*Muttering.*) Oh God! I can't remember. . . .

*The clock strikes three; he listens, fascinated. The notes
die away, and the silence envelops him.*

(*Loudly.*) It's gone! (*Rising, in a panic, and staggering about
the room like an animal in a cage.*) It's gone – I can't remember – (*sinking on* CATTRIN's *bed*) – it's gone——

The telephone rings at his elbow. He takes it mechanically.
Hello. . . . Try what on? The crown? Nathan's. . . .
(*Eagerly.*) Oh, it's you, Barty . . . no, don't ring off –
(*shouting*) – for God's sake don't – ring – off! . . . all right,
just nerves. . . . Where are you going to now, Barty?
The club? . . . For the afternoon? . . . I don't know yet.
I may have a sleep . . . or I may . . .

*His voice trails away as he hangs up. For a moment he
does not move, then he sees the roulette wheel on the floor
before him. As if in a trance, he sinks to the floor, takes
the ball from a slot at the side, gives the wheel a vicious
twist, and spins the ball. Silence, except for the endless
rhythmic whir of the ball as it races round and round.*

THE CURTAIN FALLS SLOWLY

ACT III

SCENE I

Three hours later. Early evening.

The room is the same; the curtains are closed, the lights on, the objects on the floor have been pushed back under the bed, and the eiderdown is trailing over the end of the sofa. BEVAN, in a light lounge suit, sits on the sofa studying King Lear, *his lips moving with strained concentration. His overcoat is folded over the desk.*

MRS BANNER enters. She is upholstered in her best, and carries a cardboard box.

MRS BANNER: Oh. (*After peering behind the screen.*) Where's Mad?

BEVAN: Mr Maddoc Thomas? Just gone out.

MRS BANNER (*going*): Thank you. . . . (*Turning back.*) Oh, it's the bobby! Never reconnised you without your clo'es. (*Sitting in the middle chair.*) I saw the dress re'earsal last night, is that the book?

BEVAN (*without raising his head*): It is.

MRS BANNER: I don't fancy it, do you?

BEVAN: Interesting stuff. Could you follow it?

MRS BANNER: Come an' go, an' yes an' no, but the in-between, oh it *is* a rum show. I never knew Shakespeare was that sort. . . . Picture o' Mad in the *Star*, d'you see? Without the beard, o' course. (*A faint reminiscent giggle.*)

BEVAN: Are you going to the first night tonight?

441

MRS BANNER: Can't, I been booked for weeks. World Film Prime-Year.

BEVAN (*reading*): Where is that?

MRS BANNER: Outside the Odeon.

    CATTRIN hurries in. She is in the same clothes as before; her hair has been imperceptibly dressed.

(*Rising.*) This box come for you dear——

CATTRIN (*taking it*): Oh good, it'll be my dress – I'm late – where's my father?

BEVAN (*rising*): Just gone out, back in a minute. Nathan's, is that the name?

CATTRIN: Oh yes, I suppose they wanted to see the crown on. (*Looking at the eiderdown, taking the box and putting it on her bed.*) He's had his rest, anyway——

MRS BANNER: 'Ad your 'air done?

CATTRIN (*looking in the mirror, volubly, her excitement growing*): The most wonderful place, Mrs Banner, cubicles, wax flowers, and my father in the *Tatler*, I just turned over and there he was, I nearly told the girl——

MRS BANNER: Excited?

CATTRIN: I feel empty, and yet if you put anything inside me, it'd bob straight up again. Half-past five – I'm rather glad he's had to go to Nathan's, keep his mind occupied——

MRS BANNER: I must get back to my Rosie. . . . (*Producing a tin from her pocket.*) A little present for your dad. (*Going.*) Toffee de Luxe.

CATTRIN: Oh, thank you, Mrs Banner——

MRS BANNER: Had it four months, never sell it now. . . .

    She goes, leaving the door open.

BEVAN: I called to say, Miss Thomas, I am all right for Friday.

CATTRIN (*crossing and placing the tin next to* MADDOC'S *bed*): Oh, thank you, Bevan, we'll arrange details in the morning——

ROBERT (*on the stairs*): Back all right?

CATTRIN (*calling*): Yes——

> ROBERT *hurries in, in evening clothes, in shirt-sleeves, carrying a hairbrush.*

ROBERT: Thought I heard you come in – (*brushing his hair before the mirror*) – Friday O.K., Bevan?

BEVAN (*as* CATTRIN *goes back to the bed*): Yes indeed. But Miss Thomas says until tonight is over——

ROBERT (*brushing*): The rest is silence, as Hamlet said – was it Hamlet, Bevan? (*Looking at the clock.*) We're all right. I thought we'd never get away from that music rehearsal——

CATTRIN: It was worth it. (*Undoing the string round the box.*) That trumpet call with the soldier crossing the sky – it'll make all the difference. I got a thrill even with a charwoman scrubbing round my feet. The trumpet call doesn't concern him, but I must tell him, in case it puts him off – remind me, Robert, will you – he's just gone over to Nathan's, I've had his tea laid out since the morning——

ROBERT (*reading his letter*): You're very chatty.

CATTRIN: Just nerves, I could go on talking till I was gagged——

> MRS LOTHIAN *hurries upstairs, out of breath; she is dressed in her best. She shuts the door with a bang;* CATTRIN *starts violently.*

(*In a fright.*) What is it – oh, Mrs Lothian . . . I'm sorry, I'm not able to cope with banging doors tonight. . . . (*Undoing the box.*) I must think about dressing——

ROBERT: See you anon——

He goes, leaving the door open. Mrs Lothian *stands at the back of the middle chair, in great distress.*

Cattrin: Shouldn't you be in the queue by now? (*Taking out the frock.*) Oh yes, it's not going to look at all bad——

Mrs Lothian: I left the queue to come here.

Cattrin: Will they let you back?

Mrs Lothian: I told them I was ill.

A pause. Cattrin *and* Bevan *stare at her.*

Cattrin (*starting up, hardly daring to speak*): It - isn't——

Mrs Lothian: It isn't your father.

Cattrin (*speechless with relief*): Oh . . .

Mrs Lothian: He's out, is he?

Cattrin: For a minute. What is it?

Mrs Lothian: You. (*To* Bevan.) Would a short walk be too much?

Bevan (*rising, on his dignity*): Not too much at all, I can take a hint.

He takes his overcoat and goes, shutting the door.

Cattrin: What's happened?

Mrs Lothian: That fast woman from downstairs came up to me in the queue. . . . All this getting married on Friday and joining Robert in three weeks - is it true?

Cattrin: Fan *would* have heard - and got it right, for a wonder. (*Taking off her coat.*) I'm sorry, Mrs Lothian, but I must dress——

Mrs Lothian: I'm sorry too, that I'm inflicting this on ye this minute, but after the play I presume you intend to break it to him, so it's now or never, and here I am.

Cattrin: But why?

Mrs Lothian: To tell ye not to do it.

A pause. They are both overwrought.

444

CATTRIN: I'm so angry I can't think of anything to say.

MRS LOTHIAN: For the first time in your life, you're not being honest.

CATTRIN: I don't know what you're talking about.

MRS LOTHIAN: Yes you do. You can't believe tomorrow's coming, did ye say? Well, unless something very special happens to the universe in the night, it *is* coming. Not only for you, but for him.

CATTRIN: If he makes a success tonight, his future is assured——

MRS LOTHIAN: I'd like to know how that alters the facts.

CATTRIN: Which are?

MRS LOTHIAN: That when he's a success he'll need you more than he did as a failure.

CATTRIN *sits slowly on the bed*. MRS LOTHIAN *goes to her*.

Why in heaven's name, when somebody's been by his side day and night for fifteen years, should he suddenly be able to do without 'em? Who on earth d'ye think is going to take your place? That little gentleman toper of his? I don't see that turning into David and Jonathan overnight. Me, that he can't abide in the same room and ye can't blame him? The smart lady downstairs?

CATTRIN: He's extremely fond of her – she's loyal and sensible——

MRS LOTHIAN: She's a slut, and ye know it. Ye've been toying with the idea of his marrying her, it wouldn't surprise me. (*As she does not reply.*) You and Robert are bigger fools even than I took ye for. (*Striding about.*) From the moment this marriage idea cropped up, ye've both treated the truth like an old corpse, pushed it to the back of your minds, and covered it in old bits o' subterfuge. 'He'll have money, he'll have his work, I'll write every day, I'll get people to drop in to see he's comfortable, he'll be all right'—— Away with ye. The truth is a hard thing, but it's there.

CATTRIN: And what is the truth?

MRS LOTHIAN (*turning to her, at the chest*): That if he is a success tonight, he would not be able to go *on* being a success, without you.

A pause. CATTRIN *rises and walks towards the desk.* I say 'wouldn't' because I know you're staying. (*Sitting on the foot of the sofa, as* CATTRIN *turns and looks at her.*) What did we say was going to be lit up again tonight – the flame of . . . genius, was it? If that light went out now, it would be a teasing thing to happen. Don't put it out, there's a good soul.

CATTRIN (*turning away*): After tonight, it'll be strong enough to carry on by itself——

MRS LOTHIAN: With a temperament like he's got? Subterfuge. How can his life ever turn into——

CATTRIN (*swinging on her, in a sudden outburst*): His life – what about *my* life? . . . (*Calmer.*) I loathe scenes. . . . (*After an effort.*) I've never indulged in self-pity, Mrs Lothian, but I've got to do it now. (*Choosing her words.*) I could have made a career in music, I let it go; I like new people, and Robert's the first I've met for eight years; I loathe dirt and disorder, and for as long as I can remember I've rubbed shoulders with both; I have a great liking for – grass, and trees, and – and the only time I've been to the country was to see a friend married. I'm fond of children. . . . For eight years, I've been a prisoner in this room, and I've served my sentence as faithfully as I knew how. I've cheered him up when he was depressed, lied to him if it made him happier, pretended he couldn't have been sick the night before because the room was as clean as a new pin – and while that's been going on, time's been going on too. Twenty-nine isn't old, but it's quite a time to catch up; there's a chance to catch up now. Before God and my conscience, that I've searched into through whole anxious nights, I have the right to take that chance. And nothing in the world is going to stop me. That's all.

MRS LOTHIAN: For a person so sure of doing the right thing, ye sound uncommon anxious to put your case.

CATTRIN: It's a fair case——

MRS LOTHIAN: Of course it's fair, but you know life is not as simple as that. Do you really see yourself as a typist that's stuck it like a Trojan and feels justified in leaving for something better? You're not his typist, my dear, you're his loving daughter. Will ye be able to look back and see a ship like that wreck and founder before your eyes?

CATTRIN: That's where you're wrong – how can you talk about a wreck? (*Sitting on the sofa back, speaking with the emphasis of self-justification.*) You see him as he was that first evening here, don't you? A year ago? In that year I've seen a miracle working on my father. He hasn't just been excited by the idea of success; he's been sitting at that table – striding about this room – with a light in his eye. And that light showed, beyond a doubt, that he's doing the supreme work he was born to do, and that only he can do. If you'd been here this morning and heard him talk about it, quite quietly. . . . You told him he'd been dead and buried for eight years, do you remember? Well, tonight he's going to live again. The typist can leave, because the business is on its feet at last.

A pause.

447

MRS LOTHIAN (*breaking it, with decision, rising and going round the sofa*): I'd better be claiming my place, if I don't want a dozen infuriated Shakespearian umbrellas in the small of my back . . . I'm not happy in my deportment, my dear, but I mean well.

CATTRIN: I know. (*Rising.*) And please forget all this, will you, for tonight, and sit back and enjoy yourself as you said you would. (*Taking her hand.*) Feeling a part of it. Because you are.

MRS LOTHIAN: We've waited long enough, haven't we? . . . Say no more.

> ROBERT *hurries back, in evening-dress, leaving the door open.*

ROBERT: Fix my tie, Cattrin, will you? (*To* MRS LOTHIAN.) You'll tell everybody round you how good the music is, won't you?

MRS LOTHIAN: When I've heard it and if I've liked it.
> *She fetches her bag from the middle chair.*

ROBERT: Thank you. Is he back yet?

CATTRIN (*arranging his tie*): Not yet – it's too bad if they keep him any longer, it was only to try the thing on——

MRS LOTHIAN (*going*): Well, it's on us now——

> *She is about to shut the door behind her when the telephone rings sharply.* CATTRIN *starts violently and looks at* ROBERT. MRS LOTHIAN *turns and looks at them.*

ROBERT: People ringing up at a time like this – I'll deal with them.

> *He goes to the telephone. Filled with a dread she cannot define,* CATTRIN *watches him.* MRS LOTHIAN *shuts the door.*

ROBERT: Hello. . . . Yes? . . .

> CATTRIN *relaxes, with a sigh of relief, and walks above the table.* MRS LOTHIAN *turns again to go.*

448

Oh good, that's fine. . . . What?

A sharp note in his voice makes the others look at him.

Are you sure? . . . All right.

He hangs up slowly.

CATTRIN: What is it? (*Loudly, going towards him.*) Robert!

ROBERT (*walking up*): Oh, nothing – I don't suppose——

CATTRIN: Something's happened at the theatre – a fire – what is it?

ROBERT: It was Nathan's, that's all. It's just that he hasn't been there.

A pause. Their eyes meet, and look away immediately.

CATTRIN: Is that all. . . . Bevan said he'd only just left here. Have they got the crown ready for him?

ROBERT: Yes.

CATTRIN: I expect it'll fit all right. I hope he takes a taxi back, though it isn't six yet——

She sees a note on the table, and picks it up.

MRS LOTHIAN: What does it say?

CATTRIN (*reading*): 'Gone to Nathan's. Back in a minute.'

ROBERT: Well, that's all right.

CATTRIN: Is it?

ROBERT: How do you mean?

CATTRIN: I thought Bevan had seen *him*. It was this he saw. It might have been here a long time. Since soon after we left. Three hours ago. . . .

A pause. Her fingers are moving convulsively.

It's a detective novel, suddenly. (*Volubly.*) Looking for clues, with everybody suspecting. . . . (*Suddenly, her nerves snapping, in a scream, as* ROBERT *strides across to her.*) Stop staring at me, both of you, what's happened, what have I done?

449

Silence. They have heard something on the stairs. They look at the door. The click of the handle. CATTRIN *looks before her; the others keep their eyes on the door. It opens softly and* MADDOC *enters with a thud; he is in his overcoat, but wears no hat. His movements are slow, and he is drunk.*

Suddenly, with a flick of the wrist (though, as it seems, without vicious intent) he bangs the door shut. The noise seems to echo through the house, and then die away. He walks slowly to the table, and sits down. A pause.

CATTRIN (*as if to herself, not daring to look at him*): Nearly there now, Tadda. . . . Covent Garden Opera House is swept and clean, the chandeliers are lit, the music's in its place, the curtain's down . . . nearly there now. . . .

No answer: she walks behind him, and puts her arms round his neck with her familiar gesture. She has still not looked at his face, and will not.

CATTRIN: Just to please me, love, will you say your first lines in the play? Just once. . . .

A pause.

MADDOC (*slowly, indistinctly, like an infant over and over again*): Baa baa black sheep . . . have you . . . any wool . . .

The clock begins to strike six.

(*A foolish smile spreading over his face.*) Any wool . . . Baa baa . . . baa baa . . .

The lights fade slowly into darkness. The curtain falls, and rises immediately on

SCENE II

Twenty-four hours later. Early evening.

The room is the same, except that the poster is gone.

MRS BANNER, FAN, BARTY, *and* BEVAN (*in uniform again and overcoat*), *in a row, glum and motionless;* BARTY *and* FAN *on the sofa,* BEVAN *in the middle chair, his helmet on the corner of it,* MRS BANNER *in the arm-chair. The wireless is on; an announcer's voice.*

THE VOICE: . . . who will meet the Duchess at the station and accompany her by car to the City Hall, where her Royal Highness will open the Exhibition at three p.m. The pictures will then be on view to the general public, daily from ten until five. Mr Maddoc Thomas. (*As all four prick up their ears and turn towards the wireless.*) As announced in the nine o'clock news last evening, last night's first performance of *King Lear* at the Royal Opera House, Covent Garden, was at the last moment postponed, owing to the indisposition of Mr Maddoc Thomas, who is suffering from acute laryngitis. Mr C. B. Cochran announces that Mr Thomas is making progress, and hopes to appear in the play at an early date. Sport. (*As* BEVAN *rises.*) There was a meeting today at the headquarters of the Football Association——

BEVAN *switches off; a despondent silence. He walks up and down.*

MRS BANNER: Never thought them announcers could ever know nobody I know, some'ow. . . .

FAN (*starting nervously as* BEVAN *passes her, in an angry outburst*): Stop walkin' about, comin' up here dressed as a bobby, give us all the creeps! . . . *What* did he say was the matter with him?

BEVAN (*sitting on the chest*): Laryngitis. An affectation of the throat.

FAN: Meaning he couldn't speak?

MRS BANNER: You 'it the nail all right there.

451

FAN: What d'you mean?

MRS BANNER: What I say. You've only got to look at Barty's face.

BARTY: Stow it, Mrs Banner, do.

FAN: What d'*you* think it was, Bev?

BEVAN: What he said, laryngitis.

MRS BANNER: Why?

BEVAN (*coldly*): Because they never tell a lie on the wireless.

MRS BANNER: They just tole one.

She rises, and starts to go.

FAN: How d'you know?

MRS BANNER (*turning to them all*): It weren't his throat. When 'e come in that last time, I thought 'e looked funny, sort o' thing, so I ups an' followed him to this door, to see what I could do to 'elp, sort o' thing – well, the clock struck six, an' then she screamed.

FAN: Cattrin?

MRS BANNER: Screamed. An' then a terrible noise, as if she was jumpin' at 'im an' beatin' 'is 'ead, sounded off 'er rocker, and the others pullin' 'er away and 'er beatin' an' shriekin' awful.

FAN (*distressed*): You shouldn't have listened——

MRS BANNER: An' then she said –(*going*) – no, I can't say it——

FAN: Oh yes you can, come on!

MRS BANNER (*turning again, and sitting in the middle chair*): She said 'This is 'ow you were the night you carried me an' fell down an' made me a cripple,' she said, an' then fainted, an' 'e never breathed, an' with Robert rushin' out to the chemist to pull the poor chap together sort o' thing – but it was no good – I never 'eard no more – I never knew she 'ad a fall, did you——

CATTRIN *enters, and shuts the door; she wears the same clothes as before, and carries a parcel. She is pale but composed: infinitely tired, and drained of every emotion. They sit without moving, staring at her guiltily. She looks from one to the other, with a weak smile.*

CATTRIN: What are you all waiting for, some seed-cake and a peep at the body?

She places her parcel and handbag on the desk and hangs up her coat.

MRS BANNER: *What* a thing to say. . . .

FAN: We came up for the news bulletin. You don't mind, dear?

MRS BANNER: 'Ow is 'e?

BEVAN: The laryngitis, you know——

CATTRIN: Still sleeping it off, I expect.

FAN: Oh Cat . . .

CATTRIN: After eight years pretending, I'm rather enjoying myself. I can say he was drunk, because he was drunk.

FAN: Where is he?

CATTRIN: Behind here listening. (*Looking behind the screen, with deliberate and bitter casualness.*) No, laid out like a log.

FAN (*rising*): I never knew you could be nasty.

CATTRIN (*at the desk, undoing the parcel she brought in*): Neither did I. I'm enjoying that too.

FAN *goes, leaving the door open.* MRS BANNER *rises.*

CATTRIN: Next please. Don't let me drive you away.

MRS BANNER *starts to go, then turns to her.*

MRS BANNER (*timidly*): One of the cleaners told my Rosie they was expectin' great things from last night——

CATTRIN (*brutally*): What in hell's name is the good of that now?

453

Mrs Banner (*helpless*): I was only tryin' to make you better, dear.

Cattrin (*taking her hand, contritely*): I'm sorry, Mrs Banner, darling. I'm inclined to overdo it a bit at first.

Mrs Banner: It upset me, y'know. For the night. I didn't go out.

Cattrin: What a shame. . . .

Mrs Banner: First prime-year I missed since my chest.

She goes, leaving the door open. Bevan *takes* King Lear *from his pocket and begins to read.* Cattrin *brings down two boxes of stockings from the desk, draws the new suitcase from under her bed, kneels and packs them into it. She sees* Barty *huddled in the arm-chair beside her, hardly daring to look round at her. Unexpectedly, she smiles at him. He can hardly believe his eyes.*

Cattrin: I was going to give you a hundred lines, but I'm letting you off after all.

Barty: You see, it was the club that started us off——

Cattrin: If it hadn't been you, it would have been somebody else, so don't let it spoil your evening at the dogs.

Barty *rises, starts to go, then turns.*

Barty: Cat – this spot of dough I'm coming into – would a third of it – make up——

Cattrin: Not really, ducky. Besides, what about your debts?

Barty (*with a grin*): Ooh, that hurt . . . I was thinking just now . . . he likes watching cricket, and it would have been a good wheeze to treat him to the Oval tomorrow, take his mind off . . . but of course, it's the winter.

Cattrin (*kindly*): Yes, Barty, it's the winter.

He looks at her, and goes, sheepishly.

Are you still free tomorrow, Bevan?

BEVAN (*reading, without looking up*): You have not cancelled the event?

CATTRIN: Same time, same place.

BEVAN: I am delighted to hear it. (*To himself.*) I had already purchased the present.

CATTRIN (*back at the desk*): Are you busy for the next half-hour?

BEVAN: Not until I go on duty——

CATTRIN (*taking a scrap of paper from her handbag*): Would you be a dear and slip down to Boots in the Strand and get all these – they kept me so long at the Consulate, and I've got a lot of packing——

BEVAN (*looking up*): The Consulate?

CATTRIN: For my passport. (*Coming down towards him.*) I'm sailing with Robert on Saturday.

BEVAN (*after a pause, back at his book*): I see.

CATTRIN: You're not still reading *King Lear*?

BEVAN (*turning down a leaf, and putting away the book*): I am a believer, Miss Thomas, in completin' a task once begun.

He takes the paper from her.

CATTRIN (*smiling*): If I could have combined you and my father, Bevan, what a marvellous Welshman I would have made.

BEVAN: Very true. (*Crossing.*) But you'll never see me at the top of the tree neither, you know. You see, Miss Thomas, I have several faults. (*Putting on his helmet before the mirror.*) And you know my besettin' one?

CATTRIN: What?

BEVAN: No sense of humour. I have tried and tried, but if it is not there, it is not there, is it?

He goes, shutting the door. A banging on the stairs.

ROBERT'S VOICE: It's all right, Bevan – I'll get it up——

CATTRIN (*opening the door*): Robert, you'll never manage it – see you later, Bevan – whose is it?

> ROBERT *staggers in in his overcoat, piloting a new (empty) wardrobe trunk, which he deposits open against the foot of* CATTRIN's *bed.* CATTRIN *follows him.*

ROBERT: A present from Mrs Lothian, no message. It's her way of owning up she was wrong.

CATTRIN: A very useful way too. I was wondering how I'd get everything in – was she furious?

ROBERT: No, she cried. . . . (*After a pause.*) It didn't go with her at all.

CATTRIN (*decisively*): What I've always wanted – hangers – laundry-bag——

ROBERT: I saw the management.

CATTRIN: Did you? That's been worrying me, how much it's costing them——

ROBERT: They said the insurance covers all that.

CATTRIN: Oh, what a bit of luck – I am glad.

ROBERT: They've been marvellous, as a matter of fact. Talking of opening Tuesday and give the old boy a second chance.

CATTRIN (*transferring objects from the suitcase to the trunk*): I'm afraid when they see him they'll realise it's too risky. His nerve's completely gone – besides, how could he face that audience knowing that every single person in it would know about last night? No, there's only one chance, and he's had it. I'm glad about the insurance, though.

ROBERT (*at the foot of her bed*): This didn't sound a bit like you . . . I know it's been desperately hurtful——

CATTRIN (*stopping her packing, and looking before her*): It's been something more unbearable than that. Rage, at being made a fool of – rage against him for making a

wicked idiotic mess of his life. There must be a limit to
the dutiful daughter's patience, and we've got to it. He
won't do any good storming and being sorry for himself,
because for a change the dutiful daughter's being sorry
for herself – (*vehemently*) – for spending her youth pouring water into a bucket with no bottom to it, and that
isn't even pathetic, it's just ridiculous.

 She packs again.

ROBERT: You're right, of course.

CATTRIN: You don't sound sure.

ROBERT: It's no good, Cattrin, I feel terribly worried
about him. He has relied on you so much, and . . . you
know Fan told him about us – and that was why he went
off the deep end, don't you?

CATTRIN (*stopping packing again*): That was bad luck,
but does it put you and me in the wrong? Don't you
think it might have crossed his mind – 'well, I'm disappointed, but I'll wait till tonight's over and at least
show her our eight years together haven't been a joke?'
No, 'come on, Barty, have the other half' – oh!

ROBERT: I don't like you like this.

CATTRIN: Neither do I, but I can't help it. (*Going to the
desk.*) Come on, we've both got a lot to do before dinner,
and I'm getting hungry – damn, I haven't settled up with
the dairy, I knew there was something——

ROBERT (*as she puts on her coat*): I can drop you – I've
got a parcel waiting for me at the tailor's – I asked the taxi
to wait——

CATTRIN (*taking her bag from the desk*): It's only on the
corner – they really got the suit ready, did they – Heavens,
what a rush——

 *He shuts the door behind them. A pause. A noise behind
 the screen.* MADDOC'S *tousled head peers slowly from*

457

*behind it; he sees the room is empty and shuffles out. He is
in his dressing-gown, the cord trailing, with no collar and
tie, unshaven, dirty, still suffering from his drinking. He
sees the wardrobe trunk, and stands a moment looking at it
impassively. He wanders into the kitchenette. The door
opens, and* FAN *enters quickly, shutting the door.*

FAN (*calling*): Mad!

*He re-appears in the kitchenette doorway, holding a
saucepan.*

MADDOC: Just a minute, Fan——

*He goes back; she wanders down to the sofa; he re-
appears without the saucepan, and comes down opposite her.
They stand a moment.*

MADDOC: I've never been to America.

FAN (*bursting into tears*): Oh Mad . . .

*She throws her arms round him. They stumble awk-
wardly on to the sofa.*

MADDOC: Good old Fan . . . there, sit down . . . I'd
forgotten how nice you smell. . . . You told me once
it was cheap scent, that's why I like it, I expect. . . .
Mmm. . . . What a long time – that's old King Lear,
Fan, kept me away, see? That's the co-respondent, Mrs
Thomas, that old fellow in the box as bold as brass with
his beard behind a veil and one of those Merry Widow
hats. . . .

They laugh uproariously, and kiss.

FAN (*sitting up*): Ages since we had a joke——

MADDOC: Except that you're not Mrs Thomas, and
we'll get married same time as them, eh? I'll get pots of
work, with my name being in the papers and everything
– I'm serious, Fan, is that all right?

FAN: You know it's always been O.K. by Fan, dear.
There, ducks . . . (*nestling up to him*) . . . okydoke?

MADDOC: You're the girl, Fan. The okydoke girl. . . . Nobody could say the conversation is taking a literary turn, but it's okydoke. . . .

FAN: We've known each other seven years, ever since that marine chap. I always thought trumps'd turn up, and when I heard Cat was getting married, I knew then we'd be next. . . . (*Sitting up again.*) Where'll we live, d'you think? Here?

MADDOC: No. Sell the damn lot, and start a new leaf. Nice little flat.

FAN: Ooh, I've always wanted a nice modern flat——

MADDOC: Marked with a cross it'll be, seventeen windows up and sixteen along.

FAN: What about a housewarming, Mad? What about Barty's face! And the fellows at the club, oh the rudery! But we got the laugh, Mad, haven't we?

MADDOC: We got the laugh on the lot of 'em——

FAN: Except they're thumbs down on parties in those flats, aren't they?

MADDOC: Ask the other tenants in, all of 'em, that'll shake 'em up——

FAN (*her head on his shoulder*): What a time we're going to have, Mad!

MADDOC: All the things we've got in common, eh? (*After a pause*). Sitting in the evenings, by the stove, reading. Quiet a bit, then talking a bit. About *Bleak House.*

FAN: *Bleak House*? Where's that?

MADDOC: Dickens. And then me imitating McCormack and making you laugh, and then the folk songs.

FAN (*sitting up*): Folk songs?

MADDOC: You singing in the old language, ynghariadi, same as when I was a little chap.

459

FAN (*at a loss, faltering*): But, Mad ... I don't know any Welsh, and I can't sing, and——

MADDOC: And you've never been to a concert, and you don't know about when I was a little chap.

FAN: No ... (*After a pause.*) It wouldn't be any good, Mad, would it?

She looks at him; he returns her look.

MADDOC (*gently, sadly*): No.

FAN: I'd have got thin and let my hair go dark, but it isn't only that, is it?

CATTRIN returns, hangs up her coat, and writes something at the desk, without looking at MADDOC. He rises and wanders into the kitchenette. FAN rises uncertainly.

CATTRIN: Don't go, Fan, I'll only be packing.

FAN: Oh, I've got a letter to write. (*Going.*) Where d'you think I heard from this morning? Penang!

CATTRIN: No! (*Smiling.*) Who said he'd lost interest?

FAN: Lost interest, my dear, if you could read it! (*Dabbing her eyes.*) He's lonely, see, so he's taken to readin', and he's given me a list to get. (*Going, thoughtfully.*) I wonder where you buy back numbers of *Punch* and *The Motor Cycle*?

She goes, shutting the door. CATTRIN takes passport and papers from the desk, and walks down. A crash of crockery in the kitchenette. She looks up sharply, shrugs her shoulders and goes on with what she was doing. MADDOC appears at the kitchenette door.

MADDOC: I've broken three saucers and an egg-cup.

CATTRIN (*not unkindly, sitting in the middle chair*): I wasn't taking any of that with me anyway.

MADDOC: Oh. Yes, I forgot.

He goes back, and returns almost immediately carrying

460

a small table of food. He comes down and places it in front of CATTRIN.

I heard you say you were hungry.

They look at each other. He smiles, weakly, with an effort.

It's supposed to be a poached egg.

She tries hard not to be touched, and succeeds: then picks at the food. He fetches a chair from the table and settles beside her.

MADDOC: Does it put you off if I watch you?

CATTRIN: No.

MADDOC: Because I want to see as much of you as I can in the time. Sunday, is it?

CATTRIN: Saturday, morning.

MADDOC: You won't mind if I see you off?

CATTRIN: I'd sooner you didn't, really. It makes it all – tiresome, don't you think?

MADDOC: It does really, doesn't it. . . . I'll go to a flick with Barty. . . . (*After a pause.*) There's just one thing worrying me. When I came back – and you pitched into me——

CATTRIN: Don't let's go into that, please——

MADDOC: Well, in the night I – dreamt it was all happening, again, only this time you said 'I'm lame because you fell with me in your arms.'

CATTRIN: What a horrible dream.

MADDOC: Wasn't it? As a matter of fact, I've dreamt it before, so for a minute I thought . . . (*Anxiously.*) You didn't say it, did you?

CATTRIN: Of course I didn't.

MADDOC: I'm so glad. I couldn't sleep after that. I am glad. . . . (*After a pause.*) You won't think too badly of me, will you?

461

*She is trying to eat, and not to listen: she succeeds less and
    less.*

MADDOC: Because that would upset me very much.
And it'd mean you weren't happy, and you must be
happy, you know, because you're doing the right thing.

CATTRIN (*pushing her plate away*): I'm sorry, I've got to
finish some labels for the boat——

MADDOC: I'll help you. . . . (*Going to the desk, bringing
down pens, ink and labels, and sitting again.*) About time
you had a chance, with a nice fellow like Robert, and
seeing the world, they tell me New York's a grand place
for young people. . . . (*Reading.*) 'Mrs . . . Robert' . . .
looks funny, eh? . . . I mean . . . (*looking at her*) . . . don't
think too badly of me because I haven't come to anything
in the end. You see, love, I was never meant to. I've got
good things in me, I know that, but the trouble is I'm
one of those freak machines with every good part running against a wonky one, and in the end nothing moves
at all. In the middle of that dress rehearsal – when I
suddenly knew I'd got to those heights Irving told me
about – I had an odd feeling, of standing at the back of
the circle – as I am now, rather dirty, down-at-heel –
watching myself on the stage and saying 'By Jove, he's
a great personality, that old boy! He's a success!' There
I was, on the stage, showing this shadowy old tramp what
was what. And of course it was the other way about –
the old tramp at the back of the circle was the real me –
because here I am, flesh and blood – whereas King Lear,
nobody'll ever see him. . . . See? Funny. . . .

CATTRIN (*writing, determined not to yield*): As the reason
nobody'll see him is that you had too much to drink
yesterday, there's no point in carrying on like Pagliacci,
is there?

MADDOC: No no. . . .

CATTRIN: Luckily, they're insured, otherwise there'd be a fortune down the drain.

MADDOC: Yes yes. . . . (*With a sudden impudent smile.*) I'm going to buy you a pair of pince-nez and a boned collar.

CATTRIN (*laughing, in spite of herself*): Tadda, you are a fool. . . .

MADDOC: That's better! I can talk to you, now. . . . You see, when Fan told me you were getting married, my first thought was 'Cattrin'll be happy, and now I'm on top we'll all be happy, they'll come over and see me play, I'll meet them in my car, get married myself, or anyway produce a haughty lady friend for the station' – shows how silly I am, doesn't it? And then Fan went. There's something terrible about a door banging. I wonder what I've done to deserve this feeling about being alone? . . . Then I started sinking . . . to the bottom of the sea. And I saw the truth. All those months, it hasn't been the great actor being waited on by his little daughter at all – it's been a strong-willed young woman pumping life into an old boy who'd started well but conked out. And she'd stopped pumping. And then I couldn't remember my part, love . . . (*his voice breaking*) . . . not a word, not a word . . . and then I thought, as you were going . . . I'm not making excuses. You see, love, you said yourself it's been a partnership.

> CATTRIN *rises abruptly, takes labels across and fastens them to the trunk.*

CATTRIN (*trying hard to be practical*): It's my fault – for not realising it was madness from the beginning – that no person has the right to make themselves indispensable to anybody else——

MADDOC: I haven't been so bad, you know. Lent fellows a lot of money in my time, had a few drinks with 'em, but I didn't do anything really wrong, did I? Look at that Mrs Lothian – she thought I was all right, didn't she? (*After a pause, suddenly.*) I wish she'd seen that dress rehearsal.

CATTRIN (*kneeling, to fasten a label on the suitcase*): I expect she does too, now.

MADDOC: I mean your mother.

A pause.

MADDOC: I've never mentioned her before, have I? She was awfully pretty and jolly and small, like you, only she had curls on her forehead. I hadn't had a drink, imagine how excited I was – tore upstairs – knocked an ink-stand over on the carpet, she wouldn't have liked that at all – and into the bedroom; they'd said not to, but I'd been thinking of her all through *Romeo*. She looked straight up at me. 'Well?' I said. 'What d'you think, Goldy?' she said – her name for me 'Golden Voice', the sort of silly thing you say – 'what d'you think, Goldy,' she said, 'I've presented you with a little leading lady.' And then she died. (*After a pause.*) It wasn't a very good joke, but it was very cheery.

He takes CATTRIN'S *plate into the kitchenette. She sits on the floor, too sorrowful for tears.*

ROBERT'S VOICE (*on the stairs*): Cattrin!

CATTRIN (*calling, mechanically*): Yes?

ROBERT'S VOICE: A present for you!

CATTRIN: A present?

ROBERT'S VOICE: Come and choose, will you?

CATTRIN (*breaking her mood, abruptly, hysterically*): A coat! Oh, Robert – let me see——

She disappears on to the stairs, leaving the door open.

ROBERT's VOICE: Which d'you think?

During this, MADDOC *comes out of the kitchenette, carrying a whisky and water; he shuffles behind the screen. The creak of the springs as he settles heavily on his bed.*

CATTRIN: This one, I rather like——

ROBERT's VOICE: A bit pale, perhaps——

CATTRIN (*coming upstairs and into the room*): Wait a minute; I've got the dress to go with it, we'll see which looks best——

ROBERT (*following her*): I think the other, if you ask me——

They come into the room, ROBERT *carrying two coats.*

CATTRIN *takes a dress from the suitcase.*

ROBERT: They're either of them going to be the smartest on the boat, so——

Their eyes meet. She lets the dress fall.

What's the matter?

She turns, sees the open kitchenette door, and closes it. She comes down to ROBERT.

CATTRIN: You called me your wife. Do you remember?

A pause.

ROBERT (*suddenly quiet and composed*): I know what you're going to say. You're not coming with me.

CATTRIN: So I can be as sentimental as I like. My darling.

A pause. He moves a step.

ROBERT: It shows you what hypocrites we are, because I've known all along you couldn't. Waiting in that Consulate, I knew. Seven o'clock this morning, I did something I've never done, went for a walk along the Embankment, to think over the happiness of preparing my life with you – but really to try and convince myself we were doing right. That's why I've gone out of my

465

way to pity him, knowing anything else would make you flare up and take his part, and we'd be up against the truth.

CATTRIN: She was right, wasn't she, about pushing it into the back of our minds. . . . (*Sitting on the edge of the arm-chair.*) How could we have thought he'd go on being a success without me – when he can't even be a failure without me? It's the little things I couldn't bear. Letters trailing into a scrawl, and knowing what it meant – postcards from Fan and Barty – cough bad again, will go out without his overcoat – pretends he doesn't miss you. . . . And then seeing him lying in doorways, rummaging in dust-bins – no, Robert, it's my right to go, but I can't do it.

ROBERT (*his manner hardening*): A bit unfair, isn't it?

CATTRIN: Of course it's unfair, but——

ROBERT (*up to her in an outburst, which she tries to hush*): If it's unfair, it's wrong, and it's your duty to fight it! . . . As we're facing the future with such honesty, let's face it with you staying with him. Now the rot has set in, he'll go on drinking just a little more every year, and he won't live as long as all that, you know – ten, fifteen years——

CATTRIN: Robert——

ROBERT: I've got to say it, it's my only chance! (*Driving at her.*) And then he'll be ill, you'll nurse him, he'll die, and you'll bury him. You'll be forty-five – fifty – a sad little spinster who 'devoted her life to her father, he drank and she was wonderful, you know, she lives in one room, used to play the piano, too old now, poor thing'. . . .

CATTRIN: It's true. But it can't change me.

ROBERT (*walking away, angry, desperate*): I might have known how hopeless it is to work on your feelings about yourself. (*Turning on her again.*) Well, since you don't mind your own future being wiped out, I'll have to do his trick, and work on your feelings about me. What about my future?

CATTRIN: It's not the same, Robert. You can look after yourself——

ROBERT: Can I? I haven't the perfect character either, you know. With you and a family to work for, my music might easily mean something, and I'd be all right. On my own, a series of tawdry affairs, squabbles, night-clubs, then a rich old woman and back where I started from, ending up this time as a bad-tempered old adventurer with a few cheap remarks and a tired talent for the piano. Nothing very tragic, but pretty poor all the same.

CATTRIN: You might meet – somebody else——

ROBERT: I wouldn't meet anybody else. (*Softening, in spite of himself, sitting in the middle chair.*) Do you remember the things I said to you that first night, just here?

CATTRIN: I know them by heart.

ROBERT: Will I ever be able to say them to – somebody else?

CATTRIN: No.

ROBERT: I'm not eighteen, and I know what I'm about. . . . It isn't even so much being in love with you. It's missing you when you're out of the room. It's thinking 'Must remember that, make her laugh'. It's an unhappy knack of yours, this making yourself indispensable. (*Putting his hand on hers.*) I need you, desperately. Come with me.

  She looks at him.

CATTRIN: For the first time ever, he talked about my mother. I've got to stay.

  A pause.

ROBERT: I knew as I was saying it, I was only trying it on. (*Rising, briskly, with great effort.*) Say no more about it, shall we? No lingering good-byes – keep on the move, keep the circulation going——

CATTRIN (*rising, seizing on his mood, with relief*): That's it – there's a lot of telephoning to do——

ROBERT: I'll cancel the registry office on the one downstairs. Will you do the shipping people and the rest on this——

CATTRIN: Yes – and I'll get Fan to take the coats back before they close – and she can have the trunk, I don't much want it in here – just keep going, shall we——

ROBERT: What's the registry office number, Gerrard——

CATTRIN: Gerrard 3482——

> *He hurries downstairs. She picks up the two coats, and follows him, leaving the door open. We hear her call 'Fan!' twice. A pause. MADDOC comes slowly from behind the screen, places his glass on the desk, and stands behind the middle chair.*

MADDOC: Some very rude things, but serve you right for listening, you old fool. . . . (*After a pause.*) And now it's up to you.

> CATTRIN *enters, shutting the door.*

CATTRIN(*pulling his arm*): I'm not going, love, after all.
> *She goes into the kitchenette. A pause.*

MADDOC (*calling*): Did I tell you what they said about me after the dress rehearsal?

CATTRIN (*calling*): What?

MADDOC (*almost to himself*): They said it was something this generation hasn't seen at all. I can't have been so bad, can I?

CATTRIN (*calling*): Cleaned your teeth today?

MADDOC: Don't think so. (*After a pause, to himself.*) I'll pop down now, shall I?

CATTRIN (*calling*): I'll put some tea on, and when I've done my telephoning, I'll roll you a cigarette.

MADDOC: Just you and me. The rest – rabbits! (*A pause. Calling her, in a panic.*) Cattrin!

CATTRIN (*coming back, startled.*) Yes?

> *He turns to her, suddenly sober, and in great distress.*

MADDOC: There's a book I want.

CATTRIN: *King Lear*, d'you mean?

MADDOC: No. I had it when I was a little chap, and I lost it. . . . You haven't seen it, since we've been here?

CATTRIN: But what sort of book, love?

MADDOC: A prayer-book. (*After a pause, earnestly.*) I want it – badly.

CATTRIN (*humouring him, patting his cheek, with a smile*): What you want still more is a nice long sleep, my boy. . . .

> *She goes into the kitchenette. He continues to speak, as if she were still with him.*

MADDOC: Cheerful again, like the old days. Very nice motto, y'know, blessed are the light of heart. . . .

> *He goes out, slowly, shutting the door carefully behind him. A pause.*
>
> *A crash of splintering wood and glass, on the stairs.* CATTRIN *emerges from the kitchenette, and looks round the room. She comes down, alarmed and puzzled. A loud scream, two floors below;* FAN'S *voice.* CATTRIN *stands, transfixed. A pause. The door bursts open; it is* ROBERT, *white and shaken.*

CATTRIN: What was that?

ROBERT: Stay here, will you——

CATTRIN (*almost in a scream, as he starts to go*): What was it?

469

He shuts the door and comes down towards her.

ROBERT: The window. . . . On the pavement – one arm's . . . moving – (*covering his eyes*) – oh God – I'll go down and see to him——

CATTRIN: There's no need. (*As he stops, and stares at her.*) I felt it, that minute. Inside me, here. (*Dazed.*) Forcing its way out. Like a bird. . . . (*Looking at* ROBERT.) I felt him die.

She stumbles. He catches her.

CATTRIN (*suddenly sobbing*): There's a crowd running up – thousands of them – and he was worth all of them put together. . . . (*In a panic.*) In one second they'll be pouring up those stairs – through that door——

ROBERT: And while we've got this second, we've got to say one thing, and make ourselves believe it. He played that first night after all——

CATTRIN (*in a sob*): But he didn't – he didn't——

ROBERT: We've got to make ourselves believe he did, and made the success of his life.

CATTRIN: They all thought he was finished, but now——

ROBERT: He's all right.

CATTRIN: He's all right.

THE CURTAIN FALLS